Doing Early Childhood Research

Doing Early Childhood Research

INTERNATIONAL PERSPECTIVES ON THEORY & PRACTICE

2nd EDITION

Glenda Mac Naughton
Sharne A. Rolfe
Iram Siraj-Blatchford

Open University Press
McGraw-Hill Education
McGraw-Hill House
Shoppenhangers Road
Maidenhead
Berkshire
England
SL6 2QL

email: enquiries@openup.co.uk
world wide web: www.openup.co.uk

and Two Penn Plaza, New York, NY 10121-2289, USA

First published 2001
First published in second edition 2010

A catalogue record of this book is available from the British Library

ISBN-13: 978-0-33-524262-7 (pb)
ISBN-10: 0-33-524262-6 (pb)

Library of Congress Cataloging-in-Publication Data
CIP data applied for

Typeset by Midland Typesetters, Australia
Printed by Everbest Printing Co, China

The McGraw·Hill Companies

Contents

List of tables and figures

TABLES

FIGURE

Contributors

Sue Atkinson-Lopez is an Indigenous Victorian and is currently an Honorary Research Fellow at the Centre for Equity and Early Childhood at the University of Melbourne. She has many years experience working across the education sector from kindergarten to higher education with both Indigenous and non-Indigenous students. She has recently successfully completed her doctoral study, titled 'Indigenous self-determination and Early Childhood Education and Care in Victoria'.

Mindy Blaise is currently a Senior Lecturer at Monash University, Australia. She has been conducting small-scale research since she was an early childhood teacher in the United States. Some of her studies have focused on gender at the writing centre, gender-bending in the kindergarten classroom, gender and sexuality during circle time, kiss-and-chase games, and the teaching and researching body. Blaise publishes widely on gender, sexuality and early childhood teaching. Her book, *Playing it Straight! Uncovering Gender Discourses in the Early Childhood Classroom* (Routledge, 2005) is an example of a small-scale classroom-based study.

Liane Brown will complete her doctoral studies in the Melbourne Graduate School of Education at the University of Melbourne, in mid-2009. Her research interests are in parenting education. She is particularly interested in the long-term effects of different kinds of parenting programs on parenting behaviours, child outcomes and parent–child relationships. She has worked as a parenting educator for over ten years, providing information and running programs in Australia and Singapore. Liane works in conjunction with preschools, primary schools, community health centres and business organisations. She also does occasional teaching at the University of Melbourne.

Margaret Coady is an Honorary Research Fellow at the Centre for Equity and Innovation in Early Childhood and a member of the Centre for Applied Philosophy and Public Ethics at the University of Melbourne. She has published widely in professional ethics and children's and families' rights. Margaret has held Research Fellowships at the Center for Human Values at Princeton University, the Rockefeller Center at Bellagio, Italy, the Kennedy Institute for Ethics at Georgetown University, and the Uehiro Centre for Practical Ethics at Oxford University.

Audrey D'Souza Juma is currently a doctoral candidate at the Centre for Equity and Innovation in Early Childhood, Melbourne Graduate School of Education, the University of Melbourne. She has worked as a faculty member and coordinator for early childhood programs at the Institute for Educational Development of the Aga Khan University. She has also been a member of the advisory committee for the review of the Pakistan National Curriculum for early childhood. She has extensive teaching and teacher education experience in varied settings in Pakistan, and has been involved in material development and curriculum planning in early childhood education, social studies education and human development programs. Her research interests are in the areas of gender, play, early childhood curriculum and pedagogy, ethnic diversity and identities.

Anne Edwards has been undertaking qualitative research in early childhood services and schools for the past 25 years. Her background is in both history and psychology, and she works with sociocultural frameworks to explore how adults support children as learners and the professional learning involved for them. Recent books include *Promoting Children's Learning from Birth to Five*, with Angela Anning (Open University Press, 2006) and, with a list of colleagues, *Improving Inter-professional Collaborations* (Routledge, 2009). She is currently Professor of Educational Studies at the University of Oxford.

Sue Emmett has been involved extensively in early childhood education, and the translation of research into the practical environment for over 25 years. Her professional experience includes early childhood teaching, leadership within early childhood services, work as an early childhood education consultant and teaching at university level. She currently holds the position of Research Fellow at the School for Social and Policy Research at Charles Darwin University, where her research interests include young Indigenous children's literacy and emotional development, including cultural perspectives on attachment. Sue will complete her PhD at Melbourne Graduate School of Education, the University of Melbourne, in 2009.

Maria Assunção Folque is a Lecturer in Early Childhood Education at the University of Évora in Portugal. She was a nursery teacher for twelve years and has been involved in teachers' associations such as the Modern School Movement (MEM)—a movement of teachers from all levels of education engaged in developing democratic schooling. Her research interests include quality in early years education, information and communication technologies (ICT) in the early years and research on pedagogy and learning. She has conducted an in-depth study of the MEM pedagogy in preschool and how it mediates children learning to learn as part of her doctorate at the Institute of Education, the University of London.

Susan Grieshaber is Professor of Early Years Education at the School of Early Childhood, Queensland University of Technology, Brisbane, Australia. Her research interests include early childhood curriculum, pedagogy, assessment and policy, with a focus on equity and diversity. Current research projects include a quantitative sociological study of family literacy practices, pedagogy and achievement of children in Grade 1 and a study of new professors in Australian universities. Sue has published widely and co-edits the international refereed journal *Contemporary Issues in Early Childhood*.

Linda Harrison is Associate Professor of Early Childhood Education at Charles Sturt University, Bathurst, New South Wales, Australia. Her research and professional work is in the area of child development, specialising in the ways that provisions and practices in child care and the early years of school influence the quality of teaching and learning experiences for children. She is a principal investigator on three longitudinal research studies—the Sydney Family Development Project,

Child Care Choices, and the Longitudinal Study of Australian Children—that have investigated the use and impact of early education and child care on children's health, development and well-being.

Alan Hayes is the Director of the Australian Institute of Family Studies, taking up his appointment in September 2004. With qualifications in psychology, he has research and policy interests in the pathways that children and their families take through life, and the role of families in supporting and sustaining development across life. The role of vulnerability and resilience in shaping developmental pathways has been a particular focus. Much of his work has focused on disadvantage, with a long-standing interest in prevention and early intervention. The impact of relationship breakdown on children is a particular interest, and the factors that impede access to opportunity continue to be a key focus. He held a Chair of Early Childhood Studies at Macquarie University, where he was also Foundation Dean and Head of Division at the Australian Centre for Education Studies (ACES). He has been the chair, deputy chair and a member of four Australian government Ministerial Advisory Councils, including the Commonwealth Child Care Advisory Council (CCCAC), the Australian Council for Children and Parenting (ACCAP), the Stronger Families and Communities Strategy (SF&CS) Partnership and the Australian Families and Children Council (AFCC). For the New South Wales government, he chaired the committee that successfully established the Institute of Teachers in 2004 and was a member of the New South Wales Child Protection Council. An Alexander von Humboldt Fellow, he has been a Visiting Professor at the Free University of Berlin and the Pennsylvania State University.

Patrick Hughes (PhD) is a Research Fellow at the University of Melbourne's Centre for Equity and Innovation in Early Childhood (CEIEC). Formerly, he was a Senior Lecturer in Communications at Deakin University, Victoria and has taught research methods, media studies and cultural studies at London University and at the Open University. Patrick has been a communications consultant to companies and governments in the United Kingdom and Australia. His work has been published in books, book chapters and articles in Australia, the United Kingdom and the United States, and he has presented papers to international academic conferences.

Glenda Mac Naughton is a Professor at the Melbourne Graduate School of Education at the University of Melbourne, where she directs the Centre for Equity and Innovation in Early Childhood. She has worked in the early childhood field for over 37 years and during this time she has worked as a practitioner and manager, and as a senior policy adviser to government, internationally and in Australia. Her early childhood research has focused on social justice and equity issues, and she has published widely from her research. Several of her books are set as texts internationally.

Karen Martin's main research interests are Aboriginal ontology and epistemology, and the intersection of schooling and Aboriginal early childhood. She has been a member of the Steering Committee with the Longitudinal Study for Indigenous Children since 2003 and currently works at the School of Education, Southern Cross University, Lismore, New South Wales, as Associate Professor in Early Childhood.

Sharne A. Rolfe is a psychologist and Senior Lecturer in Early Childhood Development in the Melbourne Graduate School of Education at the University of Melbourne. The author of *Rethinking Attachment for Early Childhood Practice: Promoting Security, Autonomy and Resilience in Young Children* (Allen & Unwin, 2004), her research focuses on the impact of early relationship experiences within family and child-care settings on children's social and emotional well-being. Her innovative clinical work and professional training programs at the interface between child welfare and statutory child protection have led to key advisory roles within the state governments of New South Wales, Queensland, Western Australia and Victoria, including serving on the Expert Review Panel that advised on the Victorian *Children, Youth and Families Act* 2005.

Iram Siraj-Blatchford is Professor of Early Childhood Education at the Institute of Education, University of London. Her recent research projects include evaluation of the Foundation Phase across Wales. She is a principal investigator of the major DCSF fifteen-year study on Effective Preschool, Primary and Secondary Education (EPPSE 3–16) project (1997–2013) and of the influential Researching Effective Pedagogy in the Early Years (REPEY) project. She is an expert in mixed-method, case study and qualitative research and analysis, and is currently principal investigator on longitudinal studies in the United Kingdom, Australia and Ireland. She has always been particularly interested in undertaking research that aims to combat disadvantage and to give children and families from these backgrounds a head start. She is a specialist early-years adviser to governments and ministers in the United Kingdom and internationally. Siraj-Blatchford is the President of the British Association for Early Childhood Education. She has published over 40 major research reports and books and over 120 peer-reviewed articles and chapters in scholarly books.

John Siraj-Blatchford is an Honorary Professor at the University of Swansea, and currently has a part-time research post at the University of London Institute of Education. He also works as an independent educational researcher and consultant, and is Director of Research and Development at Made in Me. He was previously employed at the University of Cambridge, Faculty of Education, and served as an Associate Director of the ESRC Teaching and Learning Research Program. Recent work has included contributing to the *Equalities Review Report* for EPPE 3–11, and to reviews of family-based support for early learning and integrated children's services for the Centre for Educational Outcomes. He is currently heavily involved in an OMEP/UNESCO initiative associated with identifying the role of early childhood education in sustainable development. His publications include *A Curriculum Development Guide to ICT in early Childhood Education*, *Supporting Information and Communications Technology in the Early Years* and *Developing New Technologies for Young Children*. His first book, *Educating the Whole Child*, was published in 1995 and *Supporting Science, Design, and Technology in the Early Years* was published by the Open University Press in 1999.

Louise Taylor has been working in education for 30 years as a teacher, tutor, curriculum writer, consultant and researcher. For her PhD, she worked with a small group of early education teachers in New Zealand, taking a poststructuralist feminist approach to investigate their professional learning. Louise is currently directing a learning centre for youth and adults who have been labelled by society as 'at risk'. In her workplace, the discourses of normality are challenged daily as she seeks to live out her thesis in practice. Louise is also facilitating an action research project centred around collective storytelling, where the purpose is to disrupt the taken-for-granted in order to experience the self and others differently.

Teresa Vasconcelos is a full Professor and Chair of Early Childhood Education at Lisbon School of Education (Polytechnic Institute). She has conducted ethnographic and case-study research both at the national level and internationally. She joined an international group of researchers led by Bob Stake, who developed case studies for the International Step by Step Association in Central and Eastern Europe.

Introduction

Glenda Mac Naughton, Sharne A. Rolfe, Iram Siraj-Blatchford

This book is about how to conduct research in and about the early childhood years. It is written specifically for novice and early career researchers and their mentors. It demonstrates that, while there are many different ways in which early childhood research can be approached, all research needs to be theoretically grounded, well designed, rigorously analysed, feasible, and ethically fair and just. The book attempts to show how to do this from within diverse traditions and paradigms.

In this completely updated and enlarged second edition, we have again drawn on the expertise and experience of a diverse team of international early childhood researchers who represent the multidisciplinary nature of this field of endeavour. They bring an authority, breadth and depth to the discussion that would not be possible in a sole-authored text.

We see two main reasons for publishing a book on the research process written specifically for novice early childhood researchers. First, early childhood studies are multidisciplinary, so standard texts written for students of the social sciences or the humanities are often not sufficiently broad for the needs of the early childhood field. Second, general education research texts often focus specifically on research in classrooms rather than the multitude of contexts experienced by the child from birth through to the early years of school.

Part I introduces readers to the nature of research and the research process. In Chapters 1 and 2, Rolfe and Mac Naughton attempt to 'demystify' research by emphasising that the research process is simply a tool by which we can answer important questions about early childhood. Readers are shown how to:

- select a topic
- review literature
- formulate a research issue/question
- design research
- collect data
- sample populations
- explore questions of validity
- process/analyse data
- draw research conclusions
- write research reports.

Chapter 3 introduces readers to four major research paradigms that underpin early childhood research: positivism, interpretivism, structuralism and poststructuralism. Hughes uses case studies of research on children and the media to explain these paradigms and show how they influence researchers' choice of method and their results. Chapter 4 explores the practical and theoretical issues faced by beginning researchers. Chapter 5 discusses key ethical issues that arise in early childhood research. In particular, it canvasses the ethics of researching with children and how to manage informed consent in research with children, using international comparisons to highlight how the early childhood field addresses ethical dilemmas. Chapter 6—new to this second edition—provides significant insights into the possibilities and challenges of indigenous research. As non-Indigenous early childhood researchers increasingly build research relationships with Indigenous communities and Indigenous researchers, and as the number of Indigenous early childhood researchers grows it is critical to more deeply engage with the issues raised in Chapter 6. Whilst the issues raised in this chapter are not specific to the early childhood research community they are deeply relevant to it.

Part II introduces key issues in research design and analysis. In Chapter 7, Hayes uses current examples from a large-scale study of Australian children to provide a foundational understanding of design. He discusses design options (experimental, quasi-experimental and non-experimental), the dimension of time (in retrospective, prospective, cross-sectional and longitudinal designs) and sampling issues to do with both the selection of participants and the settings of research. Harrison, in Chapter 8, provides an overview of the information needed by researchers to undertake quantitative research in early childhood. She brings this discussion to life using her own research to work through the meaning of statistical analysis, probability levels and 'statistical significance'. Her discussion explains statistical concepts and procedures, descriptive statistics, inferential statistics and computer analyses. Edwards (Chapter 9) provides an overview of the information needed by researchers to undertake qualitative research in early childhood. In Chapter 10, Grieshaber introduces a series of design principles for ensuring equity in research. Chapter 11 discusses mixed-method designs and their importance in researching early childhood. In the final chapter of Part II, Blaise overviews the challenges of designing to scale, using the example of doing a student research project.

Part III presents a collection of case studies illustrating some of the most commonly used early childhood research methods—including surveys and questionnaires, interviews with adults and children, ethnography, action research, direct observation, and new chapters on case study and quasi-experimental approaches.

In each chapter, the researcher or researchers provide a narrative describing how they conducted a specific research project and some of the decisions, challenges and pitfalls they encountered. To ensure that the novice researcher is able to readily compare and contrast methods, each writer explores questions that include: 'What were your major research questions?', 'What guided your decisions regarding choice of methods?', 'What sampling or other research design issues were there?' and 'How did you interpret what you found?'

Several devices are used throughout the book to ensure it is readily accessible, practical and user-friendly for the novice and early-career researcher:

- closure summary in each chapter of the key ideas covered
- boxed summaries, checklists and/or explanations of key concepts, processes and themes in all chapters
- post-text questions in each chapter to help readers review their learning and extend their thinking about the issues/methods raised in the chapter
- further reading lists, annotated to show how they might best be used to further understanding of the material covered in the chapter and
- a glossary of key terms at the end of the book.

PART I

THE NATURE OF RESEARCH

1

Research as a tool

Sharne A. Rolfe and Glenda Mac Naughton

Doing anything for the first time is a challenge, and starting off in research can be a daunting prospect. But along with uncertainty and some trepidation, there are often feelings of curiosity and excitement about the journey of discovery that lies ahead. Once underway, experience, knowledge and confidence build. There may be hurdles and pitfalls to be negotiated along the way, but the hardest part is often taking the first step.

In this chapter, we aim to demystify research and the research process, drawing on our combined knowledge and experience of doing early childhood research, and training research students over many years. Throughout this book, you will have the opportunity to learn from many experienced researchers working on a diverse range of topics, using a wide range of methods and approaching early childhood research from different philosophical perspectives and **paradigms**. You will also hear from some beginning researchers who share their experiences with you.

If you are already experienced in doing research, we hope this book will facilitate your attempts to demystify research for your students. In this chapter, we emphasise that research is best conceptualised simply as a tool that helps us answer important questions about early childhood—questions that would remain unanswered were it not for the willingness of academics, practitioners and participants (children and adults) to engage with the research process. Research is about uncovering and enabling the emergence of new understandings, insights and knowledge. The best research will always involve close, ongoing collaboration between those who plan the research, those who carry it out, those who participate in it, and those for whom the results have an impact. Research may be hard work, but it can also be fun. It is absolutely worthwhile.

WHY BOTHER WITH RESEARCH?

Given the skill it requires, the resources—both financial and human—it consumes and the time it takes, an important question to ask is: 'Why do research at all?' Research can have negative as well as positive impacts, as Coady in her discussion of research **ethics** (Chapter 5) describes in the case of 'Genie'. Genie was a young girl isolated in a bedroom of her parents' home for most of her childhood. After she was discovered, she became the focus of intensive research directed at understanding how these early experiences had influenced her development (see Curtiss, 1977). Although the researchers may have started out with the best of intentions, many questions have been raised about whether this research was ethical and how this highly vulnerable young person may have been affected in negative ways by the scrutiny of the researchers and the research process. The case highlights the tensions that can exist when benefits to the participants in research are weighed up against benefits to the researcher. Clearly, researchers must understand and address ethical issues that arise in research, including the need to protect the interests and ongoing welfare of research participants. Ethical concerns must lie at the heart of our decision to research and the choice of research methods. As Aubrey and colleagues (2000) write, 'researchers need to be clear about their roles and the responsibilities towards the *people* involved—including *themselves*—and to the *research process*' (2000, p. 143).

With careful attention to ethical concerns, research can make positive differences in the lives of children, and in this book you will find many examples of research that has done so. Some studies have at their core the quest to describe or to understand, and when this is the case researchers often favour **qualitative approaches** that encourage complexity and diversity in the research data. For example, Taylor's participant action research study of teacher learning (Chapter 17) highlighted the complex and diverse ways in which teachers in New Zealand understood the professional and policy contexts that influenced what they knew and how they understood themselves as learners. This included emphasising the tensions and dilemmas that the teachers' engagement with biculturalism generated within the group. Blaise's small-scale classroom study of gender and sexuality (Chapter 12) generated data from diverse sources (children, parents and teachers) and used diverse data-generation strategies (reading children's books, sharing and discussing popular toys, children's drawings and photographic documentation) to build a complex picture of how a small group of young children understand gender and sexuality in their early years. Understandings generated through research that explores diverse perspectives on the why and how of what happens enable early childhood practitioners to rethink what they do, how they do it, and how this affects children and their families in a variety of settings. These understandings also have the potential to impact on policy directions and the way governments respond to emerging social issues.

Other research seeks not only to understand but also to explain. This task lends itself to **quantitative approaches**, in which careful control is essential to conclusions about cause and effect. Examples of such approaches are described in chapters by Hayes on research design (Chapter 7) and Harrison on quantitative methodologies (Chapter 8), including the major long-term Australian study called *Growing Up in Australia: The Longitudinal Study of Australian Children* (LSAC). This carefully designed study with a large, nationally representative sample of infants and children is investigating Australian children's development and the contribution of social, economic and cultural environments to their adjustment and well-being.

The LSAC is an example of **longitudinal research**, in which data on the same children are collected at multiple points in time. Research of this kind allows examination of how certain events or experiences impact on children's well-being and development, both currently and at later stages. A well-known example of this kind of research began in 1955 on the Hawaiian island of Kauai. Extending from the middle of the twentieth century into the beginning of the twenty-first, the research followed the development and life course of nearly 700 infants who experienced various risk factors in the pre- and perinatal periods (see Werner and Smith, 2001). An important outcome of this study and other research that has followed has been identification of 'protective factors' that enable some at-risk infants to be resilient despite early disadvantage and trauma.

Another example of longitudinal research that has provided important insights into children's development is the Minnesota Study of Risk and Adaptation from Birth to Adulthood (Sroufe et al., 2005). This study of 180 children born in poverty has now continued for more than 30 years. Extensive assessments of the participants' development, and their developmental contexts (home, early childhood settings, school, etc.) were undertaken at multiple times, beginning prenatally. The study sought to identify the conditions that promote optimal, competent functioning—or are associated with developmental problems—along with sources of resilience and pathways to change. Based on their extensive research, the authors reach a number of compelling conclusions, including 'that nothing is more important in the development of the child than the care received, including that in the early years' (p. 19).

Longitudinal research can involve timeframes of many years, or just a year or two (see Emmett and Rolfe, 2009, as discussed in Chapter 18 on direct observation). Emmett and Rolfe (2009) examined the impact of an attachment-focused training program on participants' professional practice during the final year of an early childhood pre-service course and after two years of employment in the field. Collection of data at multiple time points may also occur in experimental and quasi-experimental studies that use a prospective pre-test/post-test design. An example of this approach is Liane Brown's evaluation of an attachment-based parenting program on parental sensitivity (see Chapter 20).

Research can also reveal how different cultures understand development, and challenge us to rethink Anglo-centric ways of studying, understanding and explaining children, pedagogy, curriculum and the effects of social contexts on what happens in early childhood settings. Martin (Chapter 6) focuses particular attention on patterns of silencing Aborigines in research and what it takes to build research that emphasises Aboriginal sovereignty in generating ways of being and knowing in early childhood research. Sue Atkinson-Lopez's study of Indigenous self-determination in early childhood curricula (Chapter 15) explores what it looks like in practice to build a research protocol and approach to knowledge generation that challenges Anglo-centrism within a research project. Research should challenge habitual ways of doing things, and provide reasons to modify, refocus or change. Throughout this book, you will have the opportunity to learn from various researchers whose own research has contributed, sometimes in major ways, to just these sorts of outcomes.

WHO CAN DO RESEARCH?

Many people are 'amateur' researchers, seeking to understand, explain and make sense of life experiences in whatever ways they can. Developmentalists such as Jean Piaget have outlined theories about how this process proceeds. People develop **hypotheses** and then test them out in haphazard ways with limited data. The danger of this approach is that we can become inappropriately confident about our amateur research outcomes, reaching hasty and premature conjectures dressed up as quasi-scientific conclusions. Sometimes we rely on the opinions or knowledge of others. This is also problematic, as opinions may be based on stereotypes passed down through the generations.

In contrast to these informal ways of gathering knowledge, well-designed research based on reliable and valid measures can generate meaningful, conclusive outcomes. We summarise the characteristics of high-quality research later in this chapter.

While most research, including early childhood research, is undertaken by people working in or associated with universities or educational institutions, quality research is not the sole province of university-based academics with doctoral degrees. In an early paper, Wadsworth (1984) argued strongly that those affected by research can and should do research: 'Research is a process legitimated in our society as producing knowledge and therefore ought to be in the hands of those who want to use and benefit from it—particularly when it is information about our own lives.' (1984, p. iii). Recognising this, an increasing number of early childhood courses include research training as part of their syllabus so that graduate early childhood practitioners can be researchers as well as informed consumers of the research of others.

LEARNING TO RESEARCH

When you first think about doing research and the questions you could address, you might consult experts, read about different opinions, and even talk to your colleagues and friends about their views. This may help you to clarify what it is that you really want to know. But this is not enough to generate high-quality research. Neither is intuition. Irrespective of who is researching, quality research requires knowledge, skills and experience. Reading this book is a great place to start. It is also helpful in developing the right sort of attitude—seeing research as a tool.

Seeing research as a tool

It is important to understand that research is a tool and, as with all tools, it is simply a matter of learning how to use it. Thinking about research in this way means that you as the researcher control the research process, not vice versa. You begin the process with your interest in an early childhood topic or question. Not content to accept what is already known and written about this topic, you want to know more. You may want to answer previously ignored questions, or you may want to approach old questions from a different angle. Research can satisfy your fascination, and others can evaluate and benefit from your work.

Some research topics and questions come from our personal or professional experiences. Others arise from careful reading of the published literature. If you are a student just beginning research, a topic may be provided by your lecturer or supervisor so that you can focus your attention on planning, designing and executing the research, evaluating results, drawing conclusions and writing them up. You may be invited to join an existing research group, taking part in a program of studies designed so that each, in its own unique way, adds to an emerging understanding of the topic of interest. Regardless of how you come to your topic, it is by learning to use research as a tool that you can answer the question or questions you set out to address, and inform others of what you have found. The next chapter explores these processes in more detail.

Learning to be sceptical

It is important to note that a research study rarely stands alone. An important part of the research process is **replication**. Different researchers or research groups study the same phenomenon, using the same or similar methods, in order to determine whether the same results will occur. This helps to establish the **generalisability** of results and conclusions drawn from them. Clearly if one study reports particular results, but these are not replicated in further similar studies, the initial results are thrown into question. Certainly one would want to look carefully at the details of how the studies were done to establish reasons for the discrepant results. Being sceptical of research outcomes is a good thing, just as it is to be critical in our evaluation of whatever we read or are told.

Not all research sets out to establish generalisable results. Research such as action research (Chapter 17) or case study research (Chapter 19) may seek to create change or understand a particular aspect of a specific setting. In this research, validity arises through the way in which the research is conducted and analysed rather than through its replicability and generalisability.

Becoming apprentices

One of the best ways for students to learn about research is via an 'apprenticeship' model. In this model, the student works under the guidance and direction of an experienced researcher, either on the researcher's own project or on a project that they develop together, appropriate to the resources available. Early in their course, undergraduates can, with guidance, plan and carry out small research projects, often pooling the data they collect with others who have (ideally) conducted the research in the same way.

Preparing for surprises

When we set out on any journey of discovery, we are often surprised along the way. By definition, surprises can't be anticipated. So, no matter how well planned your research, expect the unexpected! Every part of the research process may offer surprises: theories, events, well-tested methods, children and adult participants. As Murphy's Law states: If anything can go wrong, it will. Participants may not turn up, or may not complete questionnaires or surveys as promised, equipment may fail, or misunderstandings may develop among members of the research team.

There are other kinds of surprises as well. Theories can surprise you by unsettling your taken-for-granted assumptions about how the world works, and children and adults can surprise you with their responses to your research. These sorts of surprises can be exciting, fun, enlightening and reviving. They can motivate you to explore more and challenge you to think differently. Surprises are what good research is all about, and what make research meaningful and enjoyable. Sometimes the most compelling insights we gain from research come from the outcomes we least expected.

We started this chapter by saying that research is about discovery. As you begin your research endeavour, prepare for discovery, always asking 'What can I learn from this?' and 'How does this help my research?' Also realise that sometimes the question we start off with isn't the question we end up researching, and that is okay.

'GOOD' RESEARCH AND 'BAD' RESEARCH?

'Good' research does not rely on one particular method or paradigm. Researchers' views about what is a good research method will be determined by the research paradigm they espouse. There is lively debate among early childhood researchers about the different ways of approaching and doing research, and discussion of research agendas, research assumptions, methods and objectives. You will find a detailed discussion of how choice of research paradigm influences views of good research in the chapter by Hughes (Chapter 3).

Irrespective of the research paradigm you choose, there are some basic principles that underpin all quality research. For us, quality research is always ethical, purposeful, well designed, transparent, contextualised, credible, careful, imaginative and equitable.

PRINCIPLES FOR HIGH-QUALITY RESEARCH
Ethical research should be:

- ethical
- purposeful
- well designed
- transparent
- contextualised
- credible
- careful
- imaginative
- equitable

SUMMARY

- *Ethical research* is based on informed consent, does not harm participants, attempts to benefit them and makes a positive contribution to knowledge and to the broader social good. (Chapters 5 and 6 offer a more detailed discussion of these issues.)
- *Purposeful research* has clear aims and justifiable strategies for working towards these aims. We talk more about this in Chapter 2.
- *Well-designed research* is systematic and designed in a way that is consistent with its topic, theoretical underpinnings, aims, research strategies and methods. Chapters 7, 8 and 9 introduce you to processes for developing well-designed research.
- *Transparent research* allows other people to follow your research trail and the decisions you take at different points in the process. You should be scrupulous about recording what you did and why, and how you reached your research decisions, findings and conclusions, so that others can evaluate your conclusions.
- *Contextualised research* acknowledges its own philosophical, theoretical, policy and social contexts. This means that you must be able to show how your research developed in and from a specific theoretical context, and how specific policy and social contexts influenced the way you conducted your research, and what was found. Chapters 15, 16, 17 and 19 provide examples of strongly contextualised research.
- *Credible research* follows accepted principles for framing research questions, investigating them, analysing the findings and drawing

conclusions from them. Chapter 2 details broadly accepted principles for engaging in credible research.

- *Careful research* acknowledges its limited scope and its design limitations. You need to identify these limitations and be careful not to draw conclusions or inferences that ignore these limitations.
- *Imaginative research* is innovative and original. It captures the imagination of the researcher and those who hear about the research. It is unreasonable and inappropriate to expect that every research study will be entirely original. This is particularly the case for beginning researchers. Even experienced researchers, as we have already discussed, may choose to closely follow the design of an earlier study with the aim of establishing whether the results can be replicated. Most research will nonetheless benefit from you bringing your creative skills to the fore when you design and analyse it.
- *Equitable research* acknowledges the biases, interests and concerns of the researcher. You need to think carefully about how your own biases and background might impact on your research. Learning to do equitable research, as outlined in Chapter 10, is central to doing high-quality research.

Whether or not research is 'good' hinges on how well the researcher has worked through the various steps that constitute the research process. We begin to discuss these steps in Chapter 2, where we look at how you can bring the principles of quality research to life throughout each phase of your research endeavour. You will find these principles illustrated and amplified many times in the case examples presented throughout this book.

QUESTIONS FOR REFLECTION

1. Think of some examples of research that have influenced your views about young children. What do you know about how the research was conducted? Where could you find out more about this?
2. Where else have your views come from and how trustworthy do you now feel these sources are?
3. Do you know anyone who has done research? What have they told you about their experiences?
4. What do you see as the main challenges you face in learning to do research?
5. What aspects of learning to research excite you?

REFERENCES

Aubrey, C., David, T., Godfrey, T. and Thompson, L. 2000 *Early Childhood Educational Research: Issues in Methodology and Ethics*, Routledge Falmer, London.

Curtiss, S. 1977 *Genie: A Psycholinguistic Study of a Modern-Day 'Wild Child'*, Academic Press, New York.

Sroufe, L.A., Egeland, B., Carlson, E.A. and Collins, W.A. 2005 *The Development of the Person: The Minnesota Study of Risk and Adaptation from Birth to Adulthood*, The Guilford Press, New York.

Wadsworth, Y. 1984 *Do It Yourself Social Research*, Victorian Council of Social Service and Melbourne Family Care Organisation, Melbourne.

Werner, E.E. and Smith, R.S. 2001 *Journeys from Childhood to Midlife: Risk, Resilience and Recovery*, Cornell University Press, New York.

FURTHER READING

Contemporary Issues in Early Childhood is an international online journal that publishes articles which engage in contemporary debates and issues in early childhood research. It has a particular focus on interdisciplinary perspectives on childhood, and often—though not solely—publishes research framed using poststructuralist, postmodern and postcolonial perspectives, queer theory and the new sociology of childhood, and engaging diverse qualitative research methodologies. It includes research reviews, colloquia and critical commentaries, and is a good place to engage with cutting-edge scholarship in the field. Its themed editions offer new researchers a great way to explore diverse research methods and questions on topics of interest to them.

Early Childhood Research Quarterly is one of the foremost early childhood research journals. It publishes high-quality empirical, scholarly research in early childhood development, theory and educational practice. Qualitative and quantitative research, as well as practitioner and/or policy perspectives, book reviews, and significant reviews of research, are included. It is a good place to start if you are interested in perusing the diversity of empirical research questions investigated by early childhood researchers.

Goodwin, W.L. and Goodwin, L.D. 1996 *Understanding Quantitative and Qualitative Research in Early Childhood Education*, Teachers College Press, New York. This early text provides helpful content on the nature of the research process as it applies to early childhood education. Chapter 1 includes a discussion of the value of research and some early childhood topics that are the focus of much current research.

Suter, W.N. 2006 *Introduction to Educational Research: A Critical Thinking Approach*, Sage, Thousand Oaks, CA. This helpful introduction to educational research covers topics that include thinking about research, the language of research, diversity in educational research, analysing and critiquing research, and writing research proposals. The content can readily be adapted to research in early childhood.

2

The research process

Glenda Mac Naughton and Sharne A. Rolfe

Research means finding out about things. To this extent, the job of the researcher is like that of a detective. Each searches for clues to advance theories about how and why things happen and each starts their work with questions about something intriguing, mysterious or puzzling. They then use well-tested methods to gather the clues and information needed to help them 'solve', understand or explain their intrigue, mystery or puzzle. This chapter introduces you to the well-tested processes that researchers use to give shape and direction to these efforts.

Like detectives, researchers have different ideas about the best way to do their work. Some researchers pursue their research in a linear, logical and step-by-step way. In more technical terms, this is referred to as a **deductive research methodology**. It is associated with **positivist** paradigms and often uses quantitative approaches to data. Researchers who approach their work in this way generally wait until all their data are in before beginning to analyse and draw conclusions. They usually set out to test hypotheses based on theory and research already completed and carefully design their studies with this intention. An example of this sort of research approach can be seen in Liane Brown's quasi-experimental evaluation of a new attachment-focused parenting program (see Chapter 20). Other researchers have a more fluid and intuitive approach to their research. In technical terms, they engage in what is referred to as an **inductive research methodology**, often associated with **interpretivist** and **postmodern** paradigms, and frequently using qualitative approaches to data. The researcher generally tries to avoid too many preconceptions about what will be discovered, and is keen to stay close to and analyse the data, looking at the theory emerging from it and perhaps even modifying the line of inquiry in response to developing understandings. Examples of this research approach can be seen in Chapter 15 (on interviewing adults in an Indigenous early childhood program) and Chapter 17 (an action research study).

Both deductive and inductive approaches offer important—albeit different—insights into the phenomena of interest, and the approach used will usually reflect the way of looking at the world that the researcher brings to the task. Different sorts of questions also lend themselves to different sorts of approaches. The approaches are not mutually exclusive, and many researchers use a combination to gain a more complete picture of what they are interested in. The use of different methods within the same study—**triangulation**—is discussed in Chapter 9.

Regardless of the approach taken, at some point in the research process most researchers find that they need to complete the following steps if they want to generate research that is informative, ethical, meaningful, persuasive and significant:

- select a topic
- search and review the literature
- formulate a specific research issue/question
- design the research
- collect data/information
- process/analyse data
- draw conclusions
- write research reports.

In this chapter, we summarise what is involved in each of these steps. The remaining chapters show you how these steps work in more detail and how the specific approach to research that you take influences the role that each of these steps has in your research.

SELECT A TOPIC

Providing and operating high-quality services for young children is a complex undertaking. It requires good information about questions as diverse as the following:

- How do young children learn, grow and develop?

- How can we best use this knowledge to optimise children's learning, growth and development?
- How is it best to organise, fund and regulate services for young children?
- What curriculum is best suited to young children? Who should decide this?
- How can we ensure services are relevant to the diverse and complex needs of different families and children?
- How is it best to train staff to work with young children?
- What is the best way to staff services for young children?
- How should parents and the wider community be involved in decisions about the operation and provision of services for young children?
- What evidence exists about what works?
- What is the relationship between specific practices and polices and children's outcomes?

This diversity of issues, as well as the complexity within each issue, means that early childhood researchers are rarely short of possible research topics. In fact, the issue that many beginning researchers face is not finding a topic but selecting one from all their ideas and the possible directions they might take. For instance, in just ten minutes in a workshop on early childhood research, one group of Australian early childhood practitioners identified 22 research questions that they believed needed further exploration. The topics ranged from communication between different sectors within the field, to approaches to staff training and job satisfaction, through to equity issues of gender and disability. Even if you are not yet an experienced practitioner, your practicum experiences have probably left you wondering about children, their development and how best to care for and educate them. As we explored in Chapter 1, many research topics emerge from our own experiences. Another source of ideas is what we read in books and journals, especially as part of a course of study.

In the face of such diversity, how do you decide? The simple steps that follow can help you to settle on a research topic.

First, choose a topic that interests you personally. Are you interested in any of the following topics?:

- Children's learning, growth and development. What aspect of this interests you?
- The organisation and management of services for young children. What aspects of this interest you?

- Early childhood curriculum, teaching and learning. What aspect of this interests you?
- Community and parent involvement. What aspect of this interests you?
- Policies for young children and their services. What aspect of this interests you?
- Social justice issues for young children. What aspect of this interests you?
- Other issues. What are they?

Second, choose a topic that will be of interest and significance to other people. Research is about exploring relationships between events, seeking explanations about why things happen, comparing approaches to practice, predicting events, and building new understandings about policy and practice. It may highlight the complexities, shortcomings, possibilities, challenges and applicability of what we know, and do for and with young children. As you explore the research case studies in this book, you will see that each of the researchers, in different ways, has set out to research something that matters to them and to others. If your research matters to others, it has some chance of making a difference to the way we understand and practice our work with young children.

CHOOSING A TOPIC: QUESTIONS TO HELP

- Is it novel for you? Or is it something you have pondered for some time?
- Either way, will you be able to maintain your interest in it over time?
- Are the sorts of questions that may emerge from this topic area manageable with the time and resources you have?
- Do you have the relevant expertise or knowledge?
- Can you get the information you need in your daily work?
- Is it ethical?

SEARCH THE LITERATURE

Once you settle on the general topic of your research, it is important to find out what is currently known about it and how this knowledge has been gained. To do this, you undertake a search of the literature that has been published on your topic. This has three broad aims: to acquaint you with what other people know and have said about your chosen topic; to inform the formulation of your research question; and to guide your choice of design for your own study. Within these broad aims, a literature search and review involves several specific tasks. To become acquainted with the literature, you first need to find the literature that is most relevant to your own research topic.

Finding the relevant literature

Finding literature on a research topic has been made faster and easier with the availability of online databases that index and abstract research. These databases vary in the amount of detail accessible online. For instance, the Educational Resources Information Collection (ERIC) database often used by researchers in early childhood indexes two types of materials—education journals and ERIC documents. ERIC documents include unpublished items that would otherwise be difficult to access, such as theses, conference papers and government reports.

Most university libraries have staff to advise you on how best to search the online databases to which they subscribe. The libraries will generally have access to powerful electronic search engines that can quickly and effectively search through online databases for information about published research on your topic. For the beginning researcher, using online database searching with an experienced guide is a most effective way to begin your literature review.

However, before you approach your librarian for assistance with an online database search, do some preparatory work. Identify the key words or concepts in your research topic first. Most databases have a thesaurus of key terms that they use for indexing and abstracting purposes. Guidance from your library staff on how to use the thesaurus can save you lots of wasted search time.

From online database searching, you can find:

- summaries (abstracts) of research articles on your topic and details about how to access the full-text documents
- some full-text journal articles, reports and research summaries
- abstracts of books and book chapters related to your research
- conference paper abstracts.

Whilst online database searching is an efficient and effective way to access material, it is not the only way, and it has its limits. To improve the scope and currency of your search, use the following strategies:

- Talk to the information services librarian about the pros and cons of using the particular online databases to which your library subscribes. Some databases focus on specific geographic regions (for example,

ERIC is dominated by North American research) and some only index journals and not conference papers. It is important to be clear about what you are accessing.

- Search the hard-copy indexes of key early childhood journals to get a feel for what the journal publishes and access material in journals not abstracted in the major online databases.
- Learn where books related to your topic are kept in the library and scan the shelves occasionally.
- Keep an eye on the new arrivals shelf.
- Subscribe to the online contents pages notification for key journals in your area.
- Get into a routine of browsing the academic bookshops near you for recent arrivals.
- Participate in conferences related to your topic. It can take many months and sometimes years for a conference presentation to appear as a journal article. Conferences are one way of learning about who is doing what, right now.
- If you can't participate yourself, talk to people who have been to recent conferences (for example, academic staff, research students, early childhood practitioners). They may also be helpful to find out what conferences are planned and where they will be. The newsletters of professional organisations sometimes provide lists of upcoming events, including conferences. Conference organisers produce programs that provide at least the titles of papers and symposia being presented. You could then ask someone who is attending to request a copy of a paper of interest for you, or write to the author and request a copy yourself. Most conference programs provide author contact details, such as email addresses, to facilitate this. Finally, many conferences produce a book of abstracts of proceedings that usually can be purchased, even if you did not attend the conference.

USEFUL RESEARCH DATABASES FOR EARLY CHILDHOOD RESEARCHERS

- AskERIC—provides abstracts and full-text documents related to education and has a specialist early childhood collection (USA)
- Australian Education Index (Australia)

- Australian Family and Society Abstracts (FAMILY) (Australia)
- BIDS ISI Data Service—provides bibliographic data and full-text services for higher education and research (UK)
- British Education Index—an electronic and printed guide to the contents of British educational periodical literature (UK)
- Canadian Education Index (Canada)
- Child Development Abstracts and Bibliography
- Current Contents
- Educational Research Abstracts online
- Education Research Complete (International)
- Exceptional Child Education Abstracts
- Expanded Academic (with full-text component)
- Family and Society Studies Worldwide
- Google Scholar
- International Education Research Database (International)
- *Mental Measurements Yearbook*—this has full-text information about and reviews of all English-language standardised tests covering educational skills, personality, vocational aptitude, psychology and related areas
- Proquest Education Complete—has a full-text component
- PsycINFO
- QUALIDATA ESRC Qualitative Data Archival Resource Centre (UK)
- QualPage—provides resources for qualitative researchers (Canada)
- REGARD—a new database service containing a wide range of information on social science research (UK)
- Social Science Citation Index
- Social Science Plus (with full-text component)
- Sociological Abstracts
- Web of Science

The extent of your literature search

As you can see, there are many ways to access the research literature and, depending on your general topic area, you may find there is a lot of literature to consider! How extensive your literature search becomes should be guided by practical considerations, particularly the nature of the research task at hand. Some research projects are very small, perhaps undertaken as a minor assessment requirement for one subject. Your lecturer may have provided you with the key references and ask you to locate just one or two more that are relevant. For a year-long research project, a more detailed, extensive search may be warranted, and of course if you are undertaking higher-degree research, or funded research, it is your responsibility to 'know' the literature very well indeed. (For a detailed discussion of scaling your literature review to your project, see Mac Naughton and Hughes, 2008.)

FORMULATE A RESEARCH ISSUE OR QUESTION

In addition to familiarising you with your general topic area, the literature review should be seen as the vehicle by which you begin to refine the broad topic area of interest to you into a researchable question or questions. Wadsworth (1991) wrote that 'research begins with the conscious asking of questions' (1991, p. 3). We would add that it also continues and often ends with asking questions. In any event, finally deciding on your initial research question(s) is often the most challenging part of research. In our experience, this is certainly the first part of the research process with which students may really struggle. How much of a struggle it is depends on the topic area chosen. Some areas are very broad and students find it difficult to narrow the topic down to one or a small number of workable (researchable) questions. An example of this is the student who wishes to research a topic like 'preschoolers' play'. There are myriad different questions—probably thousands—that have been already investigated and probably thousands more that have yet to be researched. Other areas are quite narrow: little has been written about the topic because little research has yet been done. One example of this would be the student who is interested in the topic of 'paternal separation anxiety'—that is, how fathers feel about being separated from their infant children, for example, in the context of leaving them in child care. In this case, the topic may need very little refining to bring it down to a workable question. Either way, there will be challenges and this section aims to provide some ideas to help avoid common pitfalls at this stage of the research process.

The first step to formulating your research question involves a thorough review of the literature generated by your literature search. Reviewing the literature involves:

- identifying what other researchers know about the topic
- identifying the key arguments, themes and issues that have emerged to date from other research and theoretical writing on the topic
- identifying the key theoretical perspectives that have been used to frame research and to analyse the topic

- identifying gaps in knowledge, and contradictions and disagreements about what is known about the topic
- identifying areas of uncertainty, puzzlement or confusion in what is known.

These steps help you to refine, limit and refocus your own research by:

- reviewing how other research has been conducted on the topic
- reflecting on the difficulties and successes other researchers have noted in their own research
- noting the implications for your own research of any critiques of specific research approaches or theories
- identifying how your own research could add to the topic through discovering new information, refining or clarifying current understandings
- identifying the similarities and differences in context, method and questions between existing research and your proposed project
- ensuring that your own research is in some way(s) original and is not unknowingly replicating other people's research
- seeking support from within the literature for the specific approach or theoretical framework you want to use.

When your initial literature review is complete, you should be familiar with key writings and research on your topic. You should know about the quantity and quality of this work. You should be able to reflect on how this knowledge will inform your own research question. You should now be ready to refine your initial research questions and to formulate a research question or issue that is original and justifiable given the current state of knowledge about your topic.

If your research is using a deductive approach, your research problem and question will be defined precisely at this point. This precision should involve clear **operational definitions** of the key terms and variables that you intend to investigate. For further discussion on this point, refer to Chapters 7 and 8. Researchers using an inductive approach need to ensure that they have developed a research issue or question that enables them to describe and analyse people's social realities (see Chapter 9). Questions developed at this stage for a qualitative study may be less precise than those in a quantitative study, but it is still important to be clear about what you mean by each of your key terms and what it is that you are going to measure in your research.

REFINING THE TOPIC: SOME STEPS TO HELP

- Identify your broad topic.
- Break your large topic into sub-areas.
- Eliminate those sub-areas that interest you least.
- Choose one sub-area.
- Generate questions about that sub-area using 'how, why, what, when and where' questions.
- Reflect on the questions that are most likely to generate new and improved understandings.
- Consider the resources—financial, human and time—available to you.
- Decide on a question that is workable within your resourcing constraints and that interests you most.

(Based on Charles and Mertler, 2005; Berg, 2007; Kumar, 2005).

Your research question(s) should be meaningful, workable and relatively precise.

Refining the questions

- Are you clear about what you mean by the key terms?
- Will your question/topic require you to describe what exists, explore relationships between events or people, explain relationships or change them?
- Does your question enable you to focus on a combination of at least two of the following: people, problems, programs or phenomena?
- State your main objective and then check that the question enables you to meet it.

(Based on Charles and Mertler, 2005; Berg, 2007; Kumar, 2005)

In many studies, this part of the research process also involves developing the hypothesis or hypotheses of the study. This is the expectation of what your study will find, usually based on the outcomes of previous research.

The practicalities of deciding what is a workable research question

The resources available and the time period in which the research study must be completed are important practical considerations in refining your final research question. Some researchers have the financial resources to employ a research assistant or have very few competing demands. The question(s) they select may be different to those chosen by a researcher who will personally be doing all the work, as well as completing coursework, undertaking part-time paid work and maybe caring for a family as well. Research projects that must be completed in a few weeks will have different research questions from those that will extend over months or even years. Whichever is the case, it is absolutely essential that you take the time (hopefully in discussion with an experienced researcher) to make good decisions at this point. There is nothing more devastating for a student than to find halfway through her research time that the question she set out to answer is too complex or broad.

Many beginning researchers are far too ambitious about their research questions. This usually is because they want their research to make a major impact in terms of its conclusions. Simplifying questions may make them appear trivial, and therefore not worthwhile or less worthwhile. Two considerations should be helpful here. One is to realise that very few research studies, in and of themselves, provide major answers to major questions. Research is not like that. Even well-funded research projects are usually made up of a series of smaller studies planned in a programmatic way so that the results of one inform the next and so on. Knowledge is thus slowly and systematically built up, and it is the sum total of all the studies—and usually studies by many others as well—that will eventually lead to major breakthroughs. As a researcher, one learns to be content with making small, but meaningful, contributions to the ongoing quest for understanding or explanation.

Breaking up a complex area into a series of smaller areas and questions is good discipline for any researcher. The advantage of this is also that the student may feel more content knowing that, if progress is very good, it may be possible to include a further question or study if time and resources permit. It is far better to find that this is not possible and have sound data on one, relatively simple question, than to run out of time, or resources while trying to tackle a large, complex question.

We cannot stress enough that it is worth spending time finding workable, appropriate questions, as they drive the remainder of the research process. Your research question will influence what you research, how you research it and what you find out from your research efforts.

Organising and summarising the literature review

As you proceed through the literature search and review stages, it is essential that you organise the literature you access. When preparing a literature review as part of a thesis or research report, you need to demonstrate that you are familiar with previous thinking on your chosen topic and that you have critically engaged with it. This does not mean that you include a summary of every article or book that you have read on your topic. Instead, you organise your readings into the key themes and issues that you feel capture current and past thinking on your topic. Then you can write a summary of this literature based on examples that help you to illustrate these themes and issues. Your illustrative material should be indicative of the relative quality and quantity of material on each theme or issue you identify. The following questions can help you organise and summarise your literature and to select appropriate examples to illustrate your discussion:

- What are the key arguments, themes and issues?
- How have these changed over time?
- How many writers have explored each of these themes and issues?
- What seem to be the main points of agreement and disagreement between different writers?
- How representative of the theme or issue is the material you intend to include?

Continuing to learn from the literature

As your research continues, it is important to keep up to date with emerging ideas and new research on your topic. You can do this by setting aside a regular time every month or so to update your online searches. The time needed to do this will be reduced if you keep a computer file logbook of your searches in which you note the terms used to search each database and when you did this search. Then you can do a quick update rather than re-run your whole initial literature search. Many journals now provide monthly 'alerts' to keep you up to date with what they are publishing and it is an easy matter to join up for these online. It is also good to get into a habit of regularly browsing the new arrivals on the library shelves and in bookshops nearby.

As you continue to learn from the literature, your reading is likely to become more specialised and increasingly focused on the specific issues you are exploring in your research. It is at this point that you begin to become an 'expert' on your chosen topic and can begin to speak with authority about it.

Keeping track of literature

There is nothing worse when you are preparing your research report at the end of a long research process than trying to find the details of a reference used in your literature review some months previously. To avoid looking for the 'red book with a nice cover', be determined from the start of your research to keep good records of the literature that you have read and that is informing your research project. There are many ways to do this. You can use index cards, a logbook or computer software packages such as EndNote, Procite and Citation to manage your bibliography. Whatever system you use, always note down the full details of each piece of literature so that it can be readily retrieved when you prepare a report of your research for others. Time spent on this early in the research process is time well spent.

DESIGN RESEARCH

Careful design of research takes time, and is again time well spent. Good design will ensure that your research provides you with data that enable you to achieve what you set out to achieve—whether it is to describe, understand or explain what interests you. In other words, it is your research question primarily (as well as practical considerations like the financial and time resources available to you) that will guide your research design. Your research design should be a well laid out plan of action that you will follow throughout the conduct of your research.

For those following a deductive research process, this plan, once formulated, will rarely be deviated from. This is because the plan has been prepared to address particular questions with expected outcomes (hypotheses) and to rule out possible alternative explanations of the results obtained. To change the plan halfway would risk serious breaches of the control needed in this sort of research. For example, let's assume that a researcher is interested in how different early childhood curricula impact on children's peer relationships. Searching and reviewing the literature has led the researcher to the expectation (hypothesis) that Curriculum A is likely to facilitate positive peer relationships more than Curriculum B. Luckily for the researcher, there are two preschools in her area that use Curriculum A exclusively and two preschools in her area that use Curriculum B exclusively. She designs a study involving observations of equal numbers of children at all four preschools in terms of their peer relationships. She decides to use videotaping to collect her observations. So far, so good. If she sticks with this design, and she observes more positive peer relationships amongst the children in preschools using Curriculum A, her hypothesis is supported.

But let's say this is not what happens. Let's say that at some point in the study, when she has almost completed data collection at Preschool A and still has lots of observations to complete at Preschool B, she decides it's a waste of time to use videotaping. She decides to change her plan. She decides from now on to just sit amongst the children and write in longhand what she sees. After all, that's what she was doing back in the lab when she looked at her videotapes. Or she may decide to let someone else do the observations—for example, asking the teachers to rate the children yet to be observed using some rating scale of peer interaction. If her data end up showing more positive peer interaction at Preschool A, can she still confidently assert that her hypothesis is supported? If you think about it carefully, you will see that she cannot. She cannot reach such a conclusion because her method changed during the study. As a result, most of the data collected on children at Preschool A was collected in a different way to the data on children at Preschool B. We are left with the possibility that it was the different data-collection method that accounted for the different results. As we cannot rule this out, our researcher has at best learnt a very valuable lesson in research design, and at worst wasted her own and the research participants' time.

Researchers following an inductive approach also need to think about and plan their research strategies; however, because they constantly engage with their emerging data, they often choose to make alterations to their research plan in the light of their new insights and understandings. Remember that in this approach it is unlikely that the researcher starts with a clear hypothesis, rather remaining open to a range of possibilities and discoveries as the study unfolds.

Generally speaking, the design stage of research involves making decisions about how the study will be executed. Decisions need to be made about how the phenomena of interest will be measured, how data will be collected, how many participants will be included and what characteristics they will have. In more technical terms, considerations of **sampling**, measurement, **validity** and **reliability** must be addressed. Getting these decisions right is of such importance that Part II of this book is dedicated to these various topics. Quantitative and qualitative design issues are both considered in depth. It is important to remember that no matter what kind of research you conduct—quantitative or qualitative—principles of good design still apply. New researchers will gain enormously from the help of more experienced researchers as they develop their research design.

SAMPLING POPULATIONS

No matter how well funded your research may be, it is usually impossible to include in your study all the individuals of interest to you. This might not apply if your study is very small scale—for example, if you are only interested in studying the children in one classroom. But if this is the only group you study, then you cannot generalise your results to children beyond this group, even to those who come into that classroom next year, regardless of whether or not the teacher is the same. The reason you cannot generalise your findings in this way is because to generalise from one group to another, the group you study (your so-called sample) must be the same or very similar (that is, representative of) the larger group to whom you wish to generalise (the so-called population). This is really just good common sense. Taking a simple example, if you wanted to know what outside play activities four-year-old children in preschools (the population of interest) enjoyed most, it would make little sense to observe and/or talk to only four-year-old preschool girls. By excluding boys from the sample, you have effectively prevented any generalisations to four-year-old preschoolers in general, as well as any insights that might emerge on gender differences in play. You have limited your study because you could not compare the preferences of girls and boys which may be important and interesting data to consider.

Selecting representative samples is quite complex and entails decision-making around not only the characteristics of the participants, but also how many of them should be included (the so-called sample size). This is also a sticking point for new students of research. The simple answer is usually to include as many participants as possible based on pragmatic factors like how much time you have for data collection, the accessibility of members of the population of interest and how many resources are available to help you both collect and analyse the data. Generally speaking, more data means more time in the collection phase and more time analysing results. This is less of an issue if you are using structured assessments like questionnaires or checklists and are able to use computer programs.

Sample size and sampling plans will also vary according to whether you have chosen a quantitative or qualitative method. Qualitative data—for example, based on interviews—may involve fewer participants, because each participant generates a large amount of data that must be transcribed (usually from audiotape) and then analysed in some way. Even using computer programs for qualitative data relies on transcribed data. If you are doing the transcription yourself, it can take up to eight hours to transcribe each hour of audiotape. Qualitative researchers are also less likely to use sampling plans focused on achieving a so-called representative sample because representativeness is not their primary goal, or may not be a goal at all. They are more focused on generating deeper understanding of experiences and phenomena in specific contexts rather than generating findings that are generalisable to a wider population.

Whichever approach you use, it is critically important that you accurately describe the sample that you use, its size and characteristics when reporting your research (see below). You can then draw your readers' attention to any concerns you have with these aspects of the study and any limitations associated with them. Other researchers are then able, if they wish, to replicate your study. Increasingly, there is a move to using a mix of qualitative and quantitative approaches to data so that a study may draw on the strengths within each approach to generate knowledge.

Ethical considerations

Essential to the design phase of the research process is a sound appreciation of the ethical considerations associated with doing research. Ensuring that the study conforms to ethical standards is of paramount importance. This will include the development of appropriate Plain Language Statements (PLS) about your research and Consent Forms to be signed by participants, including children themselves (if appropriate), their parents or guardians. How to do this is discussed in depth in Chapter 5.

COLLECT DATA

Once your design has been worked out, and you have obtained approval to proceed with your research from your institution's Research Ethics Committee, it is time to collect your data. This phase of the research process is often the one where students begin to feel they are at long last researchers. The nature of your research question and the design chosen to address it will determine where you find yourself during the data-collection phase. Assuming you are the person doing the data collection, you may spend many hours in preschools or other early childhood services. While there, you may be observing children, interviewing them, observing teachers or parents, or maybe interviewing them. You may visit many preschools or other services, or you may concentrate your efforts in only one. You may spend time studying policy documents or historical texts as part of your research. Another possibility is to collect your data using mailout questionnaires or rating scales completed by teachers or parents. This may save a lot of time, but the nature of your data will be very different from that collected through interview or observation. You may find yourself collecting data in family homes or in other settings such as parks and shopping centres, or in university laboratories.

Before any of this can occur, however, you need to gain the permission of the person or people responsible for that setting as well as the consent of the participants themselves. For example, if your research involves observing children in a preschool, you will need to approach the director of the service and the management committee first. They will usually require a clear statement from you about the nature, purpose and design of the study and evidence that the relevant institutional Ethics Committee has approved it.

It is important to remember that all of these approvals—and if you are using multiple sites, even more so—take time. You should factor this in to your overall research plan, especially if you have a tight timeline for completion of your study. This is often the case. You also need to be prepared for delays if child or adult participants become ill or go on holidays. Equipment breakdown, postal delays, inclement weather and so on are all possible and, depending on your method, may act to further delay and frustrate your data-collection plans.

PROCESS/ANALYSE DATA

Once data collection is finished, the phase of data processing and analysis can begin. How this will proceed will depend mainly on whether you have used a quantitative or qualitative approach. Quantitative data involves numbers. These numbers need to be collated and then analysed using statistical procedures. Some statistical procedures are relatively simple and straightforward. These include so-called descriptive statistics, such as measures of central tendency including means (averages) and measures of variability, like the range and standard deviation. Inferential statistics, which enable the researcher to test whether their hypothesis is supported or not, may also be used. Statistical tests of this kind are more complex, and usually a computer software package would be used. Statistical analyses are discussed in Chapter 8.

Qualitative data is usually text (for example, words in an interview transcript). Data in this form can be analysed in a number of ways. Some qualitative data can be recoded into numbers, and then statistical tests used, as the data is now in a quantitative form. Or the researcher may wish to retain the complexity and diversity inherent in the text and use analysis techniques, such as content analysis, that retain these aspects. If this is chosen, there are also computer software packages that can be used to assist in the process. Qualitative data analysis is discussed in Chapter 9.

It is important to draw on your literature review to develop a conceptual/theoretical framework for analysing the data. This is another area with which students struggle. This framework is made up of concepts, built from the literature, that you will apply to organisation and selection of data as well the analysis. There are some good examples of this in Chapters 4, 15, 17 and 18.

As Wiersma and Jurs (2005) warn, it is important not be discouraged if your data are not perfect from your point of view, perhaps because they have not turned out the way you expected or wanted. Your hypotheses may not have been confirmed. Your outcomes may differ from other studies in the area. Sometimes the beginning researcher sees this as a flaw, but there are many reasons why your data have turned out the way they have. Perhaps you have made a design error, perhaps there were other mistakes along the way. Learning from these errors, and accepting the constructive criticisms of others, is important for all researchers, both novice and experienced. That is why it is so important to document how your did your study so that its limitations can be seen by you and others and your interpretations of the data developed accordingly. However, it may also be that you have made a new, important and unexpected discovery. You may have uncovered one of those surprises we talked about in Chapter 1. This may offer the promise of new insights of great significance for early childhood development or practice.

DRAW RESEARCH CONCLUSIONS

We said in Chapter 1 that research is a tool that can be used to improve the lives of young children and their families. To do this, we need to be able to draw lessons or conclusions from our research and share them with others.

Here are some simple steps and questions to guide you through the process of drawing conclusions:

- Look at your research question.
- Identify what you have learnt. What does your data tell you about this question?
- Summarise what you have learnt into key themes and issues.

- Identify the contextual, methodological, practical and theoretical limits and influences on what you have learnt. How have your method, sample size, context and conceptual or analytical framework influenced your findings?
- Note the effects of these limits and influences on your findings.
- What implications do your findings have for theory, practice and policy around your chosen topic?

WRITE A RESEARCH REPORT

The final phase of the research process is sharing your results with others. The research report is how most people do this. Your research report may take the form of a seminar, a project report, a thesis, a journal article or a conference paper, or it may be a combination of these. Irrespective of its form, your report as a beginning researcher should follow accepted conventions. These cover content, style of presentation and approaches to referencing your work.

Conventions differ from journal to journal, university to university and conference to conference. Always check the particular conventions associated with the form and context in which you will publish your results. If you don't follow the conventions for your particular institution or the journal to which you submit an article, your work can be rejected!

In most instances, the content of your report will include:

- title—the title of your research project
- your name, qualifications and institutional affiliation
- acknowledgements—sources of support and funding you have received
- abstract—a summary of the research question, methods and findings
- introduction—this sets the contexts and issues of your study, summarises key theories and findings from earlier research and may state your hypotheses or expected outcomes
- method—usually includes a description of the participants in the study, your measuring instruments (for example, questionnaires, checklists, behavioural codes) if any, and the procedures you used to collect the data. It may also include a description of your design and in some cases the limits to your research
- results—summarises the data you collected and the themes and issues in your findings

- summary, conclusion and recommendations—discussion of your findings and their implications. Here you can interpret your findings, speculate about their implications and raise questions for further research and identify the limitations of your own work.
- references—an alphabetical list of all sources you have used in your work. There are conventions about how these should be presented that you need to check for your specific context.
- appendixes—include material that is too bulky for the main body of the report but to which is important for your readers to have access (for example, it may include raw, uncollated data, copies of questionnaires or interview questions or transcripts).

Accepted styles of presentation for research reports are often very specific and detailed. They will often detail things such as:

- type style and size
- page layout including margin sizes, placement of page numbers, etc.
- heading styles
- reference style
- presentation of tables.

Learning to prepare a research report that follows accepted presentation conventions becomes easier over time. If you can get these right, people will more readily focus on the content of what you have presented and its implications.

SUMMARY

Researchers may use deductive or inductive research methodologies, positivist, interpretivist or postmodern paradigms, and quantitative or qualitative data approaches depending on the questions they are interested in. Sometimes triangulation—use of multiple methods and approaches—provides a more complete picture of the phenomenon under study. Regardless of approach, there is a series of steps—from selecting a topic through to writing the final research report—that must be followed to generate research that is informative, ethical, meaningful, persuasive and significant. This chapter has summarised what is involved in each of these steps. It notes the importance of choosing a topic that interests you, something you can be passionate about, and that is manageable given the time and resources you have to invest in your project. The process of conducting a literature review, including use of electronic databases, is described. The importance of carefully refining a research topic and research questions is overviewed, along with the practicalities of deciding what is a workable research question. Many beginning researchers tend to be overly ambitious in regard to their research aims, and it is essential to be realistic here, accepting that good research usually makes small, albeit meaningful contributions to understanding or explanation. Designing research so that it answers the questions you set out with, and collecting and analysing data appropriately, requires careful planning and involves complex processes that later chapters consider in depth. The end of the research process should be a well-written report that follows accepted conventions of scholarly writing, allowing your readers to readily focus on your content and the implications of your research.

QUESTIONS FOR REFLECTION

1. What areas do you think we need to know more about in early childhood?
2. What research questions would you like investigate?
3. What sort of research design would you use to investigate this question?
4. Which step(s) of the research process do you think you would find the most difficult? Why?
5. Which step(s) would you enjoy the most?

REFERENCES

Berg, B. 2007 *Qualitative Research Methods for the Social Sciences*, 6th ed., Thompson Gale, London.

Charles, C. and Mertler, C. 2005 *Introduction to Educational Research*, 5th ed., Pearson, Allyn & Bacon, Boston.

Goodwin, W.L. and Goodwin, L.D. 1996 *Understanding Quantitative and Qualitative Research in Early Childhood Education*, Teachers College Press, New York.

Kumar, R. 2005 *Research Methodology: A Step-by-Step Guide for Beginners*, 2nd ed., Sage, London.

Mac Naughton, G. and Hughes, P. 2008 *Doing Action Research in Early Childhood Studies,* Open University Press, Maidenhead.

Wadsworth, Y. 1991 *Do It Yourself Social Research*, Victorian Council of Social Service and Melbourne Family Care Organisation, Melbourne.

Wiersma, W. and Jurs, S. 2005 *Research Methods in Education*, 8th ed., Allyn & Bacon, New York.

FURTHER READING

Cryer, P. 2007 *The Research Student's Guide to Success*, 3rd ed., McGraw Hill Edition, Open University Press, Maidenhead. A useful how-to book for those undertaking research as part of a higher degree or via the 'apprenticeship' model. It discusses preparing for and settling into the life of the research student, developing positive relationships with colleagues and supervisors, time management, creative thinking and coping with 'flagging'. Although some of the book (for example, registering for a research degree) is specific to the United Kingdom, other parts will be helpful to research students in general. These include discussion of record-keeping, planning, recognising good research, presenting research to different fora, being part of a scholarly community and issues of originality. There is a select bibliography on relevant titles at the end. There is also a website (<www.postgrad_resources.btinternet.co.uk/student-resources00-book.htm>) where some of the materials and additional resources can be accessed.

Jipson, J. 2000 'The Stealing of Wonderful Ideas: the Politics of Imposition and Representation in Research on Early Childhood', in L. Diaz Soto (ed.), *The Politics of Early Childhood Education*, Peter Lang, New York, pp. 167–77. This chapter raises some important questions about what counts as useful research in early childhood and how we can do research that is inclusive and respectful.

3

Paradigms, methods and knowledge

Patrick Hughes

This chapter examines some major paradigms found in the early childhood field. It shows that a researcher's view of the world influences their choice of paradigm, and that their paradigm effectively determines their methods and the type of knowledge they produce. In this chapter, the relationships between paradigm, methods and knowledge are illustrated by examples of research into relationships between children and the media. However, at a broader level, these relationships are applicable to any area of research into early childhood—indeed, to any area of research in general.

PARADIGMS AS FRAMES

Different people can mean different things when they use the term 'paradigm'. Much of the term's current usage derives from Thomas Kuhn's (1970) use in his book, *The Structure of Scientific Revolutions*, and it is Kuhn's sense of the term that I will use here. Kuhn's book concerns the role of paradigms in the history of the natural sciences or physical sciences, but his arguments about paradigms also apply to research in the social sciences and humanities.

In very simple terms, a paradigm is a way to 'see' the world and organise it into a coherent whole. Just as a picture frame 'frames' a picture, a paradigm 'frames' a research topic; and just as our choice of picture frame influences how we 'see' the picture within it, so our choice of paradigm influences how we 'see' our research topic. For example, if we frame a portrait within a large, ornate, gold frame of the type used to frame 'old masters' in art galleries, we 'see' it very differently than if we frame it within the simple, chromium frame commonly used to frame family photos. Similarly, if we frame a research topic within one paradigm, we 'see' it very differently than if we frame it within another. This chapter illustrates how that framing happens by showing how researchers have framed children's relationships with the media within various paradigms, each one giving us a different view of those relationships.

Each paradigm is a specific collection of beliefs about knowledge and about our relationships with knowledge, together with practices based upon those beliefs. Any particular paradigm has three elements:

1 a belief about the nature of knowledge—what it means to say that we know something
2 a methodology—what to investigate, how to investigate it, what to measure or assess and how to do so
3 criteria of validity—how to judge someone's claim to know something.

We never see the world 'outside' of a paradigm ('frame'). Each of us (not just researchers) always and inevitably 'frames' the world as we 'see' it. Consequently, what we learn about the world will depend on how we 'see' it; and how we 'see' it depends on our choice of paradigm. Different paradigms give us different perspectives on the world, so we should try to keep an open mind about the paradigm we favour and be prepared to try different ones.

To see how Kuhn's idea of paradigms can help researchers studying early childhood, I will examine four major paradigms: positivism, interpretivism, structuralism and poststructuralism. I will describe each in terms of its three elements, then illustrate its use in research on children and media.

POSITIVISM

Positivists believe that the world consists of two levels:

1 a continuously changing surface of events and appearances
2 an unchanging foundation of order, expressed in universal laws.

Positivist knowledge

Positivists try to explain and predict their surroundings in terms of cause-and-effect relationships between (a) apparently random events and appearances and (b) an underlying order of universal laws. Those universal laws are invisible, like a building's foundations, but when we observe and record events and appearances, we can deduce the law/s that caused them. Some positivists claim that experimental research can *prove* the existence of such universal order; others argue that it can't because those underlying laws are, after all, invisible.

In very general terms, scientists are positivists and vice versa. Traditionally, scientists have claimed that scientific (positivist) knowledge is the only form of knowledge that can be proven true (or false). Other forms of knowledge (for example, myths, dreams, intuition) may be very interesting, they say, but we can neither prove nor disprove them.

Positivist methodology

Positivists argue that strict adherence to the stringent, technical and impersonal rules of scientific (positivist) investigation, such as rigorously conducted experiments in strictly controlled circumstances, produces results that simply reflect the world, unmediated or undistorted by the researcher's personal interests, prejudices, involvement and idiosyncrasies. From this perspective, knowledge that is produced according to the rules of scientific (positivist) investigation is objective knowledge, untainted by the researcher's own **subjectivity**; and such knowledge is of an objective world that exists independently of a particular researcher's perceptions of it.

Positivist validity

Positivists validate knowledge by seeking to replicate it. The impersonal rules governing positivist (scientific) research render the particular researcher who uses them irrelevant to the results. If the results of a specific positivist research project are valid, they will be replicated whenever, wherever and by whomever the project is repeated.

The following example of positivist research on children and the media can serve as a case study of positivism in practice. I will summarise the study, then explain what makes it positivist.

CASE STUDY: POSITIVISM IN RESEARCH ON CHILDREN AND MEDIA

Background

In the United States, infants—especially from poor families—are exposed to a substantial amount of television, and programming for young children is increasing dramatically. Much of that programming is marketed as 'educational', but infants' viewing is unlikely to have educational benefits unless it is associated with interactions with other people. Indeed, without such interactions, infant viewing may induce inattention and impede language development and reading ability. Such adverse effects can be reduced by 'coviewing' (parent and child watching programs together), but coviewing is uncommon, especially in poor families.

Aim

To assess verbal interactions associated with watching television and other electronic media between mothers of low socioeconomic status and their six-month-old infants.

> We tested 2 hypotheses. First, we hypothesized that although the overall rate of interactions during programs would be low, it would vary by program content, with the highest frequency among programs with educational content. Second, we hypothesized that maternal coviewing, given its role in facilitating interactions, would also be increased in association with educational content. The independent variable was media content. For the first hypothesis, the dependent variable was mother-infant verbal interaction … For the second hypothesis, the dependent variable was maternal coviewing. (Mendelsohn et al., 2008, pp. 412–13)

Methods

This study was part of a longer-term examination of early childhood development in 325 families undertaken at an urban public hospital serving at-risk families in New York. A total of 243 families agreed to participate in this short-term project, from which the researchers selected 154 families in the lowest two categories of socioeconomic status (that is, very poor) with a six-month-old child. The researchers asked the mother in each family to:

- list all the electronic media content (for example, television, videos, movies, games) to which her six-month-old child had been exposed while awake 'on the most recent typical day'

- identify the media content that her child had watched actively (in whole or in part)
- recall whether and how she had talked to her child during each item, and whether and how she had watched ('coviewed') the item with her child.

The researchers then placed each item viewed into one of four categories: 'educational young child-oriented', 'non-educational young child-oriented', 'school-age/teenage/adult-oriented' and 'unknown' (when the content was unknown). Finally, the researchers counted associations between the independent variable (program content) and the dependent variables (verbal interactions and maternal coviewing).

Results

- Almost all (96.8 per cent) of the mothers reported that their children were exposed daily to electronic media (on average, 120 minutes per 24 hours).
- In the reporting period, the children had been exposed to a total of 426 items, and they had watched 291 (68 per cent) of those items actively.
- The mothers had talked to their child during less than a quarter of programs (24 per cent, or 99 of 389 items*). Most of their talk was around 'educational young child-oriented' (43 per cent) items or 'non-educational young child-oriented' (21 per cent) items; they talked around 15 per cent of 'school-age/teenage/adult-oriented' items.
- The mothers had watched 253 (59 per cent) of the 426 items with their child. Of those 253 items, 83 (60 per cent) were 'educational young child-oriented' items, 22 (47 per cent) were 'non-educational young child-oriented' items and 149 (73 per cent) were 'school-age/teenage/adult-oriented' items.

The researchers concluded that infant-directed educational programming was only successful when accompanied by coviewing and interactions.

How was the study positivist?

- It expressed a two-level model of the world. The researchers examined apparently random surface appearances in order to deduce an underlying order, and their results reinforced that two-level model of the world. Specifically, the researchers examined the behaviour of randomly assembled mothers with infants around random electronic programming to deduce whether and to what extent electronic programming offers educational benefits—the 'order' underlying those random events. The researchers couldn't see that underlying order—they could only deduce its existence from those surface appearances. Consequently, the researchers didn't just ask, 'Are these infants learning?' Instead, they sought to deduce the answer from the mothers' recollections of whether and how they had talked with their child about a program and/or watched it with them.

- It used scientific research methods. The researchers sought to measure something that they had elicited in carefully controlled conditions, and they expressed the result mathematically. That statement may evoke a scientific experiment in a laboratory because it describes the methods of the scientist as follows:

> The researchers sought to measure something …

The 'something' was the two dependent variables—mothers' verbal interactions and coviewing—around electronic media content (the independent variable).

> … that they had elicited …

They elicited it by asking mothers questions about their children's exposure to electronic media content and their own role in that exposure.

> … in carefully controlled conditions …

They selected families according to their socioeconomic status and asked each mother to keep a record of her infant's exposure to electronic media content 'on the most recent typical day'.

> … and they expressed the results mathematically.

They presented the results of their research as numerical data expressed as percentages.

* Of the total of 426 items, 36 couldn't be classified and for one there was no information about mother–child interaction. This left 389 items to be analysed.

Source: Mendelsohn et al. (2008).

INTERPRETIVISM

Interpretivism seeks to explain how people make sense of their circumstances—that is, of the social world.

Interpretivist knowledge

For interpretivists, the social world is not just 'out there' waiting to be interpreted, but 'in here' or 'in us'—it *is* our interpretations. Interpretivists argue that, rather than simply *perceiving* our particular social and material circumstances, each person continually makes sense of them within a cultural framework of socially constructed and shared meanings, and that our interpretations of the world influence our behaviour in it. Interpretivists believe that we continually create and re-create our social world as a dynamic meaning system—that is, one which changes over time. As we continually make sense of our circumstances, we continually negotiate with others the meanings of our own actions and circumstances, of their actions and circumstances, and of social and cultural institutions and products. In short, interpretivists believe that our social world is not just waiting for us to interpret—it is always already interpreted. (Positivists, in contrast, regard the social world as an extension of the 'natural' world—'out there' awaiting interpretation by a scientist using methods and theories invented for the task.)

Interpretivist methodology

The interpretivist researcher's task is to understand socially constructed, negotiated and shared meanings and re-present them as theories of human behaviour. This requires more than just asking people, 'What do you think you're doing?' It requires the researcher to actively make sense of people's behaviour—including their own. One way to make sense of behaviour is to regard it as rule bound. To interpret a specific individual's behaviour, we ask how closely it conforms to some social rule. An action makes sense to others to the extent that it follows a social rule, and we explain what a word or an action means by describing the rule-bound (or rule-breaking) way that we use it (Winch, 1958, pp. 121–33). Another way to interpret behaviour is to argue that we *interpret* our circumstances using some form of language, rather than simply perceiving them. In this approach, language is much more than just a window on a world that exists independently of it. Instead, language *creates* our social world.

Interpretivist validity

For interpretivists, knowledge is valid if it is authentic—that is, the true voice of the participants in their research. A common way to demonstrate the authenticity of people's responses is to triangulate them—that is, to elicit them using more than one research method and check whether the responses are consistent. Interpretivists don't use triangulation to produce knowledge that is valid whenever, wherever and by whomever it is produced, as positivists do. Interpretivist knowledge is always 'local' and specific to a particular research project conducted in particular circumstances with particular participants. Thus interpretivist knowledge is valid only within tight limits—but interpretivist researchers must still be able to demonstrate the validity of their knowledge, even within those limits.

The following example of interpretivist research on children and the media can serve as a case study of interpretivism in practice. I will summarise the study, then explain what makes it interpretivist.

CASE STUDY: INTERPRETIVISM IN RESEARCH ON CHILDREN AND MEDIA

Background

In the United States, concerns about popular culture—and especially about its effects on children—are long-standing, but have become more prominent and widespread since the emergence of broadcast television in the 1950s. Paradoxically, popular culture is simultaneously dismissed as valueless and trivial, and criticised as a threat to childhood 'innocence'. In a further paradox, little research has been conducted on the place of popular culture in the lives of young children—and especially young immigrant children. Yet Lee (2009) believes that young children do more than just 'soak up' knowledge; they form their own sense of themselves and of society through social interactions—including those around popular culture:

> Children are not only learners caught up in pre-existing knowledge systems. They are also active contributors and participants who form their own sense of society. (Lee, 2009, p. 201)

Aims

To examine young Korean immigrant girls' attitudes to royalty as represented in Disney films.

Methods

Lee chose three Disney films—*The Little Mermaid*, *The Lion King* and *Aladdin*—for her study because they addressed issues of class, gender and race and because they were distributed widely and were popular with many Koreans. Then Lee assembled ten Korean immigrant girls aged between five and eight years, explained the study to them and to their parent/s, and successfully sought their participation. Two of the ten girls were Korean-American; the other eight had immigrated to the United States two to three years earlier. The parents were all Korean citizens, born and raised in South Korea (mostly in Seoul) and all middle class.

Lee divided the ten girls into five pairs, each of whom watched a Disney film with Lee, who conducted a semi-structured interview with them immediately afterwards. Over six months, each pair participated in four or five such interviews. In these conversations, the children often referred to Disney films other than Lee's chosen three, showing that they didn't interpret the chosen three simply in their own terms. Lee also noted casual conversations with each child, as well as each pair of children and their parents, and she also collected each child's notes and drawings (if any) about each film. Lee tried to ensure that she had understood each participant's views correctly by triangulating her data (for example, matching data from the interviews with data from children's notes and drawings and from their parents) and by asking the children and their parents whether she had understood their statements, drawings and notes correctly.

Results

The girls were puzzled by who became a monarch and how. They decided that succession was based on father–son kinship (thereby precluding female monarchy), but this raised another question—who nominated the first king in a society? The children couldn't answer this question, so instead they listed the personal qualities of a monarch and assessed characters in the films accordingly. (As Lee notes, in this way the children associated lower social status in a society with individual inadequacy, rather than with any 'structural' features of that society.)

At first, the girls seemed indifferent to the race or ethnicity of the characters in the films, unconcerned that none of the Disney princesses was Korean:

> Even when I asked if it would be great to have Korean princesses in the Disney films, for example, several girls said, '[Laughing] I don't care [about a Korean princess in a Disney film]', 'She [as a Disney princess] can be anyone', or 'I don't really think about things like that.' (Lee, 2009, p. 209)

Lee then asked them whether the fact that the central character in the Disney film *Mulan* was Chinese made it attractive to them. The girls responded firmly: Chinese and Korean people and cultures are very different; Korean beauty and tradition is superior to 'Americans', and the Disney films highlight that superiority, rather than undermine it.

The girls in this study didn't just passively absorb the films' cultural messages. Instead, they often reworked them in light of their experiences, assumptions and desires. Their approach to the films was critical and reflective, rather than simplistic and credulous.

How was the study interpretivist?

- It rested on the belief that we continually (re)create our social world as an ever-changing meaning system. Lee's study showed young Korean girls actively making sense of the Disney films. She sought to understand how the girls (re-)created their social world by asking them how and why the films 'said' what they did about royalty, class, gender and race.
- It examined how people make sense of their circumstances, with a focus on their relationships with (US) popular culture. Rather than follow earlier researchers and explain the Disney films' significance herself, Lee explored their significance for the girls.

Source: Lee (2009).

STRUCTURALISM

Structuralists regard the world as a collection of systems of law-governed relationships.

Structuralist knowledge

Structuralists explain the meaning and significance of something not in terms of its inherent qualities or characteristics but in terms of its relationships with other elements of a system. For a structuralist, meaning doesn't lie *within* something, waiting to be discovered through careful observation or experimentation. Instead, meaning lies in the non-observable system of relationships *between* that 'something' and something else. For example, an image, a word or a gesture doesn't mean anything in itself and by itself. Instead, its meaning is the result of its relationships with other images, other words or other gestures. Different writers have expressed this idea differently. For example:

> [A] structure is not a reality that is directly visible, and so directly observable, but a level of reality that exists beyond the visible relations between men, and the functioning of which constitutes the underlying logic of the system, the subjacent order by which the apparent order is to be explained. (Godelier, 1974, p. xix)

> Structuralism probes like an X-ray beyond apparently independently existing concrete objects, beyond an *item*-centred world, into a *relational* one. (Sarup, 1988, p. 50, emphases added)

> Structuralism shares ... attention to relations and systems as the framework for explanation. Instead of treating the world as an aggregate of things with their own intrinsic properties, structuralism and physics respectively seek to account for the social and physical world as a system of relations in which the properties of a 'thing' (be it an atom, a sign or an individual) derive from its internal and external relations. (O'Sullivan et al., 1983, p. 227)

A structuralist would argue that nothing inherent in a child explains who or what the child is. Nor is there anything inherent in a child's video that explains what it is. Instead, a structuralist would explain the meaning and significance of a child watching a video in terms of a complex system of law-governed relationships, including those between:

- the visual and audio signals that make up the video
- the sounds and images on the video and the narrative (story) they present
- the video and other media such as television, books and computer games
- the child, the video and those other media.

The term 'structuralism' refers not to a single, coherent paradigm but to a diverse collection of works in a diversity of disciplines, including linguistics, anthropology and sociology. Structuralists within these different disciplines argue that we can best understand the world not by interpreting individuals' experiences, but by elucidating the impersonal systems of relationships that bind the world together. Indeed, a structuralist would go further and argue that the world *is* those systems of relationships—they *constitute* the world, and therefore constitute each individual as part of the world. In other words, the individual doesn't explain the system of relationships—the system 'explains' the individual.

Structuralist methodology

Structuralism's different strands are bound together by the assumption that the truth is out there, waiting to be discovered by the assiduous structuralist researcher. As Harland (1987, p. 2) puts it:

> The Structuralists, in general, are concerned to *know* the (human) world—to uncover it through detailed observational analysis and to map it out under extended explicatory strands. Their stance is still the traditional scientific stance of Objectivity, their goal the traditional scientific goal of Truth. (original emphasis)

Linguistics—especially the work of linguist Ferdinand de Saussure (1959)—has influenced much structuralist research. Saussure regarded each language as a system, consisting of elements defined by their relationships with each other—that is, by their similarities to and differences from each other:

> [L]anguage has neither ideas nor sounds that existed before the linguistic system, but only conceptual and phonic differences that have issued from the system. The idea or phonic substance that a sign contains is of less importance than the other signs that surround it. (Saussure, 1959, p. 120)

Thus many structuralists argue that an idea, an act, an event or an institution is an element of a language (system); that it does not and cannot exist 'outside' of a language; and that each element's meaning and significance arises from its relationships with other elements of that language. For example:

- The meaning of a word or phrase derives from its relationship to other elements of a particular language (for example, English, Thai).
- The meaning of a sound derives from its relationship to other elements of a sonic 'language', such as a particular type of music.
- The meaning of a visual image derives from a visual 'language', such as a particular style of painting.

Thus, when we communicate by, for example, talking or singing or painting, we express only what a particular language allows us to express. In this way, what we can communicate depends not on our wishes or intentions, but on the language we use. Further, structuralists argue that each of us doesn't ('subjectively' and 'intentionally') create a language when we use it. Instead, the various systems of relationships (languages) that make up our society and culture 'create' us as individuals. Consequently, who we think we are depends on the language(s) we use to describe ourselves. For example, a structuralist would explain our understandings and feeling about urban life and rural life by examining the systematic, mutually defining relationships between the two ways of life. They wouldn't examine people's experiences, views and sensibilities about urban life and rural life because they regard each as defining the other: each means something because of its contrast with the other; neither means anything in the absence of the other. Some people criticise what they see as urban life's complications and stress by contrasting it with rural life's (alleged) simplicity and healthiness; other people criticise what they see as rural life's repetition and routine by contrasting it with urban life's (alleged) excitement and differences. This urban–rural relationship underpins innumerable film and television storylines.

Structuralist validity

A structuralist approach to validity resembles a positivist approach, in that both regard knowledge as 'out there' waiting to be discovered. However, while a positivist regards meaning as inherent or innate in something, a structuralist regards it as relational—a phenomenon derives its meaning or significance from its status as an element of a system of relationships. Consequently, to prove the validity of our knowledge of something, a structuralist demonstrates the nature of its relationship with other elements of a system, and shows how each element's meaning or significance derives from its relationships with other elements.

The following example of structuralist research on children and the media can serve as a case study of structuralism in practice. I will summarize the study, then explain what makes it structuralist.

CASE STUDY: STRUCTURALISM IN RESEARCH ON CHILDREN AND MEDIA

Background

Little Angels is a series of half-hour television programs broadcast by the BBC in the United Kingdom. In each program, a child psychologist intervenes in a family's daily life to solve problems of child behaviour (for example, tantrums, disobedience, violent or aggressive behaviour). The BBC markets the series alongside a documentary series on child development (*Child of Our Time*) and a website that offers parenting advice.

Lunt finds *Little Angels* interesting for two reasons: it rests on the 'transformation' narrative (story) that structures 'makeover' television programs; and it expresses both 'governmentality' and 'reflexive modernity'—two distinct explanations of the relative stability of contemporary (Western) societies. 'Governmentality' explains social stability as the outcome of each individual reflecting on their lives and actions, assessing them according to psychological prescriptions of 'good' and 'bad', and changing themselves where needed. 'Reflexive modernity' explains social stability as the outcome of each individual producing their identity (or identities) by consuming goods and services—including information and advice provided by public and private (commercial) institutions.

Aim

To show how the 'makeover' narrative structure of *Little Angels*, together with its psychological approach to social problems, expresses and reinforces a 'therapy culture' in which 'individuals increasingly focus on their own vulnerability and at the same time demand that social institutions respond to their psychological needs through the provision of public information and services' (Lunt 2008, p. 537).

Methods

Lunt examined several episodes of *Little Angels* to discover whether and how its structure contributed to its meaning, then examined the first episode of the first series in detail, as a case study of that relationship between structure and meaning.

Results

Lunt showed that *Little Angels* exhibits a clear narrative structure:

> The programme is tightly structured as a narrative with an initial state of disruption which is confronted with the help of an external heroic figure (the psychologist) who employs her special skills to enable the participants (the parents) to overcome their problems. (Lunt, 2008, p. 544)

This transformation narrative structures 'makeover' television programs and it structures *Little Angels* as follows:

- *Phase One: A 'Bad/Undesirable' situation.* The family is introduced through footage of children–parent conflict, interviews with the parents and a voiceover commentary. Vignettes illustrate the children's problematic behaviour, then the parents state their hopes/goals (for example, 'sometime in the evening, just peace and quiet'). Enter the expert—a clinical psychologist—who uses more footage of the family to show the parents that the root of their children's problematic behaviour is the parents' behaviour with/towards them, and then prescribes how to behave in future—'rules of thumb for behaviour loosely informed by psychological theory' (Lunt, 2008, p. 542).
- *Phase Two: The 'Makeover'.* We see the parents behaving according to those 'rules of thumb', while receiving further coaching by the psychologist.
- *Phase Three: A 'Good/Desirable' situation.* The parents tell us how much better their life is now, as a result of following the expert's advice.
- As an expression of reflexive modernity, *Little Angels* is an instance of a public institution (the BBC) offering to self-creating individuals a narrative of self-help guided by 'the expert'. *Little Angels* also expresses governmentality by emphasising individual training and self-control, by using 'surveillance technologies' (cameras recording the family's daily lives) and by presenting a social problem as a psychological one that can be 'cured' through psychological expertise:
- The narration moves from an account of the changing nature of work (dual-career families and the increasing commitments required of workers), taking in the broader social problem of family breakdown and the growing ill-discipline amongst children and the changing nature of family life in contemporary society, before introducing the idea that psychological intervention might provide an answer to parents' problems (Lunt, 2008, p. 541).

How was the study structuralist?

- It reflected and reinforced a relational, systematic model of the world. Lunt (2008) showed how the program's 'makeover' narrative structure and its psychological approach to social problems reflected and reinforced a 'therapy culture' (see above) defined by the relationships between individuals, experts and social institutions.
- It presented people's views and behaviour as 'structured' by their language—in this case, the language of psychology. Lunt showed the clinical psychologist using the language of psychology

to redefine the family's 'problem'—from children's behaviour it became parents' behaviour—and to redefine the parents—from victims of their circumstances, they became 'self-helpers' supported by an expert. In these ways, the visible relationships between the parents and the psychologist reflected the invisible relationships within the language of psychology—a language that 'created' them, rather than vice versa.

Source: Lunt (2008).

POSTSTRUCTURALISM

Poststructuralism is even more diffuse and complex than structuralism, and its adherents can adopt such different perspectives on the world that it can be hard to see just what unites them. A further complication is that 'poststructuralism' is sometimes used interchangeably with '**postmodernism**'—an equally diffuse and complex term!

Poststructuralist knowledge

For the sake of simplicity, but at the risk of over-simplifying, I suggest that both poststructuralists and postmodernists regard the world as fundamentally incoherent and discontinuous; however, where post-structuralists focus on individuals, postmodernists focus on society as a whole.

- Poststructuralists regard the individual as fundamentally incoherent and discontinuous. Consequently, they reject the view (shared by structuralists and positivists and, to an extent, by interpretivists) that individuals can develop coherent and continuous meanings of the world. For poststructuralists, everything and everyone can—and does—shift and change all the time, and the task of the researcher is to explain this constant instability without attempting to 'capture' or stabilise it.
- Postmodernists regard human societies as fundamentally incoherent and discontinuous. They reject the (modernist) view that each society is at a particular stage of a 'journey' by humanity towards some ill-defined 'goal' or 'endpoint' ('**telos**'). They also reject the (positivist) idea that science assists us on our 'journey' by revealing more and more about the world, enabling us increasingly to control it. Instead, postmodernists argue that we can only understand the world at a local level, because as we try to generalise our understandings, we

rely on 'big pictures' or '**grand narratives**' about humanity's 'progress' on its 'journey'.

I have separated poststructuralism and postmodernism to distinguish between them, but the poststructuralist idea of the incoherent and discontinuous individual makes no sense apart from the postmodern argument that societies are incoherent entities following no particular 'journey' of progress or development. Therefore, when I refer to 'poststructuralism', I am referring to a close association between poststructuralism and postmodernism. Those complexities mean that my characterisation of poststructuralism as a paradigm consists of three cautious generalisations about poststructuralism, each differentiating it from other paradigms.

The first of these is poststructuralism's research focus. Poststructuralists seek to understand the dynamics of relationships between knowledge/meaning, power and identity. (Contrast this with a positivist, who would seek to capture those knowledge–power relationships in a fixed and comprehensive formula.) Kenway and Willis (1997) put it thus:

> For post-structuralists, meaning, power and identity are always in flux. They shift as different linguistic, institutional, cultural and social factors move and stabilise together. The emphasis in post-structuralism is on the discourses which make up social institutions and cultural products ... [I]t is through discourse that meanings and people are made and through which power relations are maintained and changed. A discursive field is a set of discourses which are systematically related. (1997, pp. xix–xx)

The second cautious generalisation concerns languages (in the broad sense of 'a system defined by and governed by a set of rules'). Poststructuralists believe that individuals are social products of languages, rather than having an 'essence' ('the real me') separate from their social existence. They regard the individual as *un*stable, referring to her/him as a 'subject', 'subject position' or 'subjectivity'. The subject's instability derives from their status as both a 'product' and a 'producer' of languages—unstable systems in which the meaning of something can never be finally fixed because it may have several, different, mutually defining 'others'. Thus, the subject is continually (re-)constructed by her/himself and others, adopting one or more 'subjectivities' that may be mutually contradictory; and he or she understands the world in ways that may be inconsistent or incoherent.

Davies (1989) argues that individuals aren't unitary, coherent and stable, but complex, contradictory and dynamic:

> The individual is not ... some relatively fixed end product, but one who is constituted and reconstituted through a variety of discursive practices ... Individuals, through learning the discursive practices of a society, are able to position themselves within those practices in multiple ways and to develop subjectivities both in concert with and in opposition to the ways in which others choose to position them. (1989, p. xi)

Clearly, poststructuralists reject the structuralist argument that languages are stable systems of fixed meanings, in which something's meaning derives from its relationships (similarity and difference) with other elements of the system; and that languages' stability, consistency and coherence enable them to 'create' stable, consistent and coherent individuals.

My third cautious generalisation concerns relationships between meaning and circumstances. Poststructuralists believe that a subject's understandings of the world are associated with their particular experiences of the world—themselves associated with their social and material circumstances, such as their class, gender and race. For example, a poststructuralist might seek to show that a child's understanding of a film is associated with his or her experiences as a member of a specific class, gender and race. This explanation is oriented more to the viewer than to the film. It seeks to show how factors 'external' to the film—such as class, gender and race—are associated with how a subject understands it. In contrast, a structuralist might seek to show how a film's genre (for example, action-adventure, romance) predisposes viewers to interpret it in certain ways. This explanation is oriented more to the film than to the viewer. It seeks to show how factors 'internal' to the film—such as genre (a system)—influence how an individual understands it.

Poststructuralist methodology

In summary, poststructuralists study relationships between knowledge/meaning, power and identity, and they regard those relationships as dynamic, unstable results of interaction between:

- an unstable and dynamic 'subject' whose identity is never fixed
- unstable and dynamic 'languages', in which meaning is never fixed
- a world whose meanings are never fixed but are instead associated with the subject's social and material circumstances.

Poststructuralism's fundamental uncertainty about the world contrasts sharply with positivism and structuralism, each of which is certain that the truth is 'out there', waiting to be discovered; and with interpretivism, which is equally certain that the truth is 'in here'—always already-interpreted by people.

Further, poststructuralist researchers don't just feel uncertain about the world—after all, any researcher seeks to reduce uncertainty. Instead, poststructuralist researchers reject the idea that we can *ever* be certain about the world because its complexity and dynamism defy encapsulation, categorisation and closure. Seeking certainty about the world is as futile as trying to hold a river in your hand—its dynamism precludes its capture, and whatever you capture is no longer dynamic. Thus our understanding of the world can only ever be provisional—it is unattainable because it is ephemeral. Poststructuralists regard phenomena such as social institutions, relationships and individuals as 'products' of the discourse(s) within which we think about them, but each discourse exists only in its difference from others. Consequently, poststructuralist researchers seek to demonstrate how discourses 'produce' phenomena, and how a phenomenon's meaning and significance are associated with the particular discourse(s) within which people encounter them.

Poststructuralist validity

Like interpretivists, poststructuralists judge the validity of knowledge according to the authenticity of the research participants' voices. However, poststructuralists' emphasis on the 'local' nature of knowledge means that the limits they place on the validity of knowledge are even stricter than those of interpretivists. For example, where a structuralist would judge the validity of knowledge by situating it with a 'grand narrative' of progress or development, a poststructuralist would regard something as valid to the extent that it expressed the discourse(s) that 'produced' it.

The following example of poststructuralist research on children and the media can serve as a case study of poststructuralism in practice. I will summarise the study, then explain what makes it poststructuralist.

CASE STUDY: POSTSTRUCTURALISM/POSTMODERNISM IN RESEARCH ON CHILDREN AND MEDIA

Background

Zanker (1999) argued that the instability and incoherence brought about by the crisis in children's television in New Zealand invited critical examination of some founding assumptions of local children's programming. She showed that recent discussions in New Zealand about children's television have expressed poststructuralist/postmodern perspectives.

Aim

To critically reappraise some founding assumptions of local children's programming—'the child', 'the nation' and 'the national culture'.

Methods

Zanker examined closely the history of recent discussions in New Zealand about children's television. She showed that the radical deregulation of New Zealand television in the mid-1980s increased the proportion of (relatively cheap) imported programming at the expense of local production, creating 'a monoculture where short bursts of local material wrap around global cartoons' (Zanker, 1999, p. 99).

Zanker also examined the content of those discussions, which had rested on the argument that the founding assumptions of children's television in New Zealand—'the child', 'the nation' and 'the national culture'—are likely to disappear, or at least to change beyond recognition, in the absence of locally funded and locally produced programs. Zanker regarded this argument as the foundation of 'modernist white middle-class content, genre and even formatting' (1999, p. 94) and suggested that two developments in New Zealand society challenged it: postcolonial cultural fragmentation and market-driven popular culture.

In terms of postcolonial cultural fragmentation, Zanker questioned the value—even the validity—of terms such as 'the nation' and 'the national identity' at a time when New Zealand's population is becoming increasingly diverse:

> Identity in postcolonial New Zealand is becoming increasingly diverse, whether reflecting the resurgence of traditional tribalisms of Maori, voices from immigrant Anglo/Celtic/Pacific diasporas, or as expressed within the postmodern tribalisms of gender, ethnicity and consumerist lifestyles. (1999, pp. 94–5)

With regard to market-driven popular culture, some imported programs for children—for example, Nickelodeon's *Rugrats* and the BBC's *Teletubbies*—consistently out-rated local programs. These imports were widely regarded as 'quality' programs, and critics of publicly funded broadcasting used their popularity to question the need to fund local ('quality') programs for children from the licence fee.

Results

After examining the history and content of the arguments about children's television in New Zealand, Zanker characterised them as instances of:

- the broader, continuing arguments between supporters of commercial and public service approaches to broadcasting and
- the difference between what we would call modern and post-modern paradigms.

Zanker suggested that advocates of increased publicly funded local programming for children invoked a lost 'golden age' based on a consensus about 'the child', 'the nation', 'the national culture', and therefore the aims and content of children's television. That 'golden age' consensus rests on the modernist view that the child, the nation and the national culture are unitary, coherent and consistent entities, defined in opposition to a 'global' popular culture that threatens to obliterate them. In contrast, Zanker argued that children can actively transform the products of 'global' popular culture in the light of local circumstances if there are local 'spaces' in which to do so:

> There may be more effective means of ensuring media rights for a new 'media-centric' generation of children than nostalgically jumping back into national quotas or public-service channels … Popular culture is global and children demonstrate by their choices that it is important for them to play out in the 'forever new' breaking news of global popular culture. But it is equally important for them to have access to local spaces in which to explore, play with and transform global culture … These will constitute the new public spaces for children. (1999, p. 101)

To support her argument, Zanker cites Massey's view that commodified cultures built around brand names (for example, Nike, Barbie, Nintendo) can offer children new identities by offering them new 'spaces' and ways to be children:

> Could it be also that many children are finding their own public spaces away from parental surveillance and the constraints of a modernist childhood within the brand tribes of commodified culture? Once children had secret passwords to peer group secrets; now children's—like youth—culture is increasingly defined by postmodernism and unstable 'constellations of temporary coherence' of global fashions and local peer-group response'. (Zanker, 1999, p. 101, citing Massey, 1998)

How was the study poststructuralist?

- It examined the dynamics of relationships between knowledge/meaning, power and identity. Zanker examined how 'golden agers' in New Zealand sought to accrue power by presenting themselves as guardians of a national identity (based on particular modernist meanings of 'child', 'nation' and 'national culture') allegedly threatened by a global popular culture.
- It presented the individual as a fundamentally incoherent and discontinuous social product of languages, continually (re-)constructed by her/himself and others as one or more 'subjectivities'. Those 'subjectivities' may be mutually contradictory and may understand the world inconsistently or incoherently, but their understandings of the world are associated with their social and material circumstances. Zanker presented children as unstable 'subjects' continually (re-)constructing themselves. She argued that children can use television programs and other popular cultural products (local and imported) to explore different ways of being; that when they do, they transform 'global' cultural products into local ones; and that they need new 'public spaces' in which to do so.
- It sought to explain the subject's constant instability without attempting to 'capture' or stabilise it. Zanker didn't pose a definitive alternative to the stable, coherent model of the child implied in the modernist 'golden age'. Instead, she posed the child as a 'subjectivity' in a constant process of re-construction, evading any definitive explanation. Rather than seeking a new (antimodernist) consensus that '*This* (not that) is who the child is', Zanker said, 'This is how the child can be', and left the possibilities open.

Source: Zanker (1999).

LINKS BETWEEN PARADIGM, METHODS AND RESULTS

When we choose a particular paradigm, we also—implicitly—choose particular methods of investigation. Let's see this in each of the four paradigms we have considered, again using children's relationships with the media as the research topic:

- A positivist will investigate children's relationships with the media by, for example, surveying random samples of target populations of children, collating the data and tracking any patterns or regularities within that data. Their data will concern broad trends in their target populations, rather than the particular attitudes and actions of specific individuals within them; however, their data should be broadly applicable to anyone within their target populations.
- An interpretist will investigate children's relationships with the media by trying to understand how specific young children make sense of specific media products. Thus they will probably observe and interview children, their friends, carers and families. Their data will concern the particularities of specific children's relationships with specific media products, rather than broad trends in the population, and other people should be very cautious about using that data to explain how any other children relate to other media products.
- A structuralist will investigate children's relationships with the media by tracing the systematic relationships between different programs, adverts, promotions, and so on, and between them and other cultural products such as computer games, shopping malls, clothes and sports equipment. Their data will show how each item's meanings and significance derives from its (systematic) relationships with the others; and their data should be broadly applicable to any child who encounters one or more of those products.
- A poststructuralist would investigate children's relationships with the media by examining associations between specific media products, the influences of a particular viewer's class, gender and race on their encounters with those products, and the unstable, dynamic 'language/s' within which she or he understands those experiences and expresses them. Their data will concern the diverse ways in which specific children draw on their specific experiences and 'languages' to make sense/s of specific media products; and the consequences of their sense-making activity for these products' social meaning/s and significance/s. Consequently, their data should be broadly applicable to anyone who shares those experiences and languages. However, the links between experiences and the languages within which they are understood and expressed can be very complex, so the applicability

of the data to other people in similar circumstances would have to be demonstrated in each case, rather than assumed.

QUANTITATIVE OR QUALITATIVE RESEARCH?

Researchers often use the terms 'quantitative' and 'qualitative' to describe different methods of research, whereas in fact the terms describe different *approaches* to research, each characterised by the specific type of knowledge it produces. In general terms, quantitative research aims to produce facts and figures—some form of numerical, possibly statistical, data—about something. A very simple example of a quantitative approach to research would be counting how many people behave in certain ways. A researcher could ask a group of parents if they put their children to bed in the afternoons and then count how many say 'yes', how many say 'no' and how many give another response. The resulting knowledge would be quantitative—the numbers (the quantity) of people who responded in particular ways to the question. This very simple exercise is the basis of all quantitative surveys, each of which counts how many people respond in particular ways to particular questions.

As its name implies, quantitative research is concerned with quantities—how to measure phenomena and how to express those measurements. A researcher who takes a quantitative approach to investigating a topic—such as children's relationships with the media—aims to learn more about it. Their research is guided by the belief that our knowledge of something increases over time, step by step, piece by piece. We could say that they regard knowledge like gold dust—as you collect more and more, you get richer and richer. Taking a quantitative approach to research implies asking questions about phenomena that have answers which can be counted. For example: How frequently does a particular event occur in a society? How many people in an occupational group behave in a particular way? How much influence does an institution exert? Consequently, researchers who take a quantitative approach often work within positivism, as this paradigm 'frames' the world as a collection of apparently independent phenomena to be counted, measured and otherwise catalogued as the prelude to deducing the rules or laws underlying them and giving them coherence.

In contrast, a researcher who takes a qualitative approach to investigating a topic aims to understand it differently. Qualitative researchers generally aim to show something's meaning or significance to particular people or groups of people. A very simple example of a qualitative approach to research would be asking people to explain their attitude to a particular issue. A researcher could ask a group of parents if they regularly encourage their children to sleep in the afternoon and then ask those who said 'yes' to explain their reasons. The resulting knowledge would be qualitative—detailed descriptions of how and why individual parents responded to their child's sleeping pattern. This very simple exercise is the basis of much qualitative research, which seeks to explain events and actions through the eyes and in the words of the people involved.

As its name implies, qualitative research is concerned with the quality of the data it produces, rather than just its quantity. A researcher who takes a qualitative approach to investigating a topic—such as children's relationships with the media—aims to learn about it in terms of the people involved. In a sense, a qualitative researcher doesn't seek to learn more about the topic itself, but rather about how people understand and make sense of the topic. Consequently, researchers who take a qualitative approach often work within interpretivism or poststructuralism, as each of these paradigms 'frames' the world—in its own way—as the outcome of people's continuing 'negotiations'.

Cutting across the distinction between quantitative and qualitative approaches is the distinction between deductive and inductive methodologies. Deductive research is a 'top-down' approach: you start with a hypothesis (an idea about an issue) and collect data to prove or disprove it—'What can I deduce about my hypothesis from my data?' Inductive research is 'bottom-up': you collect data about an issue or an idea with no clear, preconceived view about the significance of that data for your issue or idea. Then you see whether your data will enable you to form an hypothesis about the issue or idea.

In summary:

- Quantitative research produces 'facts and figures'.
- Qualitative research produces 'meanings and understandings'.
- Deductive research proves or disprove a hypothesis.
- Inductive research may suggest a hypothesis.

SUMMARY

This chapter has suggested that a researcher's choice of paradigm influences their research methods and the sort of knowledge they produce. It has shown that:

- Positivists explain their surroundings by observing and recording apparently random events and appearances and then deducing the law or laws that caused them.

- Interpretivists explain their surroundings by observing and recording how each person continually negotiates the meaning of their behaviour with others, and how their interpretations influence their behaviour, then showing how negotiations and interpretations continually re-create the world as a dynamic system of meanings.
- Structuralists explain their surroundings by re-presenting them as systems of law-governed relationships, in which something's meaning and significance isn't inherent but derives from its non-observable relationships with one or more other elements of the same system.
- Poststructuralists explain their surroundings by examining the dynamic, unstable relationships between knowledge/meaning, power and identity, and deriving those relationships from the interaction between a dynamic 'subject', dynamic 'languages' and a world where meanings are associated with the subject's social and material circumstances.

QUESTIONS FOR REFLECTION

Choose an issue that you have encountered as a student and/or a staff member in early childhood services. The issue might concern, for example, your relationships with colleagues, how others see your work, or how your college, university or workplace is run. Now do the following:

1. Using this chapter's definitions, explanations and case studies concerning positivism, interpretivism, structuralism and post-structuralism, briefly outline how a researcher within each of the four paradigms might investigate the issue.
2. Using this chapter's material on the links between paradigm, methods and results, suggest the sort of knowledge about the issue that each paradigm would produce.
3. Ask yourself which approach would be most likely to resolve your issue to your satisfaction.

REFERENCES

Davies, B. 1989 *Frogs and Snails and Feminist Tales: Preschool Children and Gender*, Allen & Unwin, Sydney.

de Saussure, F. 1959 *A Course in General Linguistics*, McGraw-Hill, New York.

Godelier, M. 1974 *Rationality and Irrationality in Economics*, New Left Books, London.

Harland, R. 1987 *Superstructuralism*, Routledge, London.

Kenway, J. and Willis, S. 1997 *Answering Back: Girls, Boys and Feminism in School*, Allen & Unwin, Sydney.

Kuhn, T.S. 1970 *The Structure of Scientific Revolutions*, 2nd ed., University of Chicago Press, Chicago.

Lee, L. 2009 'Young American Immigrant Children's Interpretations of Popular Culture: A Case Study of Korean Girls' Perspectives on Royalty in Disney Films', *Journal of Early Childhood Research*, vol. 7, no. 2, pp. 200–15.

Lunt, P. 2008 '*Little Angels*: The Mediation of Parenting', *Continuum*, vol. 22 no. 4, pp. 537–46.

MacBeth, T.M. 1996 'Indirect Effects of Television: Creativity, Persistence, School Achievement, and Participation in Other Activities', in T.M. MacBeth (ed), *Tuning in to Young Viewers: Social Science Perspectives on Television*, Sage, Thousand Oaks, CA.

Massey, D. 1998 'The Spacial Construction of Youth Cultures', in T. Skelton and G. Valentine (eds), *Cool Places: Geographies of Youth Cultures*, Routledge, London.

Mendelsohn, A.L., Berkule, S.B., Tomopoulos, S., Tamis-LeMonda, S., Huberman, H.S., Alvir, J. and Dreyer, B.P. 2008 'Infant Television and Video Exposure Associated with Limited Parent–Child Verbal Interactions in low Socio-economic Status Households', *Archives of Pediatrics and Adolescent Medicine*, vol. 162, no. 5, pp. 411–17.

O'Sullivan, T., Hartley, J., Saunders, D. and Fiske, J. 1983 *Key Concepts in Communication*, Methuen, London.

Palmerton, P.R. and Judas, J. 1994 'Selling Violence: Television Commercials Targeted to Children', paper presented at the 44th Annual Meeting of the International Communication Association, Sydney, 11–15 July.

Sarup, M. 1988 *An Introductory Guide to Post-structuralism and Post-modernism*, Harvester Wheatsheaf, New York.

Winch, P. 1958 *The Idea of Social Science and its Relation to Philosophy*, Routledge & Kegan Paul, London.

Zanker, R. 1999 'Kumara Kai or the Big Mac Pack? Television for Six- to Twelve-Year-Olds in New Zealand', *Media International Australia*, no. 93, pp. 91–102.

FURTHER READING

Guba, E.G. and Lincoln, Y.S. 2005 'Paradigmatic Controversies, Contradictions and Emerging Confluences' in N.K. Denzin and Y.S. Lincoln (eds), *The Sage Handbook of Qualitative Research*, 3rd ed., Sage, Thousand Oaks, CA. Many researchers believe that paradigms are more problematic than I have presented them here. Guba and Lincoln's chapter introduces some of the problem areas.

Johnson, R.B. and Onwuegbuzie, A.J. 2004 'Mixed Methods Research: A Research Paradigm Whose Time Has Come', *Educational Researcher*, vol. 33, no. 7, pp. 14–26. As you read this, consider the relationships between methods and paradigms and whether 'mixed methods' is a paradigm in the Kuhnian sense.

4

Doing research as a beginning researcher

Audrey D'Souza Juma

As I write this chapter (early 2009), I am just embarking on the fieldwork for my doctoral research in my home country of Pakistan. In this chapter, I outline my journey as a beginning researcher and the issues I have faced in bringing my research to this point. I start with how I came to my study focus and then explore the more rigorous process of arriving at a conceptual framework that suited the needs of my study. I highlight my rationale for using feminist poststructuralism as my conceptual framework and foreground what it will mean for me to apply this framework in my own context of Pakistan. I also highlight the challenges that I face in conducting my research as my fieldwork begins.

THE BEGINNINGS: EMBARKING ON THE ROAD TO RESEARCH

I began my journey as a researcher prior to enrolling in a doctoral research program at the University of Melbourne. Prior to my doctoral studies, I had embarked on studying gender differences in girls' and boys' play with another colleague at the university at which I worked in Pakistan (Pardhan and Juma, 2007). At the conclusion of this study, we disseminated the preliminary findings at a conference in Pakistan that aimed at raising awareness about gender in the Pakistani context. Our findings were consistent with research done in minority world countries and revealed gender differences in children's choice of learning areas, movement in learning areas, choice and use of play materials, peer interaction and teachers' interactions with children. During our presentation, we were asked the question, 'So what—if the findings reflected what had been done in the West, how was this of value in a developing world context like Pakistan?'. This rather critical question got me reflecting on the kind of gender study that was needed in the Pakistani context. It also made me reflect on children's understanding and enactment of gender in Pakistan. Was there an alternate way of understanding gender relationships, another, non-Western way of understanding the gendering process? Could our initial gender study have been framed in another way? What niggled at me the most was the question of how the study had contributed to what needed to be achieved in Pakistan with regard to gender.

When I embarked on my doctoral studies, these questions loomed large. I knew from the start that my study would explore issues of gender in the Pakistani context. I began reading around the topic, and my initial conversations with my supervisors Glenda Mac Naughton and Karina Davis revolved around gender and what it meant in my own context and for me, a woman living in the Islamic Republic of Pakistan. How did I negotiate my existence in a visibly patriarchal society? What did this mean for gender equity in early childhood programs in Pakistan?

My own understandings of gender in young children's lives at this stage were in constant flux (as they still are). In the past, I had been influenced by socialisation theories, believing that children could be socialised into taking up their roles in society. However, through constant conversations and dialogue with my supervisors, and through the direction I got from them signposting a diverse set of readings on gender (Davies, 1988, 1989, 1993, 1994; Butler, 1990; hooks, 1984; Alloway, 1995; Mac Naughton, 1995, 1997, 1998, 1999, 2000), I broadened my perspectives on gender construction in early childhood. Reviewing this body of literature on poststructuralism made me wonder what the previous study would have looked like had it been analysed from the lens of poststructuralism. Would it have raised new possibilities for exploring gender differences in children's play?

In my intensive review of the literature on gender and young children, it was evident that numerous studies had been carried out on different aspects of gender. However, most of these studies highlighted the need for teachers to work with children to disrupt and challenge taken-for-granted assumptions about gender. Studies by Mac Naughton (2000) and Alloway (1995) had attempted to do so, and my own study took direction from this work. I sought to look at teachers' understandings of gender discourses and to reconceptualise their role to promote gender equity in early childhood classrooms in Pakistan. I was interested in initiating conversations around equity and gender discourses, and in looking at how these could be foregrounded in teachers' practice. My research objectives aimed at unearthing the prevalent gender discourses in early childhood classrooms in Pakistan. An understanding of this would in turn help to formulate strategies which could be used to challenge the discursive practices surrounding gender.

In those initial months of my doctoral studies, I also attended a research methods course at the University of Melbourne which further helped shape my study. We were introduced to a range of paradigms and theoretical underpinnings used in research. Doctoral candidates presented their own work and explained how they had designed their research studies. During the course of the semester, we were asked to formulate our own research questions and think about our research design. We had to present this for critique and feedback. This further helped refine and shape my thinking and my study.

From the inception of my study, Glenda Mac Naughton suggested I keep a research journal. This became an invaluable resource for recording my thinking, ideas, confusions, questions and comments. This also helped me chart my own trajectory of ideas and how they were developing over the course of time.

ARRIVING AT A CONCEPTUAL FRAMEWORK: USING FEMINIST POSTSTRUCTURALISM

As I continued my readings around poststructuralism, I was struck by the contesting and often conflicting ways of looking at it, and the lack of consensus about what exactly poststructuralism meant. I was faced with the challenge of what understandings of these theories I wanted to bring to my study. As I began framing my study, I was particularly interested in deepening my understanding of feminist poststructuralism because this theoretical framework is seen as 'politics directed at changing existing power relations between women and men in a society' (Weedon, 1987, p. 1). I read Lather's (1991) work in which poststructuralist research is seen as 'an enactment of power relations' (1991, p. 14). It is explained as 'legitimation' rather than 'procedure', which draws one nearer to 'some truth'. In poststructuralist research, one needs to seek a 'reflexive process' so as to question the 'taken-for-granted forms' and thus to 'lead us towards a science capable of continually demystifying the realities it serves to create' (1991, p. 15).

As my aim was to question the taken-for-granted gender discourses in early childhood settings in Pakistan, and to change the existing power relations between women and men in this context, this framework appealed to me, and I continued to think about this framework for my study. I was aware that, unlike other types of research, one could not pinpoint any single feminist poststructuralist way or 'method' of research. In contrast, as a methodology, feminist poststructuralism took on many ideas from a number of postpositivist approaches to knowledge, identity and change. However, with this approach—no matter what form it would take—the underlying point of emphasis would be on exploring the construction of knowledge rather than on found knowledge (Blaise, 2005, p. 54).

As I reflected on this framework, and what it could offer my study, I began formulating my rationale for using feminist poststructuralism. I began thinking about why this framework appealed to me. First, it was because, like Blaise (2005), I believe that knowledge is not found but is constructed, and that the gender discourses which are of interest to me are embedded within power relations and within the cultural and societal context. In my study, I planned to look at what these discourses were and to unearth the constellation of gender discourses in early childhood classrooms in Pakistan.

Second, feminism implies change. In line with Weedon (1987), it is a politics aimed at changing power relations by understanding the discourses of the field and what constitutes these discourses. By working towards gender equity in Pakistani early childhood settings, I would like to see these power relations shifted, if not disrupted totally, and I therefore see value in using this framework to guide my research. Like Davies (1993), I recognise that 'masculinities and femininities are constituted *in relation* to each other', and therefore 'cannot be understood independently of each other, nor does it make sense to make the possibility of change available to girls if it is not also being made available to boys. The burden of change cannot and should not lie entirely with girls.' (1993, p. x)

Third, feminist poststructuralism looks towards understanding the power relationships between people working together. According to Maguire (2006), feminist scholarship seeks 'to unsettle and change the power relations, structures and mechanisms of the social world' (2006, p. 66). In my case, this means looking at the power relationships that exist between me and the teachers in the group, and between the teachers and the children. This would be important since my interest in studying discourses and teacher talk was not possible without first looking at the power relations which are generated through talk. If the research participants and I were to understand how to disrupt the social order created through gender, we would need to understand how power works through discourses.

Fourth, in line with Davies' (1993) claim, poststructuralist theory provides possibilities of using a range of strategies with boys and girls, 'based on radically different conceptualization of the process of becoming a (gendered) person' (1993, p. 2). Davies argues that offering children discourses which open the doors for them to see the 'storylines through which gendered persons are constituted, to see the cultural and historical production of gendered persons that they are each caught up in' (1993, p. 2) can lay open possibilities for children to learn to be 'producers of culture'. This, in turn, can be used by them to 'make themselves' instead of being passive recipients who just follow unquestioningly.

APPLYING THE FRAMEWORK IN MY CONTEXT

As I continued to shape my conceptual framework based on the above assertions, I was faced with the dilemma of applying what this approach could offer in the context of Pakistan. Pakistan's birth in 1947 was on the basis of the two-nation theory which emphasised the creation of a separate homeland for the Muslim majority areas of India. Pakistan thus came into existence as the Islamic Republic of Pakistan. The laws and constitutions of the country have therefore been influenced by Islam.

Shaheed (1991) claims that 'the historical justification of patriarchy, through male interpretation of Islam, has forced many contemporary women into a reluctance of unequal and inferior position *vis-a-vis* men' (1991, p. 135). Gender practices are thus influenced and interpreted according to the tenets of Islam and Sharia.

Even though, in 1973, the constitution of Pakistan promised equal rights to all citizens irrespective of sex, women's status remained low. Patriarchy is dominant and is 'justified by invoking Islamic doctrine' (Shaheed, 1991, p. 135). Ashraf (2007) states that 'the unequal power relations between women and men as a fundamental principle of patriarchy seems to originate in the domestic realm' (2007, p. 85). This subordination of women, according to Ashraf, is the very basis of the framework of 'patriarchal relations'.

Farah and Shera (2007) highlight that the intent to achieve gender parity has been a policy aim of the country over the past 40 years. Girls' education has been given a priority in policy documents; however, not much has been achieved, and this is attributed to various factors. Farah and Shera (2007), in their review of female education in Pakistan, highlight several factors for this inequity, including sociocultural constraints, the distance of schools from each other, the quality of schools, and the lack of female role models. They also highlight attitudes prevalent in the wider Pakistani society which mirror what happens in schools. These relate to the ways in which girls are 'socialised' into subservient and dependency behaviours, and the fact that they are seen to shoulder the family's honour. Raza (2007) argues that steps have been taken by Pakistan since its inception to include women and their interests; however, the 'gender gap' still persists.

The above assertions raise many questions about how gender equity should be defined, and approached, and what meanings can be derived by both the teachers in my study and myself. Furthermore, this raises issues of how we translate gender equity in our work with children, and whether certain interpretations of Islam will influence the way in which gender equity is viewed and enacted in classrooms in Pakistan.

In addition, if the term 'feminism' were put under scrutiny in Pakistan, it would be met with mixed feelings. The term carries a very negative connotation, and gendered power relations are seldom talked about in everyday conversation. Also, while this framework has been used successfully in many studies in other countries (Davies, 1989; Mac Naughton, 2000; Blaise, 2005), I am faced with the issue of how it will translate in my context.

As is evident from my account above, when I began reading about poststucturalism, I was faced with many varied ways of framing my study. I brought my own understandings and interpretations to bear on deciding how best to frame my study of gender in Pakistani early childhood contexts, and what might be effective as a way of framing this work in my context. It was through immersing myself in the existing research and other scholarly literature, and gaining insights from work that others had done, that I was able to frame my own study. But my greatest challenge was making meaning from the many different perspectives available. I would often tell my supervisors that I was confused by my readings.

MY DECISION TO USE ACTION RESEARCH

I decided that the research approach best suited to realising the objectives of my study was qualitative since, according to Denzin and Lincoln (2000): 'Qualitative research is a field of inquiry in its own right' (2000, p. 2). Also, a qualitative research paradigm recognises that 'the fields of study are not artificial situations in the laboratory but the practices and interactions of the subjects in everyday life' (Flick, 1998, p. 5).

I decided to use action research as a methodology since this underscores a participatory and democratic process that I feel will aid the teachers engaging in this study and myself in uncovering gender discourses in classrooms. It will allow us to work towards gender equity through engaging in critical reflections through a cyclic process. It will also aid us in getting a 'holistic picture of phenomenon under investigation' (Mertler, 2006, p. 9). Since the phenomenon under investigation is a new one in Pakistan, and very little is known about it, a closer in-depth study is required.

Reason and Bradbury (2006) state: 'For many in the majority world, action research is primarily a liberationist practice aiming to redress imbalances of power and restoring to ordinary people the capacities of self-reliance and the ability to manage their own lives—to "sharpen their minds".' (p. xxii)

Action research is known to improve practices within different sites and looks on teachers as agents of change. Thus, through employing this methodology, I attempt to make 'a grassroots effect to find answers to important questions or to foster change' (Mertler, 2006, p. 6).

CHALLENGES IN CONDUCTING RESEARCH

Entering into the field, I am faced with a constellation of challenges which are shrouded in making sense of terms such as 'gender equity', 'feminism', 'poststructuralism' and 'knowledge–power relations' in the everyday context of early childhood classrooms. I envisage that there are no easy answers. The participants' and my own beliefs, and our experiences of growing up in a patriarchal society, will dictate how gender equity is viewed and how it is defined. I am cognisant that our understandings and how we position ourselves will keep shifting, and will be fraught with contradictions—as is already evident from preliminary interviews. In one such interview recently, a teacher voiced her mother's concern about participating in the research study since, according to her mother, equality between men and women is 'unthinkable'. Men have been created superior and that is the reality, and therefore one could not change the balance. However, from the majority of teachers' preliminary interviews, what is also emerging is their questioning of this imbalance by using the term 'unfair'. However, while many have pinpointed practices as being unfair, there is an inherent struggle involved in making sense of the issue of whether this is because one sex is created superior to the other, or because of society.

While we struggle with interpretations of gender and make sense of our meanings from within the contradictions before us, I see the action research methodology as an essential tool in making, aiding and shifting our understanding, meanings and interpretations of gender. I see post-structuralism as providing the lens from which to make sense of these shifting discourses. As we explore these terms together in what I hope will be a partnership through the journey of participatory action research, we face an array of challenges. How will teachers reconceptualise their role so as to promote gender equity? How equitable can their practices really be? How much of a shift can be achieved given differing religious interpretations?

The major task before us will be defining gender equity as it can apply in the Pakistani context. I envisage a range of meanings that this will take, emerging from the manifestation of gender and the meanings we derive from it and through our different readings of events in early childhood classrooms.

In a conversation with teachers regarding the existing understandings of gender, a teacher asked me: 'So what have you found out from us? Have you got some answers or have we transferred our confusion about gender to you?' I answered: 'Don't worry, we will work together through the confusion and come to some meanings.' With this conviction foremost, we move ahead.

SUMMARY

In my experience, the journey of research takes a winding course, etched with many complexities but paralleled with a sense of exhilaration. The key to engaging in any research is being prepared—as my supervisors remind me time and again. For me, it has meant thinking through what I do and being self-reflexive all the time. My journey of framing my study has been made possible because of several factors, which I share for those embarking on this path:

- Foremost for me has been the constant guidance of my supervisors. They have acted as a sounding board for ideas, confusions and questions. While one needs to do the hard work of thinking, formulating and conceptualising the study, the role of a supervisor is crucial in helping to guide and direct it.
- Being familiar with literature in your area is important. You cannot arrive at a conceptual framework if only a limited discourse has been reviewed. In order to conceptualise the study, you need to be acquainted with the whole array of literature.
- Dialoguing with others and talking about your study, especially at the conceptualisation stage, is important. Colleagues, postgraduate

circles and research methods classes can be useful avenues during this stage of research. It is only when ideas are sounded out loud that one can clarify understandings. Questions raised by critical friends and colleagues can help strengthen your thinking as they can create new pathways and directions that may not have been thought about.

- Keeping a research journal is vital, and can prove an invaluable tool. Recording ideas, questions, comments or even confusions can help to clarify your thinking and can help in meetings with supervisors.
- And finally, trying to situate the study within your context is important. Constant questioning and reflection can help avoid major pitfalls when you embark on fieldwork.

REFERENCES

Alloway, N. 1995 *The Construction of Gender in Early Childhood*, Dolphin Press, Melbourne.

Ashraf, D. 2007 'Shifting Position and Changing Image: Women Teachers' Experiences in the Northern Areas of Pakistan', in R. Qureshi and J. Rarieya (eds), *Gender and Education in Pakistan*, Oxford University Press, Karachi, pp. 78–105.

Blaise, M. 2005 *Playing It Straight: Uncovering Gender Discourses in the Early Childhood Classroom*, Routledge, New York.

Butler, J. 1990 *Gender Trouble: Feminisms and the Subversion of Identity*, Routledge, New York.

Davies, B. 1988 *Gender, Equity and Early Childhood*, Curriculum Development Centre, Canberra.

——1989 *Frogs and Snails and Feminist Tails: Preschool Children and Gender*, Allen & Unwin, Sydney.

——1993 *Shards of Glass: Children Reading and Writing Beyond Gendered Identities*, Allen & Unwin, Sydney.

——1994 *Poststructuralist Theory and Classroom Practice*, Deakin University Press, Geelong, Vic.

Denzin, N. and Lincoln, Y. 2000 'Introduction: The Discipline and Practice of Qualitative Research', in N. Denzin and Y. Lincoln (eds), *Handbook of Qualitative Research*, Sage, Thousand Oaks, CA, pp. 1–28.

Farah, I. and Shera, S. 2007 'Female Education in Pakistan: A Review', in R. Qureshi and J. Rarieya (eds), *Gender and Education in Pakistan*, Oxford University Press, Karachi, pp. 3–40.

Flick, U. 1998 *An Introduction to Qualitative Research*, Sage, London.

hooks, b. 1984 *Feminist Theory from Margin to Center*, South End Press, Boston.

Lather, P. 1991 *Feminist Research in Education: Within/Against*, Deakin University Press, Geelong, Vic.

Mac Naughton, G. 1995 *The Power of Mum! Power and Gender at Play*, Australian Early Childhood Association, Watson, ACT.

——1997 'Feminist Praxis and the Gaze in the Early Childhood Curriculum', *Gender and Education*, no. 9, pp. 317–26.

——1998 'Improving Our Gender Equity "Tools": A Case for Discourse Analysis', in N. Yelland (ed.), *Gender in Early Childhood*, Routledge, London, pp. 149–74.

——1999 *Saris and Skirts: Gender Equity and Multiculturalism*, Australian Early Childhood Association, Watson, ACT.

——2000 *Rethinking Gender in Early Childhood Education*, Allen & Unwin, Sydney.

Maguire, P. 2006 'Uneven Ground: Feminisms and Action Research', in P. Reason and H. Bradbury (eds), *Handbook of Action Research*, Sage, London.

Mertler, C. 2006 *Action Research: Teachers as Researchers in the Classroom*, Sage, Thousand Oaks, CA.

Pardhan, A. and Juma, A. 2007 *Gender Differences in Boys' and Girls' Play*, Aga Khan University–Institute for Educational Development, Karachi.

Raza, F. 2007 'Reasons for the Lack of Women's Participation in Pakistan's Workforce', *Journal of Middle East Women's Studies*, vol. 3, no. 3, pp. 99–102.

Reason, P. and Bradbury, H. (eds) 2006 *Handbook of Action Research*, Sage, London.

Shaheed, F. 1991 'The Cultural Articulation of Patriarchy', in F. Zafar (ed.), *Finding Our Way: Readings on Women in Pakistan*, ASR Publications, Lahore, pp. 135–58.

Weedon, C. 1987 *Feminist Practice and Poststructuralist Theory*, Blackwell, Oxford.

5

Ethics in early childhood research

Margaret Coady

> ... the only safe way to avoid violating principles of professional ethics is to refrain from doing social research altogether. (Bronfenbrenner, 1952, pp. 452–5)

This statement by one of the leading theorists of child development is challenging. Though research is essential if our understanding of human development is to be advanced, the history of research is littered with examples of harm caused by researchers to their subjects. Bronfenbrenner's comment was made soon after the Nuremberg War Trials had revealed the horrors of research in the Nazi concentration camps. As a result of these revelations, the Nuremberg Code (Annas and Grodin, 2008) was promulgated; this has been incorporated into many codes governing research. The first statement in this code is that, in research, 'the voluntary consent of the human subject is absolutely essential'.

Children are heavily represented among victims of research, as are other socially powerless groups, such as prisoners, the mentally disabled and those living in poverty. The likelihood of being a research victim increases if one suffers from more than one of these vulnerabilities. While most of the horror stories of research come from the medical field, the results of unethical research in the social sciences, though not so dramatic, can also result in extreme harm. In many cases, the researchers are genuinely trying to establish important data. One example is of a thirteen-year-old girl who had been severely deprived of social contact. She was found in Los Angeles in the 1970s, and presented an ideal opportunity to test the hypothesis that there is a sensitive period for language learning. Genie, as she was named by the researchers, was finally returned to very unsatisfactory care conditions when the research grant ran out (Rymer, 1994, p. 206).

In Genie's case, the focus shifted from benefit to the child to benefit to research. In David Elkind's words (quoted in Rymer, 1994, p. 206), 'the child was the centre of people's careers and grant-getting'. It is just one case which demonstrates the difficulties of combining the role of researcher with that of carer, teacher, doctor or therapist in the one person. The researcher may well be interested in benefiting the participants and finding important data for social good, but inevitably part of the motivation of the researcher is in furthering career and status. Research institutions also have an interest in grants and status, as well as in producing socially valuable data (McNeill, 1993, p. 166), and the good of the research participants can be forgotten.

While it is important to bear in mind the warnings provided by these historical examples and the reality that the researchers' interests may obscure the interests of the child, it must also be acknowledged that research benefits children. Without such research, we would know less about children's points of view, their wants and needs and their possibilities. A balanced approach is therefore necessary. The researcher needs to be aware of the possible ethical downfalls while being assured that the research has value for children.

INFORMED CONSENT

Informed consent of the participants, as the Nuremberg Code stressed, is the key to ethical research. The idea of informed consent is based on the ethical view that all humans have the right to autonomy—that is, the right to determine what is in their own best interests.

REQUIREMENTS FOR INFORMED CONSENT

The participants must be told in words they can understand:

- the nature of the research
- exactly what will be expected of them
- any possible risks of the research

- that they can withdraw from the research at any stage and withdraw any unprocessed data.

In addition, the participants must not be pressured by financial or other inducements to take part in the research.

Most research institutions require that the method of gaining informed consent be in writing and approved by the institutional ethics committee in advance.

CHILDREN AND CONSENT

If we were to take the Nuremberg Code literally, no research using children as participants would be admissible. Not all early childhood research involves using children as participants, as the various chapters in Part III indicate. Much early childhood research focuses on the early childhood staff, or parents, or some other adults. But much important research does involve children as participants. According to legal definitions of informed consent, children cannot give consent. The child's legal guardian can give consent on behalf of the child. However, it is good practice—and in keeping with the United Nations Convention on the Rights of the Child—to ask the child also to give consent, or 'assent' as it is known in these circumstances.

While in almost all cases of research with children it is imperative to gain the consent of the parents, there can be problems with parental consent. There have been cases where parents have agreed to children being participants in research which has had poor outcomes for the children (Emanuel et al., 2008). In addition, the parents may not be present for all of the research, and so not be fully aware of what goes on and not be able to exercise their right to withdraw the child or their data from research. This is particularly true where the research is conducted in an institution. It is desirable that the child's state should be monitored during the course of the research, ideally by somebody outside the research team—a parent, a teacher or a carer—in order to ensure that the child's best interests remain paramount throughout the course of the research.

People who are experienced in working with children may need to be involved in the gaining of assent for children's participation in research. Pictures and diagrams are sometimes used by researchers to convey to the child the nature of the research, and by the child to indicate their feelings about involvement.

DECEPTION IN RESEARCH

If participants are deceived as part of a research project, they cannot give proper consent, since they have not been fully informed. Most codes of research ethics see deception of the participants as an ethical problem. However, some important research could not be carried out without some form of deception. In fact, the process of approving pharmaceutical drugs demands so-called 'double-blind' experiments which constitute a form of deceit of the participants. These are the tests where one group is given the 'treatment' and the other is given a placebo. The participants are randomly assigned either to the treatment group or the placebo group. While these kinds of studies are more common in medicine, they frequently occur in education or psychosocial research, and there is a 'scientific' justification for them. These double-blind experiments may be ethically acceptable if potential participants are told about the treatments and the placebos. The participant can then agree to be deceived, or at least to not be fully informed to this extent.

Other examples of research involve much more serious deception. Such deception may be justified by the importance of the findings. One example of such research involved covert videorecording of parents interacting with their children in hospital (Southall et al., 1995). The children had been admitted for what is termed ALTE (Apparent Life Threatening Events). The video evidence showed that, in 33 of the 39 cases, parents abused their children in hospital to the extent of attempted suffocation or poisoning or breaking of limbs. Since a majority of the parents were later diagnosed with mental illness, and since the admitted children had siblings who would also presumably have been helped, if not saved, by the knowledge provided through the research, it was argued that the great benefit obtained through this experiment outweighed the deception. However, it was certainly a very controversial piece of research.

What of research where children are deceived? One such case (Hoagwood et al., 1996, p. 202) had as its aim the examination of children's eyewitness memory. Four-year-olds were videotaped playing individually with a research assistant posing as a babysitter. A week later, half the children met individually with a research assistant posing as a police officer who suggested to them that the babysitter from the previous week may have done some 'bad things' and asked for their account of what had happened. Later, all the children were questioned. One of the hypotheses in the research was that those who had met with the authority figure would be more likely to say the 'babysitter' had acted badly.

Some of the questions that need to be asked about this research are whether the research is important, whether the information can be gained in any other way that does not involve deception, how the children would be affected by being deceived, whether the children should be 'dehoaxed' after the research and whether the parents should be informed in advance of the deceptive nature of the research, thus possibly contaminating the research by suggesting the truth to the child participants.

CONFIDENTIALITY AND PRIVACY

Most professionals working in the early childhood area are well aware of the need for maintaining confidentiality about children and their families. Out of respect for the privacy of the participants, confidentiality is also promised in most consent forms for research.

In research, specific procedures and protocols are needed to keep data confidential. These procedures include coding of data and keeping the key to the code separate from the data, keeping data in secure, locked storage, making sure that only those researchers authorised by the appropriate ethics committee have access to the data, and making sure that reports, articles and conference papers do not contain identifying material. What is often forgotten is that participants can be identified through photos, videotapes and even audiotapes. If photos, videotapes and audiotapes are to be used in publications or conference presentations, consent to this needs to be given by both parents and children. Even with such consent, it can be ethically tricky to publish research data that contains images of child participants, since charming children agreeing at age three to be shown on a videotape may object strongly to the same video when they believe at age eight that they look foolish on it!

CONFIDENTIALITY AND CHILD ABUSE

For researchers, there is a strong presumption in favour of confidentiality. However, there are also reasons in some cases for overriding this presumption and breaching a participant's confidentiality. It is quite possible, for example, that the researcher will come across evidence which suggests a child is being abused. In such a case, the researcher needs to consider the following questions:

- Am I mandated to report suspected child abuse?
- If I am, have I made this clear when getting informed consent from the participants? The researcher should point out to participants, in advance of their giving consent, where there are legal limits to keeping matters confidential.

- If I am not mandated to report child abuse, then should I nevertheless report?
- How serious is the promise of confidentiality made to the subjects? Does the potential damage to the child and the possibility that reporting the suspected abuse can prevent it continuing, outweigh the promise of confidentiality?

In research connected with child abuse, it is important to ensure that the research does nothing to make a bad situation worse.

THE RISK/BENEFIT EQUATION

In approving a research project, an important factor to guide decision-making about its ethics is the risk/benefit equation. The idea here is that the greater the benefit to be gained from a piece of research, the more risks are acceptable. If a piece of research was almost certainly going to lead to a cure for childhood leukaemia, the risk of a small amount of pain to child subjects of research who gave blood for the research would be allowable. If the value of the research was not high, then any risk—even a slight one—would be questioned.

Risks of research on children can include psychological risks, ranging from a feeling of temporary worry to longer lasting emotional disturbance, and include upsetting relationships within a family. In research on attachment, the temporary upset shown by a baby separated from its mother would probably be acceptable, but only if the research was seen as providing new and significant data. Researchers cannot go around tormenting babies just to demonstrate their research skills! Risks in research on families can include legal risks, breakdown of relationships in families, and even physical risks where there are violent members in the family. Risks in research on professionals include damage to workplace relations, loss of jobs, loss of reputation and legal risks following from these.

The likelihood of the risk occurring also has to be calculated. If there was a high likelihood and the possible consequence was very serious (death or serious harm to a participant), the research should not be allowed.

CULTURAL ISSUES IN ETHICAL RESEARCH

Some researchers treat minority groups as curiosities rather than as people, or as **objects** to be researched, rather than **subjects**, with all that entails about subjectivities. This kind of attitude is prominent in much nineteenth century research into indigenous peoples. However, it is also a phenomenon that still exists.

Cultural differences between researchers and the researched may lead to misunderstandings by the researcher as well as by the person being researched. The participant may misunderstand what is involved in a research project because of language difficulties (in many cases, having a translator is absolutely essential), or because of cultural understandings. The participant may believe that access to educational and other important benefits may depend on agreeing to participate. Researchers may misunderstand the different cultural understandings of family and family responsibilities, of relationships, and of appropriate behaviour in different situations, and as a result may insult or offend or even terrify the subject without intending to do so.

Some argue that informed consent procedures should vary from one cultural group to another. In one sense, this is obviously true. Participants must be informed about the research in a language and by a means which they understand. But some writers further suggest that some cultural groups do not value informed consent or that the informed consent should be given by the leader of the family or, where appropriate, the tribe, since it is argued that the idea of autonomy or the right of the individual participant to consent is a Western middle-class notion.

An important study (Leach et al., 1999) in this regard was conducted in The Gambia. The subjects were mothers who were asked to consent to their children being given the HIB vaccination. Interviews were conducted with the 137 mothers who had agreed to the vaccination and the 52 who had refused the vaccination. In spite of being from a developing country, having very little education and living in rural areas, these women showed an understanding of the consent procedure and its rationale which was very similar to the understanding of those in a Western middle-class group. They valued autonomy and wanted to be free to give informed consent or refusal to their children having HIB vaccines. The researchers conclude that the principles of informed consent were affirmed by this community.

It is easy and dangerous to under-estimate or pre-judge the abilities and concerns of the participants in a situation which is very different from that experienced by the researcher.

RESEARCH INVOLVING INDIGENOUS GROUPS

Because of histories of lack of understanding and respect of researchers for indigenous peoples, research on such groups is now very sensitive. In Canada, the Interagency Advisory Panel on Research Ethics advises on the development of ethical policy in research in Canada and this includes advice on research involving indigenous people <www.pre.ethics.gc.ca/eng/policy-politique/initiatives/draft-preliminaire/chapter9-chapitre9>. In Australia, formal guidelines on ethical matters in Aboriginal and Torres Strait Islander health research have been set up by the National Health and Medical Research Council. These guidelines are available on the following website: <www.nhmrc.gov.au/publications/ethics/2007_humans/section4.7.htm>. The guidelines cover a range of matters, including full consultation with the community, gaining consent both from individual subjects and from the community, ensuring that Aboriginal women are present during all work dealing with children, and the use of any pictures strictly in accordance with the wishes of the community. Chapter 6 in this book discusses these issues in greater detail.

SUBMITTING ETHICS APPLICATIONS TO ETHICS COMMITTEES

Research undertaken within institutions will probably need to be approved by the institution's ethics committee. If more than one institution is involved in the research, there may be applications to, for example, both hospital and university, or school and university. Though the requirements of the institutions may be slightly different, they should be compatible, and will cover areas such as the vulnerability of subjects, informed consent, risk assessment and confidentiality.

ETHICS COMMITTEE APPLICATION REMINDERS

- Try not to regard your ethics application as just another legalistic hurdle to be crossed. Ideally, ethics committees should be encouraging ethical research rather than acting as obstructive police. Such committees are certainly important in providing another perspective to researchers whose main concern is successful completion of the research.
- Give a thorough though concise description of what you plan to do, avoiding jargon and technical detail particularly in the plain language description of the project. Include exactly what will be expected of the subjects and how much of the subjects' time it will take. It is particularly important to include how

much of children's time it will take. The fact that children are 'captive' in institutions does not mean their time can be used at the whim of others.

- Do not forget that digital image and sound files, videotapes and audiotapes are identifying material. Show how you intend to maintain confidentiality if you are using such files and/or tapes.
- The research ethics application form will ask you whether you are in a dependent relationship with any of the participants. It often happens in early childhood research that the researcher wants to use as participants the children and/or families in the centres in which they work, or the colleagues with whom they work. In these cases you need to **show**, not just assert, that the participants will not feel any pressure to participate and, in the case of colleagues, that their working conditions can be in no way adversely affected by their agreeing to participate.
- Remember that the participants, whether they are school children, children in child care or adults, are doing the researcher a favour in agreeing to take part in the research.

RESEARCH METHODOLOGIES

The application forms for most institutional ethics committees are better geared to quantitative research, often of a medical nature. However, ethics committees are increasingly more sensitive to a range of different research paradigms. If the research involves open-ended, in-depth interviews, most ethics committees would be satisfied with a description of why this is necessary and an account of the kind and scope of questions to be asked.

Feminist thinkers, in particular, have been sensitive to the inequalities of power between researcher and participant. However, the attempt to remedy these inequalities in some action research can lead, in a few cases, to a pretence of equality. The researcher needs to be realistic about the inequalities of power involved in a particular employment situation. A carer may feel unable to refuse involvement in the research if she believes that it will affect her career prospects. There may also be problems about maintaining confidentiality in action research since the group of participants normally works closely together. The particular ethical issues in action research need to be thought through carefully before the research begins. Special care needs to be taken in acknowledging the contributions of all in any publications or presentations, and each member of the research team should be fully informed in advance about the details about the research and the expectations of the different roles (Mac Naughton and Hughes, 2009, p. 84).

CONCLUSION

Attention to the ethical aspects of research can in some instances impede research. There are even certain pieces of research which are 'forbidden' in the sense that, while possibly yielding valuable data, they are so harmful to the subjects that they should not be performed. In other cases, research has to be limited out of respect for the subjects—for example, when accepting a participant's right to withdraw. However, in general, concern for ethics both in the planning and the execution stage of research can add to the quality of the research. While at the time it seems an added burden, even the submission of an ethics application means that the researcher must think through the whole process of the research and its implications before commencing, with the result being better thought-out research as well as greater protection of the rights of the participants and of all those affected by the research.

SUMMARY

This chapter has examined how research is not neutral because all research has embedded in it particular assumptions and ways of viewing the world; particular positioning to knowledge, knowing and meaning making and then the types of research relationships that are possible. When assumptions, positioning and relationships in research are not made conscious, examined and addressed, power inherently remains with the researcher. Just as it is necessary to understand where and how power relationships occur in early childhood research between adults and children, it is equally necessary to understand where and how this happens in research that involves Aboriginal people.

Research that involves Aboriginal people is complex because it requires working within multiple contexts where the power differentials are not just doubled, they are multiplied. This increases the places where Aboriginal people can be erased, silenced, marginalised.

As a result of challenges to Aboriginal research in terms of critical theory, postcolonialism and decolonisation, Indigenist research has emerged. The terms reflects the different sets of assumptions, positioning and researcher relationships from those of research 'on' to research 'with' or 'by' Aboriginal people. Indigenist research holds Aboriginal world-view, knowledge, values and relatedness as core to all research decisions towards achieving Aboriginal sovereignty.

In order to understand how research can be different, to know how to make it different, any research that involves Aboriginal people must make conscious and purposefully act on changing the power dynamics to deliver equity and achieve equality.

QUESTIONS FOR REFLECTION

1 Have you been a participant in a piece of research? Did you consent to taking part and what were your reasons for taking part?
2 What kind of benefits could ethically justify subjecting a child to some risk in research?
3 On what occasions can you envisage having to breach confidentiality in your research?

REFERENCES

Annas, G.J. and Grodin, M. 2008 'The Nuremberg Code', in E.J. Emanuel et al. (eds), *The Oxford Textbook of Clinical Research Ethics,* Oxford University Press, Oxford, pp. 267–88.

Bronfenbrenner, U. 1952 'Principles of Professional Ethics: Cornell Studies in Social Growth', *American Psychologist*, vol. 7, pp. 452–5.

Emanuel, E.J., Grady, C., Crouch, R.J., Lie, R., Miller, F. and Wendler, D. (eds) 2008 *The Oxford Textbook of Clinical Research Ethics*, Oxford University Press, Oxford.

Hoagwood, K., Jensen, P. and Fisher, C. (eds) 1996 *Ethical Issues in Mental Health Research with Children and Adolescents*, Lawrence Erlbaum, Mahwah, NJ.

Leach, A., Hilton, S., Greenwood, B.M., Manneh, E., Dibba, B., Wilkins, A. and Mullholland, E.K., 1999 'An Evaluation of the Informed Consent Procedure Used During a Trial of a Haemophilus Influenzae Type B Conjugate Vaccine Undertaken in The Gambia, West Africa', *Social Science and Medicine,* vol. 48, pp. 139–48.

Mac Naughton, G. and Hughes, P. 2009 *Doing Action Research in Early Childhood Studies*, Open University Press, Berkshire.

McNeill, P. 1993 *The Ethics and Politics of Human Experimentation*, Cambridge University Press, Cambridge.

Rymer, R. 1994 *Genie: A Scientific Tragedy*, Penguin, London.

Southall, D., Plunkett, M., Banks, M., Falkov, A. and Samuels, M. 1997 'Covert Video-Recordings of Life-threatening Child Abuse: Lessons for Child Protection', *Pediatrics*, vol. 100, no. 5, pp. 735–60.

WEBSITES

National Statement on Ethical Conduct in Human Research 2007 National Health and Medical Research Council, Australian Government NHMRC: <www.nhmrc.gov.au/publications/ethics/2007_humans/contents.htm>.

Values and Ethics—Guidelines for Ethical Conduct in Aboriginal and Torres Strait Islander Health Research: <www.nhmrc.gov.au/publications/synopses/e52syn.htm>.

FURTHER READING

Emanuel, E., Grady, C., Crouch, R., Lie, R., Franklin Miller, F. and Windler, D. (eds) 2008 *The Oxford Textbook of Clinical Research Ethics*, Oxford University Press, Oxford. The contributors to this book cover a wide range of issues of interest to researchers working in early childhood. These include accounts of some of the more scandalous episodes of research on children, as well as sections on the ethical issues involved in research on ethnic and minority populations, on children, on captive populations, a chapter on the ethics of giving incentives to participants, and hints about choosing participants.

Grodin, M.A. and Glantz, L.H. (eds) 1994 *Children as Research Subjects: Science, Ethics and Law*, Oxford University Press, New York. This book, entirely devoted to the topic of children as subjects, is particularly useful on issues of risk to children in research.

Hoagwood, K., Jensen, P. and Fisher, C. (eds) 1996 *Ethical Issues in Mental Health Research with Children and Adolescents*, Lawrence Erlbaum, Mahwah, NJ. This book interprets mental health broadly and looks thoroughly at issues such as risk-benefit analysis and honesty in research.

Mac Naughton, G. and Hughes, P. 2009 *Doing Action Research in Early Childhood Studies*, Open University Press, Berkshire. This book has suggestions about how to overcome the particular ethical challenges posed by action research.

The research departments of most research institutions can provide lists of principles to be followed in research and particular requirements for making submissions to the relevant institutional ethics committee.

6

Indigenous research

Karen Martin

> In 1993 and 1994, the Quandamoopah peoples of Moreton Bay in Southeast Queensland, Australia were required to provide evidence for a native title application, which required a lot of anthropological, legal and historical research. I first watched with interest that changed to anxiety, the ways in which our knowledges and beliefs were gathered, interpreted and presented for this claim. It became increasingly evident that the findings were measured against predetermined categories defined within these anthropological, legal and historical disciplines. Deliberate or not, this research made me question who I was, my rights, my knowledges and my role as a Quandamoopah woman. I was made to feel that I didn't belong because my experiences were not 'valid' or valued in these procedures. I soon learned that I was not alone in these experiences as other Quandamoopah people shared the same concerns and frustration privately and publicly at community meetings. Others still chose not to participate. But I knew three things: that somehow this Aboriginal research was wrong; from an unwavering belief in my Ancestral relatedness to Quandamoopah that this was a harmful untruth; and that it had to be challenged in order to be changed.
>
> Karen Martin

INTRODUCTION

As can be seen from this story, research is not neutral. Research can help understand problems, or it can perpetuate problems. This is particularly evident in research that involves Aboriginal people because the power dynamics exist in multiple ways and almost always benefit the researcher more than the researched (Martin, 2008). Therefore, research is a tool of **colonialism**. It can erase, erode, silence or marginalise Aboriginal people. Unless these power dynamics are first made conscious, then made explicit and then addressed, research will never deliver on the promise of equity and equality. This is evident in the above **native title** application procedures and in native title research.

This chapter examines Aboriginal research within Australia. It is acknowledged that, while similarities exist with the experiences of other Aboriginal, First Nations and Indigenous peoples throughout the world, there are just as many distinctions due to the historical, cultural, social and political contexts. Prior to the mid-1990s, almost all Aboriginal research was done without permission, consultation or the genuine involvement of Aboriginal people (Rigney, 2001). Beginning with British invasion in the 1770s and continuing to the present, natural scientists (such as biologists, geologists and botanists) and social scientists (such as anthropologists, archaeologists, educators and psychologists) have conducted research in Aboriginal lands, on Aboriginal people and at times both, without their knowledge, consent, involvement or benefit (West, 2000). In areas such as health, education and justice, Aboriginal people have been over-researched but there have been minimal benefits or changes to the outcomes for them (Calma, 2008, 2009). Justifiably, Aboriginal people are suspicious of research and of researchers because too much has been done, and too many have not delivered on their promises and have taken more than they have given.

All research has embedded particular **assumptions** and ways of viewing the world; particular **positioning** to knowledge, knowing and meaning-making; and the types of **research relationships** that are possible (see Chapter 3). Every research decision therefore emanates from the researcher's world-view, knowledge and moral systems. These decisions pertain to: the research topic; the research contexts; the research participants; the methodology and the methods; the framework for analysis and interpretation; and equally the decisions made in writing up and the dissemination of the findings. The **assumptions** a researcher holds about a particular topic, the way they have come to know and give meaning to this topic and how they give value to this topic have already shaped the research in unconscious, unstated and unexamined ways. They have become a normal way of thinking about a topic, issue, experience or belief.

Therefore, when undertaking research involving Aboriginal people, these unconscious, unstated and unexamined assumptions are the factors by which the researcher manages the power differentials inherent in Aboriginal research to either perpetuate problems, or understand them in order to work towards changing them.

POWER IN ABORIGINAL RESEARCH PATTERNS: ERASURE, SILENCING, AGENCY AND SOVEREIGNTY

In this chapter, Aboriginal research is defined as research involving Aboriginal people as objects, subjects, participants, partners or researchers. It identifies and discusses the way power exists in particular types of Aboriginal research in Australia over time and the patterns that are evident in the assumptions, **researcher positioning** and **research relationships**. While these three components are often treated separately, they are actually interrelated, and provide the means by which it is possible to determine how power is exercised or addressed. This is not a two-dimensional or uni-directional situation; rather, it is multi-layered and dynamic because the research decisions are numerous and interrelated, and occur in multiple contexts.

Therefore, by looking at these patterns in the assumptions, positioning and research relationships, it is also possible to determine where change in Aboriginal research has occurred. This is important in understanding how research is not neutral, how a researcher is not neutral and how the relationships with Aboriginal people in research are also not neutral. Just as it is necessary to understand where and how power relationships occur in early childhood research between adults and children, it is equally necessary to understand where and how this happens in Aboriginal research in order to understand how it can be different and to make it different (Mac Naughton and Davis, 2001). It must be remembered that when the research involves Aboriginal early childhood education, then the power relationships are further multiplied, not just doubled, because there are additional points where power can be misused or used effectively (see Chapter 15).

While it is the patterns that are examined here, these are discussed in reference to notional timeframes to contextualise and facilitate understanding. Thus the timeframes are indicators that show when particular shifts occurred and became prominent as different ways of conducting Aboriginal research. The patterns, however, are not confined to one timeframe as their features may have emerged in a previous timeframe or persisted into later timeframes. Hence, the features of some patterns never totally disappear, but merely become less prominent. The four patterns of Aboriginal research are: ***Terra nullius*** **Aboriginal research**—patterns of Aboriginal erasure; **Traditionalising Aboriginal research**—patterns of Aboriginal silencing; **Collaborative Aboriginal research**—patterns of **Aboriginal agency**; and **Indigenist research**—patterns of **Aboriginal sovereignty**.

Terra nullius Aboriginal research: Patterns of Aboriginal erasure, 1770s–1920s

> Whilst others visited many places within the lands and waterways that were to become known as 'Australia', it was in 1770 that Lieutenant James Cook declared this land *terra nullius*—meaning 'empty land' or 'land belonging to no one' (Cunneen and Libesman, 1995). Core to the edict of *terra nullius* is the non-Aboriginal assumption of superiority and subsequent power to take the land and hence erase Aboriginal ownership of the land. In this relationship, Aboriginal people are not regarded as human; therefore, non-Aboriginal people do not have to ask or consult them on any matters pertaining to their lives, beliefs, customs, knowledges or family. For example, when the term 'Aboriginal' was applied by non-Aboriginal people, it erased the significant diversity amongst the 260–280 language groups consisting of 600–800 clan identities.

Terra nullius Aboriginal research is based on the assumption that Australia, as it was so named, was a frontier to be explored and exploited. Any 'discovery' could be claimed, taken, owned or sold because non-Aboriginal researchers believed they did not have to ask the permission of Aboriginal people. Aboriginal people were either erased from the landscape altogether, or constructed as sub-human, and situated amongst the flora and fauna. The collection of Aboriginal artefacts, including Aboriginal remains, was condoned to prove or disprove Aboriginal humanity. This assumption was part of a wider ideology of biological racism that was prominent in this same period throughout the world. Thus museum displays, until more recent times, portrayed Aboriginal people as quirks of human evolution and exhibited them amongst the equally quirky exotic Australian animals and plants, such as the banksia, kangaroo, platypus, echidna and koala.

In *terra nullius* Aboriginal research, the researcher positioning is as the objective non-Aboriginal researcher conducting research 'on' the Aboriginal research specimen. The position is one of dominance, and of social, intellectual and cultural objectivity that either erased Aboriginal people or constructed them in particular ways, making them visible only in certain ways. The images of Aboriginal people as the 'noble savage', the 'ancient warrior', the 'dusky maiden' or 'living in harmony with nature' are constructions arising from *terra nullius* research, as are the constructions that Aboriginal people were part of the 'missing link', had 'low, animal intelligence' and were 'treacherous and evil'. The researcher positioning is described as research 'on' Aboriginal people.

Relationships existing at the time of invasion and early colonisation were the same in *terra nullius* research—namely, that Aboriginal people were believed to be sub-human and were therefore treated as such. The collection not just of Aboriginal artefacts such as spears, shields and baskets, but also of Aboriginal human remains, typifies this relationship.

One example of the assumptions of researcher relationships with Aboriginal people, is provided below. It is from the journal of Elphinstone Dalrymple, a geologist commissioned in the late 1800s by the Queensland government to survey the lands in the far northern regions of the state to ascertain the potential of its natural resources for mining and agricultural development.

> Mr. Johnstone found in a large bark gunyah of the blacks, a curious and interesting specimen of defunct humanity, viz., the body of a black gin, doubled up and tied like a roll of spiced beef, and of the same color and somewhat of the same smell … Mr. Johnstone brought it on board, and I have had the pleasure of placing it in the Brisbane Museum. Mr. Johnstone left a couple of blankets and a tomahawk for the bereaved relatives, who would doubtless rightly appreciate the exchange. The head of this mummy is small—the animal organs being developed to distortion, the mental being next to nil; in fact, it is of the very lowest type of human formation. (Dalrymple, 1874 pp. 28; no. 406)

Traditionalising Aboriginal research: Patterns of Aboriginal silencing, 1890s–1970s

> As non-Aboriginal researchers and members of the general Australian population assume Aboriginal people are 'dying out' or losing racial purity, a shift in relationships emerges in this timeframe. There is a continuance of the **biological racism** from the previous *terra nullius* phase and so traditionalising Aboriginal research was driven by the urgency to record and preserve everything about Aboriginal people.

The key assumptions of this period were that, after decades of experimental and positivistic research 'on' Aboriginal people, they were now viewed as humans. That is, Aboriginal people were made visible in research, but they were also made voiceless by research.

There was a shift to now record the social categories and detail the grand structures of Aboriginal kinship and mythology (Beckett, 1994). Thus began the obsession with research on 'traditional' or 'non-traditional' Aborigines, according to their adherence to these grand structures. Those in Central Australia, Far North Queensland, the Northern Territory and Western Australia became the focus of researchers, seen as being 'real' Aboriginal people based on anthropological categories of race and culture. The former, 'traditional Aborigines', were constructed as more 'real' or 'authentic' Aboriginal people, the latter, 'non-traditional Aborigines', deemed 'better able' to be assimilated into Australian society. Increasingly, traditionalising Aboriginal research was funded as a means to achieve Aboriginal assimilation and solve the 'Aboriginal problem'. This type of Aboriginal research was also used to inform government policy:

> Aboriginal psychology and intelligence are talked about but not scientifically understood. It is a three-sided task, to be tackled by physical anthropology, psychology and social anthropology. It is urgent because both public opinion and Government policy demand up-to-date educational facilities for all Aborigines, full-blooded and mixed blood. (Elkin, 1963, p. 21)

Researcher positioning remained positivistic and objective so that Aboriginal people could be viewed and their behaviours and beliefs interpreted according to non-Aboriginal research paradigms or disciplinary knowledge such as anthropology, archaeology, linguistics and history.

For some non-Aboriginal researchers, 'going native' became popular as a methodology where they lived for lengths of time with Aboriginal people, researching, recording and interpreting their daily lives, languages, customs and beliefs. However, the need to maintain researcher objectivity was core to recording valid data, and while the methodology shifted in this phase, the researcher assumptions and positioning did not. This positioning is one of the non-Aboriginal scientist adhering to strict disciplinary codes and research paradigms. It is best described as research 'of' or research 'about' Aboriginal people.

Researcher relationships with Aboriginal people are constrained by the assumptions and researcher positioning in traditionalising Aboriginal research. The non-Aboriginal researcher is the 'expert' and 'authority', researching Aboriginal people as objects of the research—visible but voiceless. Inherent in this relationship is the belief that it is the right of the non-Aboriginal researcher to gather this data, and therefore this does not require the consent of Aboriginal people. Through traditionalising Aboriginal research, Aboriginal people were ideologically fixed in time as 'primitive', separated from their knowledge systems, marginalised in colonial consciousness and physically, socially, legally, historically and economically excluded to the fringes of colonial society.

Collaborative Aboriginal Research: Patterns of Aboriginal agency, 1970s–1990s

> As wider societal changes occurred, this generated a rethinking of Aboriginal research, and ways to achieve greater involvement of and benefits for Aboriginal people. Models of collaborative research were emerging as successful with other groups such as women and socioeconomically disadvantaged groups, and were now seen as a means to facilitate involvement of Aboriginal people as more than 'the researched' but as having some agency in the research itself (Williams, 2001). This challenged the assumptions of previous forms of Aboriginal research, where researchers saw no need to talk with Aboriginal people unless it was a required part of the data-collection process.

The basic assumption of collaborative Aboriginal research is the necessity of involving Aboriginal people in the research. This collaboration varied, as in some models of research Aboriginal people were used to inform the Aboriginal research participants of the project, or employed to collect data, or were listed as co-authors in the reporting of the findings. However, most changes were restricted to methodology and methods for data collection and dissemination: this data was still analysed and interpreted by the researcher's disciplinary knowledge, values and beliefs. When the underlying assumptions have not been examined and addressed, the power dynamics are not challenged and Aboriginal agency is limited. Depending on the degree of Aboriginal agency achieved, collaborative Aboriginal research remained research 'about', or sometimes 'with', Aboriginal people. As Bishop (2005) argues:

> ... differential power relations among participants, while construed and understood as collaborative by the researcher, may still enable researcher concerns and interests to dominate how understandings are constructed (2005, p. 123).

Subsequently, even with some Aboriginal collaboration, the researcher positioning is maintained as 'expert', with the researcher continuing to view, interpret and (mis)represent Aboriginal world-views, cultures, experiences and knowledges. This adherence to particular research methodology and methods often acts in opposition to this collaboration whereby the benefits for the researcher will inevitably outweigh those of the Aboriginal participants (Ivanitz, 1999).

True collaboration equates to full Aboriginal agency, and this is not possible when power is afforded to researchers. When the research relationships also remain unexamined and unchallenged, as in some models of collaborative Aboriginal research, Aboriginal agency can still be limited to no more than that of consenting subjects. In other models, Aboriginal agency is evident in all stages of the research—making decisions, contributing and benefiting from the research in overt, ongoing and equal relationships.

There are various models of collaborative Aboriginal research, each addressing to varying degrees the power in the assumptions, and researcher positioning, to produce a range of collaborations between researcher and research participants to achieve a particular level of Aboriginal agency. The actual benefits for Aboriginal people significantly outweigh the actual costs—not just economic costs, but also emotional, cultural, physical, social and intellectual costs. Essentially, Aboriginal agency is possible when Aboriginal people are co-partners in the research, co-researchers and co-benefactors (Chase, 1995; Smith, 2000).

Aboriginal research is a tool of colonialism that works at first to erase, then to silence and then to marginalise Aboriginal people. While the shifts in Aboriginal research incorporated Aboriginal collaboration, this did not always achieve Aboriginal agency. Hence a critical mass of

Aboriginal scholars, both within and external to Australia, challenged this situation, asserting the need for Aboriginal sovereignty in research.

Indigenist research: Patterns of Aboriginal sovereignty, 1990s to present and future

> Aboriginal sovereignty is defined as the power inherent in the rights of Aboriginal people as the First Peoples of a particular country, and inherent in the relatedness of Aboriginal people to all things in this country of past, present and future (Martin, 2008). According to Moreton-Robinson (2007), Aboriginal sovereignty is:
>
> > ... embodied, it is ontological (our being) and epistemological (our way of knowing), and it is grounded within complex relations derived from the intersubstantiation of ancestral beings, humans and land. In this sense, our sovereignty is carried by the body and differs from Western constructions of sovereignty, which are predicated on the social contract model, the idea of a unified supreme authority, territorial integrity and individual rights. (2007, p. 2)

Three bodies of scholarship are involved in challenging existing Aboriginal research, namely: **critical race theory**, **postcolonial theory** and **Indigenist theory**. Each makes a major contribution to the shift in the assumptions, positioning and research relationships. It is not possible to describe the development of these major bodies of knowledge in depth because there is much to consider, so each is examined for its challenges to Aboriginal research and its contributions to achieving Aboriginal sovereignty. Critical race theory is discussed in relation to the challenges and critique of research; postcolonial theory is discussed in relation to the **decolonisation** of research; and Indigenist theory is discussed in relation to the articulation of Aboriginal sovereignty in research.

Critical race theory, with its roots in critical theory, examines the power in any given relationship (Coomer, 1984; Agger, 1991) to confront injustices (Kincheloe and McLaren, 1998), transform social order and produce action (Denzin and Lincoln, 1998). Researchers are required to 'place their assumptions on the table' (Kincheloe and McLaren, 1998, p. 265). When applied to research, critical race theory challenges researchers to see the imbalances of power where these involve race, culture, ethnicity and the identities of the researcher and the researched.

A key challenge to researcher assumptions is to understand that they are working within additional contexts with additional sets of demands in terms of race, ethnicity and identity (Ladson-Billings, 2000; Moreton-Robinson, 2000; Stanfield, 1998; Nicoll, 2004). Critical race theory thereby requires researchers to make explicit these additional dimensions in order to understand how power is racialised and resides with the researcher, and how it must be critiqued in order to work out of new relationship to self as researcher, to knowledge brought to and gained within the research, and to research itself.

However, Stanfield (1998) warns that, while critical race theory is valuable and necessary for the critique of research, it offers little in terms of its reconstruction. That is, it offers a researcher little in the way of how to think differently about research, beyond their own beliefs, knowledge and world-view, to avoid perpetuating the very same power differentials based on race—of the researcher and the researched:

> Until we engage in efforts to critique and revise the paradigms underlying qualitative research strategies … critiquing racialized ethnic theories, methods, styles of data interpretation, and patterns of knowledge dissemination will remain grossly incomplete … At most we have a developing literature for dominant researchers on how to be more sensitive in doing qualitative research in settings involving people of color. (Stanfield, 1998, p. 350)

Here, Stanfield defines one of the limitations inherent in collaborative Aboriginal research. Although the strategies were changed, these were not critiqued, and thus the power remained unchallenged. Even where it was stated, it was often misidentified and the research decisions became misdirected. Knowing about something doesn't always provide the means to know how it can be different. This is where postcolonial scholarship is of value.

A move towards a postcolonial research paradigm 'would accept knowledge from differing cosmologies as valid in their own right, without them having to adhere to a separate cultural body for legitimacy' (Duran and Duran, 2002, p. 87). Postcolonialism is similar to postmodernism in that it seeks to reduce or eradicate the impacts of the grand narratives established and maintained in positivism and constructivism (Mac Naughton and Davis, 2001; Tuhawai Smith, 1999). The emphasis is that, as a tool of colonialism, research perpetuates the position of colonisers over colonised—namely, non-Aboriginal over Aboriginal. As Smith (2005) puts it:

> The decolonization project in research engages in multiple layers of struggle across multiple sites. It involves the unmaking and deconstruction of imperialism, and its aspect of colonialism, in its old and new formations alongside a search for sovereignty; for reclamation of knowledge, language, and culture; and for the social transformation of the colonial relations between the native and the settler (2005, p. 88)

An assumption of postcolonialism is that colonialism must be challenged and research must be decolonised using Aboriginal terms of reference. The scholarship of postcolonialism is to take the critique further, as argued above by Stanfield. The process of decolonisation requires researchers to restructure this with the deliberate understanding of how colonialism is manifested, not just in society but in knowledge reproduction such as research.

In terms of Aboriginal research, postcolonialism requires the researcher to know about, and make decisions to not perpetuate, the types of power differentials that have been identified within the assumptions, positioning and research relationships of *terra nullius*, traditionalising and collaborative Aboriginal research. Furthermore, postcolonialism is invaluable for Aboriginal people to understand how pervasive and persuasive colonialism is within research, and to be aware that decolonisation can best be realised through the use of Aboriginal world-view, knowledge and values. Again, Bishop (2005) is helpful on this point:

> ... when [I]ndigenous cultural ways of knowing and aspirations ... are central to the creation of the research context, then the situation goes beyond empowerment to one in which sense making, decision making, and theorizing take place in situations that are 'normal' to the research participants rather than constructed by the researcher (2005, p. 126).

The spaces created by this decolonisation of Aboriginal research enable Aboriginal ways of viewing, knowing and giving meaning to be core in terms of research assumptions. Decolonisation is crucial to the achievement of Aboriginal sovereignty (Bishop, 2005; Edwards, 2009). When Aboriginal sovereignty is not a consideration of Aboriginal research, the previous patterns of the assumptions, the researcher positioning and research relationships go unchanged (Wilson, 2001).

As a result of these challenges, Indigenist research emerged with different sets of assumptions, positioning and relationships. The term reflects the interrelationship of critical theory, critical race theory and an Aboriginal world-view, knowledge and values. Hence Indigenist research has three interrelated conditions. The first is to constantly critique the power and procedures of research, particularly its assumptions, methodology and methods. The second is to decolonise research, so that the power is addressed. The third is the transformation of research through Aboriginal sovereignty, an Aboriginal world-view, knowledge and values (Martin, 2008; Wilson, 2008). Indigenist research is Aboriginal sovereignty through respecting and centring Aboriginal ways of viewing the world and all things in it, of knowing, giving meaning to and valuing the world, and in the ways this is expressed.

A key assumption of Indigenist research is that all things exist in relatedness (Arbon, 2008; Martin, 2008; Wilson, 2001, 2008; Yunupingu, 1994). Relatedness honours Aboriginal social mores and fulfilment of rites as essential processes through which Aboriginal people situate themselves and behave when in our own lands and in the lands of other Aboriginal groups (Arbon, 2008; Edwards, 2009; Yunupingu, 1994). Indigenist research is liberatory in redressing the existing social, political, education and economic inequities within wider Australian society.

Indigenist research is transformative in that the researcher is positioned in relatedness to knowledge of self and of others. By critiquing, decolonising and instating relatedness as a premise, the voices, experiences and meanings Aboriginal people give to the world are privileged (Huggins, 1988; Rigney, 2001; Weber-Pillwax, 2001). This ensures that the research benefits Aboriginal people (Moreton-Robinson, 2000; Tuhawia Smith, 1999).

Likewise, the researcher relationships are underpinned by relatedness, which implicitly restores and serves Aboriginal sovereignty. In reclaiming, renaming and re-presenting Aboriginal world-views, knowledge and values through research, the power is addressed, if not neutralised (Rigney, 1997, 2001; Duran and Duran, 2002; Weber-Pillwax, 2001; Wilson, 2001; Youngblood Henderson, 2002).

> To know your [S]tories of relatedness is to know who you are, where you are from and how you are related. Whether these Stories have been distorted or forgotten, they still exist then the task becomes one of finding how this happened in order to reclaim them. (Martin, 2008, p. 83)

CONCLUSION

In this examination of the assumptions, researcher positioning and research relationships of Aboriginal research over time, it is possible to determine the power inherent in research to erase and silence Aboriginal people, and also to achieve Aboriginal agency and sovereignty. While some shifts have occurred within Aboriginal research in Australia over time, these are too often limited to some aspects of the methodology but more particularly the methods of data collection. Rarely is the interrelationship of the research assumptions, the researcher positioning and the research relationships examined as a site of power. Until such time as this is addressed, it will continue to inevitably work against Aboriginal agency, and especially Aboriginal sovereignty. Indigenist research is vital. It is a new research paradigm based on old knowledge that challenges, engages, connects and changes more than it measures, categorises, interprets and generalises. Where erasure and silencing were once dominant as Aboriginal research models, patterns of Aboriginal agency and sovereignty are now a reality.

SUMMARY

- Research is not neutral.
- When assumptions, positioning and relationships in research are not made conscious, examined and addressed, the power inherently remains with the researcher.
- Research that involves Aboriginal people is complex because it requires working within multiple contexts. Therefore, the power differentials are not just doubled; they are multiplied, and a researcher must know about and act on most, if not all, of these to achieve Aboriginal agency.
- Indigenist research holds Aboriginal sovereignty as core to its assumptions, researcher positioning and research relationships with Aboriginal people.

QUESTIONS FOR REFLECTION

1. The discussion in this chapter gives an Australian focus. What similarities or differences do you know about research with other Aboriginal, First Nation or Indigenous people in other countries?
2. If you wanted to undertake research with Aboriginal people, how would you make conscious and then examine the assumptions you would bring with you?
3. In what ways is it possible to erase or make silent Aboriginal people in research?
4. After reading this chapter, how differently will you make your research decisions, even if this isn't with Aboriginal people?

5 What connections between the concepts and discussions in this chapter can you make to those in other chapters?

REFERENCES

Agger, B. 1991 'Critical Theory, Post Structuralism, Post Modernism: Their Sociological Relevance', *Annual Review Social*, vol. 17, pp. 105–31.

Arbon, V. 2008 *Arlanthirnda ngukarnda ityirnda—Being, Knowing, Doing: De-colonising Indigenous Tertiary Education*, Postpressed, Brisbane.

Beckett, J. 1994 'Aboriginal Histories, Aboriginal Myths: An Introduction', *Oceania,* vol. 65, no. 2, pp. 97–115.

Bishop, R. 2005 'Freeing Ourselves from Neo-colonial Domination in Research: A Kaupapa Maori Approach to Creating Knowledge', in N.K. Denzin and Y.S. Lincoln (eds), *Sage Handbook of Qualitative Research*, Sage, London, pp. 109–38.

Calma, T. 2008 *Social Justice Report 2000*, Human Rights & Equal Opportunity Commission, Sydney.

——2009, *Social Justice Report 2008*, Human Rights & Equal Opportunity Commission, Sydney.

Chase, A. 1995 'Land Issues and Consultation: Lockhart River Community', in J. Cordell (ed.), *Indigenous Management of Land and Sea and Traditional Activities in Cape York Peninsula*, Cape York Peninsula Land Use Strategy, Office of the Coordinator General of Queensland, Brisbane, Department of the Environment, Sport and Territories, Canberra, and the University of Queensland, Chapter 7.

Collard, L. and Pickwick, T. 1999 'A Nyungar at Research', in *Proceedings of the Indigenous Research Ethics Conference*, James Cook University, Townsville, pp. 29–37.

Coomer, D. 1984 'Critical Science: Approach to Vocational Education Research', *Journal of Vocational Education Research*, vol. 9, no. 4, pp. 34–50.

Cuneen, C. and Libesman, T. 1995 *Indigenous People and the Law in Australia,* Butterworths, Sydney.

Dalrymple, E. 1874 *Narratives and Reports of the Queensland North-east Coast Expedition 1873*, Government Printer, Brisbane.

Denzin, N.L. and Lincoln, Y.S. 1998 'Major Paradigms and Perspectives' in N.K. Denzin and Y.S. Lincoln (eds), *The Landscapes of Qualitative Research: Theories and Issues*, Sage, London, pp. 185–93.

Duran, B. and Duran, E. 2002 'Applied Postcolonial Clinical and Research Strategies', in M. Battiste (ed.), *Reclaiming Indigenous Voices and Vision*, University of British Columbia, Vancouver, pp. 86–100.

Edwards, S. 2009 'Me Titiro Whakamuri kia Marama ai tatou te Wao nei: We Should Look to the Past to Understand the Present', *Journal of Australian Indigenous Issues*, vol. 12, pp. 33–45.

Elkin, A.P. 1963 'The Development of Scientific Knowledge of the Aborigines', in W.E.H. Stanner and H. Sheils (eds), *Australian Aboriginal Studies: A Symposium of Papers Presented at the 1961 Research Conference*, Oxford University Press, Melbourne.

Gibbs, M. and Memon, A. 1999 'Indigenous Resource Management: Towards a Strategy for Understanding Collaborative Research', paper presented to International Symposium on Society and Resource Management: Application of Social Science to Resource Management in the Asia-Pacific Region, Brisbane.

Guba, E. and Lincoln, Y. 1994 'Competing Paradigms in Qualitative Research', in N.K. Denzin and Y.S. Lincoln (eds), *Handbook of Qualitative Research*, Sage, London, pp. 163–88.

Huggins, J. 1998 *Sister Girl*, University of Queensland Press, Brisbane.

Ivanitz, M. 1999 'Culture, Ethics and Participatory Methodology in Cross-cultural Research', *Australian Aboriginal Studies*, no. 2, pp. 46–58.

Kincheloe, J.L. and McLaren, P.L. 1998 'Rethinking Critical Theory and Qualitative Research', in N.K. Denzin and Y.S. Lincoln (eds), *The Landscapes of Qualitative Research: Theories and Issues*, Sage, London, pp. 260–99.

Ladson-Billings, G. 2000 'Racialized Discourses and Ethnic Epistemologies', in N.K. Denzin and Y.S. Lincoln (eds), *Handbook of Qualitative Research*, Sage, London, pp. 257–77.

Mac Naughton, G. and Davis, K. 2001 'Beyond "Othering": Rethinking Approaches to Teaching Young Anglo-Australian Children about Indigenous Australians', *Contemporary Issues in Early Childhood*, vol. 2, no. 1, pp. 83–93.

Martin, K. 2003 'Ways of Knowing, Being and Doing: A Theoretical Framework and Methods for Indigenous and Indigenist Research', in K. McWilliam, K.P. Stephenson and G. Thompson (eds), *Voicing Dissent, New Talents 21C: Next Generation Australian Studies*, University of Queensland Press, Brisbane, pp. 203–14.

——2008 *Please Knock Before You Enter: Aboriginal Regulation of Outsiders and the Implications for Research*, Postpresssed, Brisbane.

Moreton-Robinson, A. 2000 *Talkin' Up to the White Women*, University of Queensland Press, Brisbane.

——2007 'Introduction', in A. Moreton-Robinson (ed.), *Sovereign Subjects: Indigenous Sovereignty Matters*, Allen & Unwin, Sydney, pp. 1–11.

Nicoll, F. 2004 'Are You Calling Me a Racist? Teaching Critical Whiteness Theory in Indigenous Sovereignty', *borderlands*, vol. 3, no. 2, <http://www.borderlandsejournal.adelaide.edu.au/vol3no2_2004/nicoll_teaching.htm>, accessed 25 October 2005.

Rigney, L.I. 1997 *Internationalisation of an Indigenous Anti-Colonial Cultural Critique of Research Methodologies: A Guide to Indigenist Research Methodology and its Principles*, paper presented at the Research and Development in Higher Education: Advancing International Perspectives, HERDSA Annual Conference, Higher Education Research and Development Society of Australia.

——2001 'A First Perspective of Indigenous Australian Participation in Science: Framing Indigenous Research Towards Indigenous Australians' Intellectual Sovereignty', *Kaurna Higher Education Journal*, vol. 7, pp. 1–13.

Smith, N. 2000 *Collaborative Research Possibilities in Cape York: A Report to the Tropical Savannas CRC*, Balkanu Cape York Development Corporation, Key Centre for Tropical Wildlife Management & Centre for Indigenous Cultural Resource Management, Cairns.

Standfield, J. 1998 'Ethnic Modelling in Qualitative Research', in N.K. Denzin and Y.S. Lincoln (eds), *The Landscapes of Qualitative Research: Theories and Issues*, Sage, London, pp. 333–58.

Tuhiwai Smith, L. 1999 *Decolonizing Methodologies*, Zen Books, Otago.

——2005 'On Tricky Ground: Researching the Native in the Age of Uncertainty', in N.K. Denzin and Y.S. Lincoln (eds), *Sage Handbook of Qualitative Research*, Sage, London, pp. 85–107.

Weber-Pillwax, C. 2001, 'Coming to an Understanding: A Panel Presentation—What is Indigenous Research?', *Canadian Journal of Native Education*, vol. 25, no. 2, pp. 166–74.

West, E. 2000 'The Japanangka Teaching and Research Paradigm: An Aboriginal Pedagogical Framework', *Indigenous Research and Postgraduate Forum*, Aboriginal Research Institute, University of South Australia, Adelaide.

Williams, S. 2001 'The Indigenous Australian Health Worker: Can Research Enhance Their Development as Health and Community Development Professionals?' *Aboriginal and Islander Health Worker Journal*, vol. 25, no. 1, pp. 9–11.

Wilson, S. 2001 'What is an Indigenous Research Methodology?' *Canadian Journal of Native Education*, vol. 25, no. 2, pp. 175–9.

——2008, *Research is Ceremony: Indigenous Research Methods*, Fernwood, Ontario.

Youngblood-Henderson, J. 2002 '*Ayukpachi:* Empowering Aboriginal Thought', in M. Battiste (ed.), *Reclaiming Indigenous Voices and Vision*, University of British Columbia, Vancouver, pp. 248–78.

Yunupingu, M. 1994, 'Yothu Yindi: Finding Balance', in *Voices from the Land: Le Boyer Lectures*, Australian Broadcasting Commission, Sydney, pp. 1–11.

FURTHER READING

Australian Institute of Aboriginal and Torres Strait Islander Studies 2000 *Guidelines for Ethical Research in Indigenous Studies*, <www.aiatsis.gov.au>. This document identified three core principles of ethical research that involves Aboriginal people. These are explained in terms of eleven guidelines whereby researchers can first avoid unethical research, second examine their own power and privilege, and third make conscious the points where Aboriginal agency can be achieved.

Department of Aboriginal and Torres Strait Islander Policy and Development 2000 *Protocols for Consultation and Negotiation with Aboriginal People*, Queensland Government, Brisbane. This document is an easy-to-read guide on understanding and acting in respectful ways with Aboriginal people. It outlines a broad history of Aboriginal people as well as identifying and discussing the more important protocols for visiting, conducting meetings (and research) for respectful and productive consultation to ensure Aboriginal agency.

PART II

ANALYSIS AND DESIGN

7

Design issues

Alan Hayes

PLANNING PREVENTS PROBLEMS

Research design is simply a matter of planning. Good ideas and incisive research questions are important, but may not necessarily translate into a feasible study. There are many options and alternatives to consider when designing a research project. Among other things, one needs to consider what is to be researched and how, when and where the research is to take place, who will participate, what data will be collected and how these will be analysed.

This chapter provides an outline of the design process. It first defines the concept of research design and explores the links between research questions and decisions about design. Next, it discusses some of the major options available (experimental, quasi-experimental and non-experimental), focusing on the concept of causation. The chapter also addresses the dimension of time, considers retrospective and prospective approaches, and compares and contrasts cross-sectional and longitudinal designs. An important consideration is who is to participate in the research, and this focuses attention on approaches to sampling (random sampling, stratification and two-stage random sampling, along with non-random techniques such as systematic, purposive and convenience sampling). Specific methods of data collection are not discussed, as these are covered in later chapters. The chapter ends with a brief consideration of some further practical issues related to the design process.

Australia's flagship longitudinal research on young children—Growing Up in Australia: The Longitudinal Study of Australian Children (LSAC)—is used to illustrate some of the design issues discussed. The aim of the chapter is to demystify design and make it accessible to those who have a minimal background in research.

SETTING THE DISCUSSION IN CONTEXT

It is important to acknowledge the research tradition that underpins this chapter. The discussion is framed within the positivist paradigm of research, reflecting the background and experience of the author. Nonetheless, many of the issues raised, and how they might be approached from a design perspective, are relevant for those working within different paradigms. Useful insights into design issues for research framed by non-positivist paradigms are also provided elsewhere in this book (see Chapter 9) and in other publications (see, for example, Denzin and Lincoln, 2005; Kirby, Greaves and Reid, 2006; Liamputtong and Ezzy, 2005). Early childhood research can be informed by and combine elements of these various approaches. All frameworks, and the methods favoured by each one, provide valuable insights into the important questions that early childhood researchers address. Chapters 8 and 9 outline quantitative and qualitative designs and analyses respectively.

DESIGN DEFINED

Research design is a matter of options and choices, and as such is the creative process of translating a research idea into a set of decisions about how the research will proceed in practice. The design process seeks to balance several aspects, including the broad topic studied, the original ideas that underpin investigation of it, and the translation of initial thoughts into researchable questions (Ezzy, 2006). This first stage in thinking is typically informed by the work that has been undertaken previously on the topic. This usually involves conducting a review of the previous literature and identifying whether there are key theories presenting plausible explanations of the phenomena to be studied. The review stage also informs choices about the methods that seem most appropriate to the data, as well as how these will be analysed, interpreted and communicated.

In early childhood research, as in other areas of the social and behavioural sciences, there is rarely a single correct way of conducting any research project. Again, it is a matter of options and choices as to the approach considered most appropriate for any study. In contrast to the physical sciences, where considerable experimental control is possible, it is often very difficult to achieve the same degree of control of the behaviour of people—especially when infants and young children are involved (McCartney, Burchinall and Bub, 2006). This lack of precise control means that there is always some degree of uncertainty surrounding the conclusions that are drawn from even the most carefully designed study. Ethical considerations also limit the types of experimental manipulations that can be undertaken in the social, medical or biological sciences, as opposed to the physical sciences. Of course, the physical sciences confront issues of uncertainty and lack of control, although these are too often conveniently overlooked.

In texts on research methods, design is often presented in a way that seems complex and unduly surrounded by scientific and statistical mystique. In fact, research design is a straightforward, practical process of logically considering the relative merits of a range of approaches to the problem to be researched. It is the process by which the topic is turned into a researchable project. Following consideration of key issues such as whether the topic is within the researcher's competence, the design process involves identifying the possible alternative ways in which the project might be undertaken and evaluating their relative merits.

THE 'WHAT' AND 'HOW' OF RESEARCH

How research is to be designed and undertaken depends on the specific focus of the investigation. The first step in design is clarifying the topic and identifying the specific focus of the research (Walter, 2006). Just as an architect's design for a building depends on the clarity of the brief provided by the clients and their specific requirements, research cannot be well designed unless what is to be researched is clear. Many projects may involve stages that successively build upon one another but, at the very least, the initial stage of the project requires refinement of the specific research questions and scope to ensure that the planned investigation is researchable and feasible.

REFINING THE TOPIC

Having decided on a general area to research, the design process begins with refinement of the general topic. Typically, the initial formulation of the area of interest is too broad to be researchable within the resources and time available to the researcher. It may also involve too many facets to be addressed within a single study.

The researcher needs to break the general topic into a number of subtopics and consider the logical order in which these might be addressed. This process is illustrated in the following discussion of the development of knowledge about the links between young children's social experiences in early life, their brain development and their social behaviours.

THE DEVELOPMENT OF KNOWLEDGE: SOME OLD FOUNDATIONS OF THE NEW BRAIN RESEARCH

The broad topic

To what extent is brain development in early childhood influenced by social experience and the quality of early nurturing?

The significance of the topic

In its broadest sense, this topic casts light on the relationship between heredity and environment. If brain development is shown to be influenced by experience, this would provide important evidence of how inherited characteristics are modified in interaction with the environment and the particular experiences it provides. More specifically, it would demonstrate the importance of early childhood as a time in which changes occur that influence later development in fundamentally important ways.

The old foundations

Until recently, it was not possible to examine brain structure and functioning directly. Rapid advances in imaging technology have stimulated the recent explosion of interest in brain development in the early years of life. These advances have enabled direct observation of brain functioning and the production of high-resolution images of the brain (Perry, 2006).

The recent research is built on some older research that provided the important first step in addressing the larger question posed above: To what extent is brain development in early childhood influenced by social experience and the quality of early nurturing?

To establish that infants can be influenced by social experience required research into their competencies, particularly their sensory and perceptual capabilities. The early research was based on clinical observation and the development of infant tests by Gesell (1952) and others (Cattell, 1934).

In the 1960s and 1970s, there was a renewal of interest in infant development (White, 1971), and a series of ingenious experiments laid the foundations of knowledge about infant visual acuity and perceptual development, demonstrating their capacity to identify familiar and novel faces from the first weeks of life. Much of this work had built on equally groundbreaking research by Hubel and Weisel (1962) into the role of experience in shaping the visual system of cats. Again, a well-designed experiment enabled these researchers to show that the early experiences of kittens directly affected their visual development. These studies also showed that some of the earlier clinical observations had, in fact, under-estimated the pace of development and the degree of competence that infants demonstrate at birth and in the first year of life.

In parallel, researchers examined infants who had been deprived of social contact in early life, and compared and contrasted their development with children growing up in families where social contact was of an appropriate nature.

New insights and some possible directions for further research

What design options are there for further research that builds on the accumulated knowledge of brain development in early life? At the outset, it might be necessary to develop a valid and reliable scale to measure social experience, given the possible shortcomings of the existing scales. The first study might involve the assessment of the newly developed scale against previous scales, and of its capacity to reliably identify differences in the quality of children's social experience, as well as the relationship of scores on the scale to other measures, such as observational data on the characteristics of their home environments. In addition, it might be important to evaluate a range of methods for accurately capturing social behaviours of the children. The range of possibilities might include parent or early childhood staff reports of their direct observation of the child's experiences within the home or early childhood services. These aspects of the project would need to be completed before the main study could be undertaken.

The above discussions highlight how a process of investigation can involve stages of development of the topic, parallel strands and a range of design options to address the questions at each stage and within each strand.

For reviews of the brain research literature and the historical development of knowledge in this area, see Couperus and Nelson (2006), Cynader and Frost (1999), Hayes (2007), Perry (2006) and Stiles (2000).

TWO BROAD TYPES OF RESEARCH

In general terms, research can be classified as either non-experimental (sometimes termed 'observational') or experimental (Schneider et al., 2007; Shadish, Cook and Campbell, 2002). The difference between the two, broadly speaking, comes down to the extent to which the researcher actively controls the situation. A continuum exists from unobtrusive observation in naturalistic settings, where the researcher remains as aloof as possible from the action, to experimental methods, where the researcher directly controls the situation. Between these extremes are approaches that differ in the extent of involvement and control exercised by the researcher.

In the popular imagination, research is synonymous with experiments controlled by the stereotyped 'mad scientist'. This conception of science ignores the fact that scientific knowledge is predominantly built on foundations of observation (Schneider et al., 2007). In the social sciences, this is typically observation of the behaviour of children and/or adults, including observation, recording and analysis of their verbal behaviour (the cornerstone of much qualitative research). The choice of whether or not to base the research on experiment comes down to whether the study is focused on explaining the causes of events, and as such whether or not it addresses causal hypotheses.

HYPOTHESES OR NOT?

The extent to which the topic can be framed as a set of hypotheses needs to be the first consideration (Shadish, Cook and Campbell, 2002). Not all research projects involve the testing of hypotheses. Much valuable research involves observing or documenting things that occur in everyday life with the aim of understanding, rather than explaining.

Hypotheses are predictive statements containing a possible explanation of some phenomenon. They are typically, though not exclusively, couched in terms of cause and effect and presented as a statement such as: 'Parental neglect negatively influences brain development.' In this instance, the cause—neglect—is presumed to have an effect, in this case on brain development in infancy.

The original hypothesis might derive from clinical observations of young children who have experienced severe neglect and/or abuse. But how does the presumed effect of neglect impede brain development in infants? Is it a product of their nutrition, their mothers' nutrition during pregnancy, or both? Is it a product of impaired attachment relationships that typify neglectful families? Or is it an interaction between nutritional and social factors? What is the relationship between neglect and abuse? Does neglect increase the probability of abuse? Given that it is estimated that 190 million children, or 40 per cent of the world's population of children under five years, are currently living in circumstances that provide inadequate nutrition, this is a most important research topic.

How might one address such a topic? There are several possibilities, but some of these are ethically constrained. For example, it would be highly unethical—and, moreover, illegal—to neglect children for the purpose of research.

EXPERIMENTAL DESIGNS

One possible design for such a study might involve an **experiment** using non-human subjects. For example, animals such as rats could be reared under systematically different conditions and their brain development evaluated after a standard time, controlling for as many relevant factors as possible (including the strain of rats, their genetic characteristics, nutrition during pregnancy and the rearing conditions since birth). The rats would be randomly assigned to the different conditions (or treatments) in the experiment. Random assignment means that each subject has an equal chance of being assigned to a particular treatment group. By controlling as many of these relevant factors as possible, and randomly assigning the animals to treatments, the researcher seeks to increase the chance that the effect that is measured can only be attributed to the hypothesised cause, or combination of causal factors.

In the simplest form of experimental design, there will be two groups (Haslam and McGarty, 2004). In the example above, the rats assigned to the **treatment group** (in this experiment, it might be a low level of nutrition, as one indicator of neglect) will be compared and contrasted with a **control group** that receives a level of nutrition within the range normally needed by rats of this age and body weight. Nutrition would be regarded as the **independent variable**.

Rearing conditions (such as cage type, lighting, temperature, noise levels, food type and presentation, and any other relevant variables) would be controlled to be, as far as possible, identical for each group, as previous research might have shown them to influence the behaviour of this strain of rats. These factors are called relevant variables.

The effect of nutrition on brain development would be the focus of this particular small group study. Brain development would be hypothesised to vary depending on the level of nutrition, the variable that is free to be controlled by the experimenter. The outcome, in this case brain development, would be regarded as the **dependent variable**, as it 'depends' on nutrition.

If the effect can be demonstrated, under very similar circumstances, by other researchers, one can be confident of the causal role of early experience on early brain development. The process of repeating the experiment, ideally with different researchers conducting the experiment in different laboratories, is called replication (Haslam and McGarty, 2004). In science, and especially in the social sciences, replication is necessary to ensure that the results were not a product of chance factors or due to some causal factors, unrelated to the hypothesis, that occurred in conducting the experiment on the first occasion. If the results from different researchers in different locations are similar, one may have greater confidence in the initial hypothesis.

The animal experiment might be regarded as valid in its design and in the way that it was conducted, but it still might be of limited value in understanding human infants and the effect of early experience on their brain development. Of course, important ethical constraints also apply to the experimental use of animals.

QUASI-EXPERIMENTAL DESIGNS

Most readers of this book will be more interested in studying children than rats. Given the ethical and legal constraints that apply to experimental manipulations of children's nutrition and social experience, however, how might one study this topic in early childhood? One way might be to conduct a quasi-experiment (Cook and Campbell, 1979; Mark and Reichardt, 2004; Shadish, Cook and Campbell, 2002). The defining feature of such a design is that random assignment to treatments is not possible, although in real life groups can be identified that naturally vary in their levels on the variables of interest.

With reference to the present example, it might be possible to describe precisely differences in nutritional levels and social experience in various groups of young children, and measure each child's brain development using the new imaging techniques. From this, the researcher might be able to infer that any differences that are detected in brain development across the groups are caused by the pre-existing differences in nutrition and social experience.

While providing a less powerful demonstration of the cause and effect relationship, in many areas of the social sciences, education and early childhood, the most that can be aspired to is quasi-experimentation. The problem with not being able to assign participants randomly to treatment groups is that many other factors may be systematically related to the groups. A group that is malnourished, for example, may have associated medical problems or be at higher risk of other problems such as abuse (Weatherburn and Lind, 1997; Perry, 2006).

NON-EXPERIMENTAL DESIGNS

Often, it might not be possible to conduct even a quasi-experiment. It might be feasible, however, to measure the variations that occur within a group of children and explore the relationships of these variations to the measures of their brain development. One such non-experimental design, which analyses the relationship but does not conduct an experiment to determine that one variable (or set of variables) causes the other, is called a correlational study.

Unlike a controlled experiment, a correlational study is not capable of concluding that one factor is the cause of the other. The hypothesis might be: 'Early experience of neglect is related to brain growth.' The difference in these two ways of stating the hypothesis may seem subtle, but it is fundamentally important. It is a major temptation to interpret correlation as causation (Haslam and McGarty, 2004; Mark and Reichardt, 2004). However, to say two things are related or associated does not provide evidence that one causes the other. They may be related via a third variable. Neglect and brain growth, for the present example, might be related to the third variable of social experience. Correlational approaches seek to ascertain the extent of the relationship of variables within a group.

QUALITATIVE STUDIES

As argued above, in the social sciences there may be far more uncertainty and lack of control than in the physical sciences. For example, the key variable may actually be the interpretation of experience, more than the experience *per se* (Denzin and Lincoln, 2005; Strauss and Corbin, 1990). Rather than conducting an experiment or undertaking a correlational study, the researcher might wish to conduct a qualitative study to provide information about the perceptions or beliefs of mothers who differ in the quality of their care for their infants (from identified neglect to high-quality care). The survey might probe the mothers' knowledge and ideas about child development, attachment, play, nutrition, behaviour management and other potentially relevant dimensions of parenting.

Alternatively, it might seek to explore the beliefs without imposing any frame on the data collection, by using an interviewing technique without previously determined categories (Fontana and Frey, 2005; Sproule, 2006). Such a study is less likely to be framed in terms of hypotheses about cause and effect.

THE 'WHEN', 'WHERE' AND 'WHO' OF RESEARCH

Time, place and persons are other key aspects of research design. With regard to time, studies can focus on the past, the present or the future, depending on the nature of the research questions being addressed and the purpose of the project. Place is important, particularly in studies of young children, as settings and contexts may exert considerable influence over children's behaviour, especially when children are not familiar with them. Who participates is also a key dimension, and again relates to the focus of the study as well as the extent to which the conclusions of the research are representative of the wider population and can be generalised to groups other than those who participated in the research.

Time's arrow: Present, past and future orientations

Much research is focused in the present, as time and its passage tend not to be key dimensions of many studies. The research might explore current behaviour, attitudes, beliefs or values. The exception is research that focuses on developmental phenomena, which are inherently bound to time. Developmental research can be regarded as a 'time science'.

Of course, researchers face the same realities of limited time that confront most of us, and this in part explains the appeal of designs that can be completed in a short timeframe. In order to truncate the time required to undertake studies of development, **cross-sectional designs** are often the option of choice. These typically involve selecting groups of participants at different ages and interpreting differences in performance across the age groups as evidence of developmental change. The simplest of these designs might involve comparison of two groups (say, younger and older infants or children). More complex designs might involve multiple age groups.

The difficulty with such designs is that differences across the groups might not solely be the result of developmental changes related to age (Miller, 1987). Other variables, such as life circumstances or experiences, might also differ for different age groups. Changes in obstetric practices or approaches to infant care might result in systematic differences in infants that might be confounded with 'true' developmental changes (changes due solely to age). If the age groups span years, as has often been the case in projects studying trends in intellectual development or cognitive processes such as memory, the effects may be even more marked. A group of six-year-olds may have a fundamentally different set of early life circumstances and developmental experiences to a group of 90-year-olds who have lived through the Great Depression, two world wars and a radically different set of early childhood and later educational experiences. To make matters even more complex, the 90-year-olds represent the sample of those from their birth cohort who have survived to that age, and may be a small proportion of those who were alive when they were six years old. Differences across age groups are referred to as cohort effects (Baltes and Schaie, 1974, 1976; Miller, 1987). While these differences may be real, the conclusion that they illustrate the process of development may not be valid.

Another strategy to study developmental effects involves exploring the past experiences of groups and reconstructing their developmental pathways. Research that focuses on the past collects information retrospectively (retrospective studies). Historical information is commonly collected, and is an example of retrospective data. Using the example related to brain development, the study might take children who are showing signs of impaired brain development and focus on their previous history of care and nutrition. While it is tempting to see such **retrospective research** as providing evidence of causation, this risks reaching inappropriate conclusions. Hypothetically, it might be the case that many children who suffer early deficits of nutrition and/or care do not go on to show lasting impairment of brain development. Again, as Sameroff and Chandler (1975) argued some time ago, retrospective data may not provide valid evidence of developmental causation.

Studies designed to follow the participants through time can provide compelling evidence of causation (Miller, 1987; Pickles and Rutter, 1991). Prospective studies are a powerful way to establish the causal pathways for outcomes in children's development. Such studies can involve experimental designs with measurement before some intervention (pre-testing) and of outcomes following the intervention (post-testing). With regard to the brain development example, a pre-test/post-test design might involve initial measurement of at-risk children's brain development prior to their involvement in a social stimulation intervention project, along with nutritional supplementation and follow-up assessments after involvement in the intervention for a period of, say, a year. Comparison of measurements at the same times for matched comparison groups receiving either nutritional supplementation or social stimulation (but not both) would provide a test of the relative contributions of each factor separately.

Another type of prospective design involves longitudinal research. A longitudinal study, as compared to an experimental follow-up study, typically involves investigation of naturally occurring changes on repeated occasions over a substantial period of time (Miller, 1987). What constitutes a substantial period of time depends in part on the period of development under study. In early infancy, for example, the rate of change may be so rapid that a longitudinal study can be undertaken over a period of months or weeks, depending on the focus of the study. The key advantage of prospective, longitudinal designs is that they enable the behaviour and capabilities of individuals to be tracked as they develop. They also provide an elegant way of addressing questions related to stability and change in development both for individuals and for groups (Olweus and Alsaker, 1991; Pickles and Rutter, 1991). Of course, if only a single cohort is involved, the results are specific to that group.

An ingenious way of enhancing the power of a longitudinal study is to recruit multiple cohorts (in the following example, those born in 2000–01 and those born in 2003–04, or four- to five-year-olds and newborns to one-year-olds) at the commencement of the study and assess their development at regular intervals, say every one to two years (Bergman, Eklund and Magnusson, 1991; Gray and Smart, 2008). In this way, any similarities and differences in development among the cohorts can explicitly be measured, as well as the stability and change within each cohort as time passes. Like all matters of design, the manner in which time is handled depends on the topic and the resources available for the study. Appendix 7.1 provides an overview of the design of Growing Up in Australia: The Longitudinal Study of Australian Children (LSAC).

Table 7.1: Age of cohorts, Waves 1–4

Cohorts	Wave 1 (2004)	Wave 2 (2006)	Wave 3 (2008)	Wave 4 (2010)
B (infant)	0–1 years	2–3 years	4–5 years	6–7 years
K (child)	4–5 years	6–7 years	8–9 years	10–11 years

THE IMPORTANCE OF PLACE

In the lay imagination, research often conjures images of experiments conducted in musty laboratory settings, cluttered with strange apparatus.

In practice, however, research takes place in as many settings as one can imagine. Early childhood research is more likely to occur in settings other than laboratories, such as children's homes, early childhood services or schools.

The advantage of laboratory settings is that they allow greater standardisation and control of the conditions for the experiment. In turn, standardisation and control mean that the experiment ought to be able to be replicated across laboratories, provided the same physical and procedural conditions are established for the research. The disadvantage is that the conditions in the laboratory may not match those likely to apply in the world beyond.

In research with young children (and people generally), their behaviour may be altered by the laboratory environment and they may act in ways that they normally would not in their own surroundings. Typically, early childhood researchers will seek to study behaviour in naturalistic settings, and as unobtrusively as possible, as everyday settings can suffer similar problems to laboratory settings if children are required to perform activities and tasks that are out of the ordinary (Hayes, 1980). The issue of place is complex, and depends on the purpose of the research and the extent to which issues of generalisability of the findings to everyday settings are focal.

SELECTING PERSONS TO PARTICIPATE

Addressing the what, how, when and where questions takes place with reference to a further question: 'Who will participate?' In early childhood research, the possibilities for participants are extensive. Infants or young children might be the focus—although, depending on the purpose of the study, the participants could also be members of their family, peer group or people from their neighbourhood, early childhood staff, students training to work with young children or members of the wider community, among others. It is not uncommon for more than one of these groups to be involved. This is particularly the case if interactive phenomena such as communication, including teaching or learning interactions, are the focus of the study. The participants in this instance might be a mother or father and their young child, or a toddler and her carer, or a preschool student and his teacher.

In considering the participants, variables such as age, gender, family structure (two-parent versus single-parent families, families with only one child or couples without children), social status (as indicated by educational background, occupation and/or income level), ethnicity, home language and any special characteristics (such as giftedness or disability or specific medical conditions) may need to be taken into account, among others. The participants might also be defined by where they are rather than who they are, and the key characteristic might be, for example, whether or not children are currently attending early childhood services. In short, a wide range of characteristics of the participants may need to be considered when designing the project.

The number of participants is another aspect that must be decided. The options here span from a single individual (Hersen and Barlow, 1976; Tawney and Gast, 1984), if the study is to be a case study of one person, through to a large-scale study of an entire population. It is rarely possible, however, to study all of the members of a population, such as the world's three-year-olds. It would require time, money and personnel way beyond the realms of possibility. A population is all of the members of some group (Fraenkel and Wallen, 2003). Of course, populations vary greatly in size and some, such as children with a rare medical condition, are by definition small.

When the study of a population is not feasible, researchers resort to sampling from the population. Earlier in this chapter the concept of the **random sample** was introduced in discussing experimental designs. The defining feature of such a sample was that each member of the population has an equal chance of being selected to participate in the study. While it is beyond the scope of this chapter to provide a detailed discussion of sampling, the major types of sampling will be described briefly.

It is not always possible to sample individuals randomly. For some purposes, one wants to ensure that the sample is representative, in terms of the proportions of the sample from each sub-group within a given population (Fraenkel and Wallen, 2003). For purposes of illustration, 30 per cent of a given population might be from homes where a language other than English is spoken. The sampling strategy would ensure that these subgroups, or strata, are proportionally represented in the sample (70 per cent from an English-speaking home background and 30 per cent from non-English speaking homes). Within these two strata, the sampling would still be random. This approach is described as **stratified random sampling**.

Again, when random sampling of individuals is not possible, it might be necessary to sample some whole group, or cluster of individuals, randomly. The group might be from some particular early childhood service. This technique is referred to as **cluster random sampling** (Fraenkel and Wallen, 2003). Another variant combines cluster and individual random sampling in a two-stage process. For purposes of illustration, the researcher might randomly select twenty child-care centres, and within each randomly select five children to give a sample of 100 children in total.

At times, however, random sampling will not be possible for a range of reasons, some related to practical limitations, others related to the purpose of the study. The options for non-random sampling include systematic sampling—say, of every fifth child on a class list; convenience sampling—say, of two child-care centres that are accessible to the researcher; or purposive sampling, where the sample is based on prior knowledge of the group—say, of children who demonstrate particularly creative play and are selected for a study comparing them to a sample of those who are regarded as closer to the average (Fraenkel and Wallen, 2003). Unlike random sampling, however, each of these techniques is more likely to introduce the risk of bias into the sample.

Again, the issues of who will participate in a particular study involve many decisions that relate to other aspects of the project, such as purpose, approach, time and place.

GETTING REAL: FROM THE ABSTRACT TO THE CONCRETE

The process of designing a research project is one of turning abstract ideas for research into a set of feasible, practical research procedures. It involves a set of decisions that take the researcher from imagining an ideal study to addressing the complexities of real research, with real people, in real settings and with real limits on resources.

Design is a process of choice among many possibilities. It requires logical consideration (and elimination) of alternatives. The order of these decisions is not necessarily as presented in this discussion. As has been illustrated, the decisions are interdependent and there is great scope for flexibility. Design is the 'thought work' prior to deciding on an approach, methods and procedures for a research project. From personal experience, conducting a small-scale trial, or pilot, of the chosen approach, methods and procedures is a vital step in reassuring oneself that the choices and decisions are the most appropriate and practically feasible ways to address the research questions for the project. Ultimately, however, issues of feasibility, practicality and ethics are the key determinants of whether or not a particular design can be implemented.

SUMMARY

Design involves the processes of:

- refining the topic and framing researchable questions ('what' will be researched)
- deciding among alternative approaches to the research ('how' the research will be undertaken)

- considering issues related to time, place and persons ('when', 'where' and 'who')
- choosing methods of data collection and analysis
- evaluating the feasibility and practical constraints on the design
- modifying the design in the light of pilot testing

QUESTIONS FOR REFLECTION

1. Discuss the process of research design and compile a list of the factors that might need to be considered in designing a research project.
2. Consider the topic: 'The effect of social play on children's development in early childhood' and complete the following tasks:
   (a) Develop a set of three researchable questions.
   (b) For each question, choose two alternative approaches to researching it.
   (c) For the project as a whole, consider the following:
      - the dimension of time and how this will be handled
      - the place, or places, where the research might take place in order to address the research questions you have framed
      - the likely participants, their characteristics and a sampling strategy to guide their recruitment
      - with reference to the other relevant chapters of this book, the data-collection methods and techniques that might be used in your project
      - the practical limitations that need to be considered in implementing your research design.

ACKNOWLEDGMENTS

I gratefully acknowledge the assistance of my colleague, Carole Jean, in identifying relevant literature, and that of my very valued executive assistant, Nancy Virgona. Any shortcomings are entirely my own.

REFERENCES

Baltes, P.B. and Schaie, K.W. 1974 'The Myth of the Twilight Years', *Psychology Today*, vol. 7, pp. 35–40.

——1976, 'On the Plasticity of Intelligence in Adulthood and Old Age: Where Horn and Donaldson Fail' *American Psychologist*, vol. 31, pp. 720–5.

Bergman, L.R., Eklund, G. and Magnusson, D. 1991 'Studying Individual Development: Problems and Methods', in D. Magnusson, L.R. Bergman, G. Rudinger and B. Törestad (eds), *Problems and Methods in Longitudinal Research: Stability and Change*, Cambridge University Press, Cambridge, pp. 1–27.

Cattell, R. 1934 *Your Mind and Mine: An Account of Psychology for the Inquiring Layman and the Prospective Student*, George G. Harrap, London.

Cook, T.D. and Campbell, D.T. 1979 *Quasi-experimentation: Design and Analysis Issues for Field Settings,* Houghton Mifflin, Boston.

Couperus, J.W. and Nelson, C.A. 2006 'Early Brain Development and Plasticity', in K. McCartney and D. Phillips (eds), *Blackwell Handbook of Early Childhood Development*, Blackwell, Malden, MA, pp. 85–105.

Cynader, M. and Frost, B.J. 1999 'Mechanisms of Brain Development: Neuronal Sculpting by the Physical and Social Environment', in D.P. Keating, and C. Hertzman (eds), *Developmental Health and the Wealth of Nations: Social, Biological, and Educational Dynamics*, Guilford Press, New York, pp. 153–84.

Denzin, N.K. and Lincoln, Y.S. (eds) 2005 *The Sage Handbook of Qualitative Research*, 3rd ed., Sage, Thousand Oaks, CA.

Ezzy, D. 2006 'The Research Process', in M. Walter (ed.), *Social Research Methods: An Australian Perspective*, Oxford University Press, Melbourne, pp. 29–51.

Fontana, A. and Frey, J.H. 2005, 'The Interview from Neutral Stance to Political Involvement', in N.K. Denzin and Y.S. Lincoln (eds), *The Sage Handbook of Qualitative Research*, 3rd ed., Sage, Thousand Oaks, CA.

Fraenkel, J.R. and Wallen, N.E. 2003 *How to Design and Evaluate Research in Education*, 5th ed., McGraw-Hill, New York.

Gesell, A. 1952 *Infant Development: The Embryology of Early Human Development*, Hamish Hamilton, London.

Gray, M. and Smart, D. 2008 'Growing Up in Australia: The Longitudinal Study of Australian Children is Now Walking and Talking', *Family Matters*, no. 79, pp. 5–13.

Haslam, S.A. and McGarty, C.M. 2004 'Experimental Design and Causality in Social Psychology Research', in C. Sansone, C.C. Morf and A.T. Panter (eds), *The Sage Handbook of Methods in Social Psychology*, Sage, Thousand Oaks, CA, pp. 237–64.

Hayes, A. 2007, 'Why Early in Life is Not Enough: Timing and Sustainability in Prevention and Early Intervention', in A. France and R. Homel (eds), *Pathways and Crime Prevention: Theory, Policy and Practice*, Willan Publishing, Cullompton, Devon, UK.

——1980, *Visual Regard and Vocalizations in Mother–Infant Dyads*, unpublished doctoral thesis, Macquarie University, Sydney.

Hersen, M. and Barlow, D.H. 1976, *Single-case Experimental Designs: Strategies for Studying Behavior Change*, Pergamon Press, New York.

Hubel, D.H. and Weisel, T.N. 1962 'Receptive Fields, Binocular Interaction, and Functional Architecture in the Cat's Visual Cortex', *Journal of Physiology*, vol. 160, pp. 106–56.

Kirby, S.L., Greaves, L. and Reid, C. 2006 *Experience Research Social Change: Methods Beyond the Mainstream*, Broadview Press, Peterborough, Ontario, Canada.

Liamputtong, P. and Ezzy, D. 2005 *Qualitative Research Methods*, 2nd ed., Oxford University Press, Melbourne.

Mark, M.M. and Reichardt, C.S. 2004 'Quasi-experimental and Correlational Designs: Methods for the Real World When Random Assignment Isn't Feasible', in C. Sansone, C.C. Morf and A.T. Panter (eds), *The Sage Handbook of Methods in Social Psychology*, Sage, Thousand Oaks, CA, pp. 265–86.

McCartney, K., Burchinal, M.R. and Bub, K.L. 2006 'Best Practice in Quantitative Methods for Developmentalists', *Monographs of the Society for Research in Child Development*, Serial No. 285, 71 (3), pp. 1–8.

Miller, S.A. 1987 *Developmental Research Methods*, Prentice-Hall, Englewood Cliffs, NJ.

Olweus, D. and Alsaker, F.D. 1991 'Assessing Change in a Cohort-Longitudinal Study with Hierarchical Data', in D. Magnusson, L.R. Bergman, G. Rudinger and B. Törestad (eds), *Problems and Methods in Longitudinal Research: Stability and Change*, Cambridge University Press, Cambridge, pp. 107–32.

Perry, B.D. 2006 'Applying Principles of Neurodevelopment to Clinical Work with Maltreated and Traumatized Children: The Neurosequential Model of Therapeutics', in N.B. Webb (ed.), *Working with Traumatized Youth in Child Welfare*, Guilford Press, New York, pp. 27–52.

Pickles, A. and Rutter, M. 1991 'Statistical and Conceptual Models of "Turning Points" in Developmental Processes', in D. Magnusson, L.R. Bergman, G. Rudinger and B. Törestad (eds), *Problems and Methods in Longitudinal Research: Stability and Change*, Cambridge University Press, Cambridge, pp. 133–65.

Sameroff, A. and Chandler, M.J. 1975 'Reproductive Risk and the Continuum of Caretaking Casualty', in F.D. Horowitz, M. Heatherington, S. Scarr-Salapatek and G. Siegel (eds), *Review of Child Development Research*, vol. 4, University of Chicago Press, Chicago, pp. 187–244.

Schneider, B., Carney, M., Kilpatrick, J., Schmidt, W.H. and Shavelson, R.J. 2007 *Estimating Causal Effects Using Experimental and Observational Designs*, American Educational Research Association, Washington, DC.

Shadish, W.R., Cook, T.D. and Campbell, D.T. 2002 *Experimental and Quasi-experimental Designs for Generalized Causal Inference*, Houghton Mifflin Company, Boston.

Sproule, W. 2006 'Content analysis', in M. Walter (ed.), *Social Research Methods: An Australian Perspective*, Oxford University Press, Melbourne, pp. 113–33.

Stiles, J. 2000 'Neural Plasticity and Cognitive Development', *Developmental Neuropsychology*, vol. 18, no. 2, pp. 237–72.

Strauss, A. and Corbin, J. 1990 *Basics of Qualitative Research: Grounded Theory Procedure and Techniques*, Sage, Newbury Park, CA.

Tawney, J.W. and Gast, D.L. 1984 *Single Subject Research in Special Education*, Charles E. Merrill, Columbus, OH.

Walter, M. (ed.) 2006 *Social Research Methods: An Australian Perspective*, Oxford University Press, Melbourne.

Weatherburn, D. and Lind, B. 1997, *Social and Economic Stress, Child Neglect and Juvenile Delinquency*, New South Wales Bureau of Crime Statistics and Research, Sydney.

White, B.L. 1971 *Human Infants: Experience and Psychological Development*, Prentice-Hall, Englewood Cliffs, NJ.

FURTHER READING

Fraenkel, J.R. and Wallen, N.E. 2003 *How to Design and Evaluate Research in Education*, 5th ed., McGraw-Hill, New York. This volume provides a very clear discussion of issues related to design options for educational research.

Walter, M. (ed.) 2006 *Social Research Methods: An Australian Perspective*, Oxford University Press, Melbourne. This edited book provides an overview of quantitative and qualitative research design and methods, with chapters contributed by Australian academics.

APPENDIX 7.1: AN EXAMPLE OF THE DESIGN 'GOLD STANDARD' FOR STUDYING DEVELOPMENT IN EARLY CHILDHOOD AND ACROSS THE LIFECOURSE.

Framing the research questions

How are Australian children developing? How do factors in family, child care and early education contexts influence development? To address these broad questions the Australian government has funded a major long-term research study—Growing up in Australia: the Longitudinal Study of Australian Children (LSAC). While cross-sectional studies can provide useful information on some research questions, many developmental questions can only be answered using a longitudinal approach. Longitudinal designs capture the dynamics of change in individuals, their families and communities. As such, they can provide insights into the effects of early experience on outcomes later in life.

The LSAC study provides a uniquely valuable lens through which to observe the development of the current generation of Australian children, and to investigate the contribution of social, economic and cultural environments to their adjustment and well-being. The aim is to improve understanding of the factors that enhance or impede development, to identify opportunities for early intervention and prevention, and to inform policy and practice relating to young children and their families. The study explores the diverse pathways followed by children as they develop.

Multiple facets of children's development, health and well-being are examined, including physical health, social, cognitive and emotional development. The study seeks to understand the risk and protective processes underlying children's development, and the contexts in which they are raised, particularly their family, child care, school, neighbourhood and community experiences. The study also focuses on the parenting practices and the quality of co-parental relationships to which children are exposed, and the quality of care received in differing types of non-parental care.

Refining the research questions

In designing the study, the two broad questions were refined to give a set of fourteen key research questions, focused on the themes of child and family functioning, health, child care, and education:

1. What are the impacts of family relationships, composition and dynamics on child outcomes and how do these change over time?

2 What can be detected of the impacts and influences of fathers on their children?
3 How are child outcomes affected by the characteristics of their parents' labour force participation, their educational attainment and family economic status, and how do these change over time?
4 Do beliefs and expectations of children (parental, personal and community, in particular parents' and child's expectations of the child's school success, parents' workforce participation, family formation and parenting) impact on child outcomes, and how do these change over time?
5 How important are broad neighbourhood characteristics for child outcomes? Does their importance vary across childhood? How do family circumstances interact with neighbourhood characteristics to affect child outcomes?
6 How important are family and child social connections to child outcomes? How do these connections change over time and according to the child's age? Does their importance vary across childhood?
7 What is the impact over time of early experience on health, including conditions affecting the children's physical development?
8 What is the impact on other aspects of health and other child outcomes of poor mental health, including infant mental health and early conduct disorder? How does the picture change over time?
9 How do socioeconomic and sociocultural factors contribute over time to child health outcomes?
10 What are the patterns of children's use of their time for activities such as outdoor activities, unstructured play, watching television, and reading, and how do these relate to child outcomes including family attachment, physical fitness level and obesity, social skills and effectiveness over time?
11 What is the impact of non-parental child care on the child's developmental outcomes over time, particularly those relating to social and cognitive competence, impulse control, control of attention and concentration, and emotional attachment between child and family?
12 What early experiences support children's emerging literacy and numeracy?
13 What factors over the span of the early childhood period ensure a positive 'fit' between children and school, and promote a good start in learning literacy and numeracy skills in the first years of primary education?

14 What are the interactions among factors in family functioning, health, non-parental care and education that affect child outcomes?

LSAC was initiated and funded by the Australian government's Department of Families, Housing, Community Services and Indigenous Affairs (FaHCSIA), and is managed in partnership with the Australian Institute of Family Studies, with data now collected by the Australian Bureau of Statistics. An advisory group of some of Australia's leading early childhood, developmental and child health researchers guides the design and selection of content for LSAC.

Design considerations

A cross-sequential design was chosen for LSAC in which two cohorts of children are being followed, starting from when the children were aged from birth to one year and four to five years. The newborn to one-year-old cohort is described as the B (baby) cohort and the four- to five-year-old cohort as the K (kindergarten) cohort (see Table 7.1 above).

The two-cohort design enables information on the children's development over the first ten or eleven years of life to be collected in six years. Additionally, these two cohorts can be compared at overlapping ages, to gauge the effect of growing up in differing social contexts and policy settings. The overlapping of cohorts will first occur in Wave 3 (at four to five and six to seven years) and will then occur for each subsequent wave (shown by the arrows in Table 7.1).

Who participates and how were they sampled?

As the focus of the study is on children's development, 'the child' was the sampling unit of interest. The Medicare Australia enrolments database provided the sampling frame. A sample of more than 18 500 children within particular birth dates was taken from the Medicare administrative database during 2004. The sampling process involved the following steps. First, a sample of children was drawn via a random selection of 330 postcodes. Next, within these postcodes, children and families were randomly selected for invitation into the study. A stratification process was used to ensure that the numbers of children were in proportion to the population of children in each state/territory and within and outside each capital city.

A total of 10 090 children and their families participated in Wave 1; approximately half of the children were infants (aged three to nineteen months) and half were four to five years old. The sample is broadly representative of all Australian children (citizens and permanent residents) in each of two selected age cohorts: children born between March 2003 and February 2004 (B cohort) and children born between March 1999 and February 2000 (K cohort). Children in some remote parts of Australia were excluded because of the extremely high data-collection costs in these areas.

The LSAC sample is broadly representative of the population, with no large differences from ABS Census data on most characteristics. Variables with a close match to Census figures include mother's and father's country of birth, and study child gender. Children with mothers or fathers who have completed Year 12 are a little over-represented in the sample. Infants with no siblings are under-represented (by three percentage points), while four- to five-year-olds in couple families are over-represented and those in sole-parent families are under-represented (each by four percentage points). The sampling strategy is referred to as clustered stratified sampling.

What information is collected, from whom and how often?

Reports from multiple informants are sought in order to obtain information about the child's behaviour across differing contexts, and to reduce the effects of respondent bias. Information is being collected from the parents who live with the child (biological, adoptive or step-parents), the child (using physical measurement, cognitive testing and interview depending upon the age of the child), home-based and centre-based carers for preschool children who are regularly in non-parental care, and teachers (for school-aged children). From Wave 2, information is also being sought from parents who live apart from the child but who have contact with them.

Face-to-face interviews are conducted with the primary carer of the child (Parent 1). At Wave 1, this was the child's biological mother in 97 per cent of families. Data is also collected by questionnaire from the other resident parent (biological, adoptive or step-parent) and questionnaires are sent to home-based carers, centre-based carers and teachers. In addition, the interviewers record some observations about the neighbourhood, family and child.

The main waves of data collection are conducted every two years, with the first wave of data collection occurring in 2004. In Wave 1, for the B cohort (infants), physical measurements of the child were taken (weight and head circumference) and, for the K cohort (four- to five-year-olds), physical measurement and cognitive and language assessments were completed during the home visit. In Waves 2 and 3, height, weight and waist measurements were taken for both cohorts. The K cohort underwent further cohort cognitive testing in Waves 2 and 3. In Wave 3, the B cohort's cognitive testing repeated the Wave 1 K cohort assessments. From age six to seven onwards, the child is interviewed.

A novel feature of LSAC is the use of time-use diaries to collect data on a child's activities throughout two 24-hour periods, divided into fifteen-minute blocks. For each fifteen-minute block, options are presented in four categories. These are:

- what the child was doing
- where the child was
- who was in the same room, or nearby if outside and
- whether someone was being paid for this activity to take place (in Wave 2, for the K cohort, this was replaced by whether the activity was part of the child's homework).

Accessing the data

The LSAC data set is publicly available, subject to an application process and the granting of a deed of licence. Data user training workshops are regularly held to assist users to gain familiarity with the data set. LSAC is an invaluable resource for researchers, including research students in early childhood.

Source: The above is based on the most recent overview of LSAC by Gray and Smart (2008). Further information on the study is available from <www.aifs.gov.au/growingup>.

8

Quantitative designs and statistical analysis

Linda Harrison

This chapter summarises the main features of quantitative research and associated methods of statistical analysis. Underlying assumptions of quantitative research, types of measurement and statistical procedures are illustrated by examples drawn from the author's investigations of the use and impact of non-parental child care. It is anticipated that the reader will come to appreciate the purpose and benefits of quantitative research designs, be more able to read and critique quantitative studies, and gain an understanding of why this approach is the preferred choice for some types of research question. Reference is made to recent research to familiarise readers with the usefulness and currency of quantitative designs for addressing a range of questions in early childhood education and care.

EXAMPLE: CHILD-CARE RESEARCH

The research examples on which we draw throughout this chapter are taken from three different studies: the Sydney Family Development Project (SFDP), the Longitudinal Study of Australian Children (LSAC) described in Chapter 7 and the Child Care Choices (CCC) project. Each of these studies has used a non-experimental quantitative design to investigate children's experiences of non-parental child care over time, and the impact of different aspects of these experiences on the children's development.

The SFDP sought to reassess the commonly held view, based primarily on research evidence from the United States (see Belsky, 1988; NICHD ECCRN, 2005), that early and extensive experience of child care is associated with negative outcomes for children, such as an insecure infant–mother attachment relationship (Belsky and Isabella, 1988), more aggressive behaviour towards peers (NICHD ECCRN, 1998) and more non-compliant behaviour towards adults (NICHD ECCRN, 1998, 2003), by investigating an alternative explanation, based on the expectation that Australia's systems for quality assurance (that is, state/territory regulations and a system of accreditation for all child-care services) would mitigate any negative effect of child care (Love et al., 2003; Harrison and Ungerer, 1997/2003).

The LSAC seeks to document the breadth of children's early experiences to understand the factors impacting on health and development across the childhood years (Sanson et al. 2002). It collects detailed records of child-care attendance, family characteristics, and child development and well-being in a large, nationally representative sample of babies and preschool-aged children and their families. The LSAC provides a unique opportunity to examine different patterns of child-care attendance (Harrison and Ungerer, 2005) and the links between child care, family circumstances, and children's learning and social development (Harrison et al. 2009; Harrison, 2008).

The CCC project was designed for a specific purpose: to address the problem, identified by child-care practitioners and policy-makers, of an increasing trend for children to use multiple child-care settings across the week, and for child-care arrangements to be changed frequently over time (Bowes et al., 2004; Bowes et al., 2003). The aim was to investigate the extent to which families' patterns of care use were due to choice, or to financial or other barriers, and to assess any impact of multiple/changeable care on children's development.

DEDUCTION AND INFERENCE

The approach taken in quantitative investigations follows the processes of deductive reasoning. The researcher identifies a set of specific questions, expectations or hypotheses, along with specific methods by which these will be collected and measured. The data are analysed in relation to the research question to prove or disprove the researcher's hypotheses. Explanation, interpretation and significance of the findings for the wider population are deduced through this process of interpretation and analysis.

When the assumptions of quantitative research are wholly adhered to, the researcher is able to infer causal relationships. **Causation** is not an essential component in quantitative research (many studies describe relationships without testing causal effects), but quantitative designs are required when the researcher seeks to establish causation. Cook and Campbell (1979) identify three criteria as necessary for inferring cause:

1 An observable relationship between the presumed cause (X) and the effect (Y)—that is, between the independent or predictor variable(s) and the outcome, the dependent variable(s). However, evidence that X and Y are related does not necessarily mean that X causes Y. It could be that Y has 'caused' X, or that there is another factor influencing both X and Y.
2 Evidence that the cause precedes the effect. Researchers need to be wary, however, of assuming that longitudinal data will necessarily confirm a causal relationship.
3 The need to control for or rule out alternative causes, by considering other factors that may explain the relationship between X and Y. Cook and Campbell (1979) emphasise that *probable* causal connections should be sought and ruled out; it is not possible or even desirable to explain all causal forces.

CHARACTERISTICS OF QUANTITATIVE RESEARCH

Readers will have already gained some insights into the features of quantitative research from previous chapters—specifically, its location within a positivistic paradigm, its connection with experimental designs, and the importance of researcher-imposed controls. Quantitative research proceeds systematically through a series of stages:

1 defining the question(s), the concepts/constructs that will be addressed and the timeframe for the study
2 defining the population that can best inform the research question(s) and determining the method for selecting a sample of that population
3 identifying the set of dependent and independent variables that will be included to describe the concepts/constructs
4 selecting appropriate measures and procedures (for example, questionnaire, interview, observation, test, etc.) to accurately assess or describe each of the variables
5 recruiting the sample and sites for the study
6 collecting the data through the application of the selected measures

7 analysing the data
8 interpreting the findings, drawing conclusions, noting limitations.

Throughout this process, the researcher plans for, and relies on, working with data that are numerical in form. Measurement and statistical analysis are essential to quantitative designs. In most quantitative research, data are summarised and analysed using computer software packages, such as SPSS (Statistical Package for the Social Sciences), SAS (Statistical Analysis System) or specialised systems such as Amos for structural equation modelling, according to the types of analyses that are required. Data entry in Excel is generally sufficient as it can be 'read' by other software systems. Readers wishing to find out more about these software packages might turn to Colman, Pulfor and Corston (2007), Field (2009) or other recent statistics texts for details of these procedures.

ASSUMPTIONS OF QUANTITATIVE DESIGNS

Quantitative research designs draw on the assumptions of the traditional scientific approach—that is, 'objectivity, reliability, generality and reductionism' (Burns, 2000, p. 4). Research questions are investigated objectively, giving due attention to alternative explanations of observed events. Phenomena are defined as, or reduced to, a set of specific, measurable components or variables. The methods used to assess these variables are scrutinised as to the reliability and validity of the information they provide. The results are examined as to their relevance, or generalisability, to the population as a whole. Quantitative studies must attend to four key assumptions: objectivity, reductionism, reliability and generality.

Objectivity

By being objective, the researcher aims 'to discern *what actually is the case*', such that even if a hypothesis seems to be supported by the data, alternate hypotheses will also be tested (Burns, 2000, pp. 4–5). The researcher must give due attention to alternative explanations by attending to a range of possible influences on the phenomenon being studied. This poses a major challenge for the researcher. The solution is to introduce 'controls' into the research design to limit the range of possible influences. This may be done in any of the three following ways.

Controlled conditions

In experimental research designs, the researcher controls or manipulates the conditions of the investigation and randomises the assignment of subjects to different conditions, in order to eliminate or limit the effects of other possible influences on the outcome. This approach is used in randomised control trials designed to test the effects of an intervention program.

EXAMPLE: 'MODEL' EARLY CHILDHOOD PROGRAMS

The Carolina Abecedarian project (Campbell and Ramey, 1994) and High/Scope Perry Preschool Program (Schweinhart and Weikhart, 1997) are often cited as evidence for the benefits of high-quality early childhood education for children from disadvantaged backgrounds (Currie, 2001; Heckman, 2006). In these studies, children in the selected sample were randomly assigned to a 'treatment' (receive the intervention) or 'control' (do not receive intervention) group. Randomisation effectively controls for any pre-existing differences. This allows the researchers to be 'reasonably certain' that the differences in the outcomes for each group are the result of the experimental intervention rather than being due to other differences in the groups (Currie, 2001).

Controlled sampling

When random assignment is not possible, as in quasi-experimental or non-experimental studies, the researcher can control or neutralise the influence of pre-existing differences in subjects by limiting the scope of the study to a specified group. In this case, the controls hold constant the effect of particular independent variables that are likely to impact the outcomes. However, controlled sampling affects the generalisability of the findings to broader populations, which the researcher must note in discussing the results.

EXAMPLE: SYDNEY FAMILY DEVELOPMENT PROJECT (SFDP)

In this study, the effects of child care were examined in a sample of English-speaking couples expecting their first child. Infants who were born after a full-term pregnancy and did not have any diagnosed health problems or impairment at birth were included in the study sample. The restricted sample controlled for possible influences on developmental outcomes of the child's position in the family, prematurity and neonatal difficulties.

Statistical controls

The researcher may take account of pre-existing differences in the sample population by including a range of relevant 'controls' in the research design, such as family background, socioeconomic status, child gender or other characteristics. These variables are assessed in addition to the variables of primary interest. Preliminary stages of data analysis are used to assess the relationships between the control variables and the variables that have been selected to describe key constructs. In the final analyses, statistical procedures are used to systematically take account of the effects of the control variables while testing the effect of the independent variables on the outcome, the dependent variable.

EXAMPLE: CHILD-CARE RESEARCH

In the SFDP, LSAC and CCC studies, the effects of child care are examined in combination with other factors that are expected to (1) influence families' use of child care and (2) be related to children's developmental outcomes. These include, for example, parental age and education, family income, cultural background, the number of siblings living in the household, maternal well-being and child temperament. Variables describing these factors are part of the study design and are controlled for statistically when examining questions relating to the effect of child care.

Reductionism

In quantitative research, the key concepts/constructs that are of interest to the researcher are reduced to a set of specific, observable variables that can be described or assessed—that is, the researcher 'operationalises' the research question by reducing concepts to their measurable components. An operational definition 'assigns meaning to a construct or a variable by specifying the activities or "operations" necessary to measure it' (Kerlinger, 1986, p. 28).

EXAMPLE: CHILD-CARE RESEARCH

Child care in the SFDP, LSAC and CCC studies is 'reduced' to a number of key constructs, including type, amount and stability of care. Type is broadly defined by two categories: formal government-regulated child-care services, such as child-care centres and family daycare, and informal non-regulated arrangements, such as babysitters, relatives and nannies. Amount of care is defined in terms of number of hours per week. Stability of care is described by the number of new care arrangements that children begin during a set time period, which includes multiple arrangements and changes to existing arrangements.

These three studies are designed to follow children's development and well-being longitudinally. In the case of the SFDP, child outcomes were defined at four time points and represented how well children were doing on key developmental tasks: infant–mother attachment at age one year; behaviour problems at age 2.5 and five years; academic and behavioural adjustment to the first year of school at age six years.

Reliability

'Reliability' and 'validity' are terms that refer to the effectiveness of the measures that the researcher uses to describe or assess each variable, and the extent to which these measures meet criteria for scientific rigour. Reliability is assured when measures achieve stability, internal reliability, and inter-observer consistency (Bryman, 2008, pp. 149–50). The information provided by the assessment instruments should be stable or consistent over time. The instrument, if described by a scale, must have **internal reliability**. In other words, measures that are derived from multiple items or indicators must demonstrate that scores on one item are related to scores on the other items in the scale. This ensures that scale measures are aggregates of a number of coherent indicators. Inter-observer consistency refers to the judgments researchers make when collecting observational data or categorising information from interviews. Inter-observer reliability ensures that the variables are recorded in the same way, regardless of who has collected or categorised the data.

Validity is distinct from reliability in that it refers to what a measure really describes. The assumption of **measurement validity** addresses the question of whether the concept/construct of interest has been measured truly by the assessment instrument.

The requirements for establishing reliability and validity in assessment are complex and cannot be covered fully within the scope of this chapter. The basic issue is that **measurement error** is a reflection of the reliability and validity of the measures that are used. The quantitative researcher must aim for a low level of error by carefully selecting and pre-testing the assessment instruments. The possibility of measurement error can be reduced by using published measures that have been shown to meet criteria for reliability and validity. Researchers should also justify the measures they use by establishing inter-observer reliability (for example, for observations), testing internal reliability (for example, for questionnaires), or comparing results with established norms for children of a similar age (for example, for standardised tests).

EXAMPLE: SYDNEY FAMILY DEVELOPMENT PROJECT (SFDP)
Established measures, previously reported in other studies, were used to assess developmental outcomes in the SFDP. At age one year, the Strange Situation technique was used to code the security of infant–mother attachment (Ainsworth et al., 1978). At ages 2.5 and five years, problem behaviour was reported by mothers using the Child Behavior Checklist (Achenbach, 1991, 1992). At age six, teachers completed the Teacher–Child Rating Scale (Hightower et al., 1986), which provides ratings of children's learning difficulties, behaviour problems and sociability with peers. Before commencing the SFDP, these measures were trialled to test their relevance for an Australian sample and establish inter-observer reliability.

Generality

Generality refers to the assumption that the research has **external validity**—that is, the findings should have relevance or 'applicability … to other settings, populations, and conditions' (Goodwin and Goodwin, 1996, p. 53). To meet the requirements for external validity, the researcher must select and recruit a sample that is representative of the wider population to which the findings will be generalised. Consideration must be given to any bias in the results that may arise from the study sample, such as socioeconomic characteristics, cultural background and geographical location, through a process of statistical weighting.

EXAMPLE: LONGITUDINAL STUDY OF AUSTRALIAN CHILDREN (LSAC)

In recent years, research projects have been able to deal with the assumption of generality by recruiting a nationally representative sample. The LSAC comprises a nationally representative cohort of 5000 infants and 5000 four- to five-year-olds. Representativeness was established by comparing the LSAC sample with 2001 Australian Bureau of Statistics Census data on a number of key characteristics, including parents' ethnicity, country of birth, education and income, family size and structure, and whether the mother spoke a language other than English at home, to assess its representativeness of the population of families with an infant or four- to five-year-old. Statistical weights were developed to compensate for the differences between the final LSAC sample and the national population (Harrison et al., 2009).

Statistical weighting is also used to adjust for sampling biases in two large US representative studies, the Early Childhood Longitudinal Study—Kindergarten, and Early Childhood Longitudinal Study—and Birth (National Center for Educational Statistics). Most researchers, however, need to rely on smaller sample sizes that can only approximate the wider population. The assumption of generality is addressed by carefully describing the recruitment process and the nature of the study sample.

EXAMPLE: CHILD CARE CHOICES (CCC)

Three features of the CCC study design ensured that the sample would be reasonably representative of the wider population of children attending regulated child care.

Geographical location

Families were recruited to the study from child-care services in metropolitan and rural New South Wales. In the rural sample, all children's services in a regional and remote area of New South Wales were approached for participation. In the metropolitan sample, three recruitment areas were chosen on the basis of Australian Bureau of Statistics Census data in order to approach children's services in suburbs with families of low, medium and high income.

Type of child-care service
All licensed long daycare and family daycare services in the identified suburbs, including not-for-profit and privately owned centres, were invited to participate in the study.

Sample size and variability
A large sample (677 children: 50.7 per cent male; 49.3 per cent female) with a broad age range (four months to four years, two months) was recruited.

NUMBERS, MEASUREMENT AND NUMERICAL RELATIONSHIPS

In quantitative research, the concepts/constructs of interest are described in numerical form. Some variables may easily be defined or measured; others are more abstract and difficult to define; but whatever the construct, it must be measured or expressed numerically. In social research, four main types of measurement are used: nominal, ordinal, interval and ratio. The first two are simple non-metric measures; the latter are higher level metric measures.

Nominal

Nominal measures code, or assign, labels to variables based on a common or shared quality. Numbers are assigned to distinguish different categories or groups; they do not represent a unit of measurement, hence the term 'non-metric'. A commonly used nominal variable is child gender (for example, male = 1; female = 0). Numerical codes may also be used to denote the presence (1) or absence (0) of a characteristic—for example, Indigenous background (yes =1; no = 0).

Nominal data are reported as frequency counts for each category, as whole numbers and as a percentage of the total.

EXAMPLE: CHILD-CARE RESEARCH

Information about the type of child care children receive is coded as a nominal variable—for example, parental care only = 1; informal care with relatives or non-relatives = 2; family daycare only = 3; child-care centre only = 4; mixed formal and informal care = 5. Groups 3 and 4 can also be combined to denote formal care only.

At age one year, 54 (36.7 per cent) of the 147 children in the SFDP were attending regular child care. A similar proportion were receiving informal care (*n* = 53, 36.1 per cent).The rest were attending long daycare (*n* = 19, 12.9 per cent), family daycare (*n* = 14, 9.5 per cent) or a mixture of formal and informal care (*n* = 7, 4.8 per cent).

Ordinal

Ordinal measures also describe categories, but rank is assigned to the nominated categories, either in ascending or descending order. This type of measure describes the level of a concept/construct in terms of more or less, but does not quantify it. A commonly used example is level of education—for example, postgraduate = 5, university = 4, TAFE or other post-school qualification = 3, high school = 2, less than high school = 1. The numbers are ordered from most to least educated, but describe categorical rather than measured steps between each interval. Like nominal variables, ordinal measures are reported as frequencies (number and percentage of people in each level).

Ordered scores are also used in self-rated or observer-rated questionnaires. A commonly used system is the Likert scale, which asks the participant to rate their agreement with a statement on a five-point or seven-point scale—for example, from strongly agree = 5 to strongly disagree = 1. These scales assume an equal difference between one ranking and the next. Under certain circumstances, the scores for a number of statements can be combined and treated like interval measures (Tuckman, 1999).

EXAMPLE: SYDNEY FAMILY DEVELOPMENT PROJECT (SFDP)

At age six, children's school adjustment was measured by teachers' ratings of three areas of problem behaviour (acting out, shyness/anxiety and learning difficulties) using a five-point Likert scale (1 = not a problem, to 5 = very serious problem). Each problem area was described by multiple indicators to generate a scale. For example, poor work habits, lack of motivation and difficulty following directions were indicators of the broad concept/construct 'learning difficulties'. Prior to computing an aggregated score, the scale was checked to ensure the set of indicators met the criterion of internal reliability.

Interval

Interval measures quantify variables in terms of units of measurement, and assume equal distance between each interval and a defined arbitrary starting point. This type of measurement uses values that have numerically meaningful levels—for example, a person's level of education (years of post-compulsory study), the population of a city (number of people), the amount of time a child attends child care (hours per week) or the score a student receives on a test (0/10 to 10/10). Because interval data range from lower to higher numbers, the variables they describe are referred to as continuous measures.

Interval data can be presented as frequency counts for each interval point of the measure, but are more commonly summarised in terms of the range of scores (the minimum and maximum), the average or mean score (*M*), and the variability of the scores around the mean or standard deviation (*SD*).

When conditions for internal reliability are met, an interval measure can also be formed by aggregating a set of items measured on an ordinal (Likert) scale.

> EXAMPLE: SYDNEY FAMILY DEVELOPMENT PROJECT (SFDP)
> Teacher reported 'learning difficulties' were computed from six items rated on a 1–5 scale. Summary results for the 127 SFDP children were: *M* = 8.08; *SD* = 3.67; minimum = 6 to maximum = 27. A frequency count showed that the majority of children received very low scores for learning difficulties: 74 (58.3 per cent) had a score of 6, and 26 (20.4 per cent) had scores between 7 and 9.

Ratio

Ratio measures are similar to interval measures but have an absolute zero point. Tuckman (1999) points out that, apart from naturally occurring ratio scales, such as age and time, this type of measurement is rarely used in educational research. The exception, however, is seen in the transformation of scores for a measure into 'standardised scores' or *z*-scores. The mean (average score) for the measure is set at 0, and the unit of measurement is in standard deviations from the mean. Standardised scores are most useful when researchers want to combine variables that are measured on different units of measurement or metrics; for example, mathematics ability on a test ranging from 0 to 80 and literacy on a test ranging from 0 to 100. By transforming the scores on both tests to *z*-scores, students' results can be lawfully combined to generate an overall measure of literacy and numeracy ability.

A further example of a ratio scale is seen in standardised tests, which compare a child's 'raw' score with the 'normed' results of a large number of children of the same age to generate a 'standard score'.

> EXAMPLE: CHILD-CARE RESEARCH
> The SFDP and CCC studies used the Peabody Picture Vocabulary Test (Dunn and Dunn, 1997) to provide a reliable measure of children's language facility and cognitive functioning. The test requires children to point to one of four pictures to match a word spoken by the researcher. Children's raw scores were converted into standard scores on the basis of age (Mean = 100, SD = 15).

The four levels of measurement described above are a hierarchy, with nominal being the simplest and ratio being the most sophisticated. Data at the higher levels can be manipulated downward to create simpler level measures. For example, interval measures can be reduced to form ordinal or nominal measures—for example, by grouping ages to form categories or test scores into Pass and Fail.

> EXAMPLE: CHILD-CARE RESEARCH
> In the case of measuring the amount of child care children attend, hours per week (an interval measure) is limited by the fact that children who are not receiving care will be given a score of 0. This affects the continuity of the data. A useful technique is to form ordinal categories from the data: for example, none = 0; minimal, up to 10 hours per week = 1; part-time, 11–30 hours per week = 2; full-time, over 30 hours per week = 3.

MEASUREMENT AND ANALYSIS

The type of measures that are collected in quantitative studies determines both the extent to which comparisons across sources of data can be made, and the type of statistical analyses that can be applied to these comparisons (Hair et al., 1998). Metric measures (interval and ratio) allow the full range of mathematical procedures to be applied, whereas non-metric measures (nominal and ordinal) are restricted in their use.

Know your data and develop an analysis plan

The challenge for the researcher at the analysis stage of quantitative research is to know the data intimately. The more complex the data set, the more rigorously this maxim must be adhered to. Data analysis follows a systematic process. The researcher starts with descriptive techniques, which summarise the distribution of each variable (univariate frequencies and means). Bivariate techniques are then used to identify relationships among the set of variables. Finally, the analyses can progress to inferential techniques, which draw on multivariate as well as bivariate techniques to assess hypotheses and determine the significance and applicability of the results.

Types of measurement and associated analysis

Methods of statistical analysis are classified as **parametric** for metric data, and **non-parametric** for non-metric measures. Table 8.1 summarises the main techniques. For a more detailed explanation of these techniques, readers should turn to the referenced or other statistical texts.

Descriptive analyses (univariate)

Each variable in the data set should be checked to assess its distribution and variability. Metric data can be analysed as frequency counts for each interval point of the measure, but are more usefully presented graphically as a histogram to examine whether they are 'normally' distributed. Descriptive statistics for metric data include the mean or average score for the sample; the standard deviation (*SD*), which refers to the average amount of difference between individual scores and the mean score and is a measure of the variability of the sample scores around the mean; and the range of scores from minimum to maximum.

When numerical data are presented in their 'raw' state, means and *SD*s are expressed in 'real' terms—for example, as year of education or scores on a test. Raw data may also be transformed into standardised scores (*z*-score). In this case, the sample mean is zero and individual scores are expressed as the number of standard deviations away from the mean. The *z*-scores are either positive, above the mean, or negative, less than the mean. See Table 8.2 (bottom three rows) for an example of how descriptive data are presented.

Table 8.1: Types of measurement and associated statistical analysis techniques

Type of measurement		Statistical techniques
Metric, continuous measures		**Parametric statistics**
Ordinal scales	Univariate	Frequencies
(e.g. Likert)		Mean, standard deviation
Interval scales	Univariate	Frequencies, histogram
Ratio scales	Bivariate	Mean, standard deviation
	Inferential	Correlation
	Multivariate	Scattergram
		t-test
		Analysis of variance
		Linear regression
Non-metric, categorical measures		**Non-parametric statistics**
Nominal codes	Univariate	Frequencies, distribution
	Bivariate	Cross-tabs
	Inferential	Chi-square test
	Multivariate	Logistic regression
Ordinal codes	Univariate	Frequencies, distribution
	Bivariate	Rank order correlation
	Inferential	Cross-tabs
		Chi-square test

Distributions for non-metric data are presented as frequency counts for each category, either as whole numbers or as a percentage of the total number of subjects.

Analysis of relationships between variables (bivariate)

The next stage in a preliminary examination of quantitative data involves the examination of meaningful or expected relationships among the variables. The techniques for doing this differ according to the type of data.

Metric measures: Parametric statistics

Relationships between continuous measures are assessed using a bivariate correlation analysis, which compares subjects' scores on one measure with scores on another measure. The strength and direction of each relationship is expressed as a correlation coefficient (for example, Pearson's *r*, Spearman's *rho*). The correlation coefficient is a unitless number which can range between –1.0 and 1.0. Pairs of variables that have a positive correlation (0 to 1.0) are directly related; that is, as the scores on one variable increase so do the scores for the other. Variables that are negatively correlated (0 to –1.0) have an inverse relationship, that is, as the scores on one variable increase the scores on the other decrease. When there is no relationship between variables, this is described as a zero, or null, correlation.

Correlations can be visually illustrated using a scattergram, which graphs one variable on the X axis and the other on the y axis, and plots a point on the graph for each subject (see Kumar, 1996 and Hair et al., 1998, for examples of scattergrams). This is a useful technique for identifying 'outliers'—subjects whose scores are substantially different from most of the sample. Outliers need to be examined carefully. They may be due to errors in data entry, which can be corrected. Alternately, they may be due to 'real' cases which, particularly in correlational analyses, can unduly influence the results.

Correlational analyses test the statistical significance as well as the strength of the relationship between variables. Significance is expressed as the degree of probability (p) that the observed relationship has not occurred by chance. A p value less than .05 means that the odds of the relationship happening by chance is less than five in 100, or 5 per cent; a p value less than .01 is less than a 1 per cent chance; a p value less than .001 is less than a one in 1000 chance. Significance is conventionally set at $p < .05$. The strength of the relationship is shown by the size of the correlation coefficient (r), specifically the extent to which it is different from zero. Cohen (1988) gives the following guidelines for interpreting the size of the effect (or **effect size**) in social sciences research: small, $r = 0.1$; medium, $r = 0.3$; large, $r = 0.5$.

EXAMPLE: SYDNEY FAMILY DEVELOPMENT PROJECT (SFDP)

Correlational statistics are often presented along with descriptive statistics for metric measures in one table. An example is presented in Table 8.2. The bottom two rows report the mean (*M*) or average score for the sample—for example, mothers' average age at recruitment was 29.86 years; the standard deviation for mothers' ages was 3.91, meaning that on average mothers' ages varied around the mean by about four years. Maternal depression and child temperament, which were assessed using different measures at different points in time, have been computed as standardised scores, with a mean of 0.

The correlation matrix sets out different domains of variables: demographic (maternal age and education); maternal well-being; and child characteristics (temperament, language ability, problem behaviour). Variables within domains tend to be significantly correlated with each other—for example, mother's age is positively correlated with years of education ($r = .34, p < .01$); child temperament is positively correlated with behaviour problems ($r = .28, p < .01$). There are also significant correlations across domains. Mothers who reported more depressive symptoms perceived their infants as being temperamentally more difficult ($r = .24, p < .01$), and children whose mothers were older or more educated achieved higher scores for language/cognitive ability ($r = .35$ and $.32, p < .01$).

Non-metric measures: Non-parametric statistics

Relationships between nominal variables are examined by comparing the number and per cent of subjects distributed across the different categories in a **contingency table**. Typically, the number of categories for each variable ranges from two to five; larger numbers of groups become difficult to interpret. A comparison of nominal variables with two categories would be illustrated in a 2 × 2 table; a comparison of a two-category nominal variable with a four-category variable would require a 2 × 4 table.

EXAMPLE: SYDNEY FAMILY DEVELOPMENT PROJECT (SFDP)

Non-metric measures were used to code type (three categories) and hours (four categories) of child care. The relationship between type and hours of care is summarised in Table 8.3, which sets out the number and proportion of children receiving parental, informal and formal care for increasing amounts of care (none, minimal, part-time, full-time) in a 3 × 4 table. Inspection of the distributions suggests a relationship between type and amount of care. The infants who received informal child care (relatives, babysitters) were similarly distributed across the categories of minimal (9.5 per cent), part-time (15.6 per cent) and full-time (10.9 per cent) hours of care. In contrast, infants who attended formal care settings (child-care centre or family daycare) were less likely to be receiving minimal hours (3.4 per cent) compared with part-time (12.9 per cent) or full-time (10.9 per cent) hours. Note also that some of the infants in the parental care group were reported by their mothers as receiving minimal (4.8 per cent), part-time (2.7 per cent) or full-time (0.7 per cent) child care. This care was provided by fathers.

Table 8.2: Descriptive statistics and inter-correlations between family and child characteristics

	1 **M. age**	2 **M. edn**	3 **M. depr**	4 **C. temp**	5 **C. prob**	6 **C.PPVT**
Demographic						
1 Maternal age						
2 Maternal education (years post-compulsory)	.34*					
Maternal well-being						
3 Depression (z-score) high = more depressed	–.09	–.10				
Child characteristics						
4 Temperament (z-score) high = more difficult	–.04	.00	.24*			
5 Behaviour problems high = more problems	–.00	–.14	.24*	.28*		
6 Cognitive/language ability (PPVT standard score)	.35*	.32*	–.11	–.16	.02	
Number of subjects (*N*)	147	147	147	145	132	125
Mean (*M*)	28.86	5.14	0.00	0.02	9.80	112.72
Standard Deviation (*SD*)	3.91	1.92	0.65	0.92	7.19	13.14

* $p < .01$

Inferential statistics

Inferential analyses are required when the researcher seeks to test hypotheses, establish causation or make generalised statements about the significance of the results for the wider population. Inferential statistics examine the relationships between the dependent variable and the independent and control variables, by drawing on multivariate methods

Table 8.3: Type of care by amount of care received at age one year

	Weekly hours of care				
Type of care received	**None**	**Minimal 1–10**	**Part-time 11–30**	**Full-time over 31**	**Total**
Parent only	42	7	4	1	54
	28.6%	4.8%	2.7%	0.7%	36.7%
Informal only	0	14	23	16	53
	0.0%	9.5%	15.6%	10.9%	36.1%
Formal only or with informal	0	5	19	16	40
	0.0%	3.4%	12.9%	10.9%	27.2%
Total	42	26	46	33	147
	28.6%	17.7%	31.3%	22.4%	100.0%

of analysis to simultaneously assess the contribution, and significance, of these variables. Pathways of influence—that is, whether a variable has a direct or an indirect effect on the dependent variable—can also be tested (Baron and Kenny, 1986).

Inferential analyses progress through a series of stages, with bivariate tests preceding and preparing the way for multivariate tests. In the following sections, hypothesis testing analyses are presented in three stages, using chi-square, analysis of variance, and multiple regression tests of significance.

The chi-square (χ^2) test is used for data presented in a contingency table to assess whether the observed distribution would occur by chance alone (Bryman, 2008). The significance of the chi-square value is influenced by the number of cells in the table, or **degrees of freedom** (*df*), which is calculated by multiplying the number of columns—1 by the number of rows—1.

Analysis of variance (ANOVA) is used to test the degree of association between a continuous variable (interval or ratio) and a nominal or ordinal variable. ANOVA allows the researcher to test the hypothesis that the groups identified by the nominal/ordinal categories have the same mean, or conversely to determine whether there is a significant difference between groups. ANOVA produces an *F*-statistic (the between-groups variance divided by the within-groups variance, or *F*-ratio. The degrees of freedom are expressed as two figures: the number of groups—1; the number of subjects—1. When the *F*-ratio achieves significance, the group means differ from one another. In other words, the scores on the continuous variable differ for different categories of the categorical variable. Note that either variable can be the dependent or independent variable.

Multiple regression is a statistical technique used to assess the combined effects of a number of independent variables, or predictors, on the dependent variable. The contribution of each independent variable is specified in the final statistics. This method allows the researcher to statistically control for the effects of a number of alternate predictors while assessing the unique contribution of key variables. Multiple regression is suitable for outcomes that are continuous, or metric, measures (see Edwards, 1976; Hair et al., 1998).

Logistic regression is the preferred method for multiple regression when the outcome measure is non-metric, specifically when a binary or two-category dependent variable is used. Logistic regression assesses the likelihood of obtaining the observed outcome distribution in relation to the predicted or expected distribution. The overall statistic tests the 'goodness of fit' or the effect of all variables included in the model; this is expressed as the model chi-square (Hosmer and Lemeshow, 1989).

Multivariate methods of statistical analysis are highly complex, and readers are advised to look at other texts, such as Cook and Campbell (1979), Hair et al. (1998) and to Baron and Kenny (1986) for an explanation of moderator and mediator effects in causal pathways.

EXAMPLE: SYDNEY FAMILY DEVELOPMENT PROJECT (SFDP)

This stage of the analysis examined the relationships between the dependent variable, infant–mother attachment security, and the independent variable, amount of child care received. Note that the dependent variable is non-metric: children were assigned to one of two attachment groups, secure and insecure, based on the results of the Strange Situation assessment. The independent variable was an ordinal measure, with three levels: minimal, part-time and full-time hours of care. A 2 × 3 table summarised the relationship between the variables (see Table 8.4). Results showed that secure attachments were more likely when children attended part-time (73.8 per cent secure) or full-time (67.7 per cent secure) hours of care, and less likely when children attended for minimal hours (36.8 per cent secure). A chi-square analysis was used to test the significance of these differences. The df was 2 (2 columns—1 × 3 rows—1). Results were significant, $\chi^2(2) = 8.04$, $p = .02$.

The next stage examined the relationship between the dependent variable, an independent variable (age of starting child care) and relevant control variables (maternal age, education and depression, and child temperament). Note that the independent and control variables are metric and distributed across a range of scores. Analysis of variance (ANOVA) tests were conducted to assess the relationship between each variable and children's security of attachment. Results, presented in Table 8.5, showed that security was associated with mothers who were older, $F\ (1,143) = 4.20, p < .05$, and more educated, $F\ (1,143) = 4.96, p < .05$. None of the other variables achieved significance.

The final stage of analysis tested the effects of child care on infant–mother attachment in combination with relevant control variables, using logistic regression analysis. Results confirmed that amount of child care and type of care were significant predictors of secure versus insecure attachment, and that these made a contribution to the outcome over and above the effects of other variables included in the test, such as maternal education. Children who were in part-time or full-time child care were more likely to be securely attached compared to children in minimal hours of care. Children attending formal child care were also more likely to have a secure attachment compared to children in informal child care. Both amount and type of child care made independent contributions to attachment security—that is, children attending formal care had an increased chance of security regardless of the hours attended, and children attending part-time care had an increased chance of secure attachment compared with children in minimal hours of care, regardless of whether they were attending formal or informal care.

Table 8.4: Security of infant–mother attachment by amount of care received at age one year

	Weekly hours of care			
Security of infant–mother attachment	**Minimal 1–10**	**Part-time 11–30**	**Full-time over 31**	**Total**
Secure	7	31	21	59
	36.8%	73.8%	67.7%	64.1%
Insecure	12	11	10	33
	63.2%	26.2%	32.3%	35.9%
Total	19	42	31	92
	100.0%	100.0%	100.0%	100.0%

Table 8.5: Security of infant–mother attachment by age of starting care and maternal and child characteristics

	Secure		Insecure		
	M	*SD*	*M*	*SD*	F-ratio (*p*)
Demographic					
1. Maternal age	29.44	4.05	28.10	3.59	4.20 (.04)
2. Maternal education (years post-compulsory)	5.41	1.86	4.69	1.93	4.96 (.03)
Maternal well-being					
3. Depression (z-score) high = more depressed	0.00	0.56	0.00	0.74	0.21
Child characteristics					
4. Temperament (z-score) high = more difficult	–0.02	0.89	0.07	0.95	0.56
Child care					
5. Age of entering care (months)	9.73	9.70	11.21	9.91	0.78

CONCLUSIONS, CAUTIONS AND QUALIFICATIONS

The conclusions and recommendations that the researcher is able to draw from inferential analyses depend not only on the results of statistical techniques, but on research design features such as hypotheses, sampling and assessment measures. As Goodwin and Goodwin (1996, p. 103) point out, 'statistical significance is not the same as practical significance'. At the final stage of a quantitative study, the researcher must make objective comments about the value and applicability of the findings.

EXAMPLE: SYDNEY FAMILY DEVELOPMENT PROJECT (SFDP)

The results of multivariate, inferential analyses achieved significance and confirmed some of the proposed hypotheses and causal connections. Recall that we had hypothesised that early and extensive experience of child care would be less likely to be associated with negative developmental outcomes in Australia, with its higher standards of quality assurance, than had been reported for US studies. Security of infant–mother attachment was found to be significantly higher in the group of children who had received care in formal settings, which are governed by standards for quality and rely on qualified early childhood staff, compared with those receiving informal care. Furthermore, secure attachments were more likely when care was more than ten hours per week. This outcome not only refuted the problems noted in the United States for 'extensive' amounts of care, but suggested that infants may benefit from having sufficient time in their care settings to feel emotionally reassured and better able to manage the experience of separation from the mother.

Our results partially met Cook and Campbell's (1979) criteria for causation. There was a significant relationship between the cause (child care) and the effect (security of infant–mother attachment); the cause (child care in the first twelve months) preceded the effect (attachment at age twelve months); and the relationship between child care and attachment held up after taking account of alternate explanations (significance was noted after controlling for maternal education and other factors). However, there may be an alternative explanation for the finding that part-time and full-time hours of care were more supportive of secure attachments than minimal hours of care. Although it is plausible that regular, predictable care is beneficial for children, there may be other explanations for the poorer outcomes for minimal hours of care. For example, it could be that mothers who keep their child care hours to a minimum feel more conflict and greater anxiety about leaving their babies in care, and this anxiety may contribute to a more problematic mother–child relationship. Further research would be needed to assess this possibility.

STRENGTHS AND LIMITATIONS OF QUANTITATIVE RESEARCH

The major strength of quantitative research designs is the potential for generalising the findings from the sample population to the larger population it represents. The assumptions of objectivity and generality, when met, enable the researcher to consider wider applications of the research findings. The potential for describing causal relationships also has implications for practice. In sum, well-designed quantitative research studies have the power to influence decisions across a wide range of areas in early childhood education.

When undertaking and reporting quantitative studies, however, the researcher must be aware of the limitations of this type of design. The assumptions of reductionism and reliability imply certain limitations. Quantitative designs reduce, or operationalise, complex constructs to a set of measurable activities or events. The results of the research must therefore be seen within the limited frame of these operational definitions. Likewise, the reliability of the measures determines the strength and applicability of the findings. The quantitative researcher cannot generalise beyond what has been measured and how well it has been measured.

The significance and generalisability of quantitative research rely on statistical analyses. This can be seen as both a strength and a limitation. Results that are based on a reasonable sample size and an acceptable level of probability are accepted as 'real'—that is, they are unlikely to have occurred by chance, and therefore the hypothesis is 'proven'. However, the conclusion is based on the sample, not on the wider population, and errors are possible. In some cases, a hypothesis is accepted as proven when it should be rejected (Type I error) and, in others, a hypothesis is rejected when it should be accepted (Type II error). Quantitative researchers must familiarise themselves with these types of errors and other statistical constraints (see Bryman 2008; Burns 2000).

EXAMPLE: SYDNEY FAMILY DEVELOPMENT PROJECT (SFDP)

The multivariate nature of the research design and the significance of the results have allowed generalisations to be made for child-care policy. One of the benefits of this research has been the very positive response that the study has attracted from the early childhood community, state government legislators and the media—not many child-care reports are 'good news stories'. Nevertheless, there were limitations that also need to be acknowledged. The design provided a broad overview of the use and impact of child care, but was not able to probe mothers' individual experiences of child care or give a deep insight into the processes of the care experience. This might have been achieved by including qualitative methods, such as an extended interview with the mothers or an observation of infants in their child-care settings.

The operational definitions also point to some of the limitations of the study. Quality of care was defined by formal versus informal types of care. A more specific definition would be one based on observable events and interactions. A further concern was that assessment of infant development was based on one measure, the Strange Situation procedure. While this is a robust measure, and one that is recognised and used internationally, reliance on one outcome has its limitations. The longitudinal nature of the study, however, which has enabled the use of multiple assessment methods at different stages of children's development, is a major strength of the research.

SUMMARY

Quantitative research is based on the following assumptions:

- Objectivity introduces controls into the research design.
- Reductionism operationalises the research question to a set of measurable variables.
- Reliability determines the accuracy of these measures.
- Generality sets criteria for sample selection.
- Measurement is a key feature of quantitative designs:
  - Independent, dependent, and control variables are defined in measurable terms.
  - The nature of the measures determines the types of statistical analyses that can be applied to the data.
  - Non-metric measures—that is, nominal and ordinal codes—name but do not quantify variables, and are analysed using non-parametric statistics.
  - Metric measures—that is, ordinal, interval and ratio scales—quantify variables and are analysed using parametric statistics.
- Analysis of data proceeds systematically:
  - Descriptive statistics summarise the distributions for each variable.
  - Bivariate statistics identify relationships among the set of variables.
  - Inferential statistics test the extent to which the results can be generalised to the wider population.
  - At the final stage of a quantitative study, the researcher interprets the value, applicability, and limitations of the findings.

QUESTIONS FOR REFLECTION

1. Using Table 8.2, find the correlation coefficient that describes the relationship between mothers' education and mothers' ratings of child temperament. Is it a direct, inverse or zero correlation? Consider why this might be so.
2. Using Table 8.3, find the proportion of children attending formal care for minimal hours per week. Consider why this figure is so

low in comparison to the proportion receiving minimal hours of informal care.

3 Compare the total number of subjects described in Tables 8.3 and 8.4. Why are there fewer children in Table 8.4?

4 Search the literature in an area of your research interest for a study that uses a quantitative design. Read the article, looking for the following components:
   - the dependent variable and how it is measured
   - the independent variable and how it is measured
   - other variables (relevant controls)
   - the population for the research and the sample
   - presentation of univariate and bivariate analyses
   - the connections between results presented in the text and in tables. Make an attempt to read and interpret the numbers presented in tabular form.
   - statistical techniques used to test the research question or hypothesis.

REFERENCES

Achenbach, T.M. 1991 *Manual for the Child Behavior Checklist/4–18 and 1991 Profile*, University of Vermont, Burlington.

——1992 *Child Behavior Checklist for Ages 2–3*, University of Vermont, Burlington.

Ainsworth, M., Blehar, M., Waters, E. and Wall, S. 1978 *Patterns of Attachment*, Lawrence Erlbaum, Hillsdale, NJ.

Baron, R. and Kenny, D. 1986 'The Moderator-Mediator Variable Distinction in Social Psychological Research: Conceptual, Strategic, and Statistical Considerations', *Journal of Personality and Social Psychology*, vol. 51, pp. 1173–82.

Belsky, J. 1988 'The "Effects" of Infant Day Care Reconsidered', *Early Childhood Research Quarterly*, vol. 3, pp. 235–72.

Belsky, J. and Isabella, R. 1988 'Maternal, Infant, and Social-Contextual Determinants of Attachment Security', in J. Belsky and T. Nezworski (eds), *Clinical Implications of Attachment*, Lawrence Erlbaum, Hillsdale, NJ, pp. 41–94.

Bowes, J., Harrison, L.J., Ungerer, J.A., Simpson, T., Wise, S., Sanson and Watson, J. 2004 'Child Care Choices: A Longitudinal Study of Children, Families and Child Care in Partnership with Policy Makers', *The Australian Educational Researcher*, vol. 31, pp. 69–86.

Bowes, J., Wise, S., Harrison, L., Sanson, A., Ungerer, J., Watson, J. and Simpson, T. 2003 'Continuity of Care in the Early Years? Multiple and Changeable Child Care Arrangements in Australia', *Family Matters*, vol. 64, pp. 30–5.

Bryman, A. 2008, *Social Research Methods*, 3rd ed., Oxford University Press, New York.

Burns, R.B. 2000 *Introduction to Research Methods*, 4th ed., Addison Wesley Longman, Melbourne.

Campbell, F.A. and Ramey, C.T. 1994 'Effects of Early Intervention on Intellectual and Academic Achievement: A Follow-up Study of Children from Low-income Families', *Child Development*, vol. 65, pp. 684–98.

Cohen, L. 1988 *Statistical Power Analysis for the Behavioural Sciences*, 2nd ed., Lawrence Erlbaum, Hillsdale, NJ.

Colman, A., Pulford, B. and Corston, R. 2007, *A Crash Course in SPSS for Windows*, Blackwell, Melbourne.

Cook, T.D. and Campbell, D.T. 1979, *Quasi-experimentation: Design and Analysis Issues for Field Settings*, Houghton Mifflin, Boston.

Currie, J. 2001, 'Early Childhood Education Programs', *Journal of Economic Perspectives*, vol. 15, no. 2, pp. 213–38.

Dunn, L.M. and Dunn, L. 1997 *Peabody Picture Vocabulary Test*, 3rd ed., American Guidance Service, Circle Pines, MN.

Edwards, A. 1976 *An Introduction to Linear Regression and Correlation*, W.H. Freeman, San Francisco.

Goodwin, W.L. and Goodwin, L.D. 1996 *Understanding Quantitative and Qualitative Research in Early Childhood Education*, Teachers College Press, New York.

Field, A. 2009 *Discovering Statistics Using SPSS*, 3rd ed., Sage, London.

Hair, J.F., Anderson, R.E., Tatham, R.L. and Black, W.C. 1998 *Multivariate Data Analysis*, 5th ed., Prentice-Hall, Englewood Cliffs, NJ.

Harrison, L.J. 2008 'Does Child Care Quality Matter? Associations Between Socio-emotional Development and Non-parental Child Care in a Representative Sample of Australian Children', *Family Matters*, vol. 79, pp. 14–25.

Harrison, L.J. and Ungerer, J.A. 1997/2003 'Child Care Predictors of Infant–Mother Attachment Security at Age 12 Months', *Early Child Development and Care*, vol. 137, pp. 31–46.

——2005 'What Can the Longitudinal Study of Australian Children Tell Us About Infants' and 4 to 5-year-olds' Experiences of Early Childhood Education and Care?', *Family Matters*, 72, pp. 26–35.

Harrison, L.J., Ungerer, J., Smith, G., Zubrick, S. and Wise, S. with Press, F., Waniganayake, M. and the LSAC Research Consortium 2009 'Child Care in Australia: An Analysis of the Longitudinal Study of Australian Children', *Social Policy Research Paper Series*, Australian Government, Canberra.

Heckman, J.J. 2006 'Skill Formation and the Economics of Investing in Disadvantaged Children', *Science*, vol. 312, no. 5782, pp. 1900–2.

Hightower, A.D., Work, W., Cowen, E.L., Lotyczewski, B.S., Spinell, A., Guare, J. and Rohrbeck, C. 1986 'The Teacher–Child Rating Scale: A Brief Objective Measure of Elementary Children's School Problem Behaviors and Competencies,' *School Psychology Review*, vol. 15, pp. 393–409.

Hollingshead, A. 1975 'Four Factor Index of Social Status', unpublished manuscript, Yale University, New Haven, CN.

Hosmer, D. and Lemeshow, S. 1989 *Applied Logistic Regression*, Wiley, New York.

Kerlinger, F.N. 1986, *Foundations of Behavioral Research*, Holt, Rinehart & Winston, New York.

Kumar, R. 1996 *Research Methodology: A Step-by-Step Guide for Beginners*, Addison Wesley Longman, Melbourne.

Love, J.M., Harrison, L.J., Sagi-Schwartz, A., van IJzendoorn, M.H., Ross, C., Ungerer, J.A., Raikes, H., Brady-Smith, C., Boller, K., Brooks-Gunn, J., Constantine, J., Eliason Kisker, E., Paulsell, D. and Chazan-Cohen, R. 2003 'Child Care Quality Matters: How Conclusions May Vary with Context', *Child Development*, vol. 74, pp. 1021–33.

National Center for Educational Statistics. n.d., *Early Childhood Longitudinal Studies*, Department of Education Institute of Education Sciences, Washington, DC, <http://nces.ed.gov/ECLS>, accessed 10 May 2009.

NICHD Early Child Care Research Network 1998 'Early Child Care and Self-Control, Compliance, and Problem Behavior at 24 and 36 Months', *Child Development*, vol. 69, pp. 1145–70.

——2003 'Does Amount of Time Spent in Child Care Predict Socio-emotional Adjustment During the Transition to Kindergarten?', *Child Development*, vol. 74, pp. 976–1005.

——2005 *Child Care and Child Development: Results from the NICHD Study of Early Child Care and Youth Development*, Guilford Press, New York.

Sanson, A., Nicholson, J., Ungerer, J., Zubrick, S., Wilson, K., Ainley, J., Berthelson, D., Bittman, M., Broom, D., Harrison, L.J., Rodgers, B., Sawyer, M., Silburn, S., Strazdins, L., Vimpani, G. and Wake, M. 2002 *Introducing the Longitudinal Study of Australian Children: LSAC Discussion Paper No. 1*, Australian Institute of Family Studies, Melbourne, <www.aifs.gov.au/growingup/pubs/dp1.html>, accessed 10 May 2009.

Schweinhart, L.J. and Weikart, D.P. 1997 'The High/Scope Preschool Curriculum Comparison Study Through Age 23,' *Early Childhood Research Quarterly*, vol. 12, no. 2, pp. 117–43.

Tuckman, B.W. 1999 *Conducting Educational Research*, 5th ed., Harcourt Brace, Fort Worth, TX.

FURTHER READING

Goodwin, W.L. and Goodwin, L.D. 1996 *Understanding Quantitative and Qualitative Research in Early Childhood Education*, Teachers College Press, New York. This very accessible text includes two chapters on quantitative research design and methodology, drawing on a range of examples from early childhood research. The final chapter makes a compelling argument for combining quantitative and qualitative components into research design.

McMillan, J.H. and Wergin, J.F. 2002 *Understanding and Evaluating Educational Research*, Prentice-Hall, Englewood Cliffs, NJ. This introductory text categorises quantitative research as experimental and non-experimental, and presents a useful summary of the key principles of each. Three research articles drawn from educational research are included in each section to illustrate different methodologies and statistical techniques. Readers are led through a series of questions to analyse and critique these studies.

9

Qualitative designs and analysis

Anne Edwards

SOFT RESEARCH FOR SOFT TOPICS?

This chapter starts with a health warning. Qualitative research is not the easy option. Whatever version of qualitative design and analysis we select, we will find ourselves coming to grips with the complexities of the social world of early childhood. This is as true of an exploration of the pedagogy of early childhood staff as it is of a focus on children's experiences. Qualitative research is therefore demanding, but thoroughly worthwhile. It gives us access to the web of interactions between, for example, child, family, early childhood services and the community, and between these and the intellectual and material resources available to each of them. In short, it allows us to build up a picture of the actions and interpretations of children and adults, and locates them in the shifting networks of complex interactions that make up the contexts which provide the constraints and possibilities for action and interpretation.

Of course, single-handedly, researchers cannot look at everything in the web at once. As individual researchers, we have to select what we want to foreground and what we will treat more lightly. This selection is a subjective one. But it is not as subjective as the selection made by the experimental researcher in the laboratory, because one virtue of all qualitative research is that the process demands the researcher be continuously open to fresh interpretations of familiar events. In summary, qualitative research tries to be responsive to what the evidence tells the researcher. Responsiveness can be seen in both design and analysis. For example, we might decide to look at the language use of a group of three-year-olds at home and in preschool, and subsequently discover differences in their parents' beliefs about childrearing that takes our attention to how parents use the resources available in their homes. The analysis of the evidence will explain how the design developed to include a particular focus on parents and the language opportunities they provide. However, qualitative research has to start somewhere. The starting point of a qualitative study largely determines how the study is designed, the methods of data collection and their analysis, and what the researcher is likely to be alert to as the study proceeds.

FROM QUESTION TO DESIGN

Let's begin with an apparently straightforward practitioner concern: 'The children in this preschool rarely settle down with books.' How might we deal with this issue as qualitative researchers? A feminist researcher using a qualitative research approach might frame the research question so that the focus is placed on the different experiences of boys and girls with books in the preschool. A developmentalist would want to explore the children's previous experiences of books. Someone interested in sociocultural approaches to learning would be wondering what the children do with books. A linguist might ask 'Where else are the children getting experience of text?' These are all very different questions, demanding different research designs and levels of detail in the analysis of the evidence gathered. Each question is also, to some extent, driven by a different theoretical framing of the situation.

Let's look at how we might tackle some of these questions to give some foretaste of the range of design options that we loosely call qualitative. The developmentalist might frame her study as a cross-sectional study of two- to five-year-olds (see Chapter 6) and select a small sample of children in each year for fine-grained observations at home and in child-care services. The socioculturalist would focus on a small group of children as a case study and undertake detailed observation while the case study children interact with or relax without books in the preschool and at home. She would also interview parents and staff, and build a picture of the relationship between the children's experiences of books at home, in school and in the community. The feminist and the linguist might also opt for a case study approach, but their focus in observations and interviews would reflect the theories that inform their specialist perspectives. For instance, the feminist would focus on gender and the linguist on language structures.

QUALITATIVE RESEARCH: ALL KINDS OF EVERYTHING?

Qualitative research has a very respectable history, but definitions of it have changed over time and so have the debates around its purposes and usefulness. In an overview of twentieth century versions of qualitative research, Denzin and Lincoln (2003) identify seven overlapping phases or 'moments' in its development over the last one hundred years. They describe the first four decades as the 'traditional period' during which anthropologists used ethnographic techniques (see Chapter 16) to create objective accounts of the lives of others. The 'others' were usually alien and strange, and ethnographers had considerable power over how these others were revealed, as a result of their claims to objectivity and the analytic frames through which they developed and wrote their accounts. Critiques of this early phase argued that these accounts were based on positivist views of social science (see Chapter 3), and seemed to colonise the experiences of the cultures being studied by reducing the diversity of the fields of study so that they would fit the researchers' frames of reference.

The second phase, lasting from the 1940s until the 1970s, and labelled 'modernist', saw the emergence of what has become a continuing tension in qualitative research. Some of the work in this period built on the first phase by more overtly seeking to meet positivist research goals, such as trying to tease out causal relationships in their data (see Yin, 1998 for an example of this). At the same time, the period saw the development of the social sciences in universities, while qualitative researchers began to work with more interpretative theories of, for example, symbolic interactionism, feminism and phenomenology. There was a growing concern with the voices of those being studied and a desire for a liberationary social science. Yet these aims were frequently subsumed within a concern to ensure that qualitative fieldwork was as rigorous as that produced by experimental studies. It was in this period that the distinction between qualitative and quantitative research was so clearly shown to be a false one, as great efforts were made by some researchers to use qualitative evidence from their studies in quantitative ways through, for example, fine-grained content analysis. A number of researchers, including the author of this chapter, continue to work with frameworks that originated in this phase. Consequently, the phase marks the emergence of new priorities that have continued to be of relevance. A number of very influential early childhood studies (for example, Tizard and Hughes, 1984; Dunn, 1988) were undertaken during this phase, and usefully combined both qualitative and quantitative analyses to produce detailed and distinctly challenging accounts of the experiences of young children at home and in preschool settings.

The tensions of the modernist period, between the rigor of quantitative analyses on the one hand and the excitement of a liberationary social science and proliferating theoretical developments on the other, led eventually to the third phase, which Denzin and Lincoln term 'blurred genres'. This development was pre-eminent in the 1980s. Here we find the theoretical and methodological diversity that makes qualitative research so difficult to label. Research methods now using a qualitative approach included biography, case study and action research informed by theories that included feminism, structuralism and interactionism. This pluralism encouraged boundary crossing, so that insights from the theories and methods found in the arts and humanities permeated the work of qualitative researchers in the social sciences. It was at this point that an interest in, for example, the work of Bakhtin was seen in the analysis of textual data (Wertsch, 1991). Parallels between the representational power of researchers and of authors of fiction led some researchers to question their right to interpret the stories told by the field. Instead, they argued, attention should be paid to gathering thick descriptions of the field, and social science should limit itself to producing what Geertz (1983) suggests is 'local knowledge'—that is, rich information about locally embedded ways of understanding and acting in the world.

The fourth phase Denzin and Lincoln label 'a crisis of representation'. This crisis is arguably still with us. This phase in qualitative research approaches is marked by the encouragement of a more reflexive form of writing that makes the researcher's voice more evident and weakens any claim to the objective interpretation of the lives of others. One outcome of this development is that there may be no attempt to separate the researcher from the field of inquiry, from the analysis and how it is written for public discussion. Instead, the writing process becomes part of a reflective research process. This integration of the identity of the researcher with the production of research texts has raised questions about the reliability of the text (that is the extent to which another researcher would produce a similar representation of the field) and its more general usefulness. Mac Naughton in Chapter 17 discusses an approach to this in poststructuralist research. Denzin and Lincoln's fifth moment is what they describe as 'the post modern period of experimental ethnography' (2003, p. 28). The sixth (post-experimental) and seventh (future) moments are, according to Denzin and Lincoln, now with us. They include jointly constructed hypertext, multidisciplinary approaches, fictional ethnographies, lack of certainty and increased reflexivity, as qualitative researchers attempt to tell the stories of the field.

This overview of qualitative research in the twentieth century offers insights into some of the dynamics in qualitative research in the social sciences in the twenty-first century. It does not, however, fully tackle the purposes of qualitative research. This, too, is a contentious area, but nonetheless one that has to be considered when designing a qualitative study as the purpose helps to shape the study. Let us look in turn at two rationales for qualitative research.

A FOCUS ON ILLUMINATION

Here the emphasis is on research as way of enlightening, for example, professional practice, by providing information which questions assumptions and offers fresh ways of interpreting familiar events. Consequently, the information that research generates is seen as a tool to be used for clarifying our thinking about the world and how we act on it (Anning and Edwards, 2006; Fleer et al., 2005; Hedegaard and Fleer, 2009). This constructivist intention can be met by qualitative research which ranges, for example, from a detailed account of a child's experience of a mathematics lesson in Denmark (Bang, 2009) to the quantified analyses of interactions between early childhood staff and children in Glasgow (Munn and Schaffer, 1993).

A FOCUS ON CRITICAL INTERPRETATION

This focus belongs to Denzin and Lincoln's fourth and fifth phases just outlined. Whereas illuminatory research aims at informative and analytic descriptions of phenomena which attempt to map the territory, critical interpretative research places the subjectivity of the researcher as writer overtly at the centre of the research process. There, the researcher makes immediate connections between phenomena in the field of study and his or her personal theorising of it. For example, a researcher's anger at the treatment of a child with disabilities in a child-care service would legitimately be written into the theorising account of the event. Lather (1993, 2001) argues that, rather than description, the concern is inscription, where researchers inscribe their accounts of the field of study with the meanings they bring to it. This approach to data interpretation is particularly prominent in the research conducted from within a poststructuralist paradigm (see Chapters 12 and 17).

The range of purposes and priorities of qualitative research make a simple definition of the approach impossible. However, a number of common themes run across the diverse field. These include concerns about the power of the researcher in interpreting the field of study; an openness both to what the field is revealing and to other disciplines; and a self-critical awareness of the processes of research. In addition, qualitative researchers usually need to attend to issues of feasibility, reflexivity and validity.

KEY ISSUES IN QUALITATIVE RESEARCH DESIGN

Feasibility

This is a priority for the single-handed researcher. Qualitative research can become so open-ended and engrossing that boundary-setting becomes difficult and the researcher is seduced into gathering just that bit more information or looking closely at that relationship as well as at this one. If too many lines are followed, the single-handed researcher will need a clone! If vast amounts of data are gathered, even if the focus is narrow, the analysis will become daunting. For instance, a one hour interview may take an hour to arrange, need an hour for travel, thirty minutes for settling in and leaving, one hour for the interview, six hours to transcribe (or longer if the typist is not expert) and often several days to analyse. It is therefore helpful to draw a timeline for the duration of the project, and use it to calculate the time available for each stage of the study and to ensure that enough time is allocated for analysis and writing.

Access to the sources of evidence is also a matter of feasibility. Ethical issues need to be considered (see Chapter 5). Parents' permission will usually be required if data on children are to be gathered. Promises of confidentiality may prove difficult to keep when writing up some studies; consequently, the design may need to be adjusted to accommodate expectations of confidentiality. Some documentary sources, such as assessments made of children, may not be as available as might be believed. Some key informants (often the most senior ones) may decline the opportunity for a taped interview. It is therefore advisable to confirm access while designing the study and, where possible, to get written confirmation. Concern with feasibility can lead to a modification of grand designs, but it usually ensures that the research is completed and written up.

Reflexivity

Reflexivity is common to most qualitative studies. However, the term carries a number of meanings, all of which are relevant to the design of a study and all of which enhance researchers' sensitivity to the field of study. Sometimes designs are left slightly open, allowing researchers to respond reflexively to unanticipated evidence by slightly reshaping the design of the study. For example, a research question might initially take the researcher to observations of how adults interact with children in early numeracy and literacy activities in several child-care services. However, the observations might pick up some distinct differences between the ways that the services organise their provision for the children. These differences may raise questions about, for example, staff supervision or key worker systems, and lead to the collection of evidence on these topics.

Reflexivity can be built into the design from the outset. For example, case studies are frequently designed so that the analysis of evidence from one source informs how evidence is collected from another. Also, designs that combine large-scale surveys and case studies, often called mixed designs, sometimes ensure that surveys explore issues picked up by the more field-sensitive case studies, and that case studies try to unravel some of the trends evident in the survey evidence. Reflexivity is clearly one of the major advantages of qualitative designs for examining the messy and constantly changing contexts of early childhood. However, it does require the researcher to see data analysis as a continuous activity, and not something that can be left until after all the evidence has been collected.

A particularly demanding form of reflexivity is reflexivity in the analysis of the data. Here reflexivity can refer to the involvement of those who have been the focus of the study being involved in checking and approving the researchers' interpretations of the evidence. This is extremely difficult to do, but is often considered an essential element of feminist and anti-racist research and research conducted from within a poststructuralist paradigm. Grieshaber (Chapter 10) discusses the importance of this for equity in research design.

Reflexivity can also refer to an understanding of the impact of the researcher on the study. The position of the researcher in the field of study has long been a concern in qualitative research, as the very presence of the researcher can distort the system being examined. Careful covert observation, where researchers became part of the field and hid their identities as researchers, was one early response. However, once the subjectivity of the researcher became overtly relevant—as it has done, for example, in feminist and anti-racist research—it was argued that the idea of entirely neutral, disengaged human observer was a myth. Therefore, it was thought to be more honest to reveal one's starting points, both personal and theoretical. Having made that revelation, it is incumbent on the researcher to demonstrate that the best-quality evidence the field can reveal has been gathered and subjected to rigorous analysis.

Self-aware, engaged and reflexive research has emerged in response to researchers' disquiet about the separation of professional researchers from the field of study and their unease about their ability to speak for those whose lives they have been studying. However, self-aware reflexivity has slightly different implications for those researchers who, as practitioners in the field, i.e. early childhood staff, are already engaged with the field. For practitioner researchers, reflexive self-awareness demands the capacity to separate oneself from the field of study and to gain the distance that allows a fresh examination of familiar events using the lenses offered by previous research studies and new theoretical perspectives. In addition, increasingly informed practitioners will change the dynamics of the field as they interpret it and respond in fresh ways. Quite clearly, all researchers working with qualitative designs need to be self-aware about the balance they want to achieve between engaged commitment to the field and the capacity to offer an informed and research-based interpretation of it.

Validity

Validity is a often a vexed issue in qualitative research approaches. This is not because qualitative studies produce invalid findings. Indeed, qualitative researchers argue that the field-sensitive evidence gathered in qualitative investigations offers more valid representations of social worlds than those found in studies which reduce the lives of others to statistically significant generalisations. The problem lies in the competing views of how validity is understood within different research paradigms. Validity has specific meanings within each research paradigm (see Chapter 3). In more qualitative approaches to research, the meaning of validity is close to that commonly found in philosophy—that is, the truth-value in a statement. Validity in qualitative research is a matter of being able to offer as sound a representation of the field of study as the research methods allow. As we have seen, the development of qualitative research as a broadly distinct version of the research process has been based on attempts to offer valid interpretations of what a study of the field reveals.

In qualitative research, the validity of the findings of a study does, therefore, not add to an argument for the probable generalisability of those findings to other settings. Instead, a statement about the validity of a study is a judgment about the extent to which it can be said that the research has captured important features of the field and has analysed them with integrity.

Capturing the features of social worlds often calls for a number of fixes on the shifts and variability of settings. The qualitative researchers' response, particularly from those who are happy with the 'modernist' label offered by Denzin and Lincoln (1994), is to attempt to build a robust picture of events through a process of triangulation. Triangulation, as the term implies, involves getting a purchase on the field of study by looking at it from a number of vantage points. Denzin's (1978) classic definition of triangulation described four main types of triangulation:

1 *data triangulation*: the use of a variety of data sources in a study
2 *methodological triangulation*: the use of multiple methods to study a single problem
3 *investigator triangulation*: the use of several researchers
4 *theory triangulation*: the use of multiple perspectives to interpret a single set of data.

Each version of triangulation is important, though not all studies will employ all of them, and certainly the more reflexive and engaged accounts of the research process may dismiss them as all equally irrelevant. Patti Lather (1993), for example, has produced five new forms of validity more in tune with a critically interpretative form of research, especially that from within a poststructuralist paradigm. But triangulation does help in the quest for rich data that attempts to reduce some aspects of bias. For example, in a study of work-based training, interviews with student child-care staff might give insights into how the students are benefiting from their work placements. On the other hand, interviews with other practitioners in the service and with the trainers can provide evidence that will inform interpretations of evidence from the students (that is, data triangulation). Similarly in a study of how children are supported as learners, observational data might point a researcher towards assumptions about how practitioners are approaching children as learners, but these assumptions need to be explored in interviews or by taping planning meetings to which the practitioners are contributing (that is, methodological triangulation). Frequently, qualitative studies employ a combination of data and methodological triangulation. For example, in a exploration of how children interact with books, observations of children might be augmented by interviews with parents and the collection of planning and assessment documents produced by early childhood staff. With feasibility in mind, single-handed researchers need to decide what is to be foregrounded as the major source of evidence and what is to provide more background information. In addition, despite the origins of the term, triangulation neither restricts nor requires the researcher to observe the phenomenon from three vantage points.

Investigator triangulation is another important feature of qualitative research. You can't always work with others when collecting evidence, but studies that claim to be robust within modernist parameters do need to demonstrate that the analysis of qualitative data has been reliable. So, for instance, as we shall see later in the chapter, it is important to show that a second researcher would have analysed the data from the field in a similar way when working with the analytic categories used in the study. For a discussion of reliability in postmodern/poststructuralist paradigms see Chapter 3.

Theory triangulation is challenging and sometimes avoided by even the most established researchers. In brief, it requires researchers to consider alternative interpretations of the data. It can usefully lead to caution in interpretation, and so prevent over-claiming from the evidence. For example, a curriculum researcher might want to explain changes in children's behaviour in terms of the new curriculum he or she is evaluating. However, a developmentalist might explain the same changes as maturation. The alternative developmental explanation has to be acknowledged, even if the design of the study had not allowed an exploration of the possibility. Indeed, the more openly reflexive and critically interpretative versions of qualitative research are often more likely to explore competing theoretical interpretations of evidence. Multiple readings of data are increasingly a hallmark of research conducted from within a poststructuralist paradigm (Tierney, 2003).

DESIGNING THE STUDY

Having considered the possibilities, tensions and constraints offered by qualitative research, it is time to design the study. The case study is the most broadly used form of qualitative research design. Here the term 'case study' is used here to include individual cases, illustrative and comparative cases, and lifestory. They all attempt to answer the question 'What is going on here?' by focusing on the particularities of lives in context. The question does not rule out the capacity to reveal causal relationships, but the prime purpose of case study is to get below the surfaces offered by one method of data collection on one element of the field in order to achieve some purchase on the complexities of social worlds.

TYPES OF CASE STUDY

So what is a case? Cases are often referred to as units of analysis—that is, the bounded systems we explore in our study. A case can be, for example, an individual, a family, a work team, a resource, an institution or an intervention. Each case has within it a set of interrelationships that both bind it together and shape it, but also interact with the external world. Stake (2003) usefully describes a case as 'an integrated system'. Case studies can be longitudinal, but more often than not they provide a detailed snapshot of a system in action.

Case study is used for one of two broad purposes. Cases can be of intrinsic interest—for example, a study of the introduction of a new way of working in a child-care service. Or they can be selected as an example of phenomena occurring more widely, in the expectation that the fine-grained exploration that case study allows will assist our general understanding of the phenomena. An English example here would be a study of how four-year-olds are coping with attendance at primary school.

Our expectations of each kind of case study are therefore different. In cases of intrinsic interest, we would focus on one case, and the interactions and meanings held by participants. We might choose to look at more than one case but our focus is inside the case and comparison of the cases is not our main concern. We frequently find that an intrinsic case raises questions about wider issues—for example, how policy is changed as it is integrated into practice—but we don't design intrinsic cases in order to generalise from them. An intrinsic case may be the starting point for further study. For example, experimental designs often start with case studies that allow the researchers to clarify their understanding of the area of study.

Cases that are selected as exemplary cases have the potential to tell us more about a wider population than might be gleaned in a survey. Exemplary cases can be selected to represent a particular category from a wider population. For example, a sample of cases in a study of the national implementation of an early childhood curriculum might include a private child-care service, a volunteer-run service and a state-run service. Here, the function of the cases would be mainly illustrative to show how each service made sense of the policy. This type of exemplary case is sometimes part of a mixed design, where cases are selected to clarify findings from a survey and perhaps to help shape the construction of a further survey instrument. In another project, exemplary cases all taken from a similar type of child-care service might be selected and the cases compared in order to build up an understanding of issues that are common to all the cases in that version of child care. Here, the function of cases would be comparative and the purpose is the identification of common themes across the cases.

In both types of exemplary case study, there may be a temptation to generalise from the cases to the wider population—that is, from the particular to the general. Most writers on case study urge considerable caution about generalisation. Stake (2003, p. 135) advises designing case studies 'to optimize understanding of the case rather than generalization beyond'. For most case study researchers, the main benefit of case study is that the familiar is seen afresh as a result of rigorous examination. For others—for example, Atkinson and Delamont (1985)—the capacity that case study has for theory-building through the comparative analysis of cases should not be forgotten, and indeed provides a major justification for the use of case study. In brief, case study can be either a design in its own right or a feature of other research designs.

CASE STUDY RESEARCH

- A research study can take an intrinsic case as its sole focus.
- Exemplary cases can be incorporated into mixed designs so that they can provide illustrative evidence to inform understandings derived from surveys.
- Exemplary cases can be compared so that more general understandings of the field can be constructed from the ground up.

Identifying the boundary of a case can be difficult. This is because, once we see a case as a system, it is necessarily connected with other social systems. Decisions on the foreground and background of the study are therefore essential. It is sometimes helpful to think of a case as a set of concentric circles in which the major focus is on the central circle with interest decreasing as one moves towards the outer ring. In an intrinsic case study of how adults and children in a child-care service interact after the introduction of a key worker system (that is, where each child has a designated member of staff as a key carer), the case would look something like this. At the centre of the case we would find the primary focus of study: children in interaction with their key workers. More than one pairing of adult and child at the centre would be needed as the case is the service rather than the child. The next circle would represent early childhood staff's expectations and pedagogy in relation to the children and their practices. The next layer, still moving outwards from the centre, might be the early childhood curriculum, its implementation and management. The next layer might tackle parental perspectives and the outer circle might address issues relating to government policies on the early experiences of the under-fours and conditions of employment for early childhood staff.

The collection of evidence would centre on the interactions between the adults and the children. Consequently, high-quality observational data would be essential. Staff and parents would be interviewed, and documentary sources would be gathered on policy, management and implementation. Exemplary cases look very similar to intrinsic cases, but feasibility is important when constructing several exemplary cases. If several cases are being explored, it may be advisable to narrow the focus—for example, to the two innermost circles in the example just given—to ensure that there is time to gather the good-quality evidence required. There is little that is more disheartening than to find that the evidence gathered from cases is too superficial to be informative.

The timing of data collection is crucial, as case studies are designed to allow exploration of interrelationships between elements of the study. Ideally, evidence from one source is analysed before themes from that source are pursued in other forms of data collection. This ideal is not always achieved, but at the very least case study researchers need to remain alert to emerging themes in their data and to write analytic memos as they gather and read through their evidence. Research diaries become a useful resource for qualitative researchers as a place to record their changing interpretations of the field of study over time. The diary can include insights from the field and from published studies.

GETTING THE BEST INFORMATION AVAILABLE

Case study calls for a balance between rigour and lightness of touch. Bromley (1986) summarises these demands when he suggests that case study requires the best information available. The words 'best' and 'available' are both important, as rich data are essential, but equally the case study researcher has to take care to avoid overly distorting the case by his or her presence. Qualitative researchers, therefore, do need to acknowledge that they will disrupt the case. Most ensure that participants in the case become used to their presence before starting to collect evidence. Sometimes the disruption can become part of the case. This can occur, for example, when the study is monitoring an intervention such as the introduction of a new set of practices. Observations of children and interviews with staff can assist the careful implementation of the new practices. However, most case studies are examining existing systems, and researchers try to avoid too much disruption. Case study researchers therefore aim at low-intrusion data-collection methods so they can do justice to the story the case is telling.

OBSERVATIONS

The least obtrusive way of collecting evidence is observation (see Chapter 18 for more detail).

OBSERVATIONS

Broadly, observations can be:

- anecdotal—that is, rich descriptions of a specific and informative event
- event sequenced—that is, noting when a particular behaviour occurs
- time sequenced—that is, collecting information at regular intervals.

Anecdotal observations can be descriptive notes of an event that appears to offer some insight into the phenomenon being studied. For example, a quarrel in the book corner over whether or not it is girls' or boys' space, or a child's reluctance to leave her parent can be written first in notes that capture the event, its context and immediate antecedents. Then, subsequent behaviours are then written up more fully, perhaps as a vignette.

Event-sequenced observations can involve a simple count with an event counter or even a system of tally counting—for example, every time a child uses a particular resource. This is a fairly crude way of collecting evidence, as it tells us nothing about the length of time or how the resource was used.

Time-sequenced observations that are useful for qualitative researchers in early childhood settings are photographs, and Sylva's target child method (Sylva, Roy and Painter, 1980). Both methods allow researchers to collect evidence from the field and analyse it inductively once it has been collected. Photographs can be used to collect time-sequenced data by taking a picture of the target child or adult at regular intervals—for example, every 60 seconds. If a digital camera is used, the pictures can be loaded onto a computer for ease of analysis.

The target child method, like photographs, involves selecting a target, which may be an adult or a child or even a small group (Edwards and Talbot, 1999). The researcher prepares an observation sheet (see Figure 9.1). The rows represent one minute of observation and five rows fit an A4 page.

In the first column the time is noted, in the second, the researcher records everything the target does in one minute, while the third column

Figure 9.1: The target observations method

Time	Observations	Analysis
10.00		
10.01		

is left blank for the analysis stage. At 10.01 the researcher moves to the second row and so on. This method is tiring, so a break after ten or fifteen minutes is recommended to enable the researcher to make sense of the scribbled notes and to write any background information on the settings that will assist later analysis. After a short break, observation can resume. The number of observations will depend on how they are contributing to the design of the study. But, as a rule of thumb, more than one observation needs to be made of a target if observations are to be a major data source.

The target method can be used alongside tape recording as the minute-by-minute breakdown allows the researcher to combine the real-time tape with the real-time observations. So why not use a video camera? The answer is that they tend to be disruptive if they are handheld, and if they are fixed they see less than the more flexible human observer. The target method is not helpful if you need to know precisely how long a behaviour lasts, but it does allow you to capture broad sequences of behaviour and their contexts.

INTERVIEWS

Interviews (see Chapters 14 and 15) allow case study researchers to explore the meanings that lie behind observed behaviours or documentary evidence. In some cases, the interviews will be the major data source and the observations will be prompts. In case study research, it is commonplace to use observations as a starting point for interviews. Most interview schedules start quite broadly and then focus down on the issues that have arisen as the case has been explored. Case study researchers often use interviews to explore their interpretations of the data and the tentative links they have been making between elements of the case as they progress towards an understanding of the case. Of course, here it is important to avoid leading questions. A simple tip is to ask 'What do you think about the key worker system?' rather than 'Do you think the system is working?' The researcher can focus the topic of the interview, but should avoid constraining the response.

DOCUMENTARY SOURCES

These are easily collected and can include material sent to users of the service, minutes of meetings, observations made of children by staff, curriculum policies, and so on.

ANALYSING QUALITATIVE DATA

Being organised is an essential attribute for the qualitative researcher. To be drowning in data is not a pleasant experience. The physical sorting of data needs to start as soon as evidence begins to accumulate. An increasing number of qualitative researchers like to put as much data as possible on to computer databases and to manipulate them there. There are also a growing number of computer programs aimed at assisting qualitative analysis. But these should be treated cautiously and only used if they give the help that is needed. Analysis should not be led by what the analysis program can do!

Qualitative analysis usually involves content analysis that is a process of combing the evidence. The comb can be quite fine, allowing detailed analysis of the transcribed interview text—for example, the type of language used to talk about children. Or it can be quite broad and pick up thematic responses—for example, beliefs about children as learners. Analysis can involve the entire text or simply segments of it. Much depends on the purpose of the study. Whatever method is used, the case study researcher needs to explain carefully how the analysis was carried out.

Sometimes the analysis is theory led. In a study of mother–child interaction, for example, a researcher might record mothers' behaviours in the second column of Figure 9.1 and use the third column to label the mothers' behaviours recorded using the categories of mothering behaviour identified by Schaffer (1977). Schaffer's categories may not fit the data, perhaps because the mothers in the present study are from a different cultural background from those who generated Schaffer's categories. The researcher would then adapt some categories or create new ones in response to the data.

Sometimes the analysis is data driven. Data-driven analysis is not easy to do well, as it involves constructing a category system from the evidence that has been collected. In fact, most data-driven analyses start with the researcher's beliefs about the focus of the study. For example, in a study of three-year-olds and number activities, the starting point for analysis would be the researcher's own grasp of how young children learn to think and act with numbers in everyday settings. This understanding may have been informed, even implicitly, by earlier research—for example by Saxe, Guberman and Gearhart (1987). Indeed, the study could not have been designed without some implicit theory of how children acquire numeracy.

Sometimes only analytic memos are required. In Figure 9.1 the third column can simply be used for writing analytic memos which will alert the researcher to the topics to be followed up in later data collection when the mothers are interviewed. (If observations are photocopied, they can be used for both categorisation and memos.) Similarly, interview evidence can prompt analytic memos which help the researcher's developing interpretations of the case.

Developing a category system

This is where the modernist qualitative researcher's rigour is tested. A category system consists of the category labels assigned to observed behaviours or, in interviews or recorded conversations, to units of talk. Each category label needs to be supported by a description that distinguishes it from the other category labels. The descriptions need to be clear enough to enable another researcher to use them to categorise a sample of some of the data and achieve a high degree of match with the original categorisation. Above 85 per cent match on categorisation by two researchers on a 10 per cent sample of a data set is usually acceptable. If the second researcher finds the categories difficult to use, they need to be refined and made clearer until they are usable. At the start of a project, the category system is an evolving document as adjustments are made to descriptors in response to the data.

Applying the categories

The first task is to identify the unit of analysis to which the categories will be applied. One version of a unit of analysis is where the behaviour or utterance begins and ends. Identification is relatively easy in observational data where behaviour is labelled at the point when it starts. With interviews, units can be fine-grained 'meaning units' (Edwards, 1997), where a unit is defined as a string of words in which a meaning is carried. For example, 'she is often late/but she's keen when she gets here' consists of two units. At the other end of the range of unit are large segments of text which represent a specific perspective on events in a more broadly thematic analysis. Again, much depends on how the data are to contribute to the story of the case.

However the evidence is analysed, the major virtue of qualitative studies is their capacity to tell a well-substantiated story. These stories are strengthened by using voices from the field, or detailed snapshots of the field, to bring to life the arguments being pursued in the research report. Organisation of qualitative evidence therefore has to allow the researcher easy access to the qualitative sources of the strong themes being discussed. For example, if a report identifies two perspectives on young children as learners in operation in one preschool, the researcher needs to be able to find examples of each interpretation to use them to briefly illustrate the argument being made. Systematic organisation of data cannot be over-emphasised!

TELLING THE STORY

Qualitative data can be transformed into quantitative data through fine-grained content analysis and findings can be statistically tested. But tables cannot represent the complexities and ambiguities of the field revealed in case study. One of the challenges of telling the tale elicited from the field is to provide an account of what is going on which is sufficiently coherent to retain a reader's interest but is also sensitive to the complexities and multiple perspectives revealed in the study.

The extent to which the story is a richly illustrated research report, or is a personal narrative, will largely depend on whether the researcher's aim is primarily to produce illuminating research or to offer a critical interpretation. Although these aims demand different modes of story-telling—the former often more like a traditional research report and the latter giving more opportunities for inventive representation—they will usually contain some common features.

COMMON FEATURES IN QUALITATIVE RESEARCH

- Openness about the researcher's theoretical and personal starting points
- An ethical concern for those whose experiences are being represented
- An attempt to reveal the richness of the field in the field's own terms
- A need for a careful system of data organisation to support the analysis
- A critical awareness of what has been learnt during the research process

SUMMARY

In this chapter I have argued that working with qualitative data is demanding but worthwhile if you want to get some grip on the complex interactions that make up the messy work of early childhood practices. However, care needs to be taken to ensure that the questions you pose, the study you design and data-collection methods you use help you reveal what matters most to you. There are several approaches to designing qualitative research and carrying out analyses and each has its own integrity. You need to decide which suits your interests and purposes and then work rigorously within the expectations of the design you have selected.

QUESTIONS FOR REFLECTION

1 Think of a practical issue that you would like to explore. Try to identify the questions that some of the following researchers might like to pursue when exploring the topic: a feminist, an anti-racist, a linguist, a developmentalist. Briefly outline the studies that two of them might undertake. How will their starting points affect how each study is designed?
2 Where would you place yourself as a researcher in the 'moments' of qualitative research identified by Denzin and Lincoln (2003) and outlined in this chapter? How easy is it to categorise yourself? Can you think of a situation where, for example, you might be both a modernist and a critical interpreter?
3 How would you explain to a civil servant who might offer you funds how your qualitative research will help the development of practice in early childhood services?
4 What would be the ethical issues to be considered when designing a case study of how a preschool handles links with children's families? (See Chapter 5 and, for example, ethical guidelines available on the websites of national research associations and psychological societies.)
5 Roughly how much time should you allocate on your timeline for data analysis and to what extent can analysis be carried out before all the evidence is collected when planning a study which will involve the following: six hours of interviews to be analysed to extract broad themes; three hours of written target child observations (30 minutes on each of six children), which will be analysed in some detail; assessment data on the six children being observed; and some background information on curriculum policies and planning?

REFERENCES

Anning, A. and Edwards, A. 2006 *Promoting Learning from Birth to Five: Developing Professional Practice in the Pre-school*, 2nd ed., Open University Press, Buckingham.

Atkinson, P. and Delamont, S. 1985 'Bread and Dreams or Bread and Circuses? A Critique of Case Study in Educational Research', in M. Shipman (ed.) *Educational Research: Principles, Policies and Practices*, Falmer Press, London.

Bang, J. 2009 'Conceptualising the Environment of the Child in a Cultural-Historical Approach', in M. Hedegaard and M. Fleer (eds), *Studying Children: A Cultural Historical Approach*, Open University Press, Buckingham.

Bromley, D. 1986 *The Case Study Method in Psychology and Related Disciplines*, Wiley, New York.

Denzin, N. 1978 *The Research Act*, 2nd ed., McGraw-Hill, New York.

Denzin, N. and Lincoln, Y. (eds) 2003 *Strategies of Qualitative Enquiry*, Sage, London.

——1994 *Handbook of Qualitive Research*, Sage, Thousand Oaks CA.

Dunn, J. 1988 *The Beginnings of Social Understanding*, Blackwell, Oxford.

Edwards, A. 1997 'Guests Bearing Gifts: The Position of Student Teachers in Primary School Classrooms', *British Educational Research Journal*, vol. 23, no. 91, pp. 27–37.

Edwards, A. and Talbot, R. 1999 *The Hardpressed Researcher: A Research Handbook for Health Education and Social Care*, 2nd ed., Longman, London.

Geertz, C. 1983 *Local Knowledge: Further Essays in Interpretative Anthropology*, Basic Books, New York.

Hedegaard, M. and Fleer, M. (eds) 2009 *Studying Children: A Cultural Historical Approach*, Open University Press, Buckingham.

Fleer, M., Edwards, S., Hammer, M., Kennedy, A., Ridgway, A., Robbins, J. and Surman, L. 2005 *Early Childhood Learning Communities: Sociocultural Research in Practice*, Pearson Australia, Sydney.

Lather, P. 1993 'Fertile Obsession: Validity After Poststructuralism', *Sociological Quarterly*, vol. 34, no. 4, pp. 673–93.

——2001 'Postmodernism, Poststructuralism and Post(Critical) Ethnography: Of Ruins, Aporia and Angels', in P. Atkinson et al. (eds), *Handbook of Ethnography*, Sage, London.

Munn, P. and Schaffer, H.R. 1993 'Literacy and Numeracy Events in Social Interactive Contexts', *International Journal of Early Years Education*, vol. 1, no. 3, pp. 61–80.

Saxe, G., Guberman, G. and Gearhart, M. 1987, 'Social Processes in Early Number Development', *Monographs of the Society for Research in Child Development*, Serial No. 216, vol. 52, no. 2.

Schaffer, H.R. 1977 *Mothering*, Fontana, London.

Stake, R. 2003 'Case Studies', in N. Denzin and Y. Lincoln (eds) *Strategies of Qualitative Enquiry*, Sage, London.

Sylva, K., Roy, C. and Painter, M. 1980 *Childwatching at Playgroup and Nursery School*, Grant McIntyre, London.

Tierney, W. 2003 'Undaunted Courage: Life History and the Postmodern Challenge', in N. Denzin and Y. Lincoln (eds), *Strategies of Qualitative Enquiry*, Sage, London.

Tizard, B. and Hughes, M. 1984 *Young Children Learning: Talking and Thinking at Home and School*, Fontana, London.

Wertsch, J. 1991 *Voices of the Mind*, Harvard University Press, Cambridge, MA.

Yin, R.K. 1998 'The Abridged Version of Case Study Research: Design and Method', in L. Bickman and D. Rog (eds), *Handbook of Applied Social Research Methods*, Sage, London.

FURTHER READING

Denzin, N. and Lincoln, Y. (eds) 2003 *Strategies of Qualitative Enquiry*, 2nd ed., Sage, London. This covers the broad range of qualitative approaches, including chapters on narrative, grounded theory and action research, which operate as useful gateways into these approaches to research.

Silverman, D. 2001 *Interpreting Qualitative Data: Methods for Analysing Talk, Text and Interaction*, 2nd ed., Sage, London. A comprehensive book, with all the detail the beginning researcher requires.

10

Equity and research design

Susan Grieshaber

This chapter recognises that research is a cultural invention and explains why. It discusses what equity, research and research design mean, and suggests that the concept of equity is enriched considerably when ideas from Indigenous, critical and politically committed research traditions are involved in research design. When research design and the processes of research are guided by principles of equity, several issues warrant investigation. These include power relations, deficit models of research, homogeneity and reflexivity. Research design that is informed by principles of equity is explicit in its political purpose of seeking socially just outcomes for the short and long term.

RESEARCH AS A CULTURAL INVENTION

Research is a cultural invention of the white Western male upper middle-class academic world, and as such represents a highly privileged position. This privileged position has been used to judge and legitimate all other approaches to research. 'Legitimate' or **dominant approaches** are those based on the principles of Eurocentric scientific rationality; they claim they are neutral, objective and value free, and profess to produce facts—or the 'truth'. Such approaches to research profess that reality is knowable, observable and can be captured scientifically. The goal is to create universal laws that can be used to govern behaviour. Most research that satisfies these criteria can be categorised as positivist because it is informed by theory and specific procedures that predict, test and confirm hypotheses; this is what we know as quantitative research.

In scientific research, the production of 'legitimate' knowledge can only be undertaken by certain people using particular procedures in specific ways, which then produces particular types of 'truth'. Thus, much of what has been called legitimate research has been 'done on' and 'done to' those who are the 'objects' of such research. This is usually justified on the grounds that the 'subjects' are members of 'socially, economically or politically disadvantaged groups and [are seen to be] in need of help or redress' (Mayall, Hood and Oliver, 1999, p. 1). Such groups tend to include Indigenous people, refugees, children, the elderly, those with health problems and anyone who is classified as belonging to a 'minority' group. According to Mayall, Hood and Oliver (1999), such people are the object of research because they are constituted as economic problems and a remedy is needed to reduce the economic burden they present for government. (This is a deficit approach, which is discussed later.) Research activity, then, is a particular cultural invention or social construction of the Western academic world aimed at investigating other social constructions and cultural inventions that are not necessarily located within the same culture, economic circumstances or historical period. Some of the difficulties encountered with this position include the imposition of Western academic ways of researching on who and what is being studied.

The approach taken in this chapter is the reverse of the dominant position. That is, research is seen as subjective, never neutral and always political, as capable of producing many 'truths' and not about creating universal facts. It questions the application of positivist aims, methods and approaches associated with natural science to the social sciences on the grounds of ontological and epistemological differences. By **ontological**, I mean world-view, or what Strega (2005, p. 201) calls 'a theory about what the world is like—what the world consists of, and why'. To Strega, epistemology is:

> ... a philosophy of what counts as knowledge and 'truth'; it is a strategy by which beliefs are justified. Epistemologies are theories of knowledge that answer questions about who can be a 'knower'; what tests beliefs and information must pass in order to be given the status of 'knowledge'; and what kinds of things can be 'known' (2005, p. 201).

The ontologies and epistemologies of positivist research are quite different from research that is founded on principles of social justice, and more capable of producing many 'truths'. Research design is influenced by the world-view or ontology of researchers and their **epistemology**, or the theories of knowledge to which they subscribe (see Hatch, 2002). It follows, then, that methodological approaches are informed by particular ontologies and epistemologies, making equity an important component of research design from the beginning. The choice of research paradigms reflects our beliefs and values about the world in which we live and the world in which we want to live.

Including equity as an integral part of research design is a topic for both qualitative and quantitative researchers, despite their differences. Feminist author Ann Oakley (1999) discusses the idea that the 'social sciences have themselves been gendered, and have thus spawned a gendered discourse about "qualitative" and "quantitative" methods' (1999, p. 161). Oakley aligns qualitative research with feminine approaches and quantitative research with masculine approaches. She points out other dualisms, contrasting the 'understanding' characteristic of qualitative (feminine) approaches with the quantitative paradigm and its association with control (masculine); and in the same vein, intuition and reason, soft and hard, subjective and objective, and so on respectively, noting that dualistic thinking is a characteristic of Western culture (1999, p. 161). Whatever the approach adopted (qualitative or quantitative), equity ought to be considered from the beginning when the research is being conceptualised. It is too late to think about it when trying to negotiate access to a research site or when gathering data.

WHAT IS MEANT BY EQUITY, RESEARCH AND RESEARCH DESIGN?

An understanding of **equity** involves notions of justice and fairness. It moves beyond equality, as equality signals understandings of parity, equivalence and making things equal, which do not necessarily equate with justice and fairness. In order to be just and fair, it is necessary to move beyond making things equal.

Both the nature of research and research design have been categorised in various ways. Although both terms conjure up many different understandings, **research** is conceptualised here as a systematic investigation of a topic or issue that is culturally specific, and which seeks information and/or solutions. It can begin with a question, concern, situation or controversy. **Research design** means the plan for what is to be investigated and how this is to be undertaken. The research design is contingent on the ontological and epistemological orientation of the researchers and is directly related to the research questions or problem, data to be collected and how this will be accomplished. This means considering who the participants will be, how they will be selected and how the data will be collected (data-gathering techniques). The research design also involves how the data are to be analysed, including measures of reliability, validity and generalisability, and how data are to be 'written up' and shared with participants. Equity issues in research design therefore incorporate notions of fairness and justice in relation to the research investigation (the systematic method of inquiry) and the whole process of how it is to be undertaken, from conceptualisation to conclusion. Concerns probed in relation to equity issues in research design include power relations, research based on a deficit model, the notion of homogeneity and some ideas for the detection of bias.

ISSUES OF EQUITY IN RESEARCH DESIGN

Power relations

Because researchers enact and participate in relationships of power, there can be no researcher neutrality. Undertaking any research activity alters the research site to an unknown degree, no matter what type of research approach is used. For instance, questions on a survey might cause people to reflect on issues or situations that they might not have considered if they had not completed the survey. Likewise, observing research sites makes a difference to what would have happened had the researcher not been present in some capacity in the context. However, what we do not know is the extent of the change that occurs. In more traditional approaches to research within a positivist paradigm (that is, quantitative research), researchers are positioned more powerfully than those who are the objects of that research, usually called 'subjects'. Approaches that attempt to challenge and renegotiate the power of researchers are more likely to be found within qualitative research, especially that informed by feminist, Indigenous and anti-racist theoretical and methodological perspectives.

More equitable power relationships between researchers and those who are researched means a redefinition of traditional relationships involved in the research process. However, this can be difficult for those used to operating within Eurocentric approaches, as it involves researchers, those who participate in research and bureaucratic policies and processes such as ethics committees. Issues of power and control must be negotiated from the inception of the project, and remain the responsibility of all those committed to research that attempts to redefine relationships of power by locating it with others rather than with researchers alone.

While we need to move beyond simplistic notions of researchers being all powerful, there are those who maintain that the balance of power remains with the researcher. For example, Hatch (2002) has commented that teachers 'often perceive themselves to be in a subordinate position in relation to educational researchers' (2002, p. 67). Others (e.g. Grieshaber, 2007) maintain that the balance of power in qualitative research can fluctuate constantly, moving from researcher to participants and back again, even in the course of a moment during the research or a sentence or two in the reporting. Researchers must be aware of how relationships of power are unpredictable and can change rapidly. The traditional power associated with researchers can be redefined by negotiating power relationships through more collaborative approaches found in critical, poststructural and social identity theories and their associated methodologies.

Critical approaches raise questions to heighten awareness of inequities and have the potential to realise social change (Lather, 2007). Research inspired by critical theory includes neo-Marxist, race-specific, feminist, praxis-oriented, Freirian participatory, action research and gay and lesbian studies (Lather, 2007). Theories with poststructural and postmodern roots use deconstruction and other methodological techniques, and have the capacity to 'Interrupt binaries; not just reverse the model' (Lather, 2007, p. 165). They include postcolonial, queer theory, postfeminist, post-race theories and cultural studies (Lather, 2007). However, as Spivak (1987) notes, theories associated with postmodern positions do not differentiate between those that perpetuate dominance and those that contest oppression, and so are 'not necessarily critical or emancipatory in their claims' (Moosa-Mitha, 2005, p. 64). Social identity theories are located within oppositional social movements (for example, anti-racist, queer, disability, Aboriginal) and have 'the elimination of oppression, as experienced by their collectivity, as its central focus' (Moosa-Mitha, 2005, p. 61). As well as analysing social reality, anti-oppressive theories have at least two things in common: a vision of social justice and an understanding that 'subordinate/dominant power relations characterize social relationships in society' (Moosa-Mitha, 2005, p. 61). Anti-oppressive or difference centred research approaches consider that 'not everything is knowable' (2005, p. 66), that difference is 'a fluid concept' (2005, p. 67) and that knowledge is 'intersubjective and dialogical' (2005, p. 67). Those who write from anti-oppressive perspectives tend to name their approaches specifically—for example, feminist anti-racist research methodologies (Dei, 2005), decolonising methodologies (Tuhiwai Smith, 1999), anti-racist research methodologies (Okolie, 2005), anti-oppressive research (Moosa-Mitha, 2005; Potts and Brown, 2005), anti-colonial research (Max, 2005), Indigenous methodologies (Kovach, 2005), the Indigenist research paradigm (Martin, 2008) and restorative research methodologies (Ball, 2005; Ball and Pence, 2006).

Characteristics of approaches that seek to challenge traditional power relationships between researchers and participants include active and respectful consultation; negotiation and involvement of participants from initial thoughts about the possibility of research to the negotiation of all aspects of it, including access, ethics, research questions, research design, data collection, analysis, ongoing contact and 'reporting'; and the recognition of rights including intellectual property (for example, who owns the knowledge/data).

Children and power relations

Until relatively recently, power relations with children involved in research were not addressed. Consent from a parent or guardian was considered adequate and children were not consulted as to their willingness to be involved. Much research with children has been based in the paradigm of developmental psychology and drawn on positivist and constructivist approaches (see Greig, Taylor and Mackay, 2007). It is much less common for research with children to draw on critical and post-oriented theories and methodologies. Positivist and constructivist approaches are worlds apart ontologically and epistemologically from critical approaches or anything that might be described as 'post'-type approaches (see Denzin and Lincoln, 2005; Hatch, 2002). This means that research with children that is informed by positivism and constructivism is far less likely to have social justice as a goal than critical and postmodern approaches. However, much has been written about research with children over the past few years, specifically in relation to ethics, consent and participation in research. On the whole, this literature draws on the theoretical perspective of the sociology of childhood, which positions children as competent actors in their everyday worlds and capable of making decisions about participating in or withdrawing from research (Farrell, 2005).

The increasingly large body of literature about participatory approaches to research involving children has become more dominant during these early years of the twenty-first century. However, it has been questioned recently because of the uncritical ways in which participatory approaches are deployed in research with children (Gallacher and Gallacher, 2008). Gallacher and Gallacher point out that, in contrast to traditional and psychological social research, participatory approaches appear to be 'emancipatory and democratic, respecting children's agency' (2008, p. 499).

That children's ideas can be accessed through participatory approaches is particularly appealing, and is seemingly an epistemological and ontological change from psychological paradigms, which have essentialised children by focusing 'on the character of children's otherness, and their progress towards sameness, that is towards adulthood' (Mayall, 1999, p. 11). But, as Gallacher and Gallacher note, the attractiveness of participatory approaches may conceal the need to think more critically about them.

While Gallacher and Gallacher (2008) raise several points, their ontology of 'emergence', 'becoming' and 'inexpertise' (2008, p. 511) deserves comment because it is more attitudinal than about 'methods or techniques', and relates to all research—not just participatory approaches with children. They put forward the notion of methodological immaturity as a way of beginning to '(re)position social research—and life more generally—as a necessarily complex, incomplete and messy process' (2008, p. 511). They suggest that researchers should proceed from positions of ignorance (rather than expertise) given that, in the context of the research they are undertaking, they come from positions of 'incompleteness and immaturity' (2008, p. 512). This is similar to the position of researchers as learners and not-knowing that is aligned with anti-oppressive research (Moosa-Mitha, 2005). There are difficulties with this position, again produced by dominant Western traditions which see immaturity, incompetence, vulnerability and not-knowing as contingencies that must be overcome. However, the upshot of Gallacher and Galacher's (2008) claims is that research, like the social world, is 'inherently unpredictable ... Methodological immaturity privileges open-ended process over predefined technique. It does not aim to discover or uncover a pre-existing world, offering instead experimentation, innovation and "making do"' (2008, p. 513). Research, then, is about relationships between researchers and participants and what occurs between the beginning and the end of the project. However, as Ball (2005) and Ball and Pence (2006) have shown, research partnerships and ethical responsibilities with Indigenous communities continue after the project has come to a 'formal' end. This is worth considering for any research.

Research using a deficit model

Research based on a deficit model involves the use of statements or norms developed with one group of participants and applied to another group. For example, Head Start programs were initiated in the United States in the 1960s to provide compensatory early education experiences for children living in poverty. Cannella (1997) argues that Head Start programs were 'grounded in the assumption that particular groups of children are deficient, that parents are responsible for these deficiencies, and that outside intervention is necessary to overcome the problems' (1997, p. 111). Since the 1960s, these programs have been the focus of continuous research, much of it aimed at showing how such programs are beneficial. While often demonstrating what have been called benefits, the research can make cultural, socioeconomic, racial and ethnic differences appear as deficits. In Cannella's (1997) words: 'Head Start would provide an environment in which "disadvantaged" children would become like their middle-class peers, would be prepared cognitively for first grade' (1997, p. 111).

In another example about children, Lubeck (1994) demonstrates that, through developmentally appropriate practice, much child development research has endorsed the belief that 'some cultural practices are preferable (and others, if not 'deficient', [are] certainly less desirable)' (1994, p. 20). Lubeck also argues that the focus in developmentally appropriate practice on 'individuals (children and family members) [has been used] in an effort to rectify social ills' (1994, p. 20). Focusing on the individual child or family locates the problem with the individual, rather than structural factors in society. The individual or family is then the target of programs aimed at rectifying the social ills identified. This is an example of how the production of normative assumptions based on a distinct segment of the population (white upper middle- and middle-class children) has been used to promulgate norms that are then generalised to society as a whole. This can happen with both qualitative and quantitative research approaches, but is less likely with the former. Research based on assumptions of deficit or disadvantage often reflects the dominant paradigm of Eurocentric scientific research.

In their critique of Eurocentric approaches, Padilla and Lindholm (1995) show that the Eurocentric paradigm rests on three assumptions:

> ... (a) the White middle-class American (typically male) is the standard against which other groups should be compared; (b) the instruments used for assessing differences are universally applicable across groups, with perhaps only minimal adjustments for culturally diverse populations; and (c) although we need to recognize the sources of potential variance such as social class, educational attainment, gender, cultural orientation, and proficiency in English, these are nuisances that can later be discarded. (1995, p. 97)

While Padilla and Lindholm are talking about quantitative educational research, their criticism is instructive for qualitative researchers as well, because it highlights the 'biases inherent in the paradigms themselves'

(1995, p. 97). They are scathing in their analysis of how research with minority students has been used, claiming that 'when minority students are included in quantitative research, it is usually with the intent of documenting low achievement of Hispanic, African American, and, to a lesser extent, Native American students in comparison to Anglo students' (1995, p. 100). Some more recent quantitative research has attempted to address this bias, but not all. It is therefore important to be vigilant about how cultural, socioeconomic, racial and ethnic differences can be classed as deficits.

Homogeneity

The notion of homogeneity can be likened to essentialism, and is also linked to research based on deficit models. Homogeneity means using a major characteristic to group items or people. This may be by virtue of a common language (for example, Spanish speaking) or nationality (for example, Israeli). In such cases, Spanish-speaking people are 'lumped together' with no consideration given to differences within the larger group such as class, socioeconomic factors, age, migration patterns, country of birth, gender, and so on. Classing any group as homogeneous can obstruct differences that are likely to be significant in research activity, making the research seriously flawed. This can impede the trustworthiness of the data, the data analysis and the validity of the research project as a whole.

Essentialism is understood as the possession of intrinsic or characteristic properties that constitute the true nature of something. Essentialist understandings can be applied to a range of constructs including childhood, women, family, gender, men and particular ethnic groups, often producing stereotypical (mis)representations that are very powerful. However, there is no permanent and essential nature to any of these constructs because they are always changing. Childhoods today, for instance, are different from those of ten, twenty or even five years ago because of global, national, regional and local differences. They also differ according to nationality, ethnicity, 'race', gender, age, class, socioeconomic status, ability, and more. Likewise, there is no permanent and essential nature of woman, family, gender, Asian people or man. To explain further, the Eurocentric humanist understanding of 'Man' is an essentialist notion because it locates women as 'other' and sets up a binary division between women and men. There are many differences among women ('race', ethnicity, class, sexuality and age, to mention a few), which cannot be reduced to an essential understanding of who and what all women are, particularly when those differences have been essentialised as binary oppositions to male characteristics. The postmodern project, together with its associated research paradigm, has been valuable for those who have been marginalised by essentialist understandings (for example, so-called minority groups, children and women) that privilege one truth, which is based on Western reasoning and objectivity. Research activity therefore needs to appreciate the heterogeneity of participants in research projects and the fact that our current social conditions are characterised by plurality, difference, ambivalence and contradictions. Ensuring that research activity reflects the diversity of particular groups being studied is a particularly important equity consideration. Whether children, ethnic groups, Indigenous people, women or aged people are involved in research, the temptation to treat the groups as homogeneous must be resisted.

DETECTING BIAS IN RESEARCH

When designing research projects, researchers rely on the resources they have available to them by drawing on theoretical standpoints and perspectives, either explicit or implicit. Interacting with the world being studied can produce particular effects on the researcher, as well as on the participants. Researchers themselves embody particular beliefs, values and interests, which are often reflected in the way the problem and questions are formulated, research is designed, data collected and interpreted, and findings shared and displayed.

Locating your own particular values, interests and beliefs that may interfere with justice and fairness in the research endeavour is an important part of researcher responsibility. This means researchers need to foreground their own investments and interests, standpoints and motivations, explicitly stating their theoretical positions and assumptions. Such foregrounding is often referred to as self-reflexivity. Self-reflexivity involves deconstructing the ways in which our desires shape the texts we produce. It also necessitates deconstructing the relations of difference—of 'race', class, gender, and so on—that have been instrumental in the design of the research process. Because researchers 'cannot assume they share the world experience of the researched' (Mayall, 1999, p. 14), being self-reflexive involves incorporating the views of those researched into the whole research process.

In more traditional research approaches, the analysis and presentation of data represent areas where the 'researched' have had least power (Mayall, 1999) as data are often removed and those who provided it have limited, if any, access to it. Potts and Brown (2005) point out that 'the term "data" in its origins means "gift"' (2005, p. 269). Thinking about data as a gift from participants is important in rethinking power relations between researchers and participants, and is a significant part of reflexivity. Being reflexive can help researchers address concerns about what is written and presented. The written and presentation aspects of any research project are inevitably a process of combining participants' experience and communication with that of the researchers, converting it into whatever has been negotiated with participants both beforehand and as the process unfolds.

Self-reflexivity in analysing research

- Research is about relationships; how have I involved participants meaningfully in the research process, including the design?
- How have my ontologies and epistemologies affected the design, process and outcomes?
- Check with participants that you have understood what they mean.
- Provide participants with transcripts, field notes, diary entries, and so on to make sure their input is represented accurately.
- Check your interpretations of what participants say with the participants themselves (as an ongoing part of the research).
- Involve participants in conversations about the analyses and seek their input.
- Make available the interpretation and analyses to participants and encourage them to respond.
- Can participants see their perspectives reflected in the study?

Eurocentric or dominant perspectives can influence the research at all stages of the process, making equity seem unimportant. As research is about relationships between researchers and participants, equity and social justice should be considered from start to finish, and include ontological and epistemological positions, initial decisions about the research design, formulation of hypotheses or research questions, consideration of variables, selection of participants, analyses, interpretation and reporting of data.

DETECTING BIAS IN QUANTITATIVE RESEARCH

In hypotheses, watch for:

- hypotheses, situations and measures that maximise group differences and ignore settings in which differences are not likely to be observed

- individual studies showing gender or race differences that are not shown in multiple studies.

In theories, watch for:

- deviance and disorder that blames mothers or individuals for life circumstances
- research on families that implies the nuclear family is the norm 'against which others are compared'
- theories that position different racial groups as inferior or as 'other'.

When it comes to variables, watch for:

- use of instruments or measures as universally applicable across groups with little alteration for gender, age or ethnic group
- describing something as negative in one ethnic group and as something quite different in another group
- confusion of gender and sexuality/sexual orientation
- use of 'white' data-gatherers in research about ethnic groups
- socioeconomic indicators not being taken into account (Quina and Kulberg, 1988, pp. 72–6).

SUMMARY

Designing research for equity means:

- being alert to how your research design might position individuals and groups who have been traditionally 'othered' in research (Indigenous peoples, ethnic groups, refugees, children, people with disabilities, women)
- recognising and reworking power relationships between researcher and participants
- analysing how homogeneity is being constructed in the research and removing it
- rejecting deficit models of research; learning self-reflexivity as a researcher
- minimising bias in the theories, questions, methodologies, methods, hypotheses, variables, participants and interpretations used during the research process.

QUESTIONS FOR REFLECTION

1. Whose interests does the research serve (who benefits—researcher, participants, community, other)?
2. Who will be involved, why and how? How is it evident that research is about relationships?

3 What are the benefits for the participants, funding bodies and researcher?
4 What have I included in the research design to avoid a conflict of interest among these three positions?
5 What is the goal of the research, and how does it relate to issues of equity and social justice?
6 How have I considered the political implications of researching with particular groups before embarking on the research?
7 How are data recognised as the intellectual property of participants and how is this reflected in my reporting?
8 What are the criteria for judging the quality of the research and who gets to decide this?
9 How have I made sure that my research design does not rely on a deficit model?
10 How is diversity within groups (such as children or Spanish-speaking people) reflected in the research design?
11 How is my research design reflexive?
12 How have I understood relations of power between the researcher and participants?
13 How do the ethics of the research allow for renegotiations of power relations between researcher and participants?

REFERENCES

Ball, J. 2005 'Restorative Research Partnerships in Indigenous Communities', in A. Farrell (ed.), *Ethical Rresearch with Children*, Open University Press, Maidenhead, pp. 81–96.

Ball, J. and Pence, A. 2006 *Supporting Indigenous Children's Development: Community–University Partnerships*, University of British Columbia Press, Vancouver.

Brown, L. and Strega, S. 2005 'Introduction: Transgressive Possibilities', in L. Brown and S. Strega (eds), *Research as Resistance: Critical, Indigenous, and Anti-oppressive Approaches*, Canadian Scholars' Press, Toronto, pp. 1–17.

Cannella, G.S. 1997 *Deconstructing Early Childhood Education: Social Justice and Revolution*, Peter Lang, New York.

Dei, G.J.S. 2005 'Critical Issues in Anti-racist Research Methodologies', in G.J.S. Dei and G.S. Johal (eds), *Critical Issues in Anti-racist Research Methodologies*, Peter Lang, New York, pp. 1–27.

Denzin, N.K. and Lincoln, Y.S. 2005 'Introduction: The Discipline and Practice of Qualitative Research', in N.K. Denzin and Y.S. Lincoln (eds), *The Sage Handbook of Qualitative Research*, 3rd ed., Sage, Thousand Oaks, CA, pp. 1–32.

Farrell, A. (ed.) 2005 'Ethics and Research with Children', in A. Farrell (ed.), *Ethical Research with Children*, Open University Press, Maidenhead, pp. 1–14.

Gallacher, L. and Gallacher, M. 2008 'Methodological Immaturity in Childhood Research? Thinking Through "Participatory Methods"', *Childhood*, vol. 15, no. 4, pp. 499–516.

Grieg, A., Tayler, J. and MacKay, T. 2007 *Doing Research with Children*, 2nd ed., Sage, London.

Grieshaber, S. 2007 *Never Certain: Research Predicaments in the Everyday World of Schools*, in J.A. Hatch (ed.), *Early Childhood Qualitative Research*, RoutledgeFalmer, New York, pp. 147–65.

Hatch, J.A. 2002 *Doing Qualitative Research in Education Settings*, State University of New York Press, Albany, NY.

Kovach, M. 2005 'Emerging from the Margins: Indigenous Methodologies', in L. Brown and S. Strega (eds), *Research as Resistance: Critical, Indigenous, and Anti-oppressive Approaches*, Canadian Scholars' Press, Toronto, pp. 19–36.

Lather, P. 2007 *Getting Lost: Feminist Efforts towards Double(d) Science*, State University of New York Press, Albany, NY.

Lubeck, S. 1994 'The Politics of Developmentally Appropriate Practice: Exploring Issues of Culture, Class and Curriculum', in B.L. Mallory and R.S. New (eds), *Diversity and Developmentally Appropriate Practices: Challenges for Early Childhood Education*, Teachers College Press, New York, pp. 17–43.

Martin, K.L. 2008 *Please Knock Before You Enter: Aboriginal Regulation of Outsiders and the Implications for Researchers*, PostPressed, Brisbane.

Max, K. 2005 'Anti-colonial Research: Working as an Ally with Aboriginal Peoples', in G.J.S. Dei and G.S. Johal (eds), *Critical Issues in Anti-racist Research Methodologies*, Peter Lang, New York, pp. 79–94.

Mayall, B. 1999, 'Children and Childhood', in S. Hood, B. Mayall and S. Oliver (eds), *Critical Issues in Social Research: Power and Prejudice*, Open University Press, Buckingham, pp. 10–24.

Mayall, B., Hood, S. and Oliver, S. 1999 'Introduction', in S. Hood, B. Mayall and S. Oliver (eds), *Critical Issues in Social research: Power and Prejudice*, Open University Press, Buckingham, pp. 1–9.

Moosa-Mitha, M. 2005 'Situating Anti-oppressive Theories within Critical and Difference-centered Perspectives', in L. Brown and S. Strega (eds), *Research as Resistance: Critical, Indigenous, and Anti-oppressive Approaches*, Canadian Scholars' Press, Toronto, pp. 37–72.

Oakley, A. 1999 'People's Ways of Knowing: Gender and Methodology', in S. Hood, B. Mayall and S. Oliver (eds), *Critical Issues on Social Research: Power and Prejudice*, Open University Press, Buckingham, pp. 154–70.

——2005 'Toward an Anti-racist Research Framework: The Case for Interventive In-depth Interviewing', in G.J.S. Dei and G.S. Johal (eds), *Critical Issues in Anti-racist Research Methodologies*, Peter Lang, New York, pp. 241–67.

Okolie, A.C. 2005 'Towards an Anti-racist Research Framework: The Case for Interventive In-depth Interviewing', in G.J.S. Dei and G.S. Johal (eds), *Critical Issues in Anti-racist Research Methodologies*, Peter Lang, New York, pp. 241–67.

Padilla, A. and Lindholm, K.J. 1995 'Quantitative Research with Ethnic Minorities', in J.A. Banks and C.A. Banks (eds), *Handbook of Research on Multicultural Education*, Macmillan, New York, pp. 97–113.

Potts, K. and Brown, L. 2005 'Becoming an Anti-oppressive Researcher', in L. Brown and S. Strega (eds), *Research as Resistance: Critical, Indigenous, and Anti-oppressive Approaches*, Canadian Scholars' Press, Toronto, pp. 255–86.

Quina, K. and Kulberg, J. 1988 'The Experimental Psychology Course', in P. Bronstein and K. Quina (eds), *Teaching a Psychology of People*, American Psychological Society, Washington DC, pp. 69–79.

Spivak, G.C. 1987 *In Other Worlds: Essays in Cultural Politics*, Methuen, London and New York.

Strega, S. 2005 'The View from the Poststructural Margins: Epistemology and Methodology Reconsidered', in L. Brown and S. Strega (eds), *Research as Resistance: Critical, Indigenous, and Anti-oppressive Approaches*, Canadian Scholars' Press, Toronto, pp. 199–235.

Tuhiwai Smith, L. 1999 *Decolonizing Methodologies: Research and Indigenous Peoples*, University of Otago Press, Dunedin, New Zealand.

FURTHER READING

Ball, J. and Pence, A. 2006 *Supporting Indigenous Children's Development: Community–University Partnerships*, University of British Columbia Press, Vancouver. Ball and Pence discuss how restorative research methodologies have been used with many First Nations communities in Canada.

Gallacher, L. and Gallacher, M. 2008 'Methodological Immaturity in Childhood Research? Thinking Through "Participatory Methods"', *Childhood*, vol. 15, no. 4, pp. 499–516. This article challenges readers to think critically about participatory approaches that have become dominant in research with children.

Potts, K. and Brown, L. 2005 'Becoming an Anti-oppressive Researcher', in L. Brown and S. Strega (eds), *Research as Resistance: Critical, Indigenous, and Anti-oppressive Approaches*, Canadian Scholars' Press, Toronto, pp. 255–86. This chapter explains what anti-oppressive research is and describes what is involved in such an approach.

11

Mixed-method designs

Iram Siraj-Blatchford

This chapter critically examines the claim that early childhood research has become dominated by positivism, technicism and the reification of dominant conceptions of quality. Following Farquar (1999), the chapter considers the standards, stakeholder, postmodern and ecological approaches to quality in early childhood education, arguing that to the extent that any paradigm may be considered dominant it would be one that at times may be considered to embrace all four of these perspectives. Mixed-method approaches and perspectives also provide a means of rising above the false dualities (of qualitative versus quantitative) and essentialisations characteristic of the 'paradigm wars'.

Early childhood researchers who recognise the part that their study may play within a broader collaborative early childhood research program may build creatively upon the findings of their peers, creating ongoing patterns (or programs) of research that may involve individual qualitative studies establishing important variables, which may then be investigated further in correlation studies that examine the impact of differences and in randomised controlled experiments that isolate the underlying variables further, and lead to the development of more focused qualitative studies to provide explanatory evidence.

INTRODUCTION

Oakley (2004) has argued strongly that the 'paradigm divide' between qualitative and quantitative research communities continues to constitute a major problem in educational research, and I would argue that this persists in being the case in early childhood research when other fields have moved beyond this false dichotomy. Oakley refers to a number of critiques of alleged 'misplaced positivism' in educational research. Research in the field of early childhood studies and education has not been immune to these criticisms, and specific concerns have been expressed regarding alleged technicism and the reification of dominant conceptions of early educational quality.

Many research students in early childhood education have been influenced strongly by the work of Dahlberg and Moss (2005) in particular, who have characterised the early childhood research field as one that is crudely positivist, aiming: 'to discover the truth, rather than create particular and provisional understandings' (p. 6). In many respects, this critique of the dominant language of quality in early childhood provides a timely warning. It is important that researchers recognise that 'quality' is a socially constructed concept. But when they argue that in the early years educational 'quality' has achieved hegemonic status and 'closure', so that research has become restricted to technical questions about effectiveness and efficiency their case may at times be overstated:

> They are not [addressing] questioning questions, which ask about value, acknowledge the probability of multiple perspectives and meanings, diversity and uncertainty, and which open up for democratic participation, dialogue and further questioning. (2005, p. 2)

It is hard to see how these criticisms can be sustained against the evidence of recent critical research reviews conducted by the US Committee on Early Childhood Pedagogy (Bowman et al., 2001); in the Outcomes of Early Childhood Education (Mitchell et al., 2008); or in *Improving Children's Attainment Through a Better Quality of Family-based Support for Early Learning* (Siraj-Blatchford and Siraj-Blatchford, 2009). Each of these major reviews provides evidence of research that has engaged with the question of what it is that constitutes quality, and research that offers practitioner and parent (if not always children's) perspectives. Yet Dahlberg and Moss (2005) argue that early childhood research has become dominated by a perspective in which educational institutions are now seen as: 'first and foremost, a site for technical practice, seeking the best methods and procedures for delivering predetermined outcomes' (2005, p. 2). One reading of Dahlberg and Moss's argument would give emphasis to their concern that the site of political and ethical discourse in early childhood education should be at a local 'micro-political' rather than at a national level. This might be read as an appeal to regaining professional autonomy and local control of the field in the face of greater national centralisation, accountability and globalisation. But, given the unprecedented level of change and funding for early childhood education and care around the world in recent years, a concomitant increase in public accountability might reasonably be expected. In this, research has certainly played a part; however, the question is whether this has become its dominant role or whether it is continuing to provide a critical enrichment of our knowledge and understanding of the field.

Farquhar (1999) has suggested that there are currently four distinct approaches to the question of 'quality' in early childhood research: 'the standards approach', 'the stakeholder approach', 'the postmodernist approach', and the 'ecological and ethnographic approaches'. While the first of these has been concerned to provide evidence to policy-makers, the stakeholder approach (Farquhar, 1990; Balaguer, Mestres and Penn, 1992) has been applied significantly to support the efforts of minority ethnic groups. Perhaps the most notable example of this has been research supporting Maori interests in cultural rejuvenation and language promotion, and in the development of the *Te Whariki* approach to early childhood education in New Zealand (Irwin, 1990; Siraj-Blatchford, 1999). As Farquar (1999) argues, the postmodernist approach (Dahlberg, Moss and Pence, 1999) may be seen as more of a critique of the standards approach than any fully developed alternative (Farquar, 1999, p. 5). These perspectives are also identified in Siraj-Blatchford and Wong (1999), where it is argued that objectivist approaches are required alongside the more relativist alternatives and that there is a need for more dialogic approaches to be taken in cross-cultural studies. Dahlberg and Moss (2005) themselves acknowledge that the increase in state interest in, for example, the United Kingdom has strongly been driven by concerns about inequality. What they fail to recognise is that a good deal of the early childhood research that they might characterise as being fundamentally about 'standards' has often applied multiple perspectives and has been driven by precisely the same concerns.

In their critique of the dominant language of quality in early childhood education Dahlberg and Moss (2005) specifically refer to the Early Childhood Environment Rating Scale Revised (ECERS-R; Harms, Clifford and Cryer, 1998) as a 'regulatory technology'. Yet, as has been argued elsewhere (Siraj-Blatchford and Wong, 1999; Sylva, Siraj-Blatchford et al., 2006), it is widely recognised that quality in preschool practice must be contextualised in a way relevant to the values of a particular society (Dahlberg, Moss and Pence, 1999). But, as Woodhead (1996) and Siraj-Blatchford and Wong (1999) have suggested, while 'quality' may in part be considered subjective, that does not mean that it should be considered arbitrary.

As Dahlberg, Moss and Pence (1999) have documented, the ECERS was originally developed in the United States in the late 1970s in a process that involved early childhood 'experts' and early childhood trainers. It was therefore predicated on US practitioner interpretations of quality and good practice. Each item on the scale describes a concrete feature of the US preschool environment or an element of practice. The quality statements reflected in the scales were drawn from the 'real-life' observations of these authorities, and their construction constitutes a genuine engagement with early childhood practice. Of course, these processes of construction, and the subsequent processes of standardisation, should not be seen as a 'one-off', up-front activity (Siraj-Blatchford and Wong, 1999). Since the 1980 publication of the ECERS, the instrument has been subject to major revisions that led to the publication of the ECERS-R (Revised) in 1998. These processes of revision are outlined in the introduction to the scale itself (Harms, Clifford and Cryer, 1998). The processes included content analyses, a review of national and international ECERS studies and feedback, through focus groups and questionnaires, from ECERS users. Moreover, there has been a vigorous research and practice literature on the ECERS.

In selecting any particular set of instruments, we do inevitably limit the possibilities for explanation that are open to us, but research tools like the ECERS can be adapted or extended to suit immediate local contexts and needs. In fact, this is precisely what happened in the case of research conducted in England for the Effective Provision of Pre-school Education (EPPE) Project (Siraj-Blatchford and Sylva, 2004). In its application in countries outside the United States, the ECERS has been subject to translation and other major revisions to suit particular cultural contexts (e.g. Tietze et al., 1996). In the United Kingdom, EPPE developed the ECERS-E (Extended) in much the same way as the original ECERS and the ECERS-R, in an extended iterative process that involved both early childhood authorities and practitioners. The ECERS-E was developed with the explicit purpose of providing more relevant 'quality' data for the UK local context (Sylva, Siraj-Blatchford and Taggart, 2006).

While there is always a danger when applying any research instrument that it may become 'reified' in the process, much more fundamentally in educational research, the research questions that we ask and any hypotheses that we test are always drawn from (however weakly or strongly defined) established paradigms, and these may be seen as value loaded in favour of particular explanations. The subsequent biases may be professional, they may originate at a local cultural level or they may even be due to more global assumptions. Social practices are inevitably taken for granted, and competent social researchers have always recognised the need to critically consider the familiar 'strange' (Erickson, 1986, see also Chapter 16). But for Dahlberg and Moss (2005), together with an increasing number of other writers, this recognition has led to an outright rejection of any form of objectivism. While we can share their scepticism regarding the possibilities for any absolute value neutrality in research, this total rejection of objectivism may be seen as a serious over-reaction. In a 2007 publication, Moss has argued the same case, and applies comparable terms when he writes about early childhood researchers adopting 'modernist' and 'foundationalist' perspectives on the one hand, and researchers applying 'postmodernist' and 'post-foundationalist' perspectives on the other. Each of these perspectives is presented as offering distinct and incommensurate paradigms that impose fundamental limitations on communication and collaboration between the respective researchers. To explain this argument further, it is useful to consider the use of the term 'paradigm' in this context further.

PARADIGMS IN SOCIAL RESEARCH

As suggested in Chapter 3, it was Thomas Kuhn (1970) who first applied the term 'paradigm' in the philosophy of science. For Kuhn, paradigms were considered to offer distinct scientific world-views, providing the basis for defining the puzzles and questions that might legitimately be pursued, as well as the criteria for assessing any solutions to them. Kuhn provided an account of the history of science that described extended periods where scientific knowledge accumulated within 'normal science' paradigms, which were grounded on axiomatic statements of 'truth' that seemed so obvious they were accepted by everyone. To take a concrete example, an elaborate science of astronomy was initially constructed around the popular axiom that the earth was the centre of the universe. Kuhn argued that paradigms of this kind were only replaced (by 'revolutionary' science) when there was substantial (anomalous) empirical evidence against them. But paradigms are often so different that researchers belonging to different camps are unable to find a common language in which to conduct a meaningful comparison: they are 'incommensurate'. Scientific paradigms might therefore be considered to act at times as competing ideologies within research communities.

Kuhn's contribution has therefore been to identify significant social processes in the production of scientific knowledge, and these have in turn provided a major source for the postmodern critique of scientific metanarratives. But while Kuhn (1991) recognised that the natural sciences involved interpretation just as much as the social sciences, he actually expressed scepticism regarding the potential application of his theory in areas of social science which he considered were typically unable to sustain any extended period of 'normal' science. While any changes in the established axioms of natural science were typically resisted, and reinterpretations only achieved as a result of a scientific revolution, he argued that many areas of social science were pursued with the specific intention of constantly seeking newer and deeper interpretations. He also argued that new interpretations would inevitably be adopted in the social sciences whenever social and political systems changed.

The suggestion that postmodernism may be considered some kind of *refutation* of modernism is also open to serious question. As Burbules (1995) has observed, when Lyotard (1984) first defined postmodernism as an 'incredulity towards metanarratives', the term 'incredulity' should not have been considered to imply any kind of denial or rejection. It was simply intended in the sense of an 'inability to believe' (Burbules, 1995, p. 2). Lyotard fully recognised that, however ambivalent its relation to modernism had become, postmodernism was not a refutation of modernism; rather, it was a product of it:

> ... it is a mistake to think that postmodernism is about the rejection of modernist conceptions of language, science, ethics, reason, and justice. Thinking that it is would require that we ask for the arguments that would support such a rejection, and ask for an account of what one is going to replace them with [and] as soon as one offers something that looks like counterarguments, or tries to offer criteria of a 'better' alternative, he or she is promptly caught up in a contradiction, for these are precisely the types of things that are being denied. (Burbules, 1995)

But for Moss (2007), anti-foundationalism and postmodernism are drawn well beyond the traditional realms of philosophical scepticism and often appear to reject the very idea or possibility of representation, adopting a more radical relativism than would be accepted by many of the authorities that he cites. Derrida explicitly rejected such a position (Caputo, 1996), and arguably Foucault implicitly did so as well (Prado, 2005). In arguing against the definition of 'quality', Moss quotes from his 1999 collaboration with Dahlberg and Pence:

> ... the concept of quality in relation to early childhood institutions is irretrievably modernist, it is part of the Cartesian dream of certainty and

> the Enlightenment's ambition for Progress and Truth. It is about a search for definitive and universal criteria, certainty and order—or it is about nothing. (Dahlberg, Moss and Pence, 1999, p. 232)

The association of modernism with foundationalism here is simply assumed, and the suggestion that educational research searches for universal truth and certainty *or for 'nothing'* is startling. It is also in part symptomatic of many recent critical discussions of quantitative methods that appear to have been trapped in a similar 'time warp' (Yu, 2003) where, for example, many basic textbooks continue to exclusively associate quantitative methods with positivism or place them within a positivist frame of reference. This is despite the discussion of numerous alternative epistemologies and methodologies, such as postpositivism, pragmatism, and scientific and critical realism, which have been discussed in numerous books and articles since the 1980s. The fact is that few, if any, social scientists today would subscribe to orthodox (or naïve) positivism. In any event, the association of the dominant forms of early childhood research with positivism may be seen as something of a red herring; the *substantive* critique that is actually made by Moss (2007) is that science is pursued according to a naïve realism.

This false duality constructed between 'naïve realism' and 'radical relativism' has been discussed by Pring (2000), who considers this form of binary thinking totally unsustainable. In any event, it is difficult to envisage how the dichotomisation can be seen as anything more than unjustified essentialisation. Realism and relativism might just as easily be considered to offer the most extreme positions in a continuum of positions that could be taken in the practice of social scientific investigation. Contemporary pragmatism offers a range of possible approaches and, as Thayer-Bacon (2003) has argued, a number of alternative positions have been (and will undoubtedly continue to be) constructed employing qualified relativism that (more or less) embrace Peirce's (1992) 'fallibilism', James' (1909) truths as 'satisfactory relations' and Dewey's (1938) notion of 'warranted assertability'. As Stephen Best (2007) has argued, feminist standpoint theory has also shown that 'postmodern epistemologies are not necessarily anti-modern; rather, at their best, they are a vital continuation of the rational and critical resources of learning developed by science, the Enlightenment, and democratic norms'.

BEYOND ESSENTIALISATION AND FALSE DUALITIES

Stephen Fuchs' (2001) sociology of cultural networks 'dissolves' (as opposed to solves) the problems of paradigmatic incommensurability (along with insider and outsider perspectives) by showing that essentialisation may itself be seen as the response of tightly connected social networks (for example, research communities) to any competition or threat to their foundations, where they act to 'isolate and shelter [their] basic certainties' (2001, pp. 16–17). In these circumstances:

> Each network will observe the other's core as a contingent construct, not as a basic natural necessity. They will behave as constructivists about the other's core practices, and as realists about their own. They will debunk each other's core as being composed of 'ideologies'—beliefs and ideas suspiciously unaware or deceitful of their 'true' motives and interests—while asserting that their own ideas and beliefs are just right and righteous, and that they capture the empirical and moral order of the world as it really is, without any construction going on at all. (2001, p. 34)

The lesson to be learnt from considering these apparent 'paradigm' struggles in this way is, as Fuchs suggests, to recognise that 'the truth of a science is its truth, not the truth of science as such. A science has only the foundations it builds for itself, and it has those until further notice, until it changes these foundations.' (2001, p. 74). Fuchs' overall argument is therefore that we should respond to the challenges of anti-foundationalism and scepticism with a sociology of foundations that explains them (or their absence): 'In this approach antifoundationalism and scepticism signal a local fragmentation in social solidarity within (weak) cultures, not a global and philosophical crisis of representation.' (2001, p. 74)

As Fuchs points out, 'paradigm incommensurability' involves a good deal more than simply people misunderstanding each other, and is more the result than any cause of a breakdown in communication. Also, the good news is that 'incommensurability is not opposed to communication, but actually encourages and energises it, by irritating the background certainties and institutional invisibilities taken for granted in each of the interacting cultures' (2001, p. 93).

From this perspective, Dahlberg, Moss and Pence's (1999) arguments may be seen to be themselves symptomatic of an inherent weakness in the culture of early childhood research. Efforts should therefore be made to reduce fragmentation through improved communication and collaboration. But a significant weakness in Moss' (2007) paper that addresses this problem directly, is that it fails to take into account the considerable efforts that are already being made to achieve this, particularly in the context of educational research employing mixed methodologies. As Tashakkori and Teddlie (2003) argue that in the United States, it has partly been the success of mixed-method research that has caused the 'paradigm wars' to be 'largely discredited'. In the United Kingdom, Furlong (2003) and others have also been suggesting for some years that we should now 'rise above such divisions'. The research carried out by the EPPE team since 1998 provides a notable example of a recent, and extremely influential, mixed-method study that has combined both sophisticated statistical and constructivist analysis, while making no foundationalist claims or assumptions (Siraj-Blatchford et al., 2006).

THE DIALECTICAL NATURE OF THE EPPE STUDY

While the positivism of the past has constituted (and still does to some extent) metaphysical status for a few hardened advocates, for the majority of social researchers and for the EPPE research team (to learn more about the EPPE research, see <www.eppe.ioe.ac.uk>), postpositivist approaches provide a means of rejecting these excesses without rejecting what they considered to be the underlying discipline of social science. Taking a scientific realist stance, the EPPE team has explicitly rejected naïve empiricism and argued that knowledge could be both fallible, partial and approximate, yet still remain 'objective' (Bunge 1993; Siraj-Blatchford et al., 2006).

The longitudinal mixed-method design of the EPPE project brought together a large-scale quantitative survey approach that involved the assessment of child development and setting quality, along with both structured and non-structured interviews and observations of practitioners and children. As Green (2005) argues, a mixed-method approach to educational inquiry engages directly with difference, and is thus able to address what she refers to as 'inherent tensions' in our work. The tensions to which she refers are concerned with the multiple audiences our research inevitably has to address; the multiple focuses upon teaching and learning program design, implementation and outcomes; and the inevitable effects of working in complex real-world contexts that have some characteristics which are unique and others shared across contexts. Green's (2005) argument is that, in all of these respects, mixed-method approaches provide a means by which differences of needs and perspectives are both respected and engaged (2005, p. 210).

The EPPE mixed-method analysis was iterative in nature as the different phases of the research and the analyses periods overlapped and facilitated in-depth discussion of emerging issues and findings. But the combination of qualitative and quantitative methods has at times itself been seen as a problem. Again, a popular argument has been that qualitative and quantitative methods are incompatible due to the inherent incompatibility or incommensurability of their underlying paradigms (Smith and Heshusius, 1986). Yet Tashakkori and Teddlie (2003) outline contenders for a distinct paradigm for mixed-methods research:

- pragmatism (Tashakkori, and Teddlie, 2003)
- the transformative-emancipatory paradigm (Mertens, 1999)
- dialectical thesis (Green and Caracelli, 1997)
- the multiple paradigm thesis (Creswell, 2003).

Scott (2007) has also made a strong argument for critical realism as both a resolution of the quantitative/qualitative divide and for combining methodologies. Perhaps most significantly, critical realism has sometimes been considered to offer the possibility of identifying the contributions of both the social structures and agencies that characterise all aspects of social life.

Yet it is interesting to note that the EPPE team never sought, nor did it ever achieve, any kind of epistemological consensus. The team members all contributed different areas of research expertise and approach. The senior members of the team met one day a week for over a decade to complete their work, and the dialogue this engendered proved fruitful in allowing emerging findings and interim analyses from the different approaches to inform and stimulate each other. The project might therefore best be considered to have operated more closely to what Green and Caracelli (1997) describe as 'dialectical'. This is a term that they attribute to Geertz (1979):

> … who argued for a continuous 'dialogical tacking' between experience-near (particular, context specific, ideographic) and experience-distant (general, universal, nomothetic) concepts, because both types of concepts are needed for comprehensiveness and meaningful understanding (1997, p. 10).

But EPPE would have to be considered a dialectical project by default rather than by prior design. It is only in retrospect that we could identify with Green and Caracelli's (2003) description of an approach that involved more than merely a mixed-method approach, but rather a 'mixed method way of thinking' (2003, p. 93). In retrospect, it is clear that we were habitually inviting each other to openly express ourselves in our own terms, to contribute to an ongoing dialogue about structures and behaviours, the particular and the general, the emic and the etic, and about our value commitments and the need for neutrality. These conversations were not (in the main) philosophical ones; as Green and Caracelli (2003) note, such conversations are related closely to the phenomenon being studied: 'But the contradictions, tensions, and oppositions are rooted in, and thereby reflect, different ways of knowing and valuing' (2003, p. 97). The practical result of these conversations was a practical, paradigmatic integration through sustained and respectful interaction. The use of mixed methods provided a study of preschool influence that was more meaningful, and provided a wider evidence base for both policy-makers and practitioners than reliance on any one form of data-gathering and approach to analysis would have achieved. Complex and pluralistic social contexts demand analysis that is formed by multiple and diverse perspectives, and this is more fruitful than reliance on only one philosophical position or methodological approach (or, indeed, belief). The EPPE conclusions were stronger for having applied a mixed-method approach within an ongoing dialogic engagement.

THE IMPLICATIONS FOR RESEARCH IN EARLY CHILDHOOD EDUCATION AND CARE MORE GENERALLY

According to McIntyre and McIntyre (2000), correlation studies dominated the quantitative work of educational researchers in the 1970s, and legitimate criticism of these approaches led to increased use of qualitative methods in the 1980s. It is interesting to note that it was these qualitative studies that bore the brunt of the critique of educational research in the 1990s. In each critique, and perhaps most significantly in the case of Tooley's (1998) report, an assumption has been made that these kinds of criticism might legitimately be levelled against publications reporting upon individual (discrete) research projects. Yet McIntyre and McIntyre cite Dunkin and Biddle (1974), who suggested that even in the 1970s, an 'ideal' *pattern* of research was widely accepted even if rarely realised. The pattern that was referred to involved individual qualitative studies establishing important variables, followed by correlation studies examining the impact of differences, and finally by randomised controlled experiments to isolate the significant variables (1974, p. 22). From this perspective, we might consider the real problem of educational research to have been more to do with the relatively early stage of development of the (educational research) scientific community and the failure of individual researchers to collaborate and build upon each other's work. It may be that more needs to be done to support the work of agencies such as the national educational research associations before individual researchers are ready to develop studies that build creatively upon the findings of their peers.

Oakley (2004) has argued that collaboration and accumulation of evidence are essential in social research: 'Unless we collect together, classify and manage knowledge in such a way that new bits of evidence can easily be added in and the picture of what we know overall then constantly revisited, we are still in the dark ages' (2004, p. 15). Arguably, there are two ways to achieve research collaboration and accumulation. In the medium and long term, it is essential that researchers develop better communication and collaboration throughout the educational research community, but in the short term, large-scale, mixed-method studies like EPPE have provided an alternative, if partial, solution.

Green (2005) argues that mixed-method approaches can create spaces for a full engagement with the challenges of understanding teaching and learning as complex processes. As Green says, in a democracy there should be space for multiple interests and methods, and the current struggles over methods are misplaced. The EPPE work has been focused upon developing better understandings to improve educational opportunities, and this has reflected our commitment to promoting equity and enhancing the quality of the early years experiences of young children, particularly those from disadvantaged groups (for example, our recent contribution of evidence from EPPE to the Cabinet Office, Equity Review Team—see Sylva, Melhuish et al., 2006). In furthering this aim, we have found that well-designed studies employing mixed-method approaches can provide an extremely fruitful way forward.

SUMMARY

I have argued that mixed-method approaches and mixed-method perspectives provide a means of rising above the false dualities and essentialisations characteristic of the 'paradigm wars'. Claims of paradigmatic incommensurability are identified as a common response of social networks (in this case, marginal methodological or philosophical research communities) to perceived threats from other competing networks. The critical claims being made against the dominant forms of educational research may therefore be seen as symptomatic of an inherent weakness in the culture of the early childhood research community. It is therefore essential that we promote greater communication across the research community and engage directly with these substantive criticisms.

The chapter critically examined the claim that early childhood educational research has become dominated by positivism and technicism, and has reified dominant conceptions of quality. The chapter shows how it is possible (and legitimate) for a researcher to accept the critique of postmodernism without becoming a postmodernist.

QUESTIONS FOR REFLECTION

1 To what extent would you consider your own work to be the product of a particular research community or perspective?
2 To what extent does any research community or perspective with which you align yourself apply its critical arguments reflexively to consider its own underlying assumptions?
3 How does your proposed research study build upon the findings of earlier research?
4 How might future researchers build upon the study that you are currently conducting?
5 What standards of evidence does your research provide that would warrant its attention from practitioners or policy-makers.

REFERENCES

Balaguer, I., Mestres, J. and Penn, H. 1992 *Quality in Services for Young Children*, European Commission for Equal Opportunities Unit, Brussels.

Best, S. 2007 'Is Science Multicultural? Postcolonialism, Feminism, and Epistemologies', <www.drstevebest.org/Essays/IsScienceMulticultural.htm> accessed 2 December 2009.

Bowman, B., Donovan, S. and Burns, S. (eds) 2001 *Eager to Learn: Educating Our Preschoolers, Committee on Early Childhood Pedagogy*, National Academic Press, Washington, DC.

Bunge, M. 1993 'Realism and Antirealism in Social Science', *Theory and Decision*, vol. 35, no. 3, pp. 207–35.

Burbules, N. 1995 'Postmodern Doubt and Philosophy of Education', *Philosophy of Education*, vol. 118, pp. 39–48.

Caputo, J. (ed.) 1996 *Deconstruction in a Nutshell: A Conversation with Jacques Derrida*, vol. 1, Fordham University Press, Bronx, NY.

Creswell, J. 2003 *Research Design: Qualitative, Quantitative and Mixed Methods Approaches*, Sage, Thousand Oaks, CA.

Dahlberg, G. and Moss, P. 2005 *Ethics and Politics in Early Childhood Education*, Routledge-Falmer, Abingdon.

Dahlberg, G., Moss, P. and Pence, A. 1999 *Beyond Quality in Early Childhood Education and Care*, Falmer Press, London.

Dewey, J. 1938 *Logic: The Theory of Inquiry*, Henry Holt and Co., New York.

Dunkin, M.J. and Biddle, B.J. 1974 *The Study of Teaching*, Holt, Rinehart and Winston, New York.

Erickson, F. 1986 'Qualitative Methods in Research on Teaching', in M.C. Wittrock (ed.), *Handbook of Research on Teaching*, Macmillan, New York, pp. 119–61.

Farquhar, S. 1990 'Quality in Early Education and Care: What Do We Mean?' *Early Child Development and Care*, no. 64, pp. 71–83.

——1999 'Research and the Production of "Worthwhile" Knowledge about Quality in Early Years Education', paper presented at the 1999 AARE—NZARE Conference on Research in Education, Melbourne.

Fuchs, S. 2001 *Against Essentialism*, University of Chicago Press, Chicago.

Furlong, J. 2003 *BERA at 30: Have We Come of Age?* presidential address to the annual conference of the British Educational Research Association, Heriot-Watt University, Edinburgh.

Geertz, C. 1979 'From the Native's Point of View: On the Nature of Anthropological Understanding', in P. Rabinow and W. Sullivan, (eds), *Interpretative Social Science*, University of California Press, Berkeley, CA.

Green, J. 2005 'The Generative Potential of Mixed Methods Enquiry', *International Journal of Research and Method in Education*, vol. 28, no. 2, pp. 207–11.

Green, J. and Caracelli, V. (eds) 1997 *Advances in Mixed Method Evaluation: The Challenges and Benefits of Integrating Diverse Paradigms*, New Directions for Evaluation, no. 74, Jossey-Bass, San Francisco.

——2003 'Making Paradigmatic Sense of Mixed Methods Practice', in A. Tashakkori, and C. Teddlie (eds), *Handbook of Mixed Methods in Social and Behavioural Research*, Sage, Thousand Oaks, CA.

Harms, T., Clifford, M. and Cryer, D. 1998 *Early Childhood Environment Rating Scale, Revised Edition (ECERS-R)*, Teachers College Press, Vermont.

Irwin, K. 1990 'The Politics of Kohanga Reo', in S. Middleton, J. Codd and A. Jones (eds), *New Zealand Education Policy Today: Critical Perspectives*, Allen & Unwin, Auckland, pp. 110–20.

James, W. 1909 *The Meaning of Truth*, Harvard University Press, Cambridge, MA.

Kuhn, T. 1970 *The Structure of Scientific Revolutions*, University of Chicago Press, Chicago.

——1991 'The Natural and the Human Sciences', in D. Hiley, J. Bohman, and R. Shusterman (eds), *The Interpretative Turn: Philosophy, Science, Culture*, Cornell University Press, Ithaca, NY, pp. 17–24.

Lyotard, J. 1984, reprint 1997, *The Postmodern Condition: A Report on Knowledge*, trans. G. Bennington and B. Massum, University of Minnesota Press, Minneapolis, MN.

McIntyre, D. and McIntyre, A. 2000 *Capacity for Research into Teaching and Learning*, Report to TLRP, <www.tlrp.org/acadpub/McIntyre,%201999.pdf>, accessed 2 December 2009.

Mertens, D. 1999 'Inclusive Evaluation: Implications of Transformative Theory for Evaluation', *American Journal of Evaluation*, Vol. 20, no. 1, pp. 1–14.

Mitchell, L., Wylie, C. and Carr, M. 2008 'Outcomes of Early Childhood Education: Literature Review', New Zealand Council for Educational Research/Ministry of Education, <www.educationcounts.govt.nz/_data/assets/pdf_file/0003/24456/885_Outcomes.pdf>, accessed 2 December 2009.

Moss, P. 2007 'Meetings across the Paradigmatic Divide', *Educational Philosophy and Theory*, vol. 39, no. 3, pp. 229–45.

Oakley, A. 2004 'The Researcher's Agenda for Evidence', *Evaluation and Research in Education*, vol. 18, nos 1&2, pp. 12–27.

Peirce, C.S. 1992 *The Essential Peirce, Selected Philosophical Writings, Vol. 1 (1867–1893)*, eds N. Houser and C. Kloesel, Indiana University Press, Bloomington, IN.

Prado, C. 2005 *Searle and Foucault on Truth*, Cambridge University Press, Cambridge.

Pring, R. 2000 'The "False Dualism" of Educational Research', *Journal of Philosophy of Education*, vol. 34, no. 2, pp. 247–60.

Scott, D. 2007 'Resolving the Quantitative-Qualitative Dilemma: A Critical Realist Approach', *International Journal of Research & Method in Education*, vol. 30, no. 1, pp. 3–17.

Siraj-Blatchford, I. 1999 'Early Childhood Pedagogy: Practices, Principles and Research' in P. Mortimore (ed.) (1999) *Understanding Pedagogy and Its Impact on Learning*, Paul Chapman, London.

Siraj-Blatchford, I., Sammons, P., Sylva, K., Melhuish, E. and Taggart, B. 2006 'Educational Research and Evidence Based Policy: The Mixed Method Approach of the EPPE Project', *Evaluation and Research in Education*, vol. 19, no. 2, pp. 63–82.

Siraj-Blatchford, I. and Siraj-Blatchford, J. 2009 *Improving Children's Attainment Through a Better Quality of Family-based Support for Early Learning*, C4EO, London, <www.c4eo.org.uk/themes/earlyyears/familybasedsupport/files/c4eo_family_based_support_kr_1.pdf>, accessed 2 December 2009.

Siraj-Blatchford, I. and Sylva, K. 2004 'Researching Pedagogy in English Pre-Schools', *British Educational Research Journal*, vol. 30, no. 5, pp. 713–30.

Siraj-Blatchford, I. and Wong, Y. 1999 'Defining and Evaluating "Quality" Early Childhood Education in an International Context: Dilemmas and Possibilities', *Early Years: An International Journal of Research and Development*, vol. 20, no. 1, pp. 7–18.

Smith, J. and Heshusius, L. 1986 'Closing Down the Conversation: The End of the Quantitative–Qualitative Debate Among Educational Researchers', *Educational Researcher*, vol. 15, no. 4, pp. 4–12.

Sylva, K., Siraj-Blatchford, I. and Taggart, B. 2006 *Assessing Quality in the Early Years: Early Childhood Environment Rating Scale-Extension (ECERS-E): Four Curricular Subscales. Revised Edition*, Trentham Books, Stoke-on-Trent.

Sylva, K., Siraj-Blatchford, I., Taggart, B., Sammons, P., Melhuish, E., Elliot, K. and Totsika, V. 2006 'Capturing Quality in Early Childhood Through Environmental Rating Scales', *Early Childhood Research Quarterly*, vol. 21, pp. 76–92.

Sylva, K., Melhuish, E., Sammons, P., Siraj-Blatchford, I. and Taggart, B. 2006 *Promoting Equality in the Early Years: Report to The Equalities Review*, Cabinet Office, London, <http://archive.cabinetoffice.gov.uk/equalitiesreview/upload/assets/www.theequalitiesreview.org.uk/promoting_equality_in_the_early_years.pdf>, accessed 2 December 2009.

Tashakkori, A. and Teddlie, C. (eds) 2003 *Handbook of Mixed Methods in Social and Behavioural Research*, Sage, Thousand Oaks, CA.

Thayer-Bacon, B. 2003 'Pragmatism and Feminism as Qualified Relativism', *Studies in Philosophy and Education*, vol. 22, pp. 417–38.

Tietze, W., Cryer, D., Barrao, J., Palacio, J. and Wetzel, G. 1996 'Comparisons of Observed Process Quality in Early Child Care and Education in Five Countries', *Early Childhood Research Quarterly*, vol. 11, no. 4, pp. 447–75.

Tooley, J. 1998 *Educational Research: A Review*, OfSTED/HMSO, London.

Woodhead, M. 1996 *In Search of the Rainbow: Pathways to Quality in Large Scale Programmes for Young Disadvantaged Children*, Bernard van Leer Foundation, The Hague.

Yu, C. 2003 *Misconceived Relationships Between Logical Positivism and Quantitative Research*, paper presented at the Annual Meeting of the 2001 American Educational Research Association, Seattle, WA.

FURTHER READING

Geertz, C. 1997 'From the Native's Point of View: On the Nature of Anthropological Understanding', in P. Rabinow and W. Sullivan (eds), *Interpretative Social Science*, University of California Press, Berkeley, CA. In this highly authoritative text, Geertz presents a clear and persuasive argument for gaining insights into the lives of others through studying their expressions: '… not by imaging myself someone else, a rice peasant or a tribal sheikh, and then seeing what I thought, but by searching out and analyzing the symbolic forms—words, images, institutions, behaviors—in terms of which, in each place, people actually represented themselves to themselves and to one another.' (p. 58).

Siraj-Blatchford, I., Sammons, P., Sylva, K., Melhuish, E. and Taggart, B. 2006 'Educational Research and Evidence Based Policy: The Mixed Method Approach of the EPPE Project', *Evaluation and Research in Education*, vol. 19, no. 2, pp. 63–82. This paper provides an account of the Effective Provision of Preschool Education (EPPE) Project and locates the study in terms of the contemporary literature on mixed-method research. It is argued that the mixed-method approach that was adopted provided evidence that usefully informed policy, whilst avoiding technicism and/or any reification of imposed conceptions of early educational quality.

Tashakkori, A. and Teddlie, C. (eds) 2003 *Handbook of Mixed Methods in Social and Behavioural Research*, Sage, Thousand Oaks, CA. This handbook provides a valuable introduction and guide to both the epistemological foundations and the concrete practices adopted in mixed-method approaches to social science inquiry.

12

Designing to scale: When size matters

Mindy Blaise

Research designs are not ready made. They are a set of procedures developed by the researcher to guide an entire study. The components of a design usually include a clearly framed question, theoretical and conceptual frameworks to guide the study, strategies for collecting and organising data, approaches to data analysis, and a plan for interpreting the analysis (Lankshear and Knobel, 2004). When doing any kind of research, regardless of the study's size or the amount of time spent in the field collecting data, these components must fit together. For those conducting small-scale studies, an awareness of the project's scope and scale in relation to their role during the research process is another layer of complexity that must be addressed in ensuring a successful study. This chapter shows how I considered the scope, scale and my researcher role when designing an exploratory study of young children's understandings of gender and sexuality (Blaise under review; 2009a). In particular, it highlights how size matters when developing a research question, using a theoretical perspective and determining data-collection strategies for doing a small-scale qualitative study.

DOING WHAT IS REASONABLE

Studies are usually considered **small scale** when data collection occurs over a short period of time, when a small number of participants are involved in a study, or when few data-collection methods are used to answer a research question. Just as early childhood education is not a 'watered-down' version of primary education, small-scale studies are not smaller or less important versions of larger investigations. They are just different, and what can reasonably be accomplished in a short amount of time must be taken into consideration when designing a study to scale.

Novice and experienced researchers conduct small-scale studies when they do not have the time to complete a larger project. For student researchers, small-scale studies are often the only option because they are manageable. For example, pre-service teachers are usually expected to carry out some form of teacher research during their early childhood teacher preparation programs. Sometimes this happens while pre-service teachers are completing a two-week placement and other times it might occur at the end of their course when they are interns and responsible for all aspects of an early childhood program. Honours students might only have one term to complete their projects and PhD candidates are under pressure to get their studies done in a timely manner. All researchers must think about what is reasonable and manageable with regard to their personal circumstances when designing a study.

DEVELOPING A RESEARCH QUESTION

Because time is an important factor, small-scale studies are often conducted as exploratory exercises with the intention of 'getting to know' something well. Researchers usually begin any project by having several ideas they want to explore. Scaling down these ideas into a researchable question is an important part of the research design process. Although my research interests include gender and sexuality, this was too broad a topic for a study that would happen over a short period of time. In fact, my timeline for generating data totalled five days. Narrowing down my topic meant that I had to consider what kinds of research questions could be answered during five days of fieldwork. I did this by developing a research question that focused on how young children talk about gender and sexuality.

Findings generated from exploratory studies might influence the development of larger projects. For instance, I carried out an initial investigation of young children's understandings of gender and sexuality in order to gain a sense of the ways in which children talked about and understood gender and sexuality. These initial findings, particularly concerning how children talked about Spiderman and Bratz dolls, have been useful for designing interview questions that I intend to employ with children regarding bodies and body image.

CONSIDERING YOUR ROLE

Research designs also include the procedures or guidelines for doing something under certain conditions. Determining what these conditions are is an important part of designing to scale. Although the amount of time spent in the field generating data will be significant for small-scale studies, another important condition is the role of the researcher throughout the study. Student researchers will need to consider the responsibilities they have while carrying out teaching and research. They will need to bear in mind what kind of data is reasonable to collect in relation to their research question, teaching roles and responsibilities. Some student researchers might create ways to integrate these two roles, while others will decide to keep their teaching and researching roles separate. Since I was neither volunteering in the early childhood room nor completing a teaching practicum where I was intending to do my research, my role was that of a researcher. Although I did not have teaching responsibilities in this early childhood room, I did need to think about my role within this setting and plan for developing rapport with the participants.

A possible limitation of small-scale qualitative research is the need for the researcher to develop rapport with participants in a short period of time. This can become problematic when researchers need to conduct their studies in unfamiliar early childhood services. If this is the case, it will be necessary to take this unfamiliarity into account when designing a small-scale study. Although I had a prior research relationship with the early childhood service where I conducted my gender and sexuality research, I was unfamiliar with the group of children and their families who participated in my project. Student researchers who are doing teacher research while completing a semester-long practicum should consider the opportunities they have for developing rapport with potential participants. In early childhood services, these potential participants can include children, their families, teachers and early childhood professionals.

Since I did not know the participants in my study, I had to build into my design ways to address this. I did this in several ways. First, I chose to conduct my study around the time that this room was having an informal social event with families and children. I attended this social function and had opportunities to meet the families and children in the room, informally discuss the research study, and talk about my researcher role. Second, I asked the teacher to formally introduce me to the children on the first day of the study. This gave me the chance to explain to the children about my role and the purpose of the research. Third, I spent the first day of the study developing rapport with the children. I did this by spending three hours in the room as a participant observer, taking part in the everyday routines, like reading and drawing with children. I also took field notes, making notes of children's names, friendship groups, adults present and the materials in the room. During this time, I also interacted with the teacher. I made sure that children saw us talking because I wanted them to see that we had a friendly and collegial relationship. Fourth, I debriefed with the teacher daily after conducting fieldwork and then met with her the following morning to share my initial findings. This was intended to support our developing research relationship and gain her perspective about the daily progress of the study, including my role and how it might be modified in order to best document children's understandings of gender and sexuality.

UTILISING THEORETICAL AND CONCEPTUAL FRAMEWORKS

Researchers must decide how they will utilise theoretical or conceptual frameworks to frame their research questions and generate data. Even small-scale studies must draw from theoretical or conceptual ideas to frame a project. Rather than using an entire theoretical framework, it is recommended instead to choose one or two conceptual ideas to guide the project, including data analysis. For instance, poststructuralist and queer perspectives framed my study and were useful for theorising children's gender and sexuality. These viewpoints regard sex, gender and sexuality as discursively constituted. More specifically, Butler's (1990, 1993) ideas on sex, gender and sexuality were pivotal to moving away from natural and universal understandings of these concepts towards working within a social and historical logic. Butler (1990) claims that gender is one of the effects of sex, and reads gender as the productive mechanism through which the sexes are themselves constituted. For Butler, gender is not a noun. In contrast, gender is considered a verb, a process or a series of acts.

Since young children are in the process of working through their theories of sexuality, it was important to remember that they might be elusive and it might be difficult for adults to locate or recognise how their ideas might be related to sexuality (Britzman, 1998). Therefore, if my study intended to explore children's sexual knowledge, then it had to reimagine how children, rather than adults, know and talk about these concepts in their everyday worlds. With this goal in mind, this study moved away from situating children's sexual knowledge as merely naming body parts or explaining where babies come from, to documenting how they talk about gender discourses. If gender is an effect of sex, as Butler's (1990, 1993) work suggests, then children's understandings of gender, especially when situated within heterosexual discourses, might be one pathway for understanding their sexual knowledge. In short, poststructuralist and queer understandings about gender and sexuality meant that children's talk could be one way to document children's understandings about gender and sexuality.

CONSIDERING WHAT, WHO AND HOW IN RELATION TO THE SCALE OF YOUR PROJECT

Although a theoretical and conceptual framework will influence the kinds of research questions asked, determining what is going to be studied within the scope and scale of the study is one of the most challenging steps in research design. It is difficult because it usually entails scaling down original ideas and refining them to coincide with both the theoretical framework and the amount of time a researcher is able to spend in the field completing their project. Scaling back is a process that happens while framing and reframing research questions. Part of the skill required when designing a study to scale is simultaneously considering a range of issues. It is about keeping an eye on the research question, in addition to where the study takes place, the kinds of data-collection strategies that will help answer the research questions, and the role of the researcher.

You will need to decide whether to use a single data-collection strategy or combine several strategies. You must only use strategies that will help answer your research question. This is why refining and reframing your research question in a way that recognises the scale of your study is important. For instance, when deciding on the types of information that I would gather for the exploratory gender and sexuality study, I focused primarily on children's perspectives. Not only was this aligned with queer and poststructuralist perspectives on sex, gender and sexuality, but it could also be done over a five-day period. I used multiple methods to generate data, including participant observations, field notes, and audiotaped small- and large-group discussions with children. All of the group discussions were audiotaped and focused on daily research activities I did with children aimed at eliciting their understandings about gender and sexuality. These daily research activities included reading children's books (*Clarice Bean, That's Me*, by Lauren Child), sharing and discussing popular toys (Bratz dolls), children's drawings, and photographic documentation.

Although this study was interested in generating children's understandings about gender and sexuality, the teacher and children's families were also consulted. Interviews and debriefs were conducted with the teacher. Although these were audiotaped, they were not transcribed until formal data collection ended. Teacher interviews and daily debriefs were strategies for strengthening the collaborative and child-centred data-collection methods used throughout the study. Choosing not to transcribe the teacher interviews and debriefs until formal data collection ended was a strategy for making the project manageable. Finally, after fieldwork, I left a daily researcher notebook in the room for parents to read. This notebook contained a summary of the research activities and initial findings. It also supported **researcher reflexivity** because it contained emerging questions I had about the small- and large-group discussions we had regarding the books I read, toys I shared, children's drawings or children's photographic documentation. I also encouraged parents to respond in the notebook by posing questions such as, 'Do you hear similar kinds of talk about being handsome, cool, pretty, or sexy at home? What kinds of dress-up games does your child like to play? Do you ever get uncomfortable when your child asks you about sex or gender?'

SKETCHING OUT THE PROJECT

Sketching out the entire project is a strategy for envisioning and planning how you will conduct your study and the pacing of the project. **Research briefs** are detailed outlines completed before the research study begins. They provide researchers with opportunities to work their way through a series of questions before developing a timeline (see boxed summary).

RESEARCH BRIEF GUIDELINES

Research purpose	Why do I want to study this?
Research question	What do I want to study? What sub-questions do I have? Are these reasonable research questions, in light of my circumstances?
Data collection	How will I collect data?
Data analysis	How will I analyse data?
Timeline	When and how will I complete the different phases of my study? Is this manageable, in light of my circumstances?
Support	Who will help me sustain this project?
Permissions	What permissions do I need to collect? What are the ethical issues I need to consider?

(Hubbard and Power, 1999, pp. 47–8)

Creating **timelines** is helpful for envisioning your researcher (and teaching) role while carrying out research in the early childhood setting. Even if you are intending to conduct a study using emergent research methods, a timeline is useful for knowing what you need to do and when you need to do it. If you are planning to do research that is generative, where analysis is ongoing and initial findings influence how the project proceeds, then this too must be built into the design. Because I wanted to find out how children understood gender and sexuality, it was necessary to encourage them to talk about gender and sexuality in their own terms. I did not set out to 'make' children talk about gender and sexuality. Instead, I used research activities that might encourage them to discuss these concepts. I wanted to find out the ways young children talked about gender and sexuality, and then build on these findings over a five-day period. As this was an emergent and generative study, I also had to build in time to initially analyse my data and plan for the next day of fieldwork. Drawing from previous research experiences, I knew that it would be impossible to transcribe the small- and large-group discussions each night, before the following day. However, it would be possible to review my field notes and listen to the audiotapes nightly, making note of critical incidents. The following day, I would then present these initial findings to the teacher at the morning debrief. It was during this time that the teacher would add her perspective to the data, findings and research process. We would then decide how to modify the original research plan and continue with the study.

The **daily research plan** kept me focused and prevented me from derailing. It also allowed me to modify the pacing of the project. Because the project was emergent, my original plan did shift as a result of the data generated and the daily teacher debriefs I had with the teacher. For example, although I originally planned to have children take photographic documentation on the last day of fieldwork, the teacher and I decided that it would be more appropriate for them to do this on the third day. This decision was made because of the children's high interest in the Bratz dolls I brought to share. The small and large group discussions about the Bratz dolls indicated that children understood them to be 'sexy', 'handsome', 'cool' and 'pretty'. The teacher and I decided to build on these ideas by asking children to take photographs of the Bratz dolls being 'sexy', 'handsome', 'cool' and 'pretty' immediately following the discussions, rather than waiting until the last day of the project.

Another change in the daily research plan occurred as a result of one girl's play with the Bratz dolls during the small-group discussion. While sitting with seven children (four girls, three boys) and discussing Leah and Bryce, the Bratz dolls I had brought to share, a girl leaned towards the dolls and started moving their bodies. According to my fieldnotes, she first took Leah and moved her arm so it was resting on her hip. She then took Bryce and placed his arm around Leah's waist. When the girl sat back down, she pointed to the dolls, and with a smile exclaimed, 'There. They are on a date.' Both the teacher and I saw this as significant and wanted to know more about what children understood about how these dolls 'fitted' or 'worked' together. In other words, we were interested in how the children talked about couples. We also wondered what else the children could tell us by using the digital cameras to photograph the dolls together. This was another reason for introducing the cameras earlier than originally planned. I wanted children to photograph how they thought the dolls 'went' together and then have conversations with them about how they positioned the dolls. This method allowed for the children to play with the dolls and position them together. At the same time, I also needed to review with children how to use the cameras. In order to do this, I photographed the dolls while talking out loud about how I was using the camera to take the photograph. I then left the camera, so children could practise taking photographs. In the end, children spent two days taking photographs of objects and things (that is, toys, books, backpacks, each other) in the room that they considered to be sexy, cool, handsome and pretty. On the last day of the study, time was spent talking with children about their photographic documentation.

Pre-service teachers who are doing student research while also completing a required practicum will need to determine how they will carry out their teaching *and* researching responsibilities. Sketching out these responsibilities might make planning for data collection more clear. It is also suggested that researchers doing qualitative research in early childhood services become familiar with the daily room routines, such as group time, 'show-and-tell' or free play. It is likely that some of these routines can be used to generate data with children (for an example of how I used show-and-tell to conduct large group discussions about gender and sexuality, see Blaise 2005, 2009b). For instance, morning and afternoon tea might be served to small groups of children sitting at a table. While children are enjoying their snack, it might be possible, appropriate and manageable to conduct informal group interviews about a particular topic under study. However, it is important to remember that this strategy might not always be useful for answering all research questions.

CREATING TIMELINES

My research designs do not become 'real' until I begin sketching them out. I start this process by creating a timeline, including how data generation will occur while I am in the field. Table 12.1 shows an example of the original timeline I created for the gender and sexuality study. Although it changed, it was useful for helping me design a manageable study. When creating a timeline, I begin with what I know. In this case, I knew I only had five days to spend in the field generating data. Therefore, I had to be realistic about what I could do over five consecutive days.

Table 12.1 Timeline for data generation

Day 1: Entering the field	Day 2: Reading stories	Day 3: Bratz dolls and photographs	Day 4: Drawing pictures	Day 5: Photographing
Developing rapport with children	Read stories and have small-group discussion	Bring Bratz dolls and have small group discussion	Children drawing pictures and having discussions	Children photographing what they like, or what they think boys and girls will like
Parent social night	Teacher debrief (before and after fieldwork)	Photographs	Teacher debrief (before and after)	Teacher debrief (before and after fieldwork)
Teacher interview	Leave researcher notebook	Teacher debrief (before and after fieldwork)	Leave research notebook	Teacher interview
		Leave researcher notebook		Leave researcher notebook

SUMMARY

This chapter has shown how size does matter when designing a small-scale study. It discussed how researchers must consider the scope and scale of their study, in relation to their researcher role when designing research. In particular, this chapter addressed the following:

- how the scope and scale must be considered when developing a research question
- how a theoretical perspective or conceptual framework might be used when doing a small-scale study
- how to determine data-collection strategies that are manageable in relation to the research question, the role of the researcher and the time spent in the field

- the importance of considering what is reasonable and manageable with regard to a researcher's personal circumstances when designing a study.

QUESTIONS FOR REFLECTION

1. In what ways will your study be considered 'small scale'?
2. How will time be a factor when designing your study?
3. What will your role be while carrying out your study?
4. What kind of data will be reasonable to collect in relation to your research question, your role in the early childhood service and the amount of time you will have to generate data?

REFERENCES

Blaise, M. under review 'Relationships and Desires: Exploring Young Children's Understandings of Gender and Sexuality', Special Issue on Sexuality, *Australian Journal of Early Childhood.*

——2009a *Young Children's Understandings of Gender and Sexuality*, final research report to the Foundation for the Scientific Study of Sexuality, Allentown, PA.

——2009b 'What a Girl Wants, What a Girl Needs: Responding to Sex, Gender, and Sexuality in the Early Childhood Classroom', *Journal of Research in Childhood Education*, vol. 23, no. 4, pp. 450–60.

——2005 *Playing it Straight: Uncovering Gender Discourses in the Early Childhood Classroom*, Routledge, New York.

Britzman, D. 1998 *Lost Subjects, Contested Objects: Toward a Psychoanalytic Inquiry of Learning*, SUNY Press, New York.

Butler, J. 1990 *Gender Trouble: Feminism and the Subversion of Identity*, Routledge, New York.

——1993 *Bodies That Matter: On the Discursive Limits of 'Sex'*, Routledge, New York.

Child, L. 2000 *Clarice Bean: That's Me*, Orchard Books, Sydney.

Hubbard, R.S. and Power, B.M. 1999 *Living the Questions: A Guide for Teacher-researchers*, Stenhouse Publishers, York, Maine.

Lankshear, C. and Knobel, M. 2004 *A Handbook for Teacher Research: From Design to Implementation,* Open University Press, Berkshire.

FURTHER READING

Blaise, M. 2005 'Performing Femininities Through Gender Discourses', in L. Diaz Soto and B.B. Swadener (eds), *Power and Research with Children*, Peter Lang, New York. This chapter shows how the author drew from Foucault's theory of discourse in order to locate five gender discourses in the early childhood classroom. This is an example of how the author uses a conceptual framework to analyse data.

Dyson, A.H. and Genishi, C. 2005 *On the Case: Approaches to Language and Literacy Research*, Teachers College Press, New York. This engaging book provides a wealth of information relevant to designing small-scale case studies. Of particular interest will be Chapter 3, 'Getting on the Case: Case Study Design', because it raises readers' awareness of the complexity of designing to scale and addresses the importance of times, spaces and participants.

Hubbard, R.S. and Power, B.M. 1999 *Living the Questions: A Guide for Teacher-researchers*, Stenhouse Publishers, York, Maine. This is an excellent resource for teacher researchers. The chapter, 'Research Plans', is useful because it provides examples of various research briefs that were completed by researchers before their studies began.

PART III

THE RESEARCH PROCESS IN ACTION

13

Surveys and questionnaires: An evaluative case study

John Siraj-Blatchford

When most people think of a survey, they imagine the kind of large-scale study carried out for the purposes of market research or the identification of political opinions. The term may even conjure up images of people with clipboards completing questionnaires door to door, or approaching hapless individuals outside supermarkets. Surveys are always carried out to describe some particular characteristic or a range of characteristics of a given population. But not all surveys are large scale, and even small populations—such as the parents and staff of a nursery—can be surveyed. This chapter provides an outline account of a three-year nursery evaluation recently conducted in the United Kingdom using interviews and questionnaires. (The design also incorporated other measures, but for the purpose of this chapter it will only be the latter that are reported.) From this case study, a number of general issues will be explored including sampling, questionnaire construction, the processes of interviewing and the design of small-scale surveys.

WHAT WERE THE RESEARCH QUESTIONS?

The nursery involved was a very successful combined centre that integrated preschool child care, education and family support. It was identified by the UK government as an Early Excellence Centre (EEC) (DfEE, 1997) and given extra funding to develop its multi-agency approach further, and to disseminate its good practice. Unsurprisingly, the government was keen to ensure that the additional funding was well spent and to this end it instituted a comprehensive national three-year evaluation of the EECs initiative. National evaluators were appointed, and an elaborate set of 'common indicators' was established to provide the central terms for an annual evaluation of each of the 33 pilot EECs (Pascal et al., 1999). The 72 indicators covered contexts, processes and outcomes. The central research questions were therefore the extent to which each of these indicators was being achieved. If we consider, for example, those indicators most relevant to parental involvement and partnership, P3 of the process indicators included:

- P3a Partnership with parents
- P3b Responsiveness
- P3c Proactive involvement of male family members. (Pascal et al., 1999, p. 52)

In addition, O2 of the Outcome/Impact indicators were:

- O2a Use of services
- O2b Social and health skills
- O2c Parenting skills
- O2d Employability (Pascal et al., 1999, p. 54).

While some of the data required in the evaluation were available through secondary sources such as local employment and social services data, a good deal had to be obtained through primary sources. The head of each early excellence centre was required to appoint a local evaluator to support this process.

All further references to this evaluation (the case study) will be concerned exclusively with the local evaluation, as any additional discussion of the national evaluation is beyond the scope of this chapter. The terms of the evaluation were exceptionally wide so that, again in the interest of brevity, only some aspects of parental partnership (P3/O2) will be reported.

HOW WERE THE RESEARCH QUESTIONS DEVELOPED?

While there was a need to provide the national evaluators with descriptive and reliable summative data, there was clearly an opportunity to work closely with the centre, thus providing a much more formative evaluation. Taking the parent involvement/partnership issue as an example, the centre was aware of the need to continuously monitor and strive to improve practice in this area. The local evaluator had also been involved in research and development projects concerned with parent partnership for some years (Siraj-Blatchford and Clarke 2000), and therefore brought her own expertise to the area.

As Cronbach (1982) has argued, the design of an evaluative investigation is something of an art. In this case, an illuminative perspective was employed where the 'attempted measurement of "educational products" was abandoned for intensive study of the programme as a whole: its rationale and evaluation, its operations, achievements, and difficulties. The innovation is not examined in isolation, but in the … context or "learning milieu".' (Parlett and Hamilton, 1987, p. 62)

HOW WERE THE RESEARCH QUESTIONS ANSWERED?

Although most large-scale surveys are aimed at gaining a small amount of information from a large number of people, a good deal of the research carried out in early childhood settings involves relatively small populations. Interviewing was therefore a very practical possibility. It was decided that parents would be interviewed, and staff and managers would complete questionnaires to provide triangulation in terms of source. Methodological triangulation was achieved by applying other methods as well, including documentary analysis, focus discussions with staff and the use of standardised rating scales.

The interviews

Interviews can be entirely structured, entirely unstructured or semi-structured (somewhere between the first two). Unstructured interviews, often referred to as a 'conversation with a purpose', are considered to provide the maximum freedom to the respondent in determining their response. In the ideal case, the interviewer will respond to the interviewee to check and elaborate upon their understanding of the chosen subject as they go along. The more structure, the more the interview is 'theory driven', whether this is in the form of hypotheses to be tested, or through the predetermined terms of an evaluation. The more closely we predefine the range of responses, the greater the opportunity for quantification, and the more we ensure each respondent is asked the same questions in the same way, the more reliable our quantitative data will end up being.

Generally speaking, in any survey there is a tradeoff—the greater the structure, the less you find out, but the more reliable the information you obtain. The less the structure; the more you find out, and the greater the validity this has, at the expense of reliability.

All this applies equally to other research instruments such as observation coding schemes and rating scales. From this perspective, ethnography (see Chapter 16) may be considered to offer the least predetermined structure and the greatest validity, while rating scales may be employed to give us maximum reliability.

Where the interview has some structure, this usually takes the form of a series of predefined questions and a sequence of prompts and probes. Semi-structured interview schedules often include all kinds of strategies employed to encourage the respondent—for instance, a respondent may be reminded of a particular past event to support their recall and/or the interviewer may at times pretend not to fully understand to prompt the respondent to say more. The most highly structured interview schedules are questionnaires, and where schedules are in this form there may be no need for an interview at all. The questionnaire would then be referred to as one for 'self-completion', and might be distributed through a simple mailing. In any event, prompts and probes can often be used to good effect. A prompt suggests to the interviewee a number of possible answers that the interviewer expects. Probes are used to encourage an expanded response from the interviewee. They may be specific questions such as 'Is there anything else you want to say about that?', they may involve repeating the last thing the interviewer said or they may involve some kind of non-verbal communication (perhaps a raised eyebrow or a period of silence). In the interests of reliability, it is usually important to ensure both prompts and probes are applied consistently across interviews.

As far as possible, questions should be short and clear and only one question should ever be asked at a time. Jargon should also be avoided as much as possible. Leading questions can often put words into the interviewee's mouth. For example, the question 'What do you think is the best activity we provide for children of this age group?' presupposes that the interviewee feels positively about some of the activities offered; in fact, they might disapprove of all the activities on offer. Perhaps the most important thing of all to avoid is a loaded question using unnecessarily emotionally charged words or phrases—for example; 'Do you approve or disapprove of the abusive practice of teaching basic literacy and numeracy skills in a formal way to under fives?'

The parent questionnaire that was constructed for the EEC evaluation had a mixture of open and closed questions, prompts and scale items for a total of 57 questions. The questionnaire began with questions eliciting demographic data such as names/ages. (e.g. 'How long has your child been at the centre?') and then asked a series of open questions about the quality/ies of centre buildings and the centre's expectations (for example, with regard to parent involvement). Parents and staff were also asked to provide their responses to these expectations. The parents were asked questions about the main qualities of the staff and about the quality of management; the staff were asked about their own qualities and those of managers. The parents were interviewed by people who were not staff of the centre, and the staff self-completed their questionnaire after a half-day training and question-and-answer session with the researcher. Parent interviews lasted about one hour; self-completion of questionnaires by staff was reported to take 40 to 90 minutes, depending on how detailed the responses to the open questions were.

The boxed extract illustrates the general pattern of questioning.

SHORT EXTRACT FROM PARENT QUESTIONNAIRE WHICH INCLUDED OVER THIRTY QUESTIONS ON PARENT INVOLVEMENT

What kinds of parent involvement does the centre encourage? For example:

23. as helper/volunteer, assistant to a trained adult, centre visits, fundraising
24. to attend workshops or other training—examples?
25. other forms of parent education—examples?
26. parent support for families under stress—examples?
27. What services are you aware of now?
28. Do you take advantage of any of these?

If yes:

29. How often do you visit . . . ask about their levels of attendance at each/any activity.
30. Do you feel that you have learnt anything from attending centre courses/activities?

If yes:

Is there any way that this may have benefited your child?

31. Do you feel that the centre activities have added anything to your own quality of life?

If yes:

Do you think any of this may give you better employment opportunities?

32. Have you made new friends as a result of your involvement?

If yes:
Do you find you are you able to help each other?
Probe: In what ways?

33. If a 'course' is referred to:
Was it set at an appropriate level?
Were you satisfied with the course?

Probe: Why?

34. How, if at all, do you feel that you have benefitted from the services provided?

Probe: for example, confidence?

35. Can you think of any reasons people might not take advantage of any of the services—even when they feel they may be valuable?

Probe: Any gender/socioeconomic/moral stigma involved? Other questions:

36. Is the child's father, or any other male member of your family, involved in bringing up the child?

If yes:
Does the centre make a deliberate effort to involve them?

1. To what extent do you think the centre is identifying your child's individual needs?
2. What do you think about the educational provision of the centre? (Siraj-Blatchford, 2000b)

Closed questions set the range of alternative responses and may involve a simple yes or no answer. This was advantageous where we wanted unambiguous data for quantification. Question 28 is therefore closed (there are a limited number of possible responses). Question 30 is another good example of this. Questions 34 and 35, on the other hand, are open-ended and provide a means of collecting more qualitative data. As can be seen, the two questioning strategies were often combined to provide a qualitative check on the interpretation of the quantitative answers. An alternative approach would have been to use scale items, where a question is followed by a range of possible options for the respondent to choose from. For example, 'The staff consider themselves successful in supporting children in developing appropriate social skills. Do you: strongly agree/agree/feel unsure/disagree/strongly disagree (select one response).'

Instructions for interviewers

A semi-structured questionnaire is incomplete; it leaves you space to 'probe' and 'prompt' and follow up interesting ideas. To ensure respondents feel comfortable, the researcher must emphasise that the information they provide is confidential and will not be used with any names of staff, parents or children. Record these interviews and explain that they are for your purposes only because you want to listen to or read them for analysis. In this case study, before beginning the interview a friendly conversation was usually begun about something neutral—for example, the weather, local traffic or even the price of shoes! Parents were interviewed individually. Where these were mostly 'mums', the researcher tried to probe whether fathers/partners (if present) would hold similar views. Most research on parent involvement seems to be with mothers (Siraj-Blatchford, 2000a).

Robson (1998) provides a useful five-point model that can be applied when designing your own interview schedule or questionnaire:

- *Introduction:* interviewer introduces herself, explains purpose of the interview, assures of confidentiality, and asks permission to tape and/or make notes.
- *'Warm up':* easy, non-threatening questions at the beginning to settle both of you down.
- *Main body of interview:* covering the main purpose of the interview in what the interviewer considers to be a logical progression. In semi-structured interviewing, this order can be varied, capitalising on the responses made (ensure 'missed' topics are returned to unless this seems inappropriate or unnecessary. Any 'risky' questions should be relatively late in the sequence so that, if the interviewee refuses to continue, less information is lost.
- *'Cool-off':* usually a few straightforward questions at the end to diffuse any tension that might have built up.
- *Closure:* thank you and goodbye. The 'hand on the door' phenomenon, sometimes found at the end of counselling sessions, is also common in interviewing. Interviewees may, when the recorder is switched off or the notebook put away, come out with a lot of interesting material. There are various possible ways of dealing with this

(switch on again, reopen the book, forget about it) but in any case you should be consistent, and note how you dealt with it (Robson, 1998).

WHAT SAMPLING ISSUES WERE THERE?

In small-scale surveys such as this example of research in action, you need to obtain the biggest response you possibly can, so whenever possible you should survey the whole population. Where this is not possible for reasons of time and/or expense, you will need to take a random or structured sample. It is worth bearing in mind that if you wish to carry out any sophisticated form of statistical analysis you will need at least 30 respondents. Remember that your responses need to be representative of the overall population, and that you need to avoid any kind of bias in the selection of (or encouraging participation in) your sample. In the case of the parent survey, some of the questions related directly to particular 'user' groups, such as sole parents, ethnic minorities and males; thus it was essential that parents from these categories were interviewed.

A number of alternative sampling strategies could have been employed:

1. *Probability sampling* occurs where the sample is designed to provide an accurate representation of the total population. This includes:
   - *simple random sampling*, where each member of the population has an equal chance of being selected
   - *stratified random sampling*, where the total population is first divided into groups considered significant to the area of study. Here the size of the subsamples is often set to reflect their size within the total population. The selection process is designed so that each member of a subgroup has an equal chance of being selected.
   - *cluster sampling*, normally applied when the variation among groups is relatively small. In cluster sampling, a random sample of groups is taken and each member within the group has an equal chance of being selected. Again it is important to recognise that group samples will need to be 30 or more if statistical comparisons are to be made.
2. *Non-probability samples* are used where there is a need to over-represent groups with certain characteristics. They are easier to set up and they are cheaper but these are advantages gained at the expense of representation. Non-probability findings cannot

be generalised beyond the sample itself. Such samples include:

- *convenience sampling*, where the respondents are selected according to convenience of access. This is entirely legitimate where the population can be reasonably considered heterogeneous in the terms set by the research question.
- *quota sampling*, where representatives from each significant group are selected in proportion to their representation in the total population
- *purposive sampling*, where members of the sample are selected according to a reasoned case for typicality.

A question every researcher will ask is, 'How large does the sample need to be if it is to be a reliable indicator of the overall population?' Unfortunately this is a statistical question that warrants a book in itself, but for a very clear and concise overview of the issues it is worth looking at Anderson (1990, Chapter 18). It is probably enough to note at this point that, even in the case of fairly heterogeneous populations, the size of the sample that is required is not proportional to the total population. The sample size of smaller populations needs to be relatively larger. According to Anderson, for example, to achieve a 95 per cent level of certainty in a population of 100 you need a sample of at least 79, whereas in a population of 1000 the sample only needs to be around 277 (Anderson, 1990, p. 202).

A recurrent problem in probability samples is non-response. However clever you are in approaching prospective respondents by letter or direct contact, there will be some who will decline the offer of participating in your survey. This can have serious implications for reliability, and it is therefore a good idea to do all that you can to reduce the occurrence. Often the reason people choose not to respond will be directly relevant to the subject under study, so that the non-response introduces serious bias. In a postal survey, the response rate is often influenced by the length and complexity of the survey, but response rates less than 40 per cent are quite common. Follow-up contacts are therefore a necessity to achieve something closer to the 70 to 80 per cent response rate generally considered acceptable. Cohen and Manion (1994) refer to the diminishing return to be expected in following up on non-response (p. 99):

- original dispatch: 40 per cent
- first follow-up: +20 per cent
- second follow-up: +10 per cent
- third follow-up: +5 per cent
- total: 75 per cent.

The same general principles apply to the response rates for other forms of research based on random sampling. It is possible to apply statistical strategies that compare the characteristics of first- and second-choice responders to provide representational justification for a low response, but these methods are controversial. In every case, the aim must be to encourage the maximum level of response at the first approach.

In the case of the parent survey, compromises had to be made from the beginning; while we knew the target total population, there were groups within that population that had to be included—yet we didn't know the size of these groups. Many were very small, but as the questions that we were asking related directly to their experiences and concerns, it was important to over-represent them in our sample. This situation, where the conceptual framework of the study must take precedence over representation, is quite common (Cohen and Manion, 1994, p. 88). A complete census would have been too expensive (in terms of both time and the budget), so a non-probability stratified random sample was employed. For this reason, we were unable to claim to present a comprehensive account of the views of the total population of parents. However, we were able to claim to have identified the range of views held by different groups with some confidence. The self-completed questionnaires from staff, following extensive consultation and the delivery and collection of questionnaires at the centre, yielded a response of over 80 per cent of the total sample.

It is always a good idea to pilot an interview. One very good way of doing this, if there is to be more than one interviewer, is to interview each other. This should also encourage greater uniformity of approach and therefore greater inter-interviewer reliability.

Even if you are interviewing on your own, it is important to always keep to the script—if respondents are treated differently, the data that are collected will not be comparable. There are a broad range of factors that can influence responses—most of the published guidance emphasises the importance of considering the way that you dress, the importance of only using standard probes and prompts, of accurate record-keeping and a consistently friendly and respectful approach.

As May (1993) argues (citing Gearing and Dant, 1990), effective interviewing involves achieving a balance between maintaining a detached and objective 'distance' and the sort of close engagement that permits intersubjective understanding:

> There is a tension in the biographical interview between, on the one hand, the need of the interviewer to establish and maintain a rapport and a trusting relationship in which the interviewee will disclose signifi-

> cant personal information and, on the other, the practical demands and constraints of any research enquiry . . . what transpires is inevitably something of a balancing act. (Gearing and Dant, 1990, p. 152)

Many novice interviewers tend to talk too much, and it is important to remember that the main object of the exercise is to be *listening*. It is worth considering your interviewing as a kind of dramatic role that you adopt, always showing pleasure in the experience, providing variation in your voice and in your non-verbal expression. Questions must never be threatening or leading, but if the respondent becomes confused or defensive it is important to recognise that your role is to reassure them and make them feel comfortable, regardless of your personal views.

WHAT WERE THE FINDINGS AND HOW WERE THEY INTERPRETED?

Given the open-ended nature of many questions, the amount of data that might be collected can be very great. Some choice and selection is therefore necessary if data are to be manageable. Miles and Huberman (1994, p. 10) provide a useful flow model that illustrates the various components of data analysis. The model shows that analysis is a continuous process that extends throughout the study. It begins even before you start to collect your data, as you select the particular subject and the analytical framework for your study. In constructing a questionnaire or interview schedule, it is inevitable that you will reject some of the many possible questions and forms of data that you might otherwise have collected. Your initial readings, your life experiences and values contribute towards this anticipatory data reduction. They also contribute towards the analysis throughout the study. It is therefore important that you carry out some degree of introspection in order to become aware of your reasons for favouring particular research questions, conceptual frameworks and data-collection techniques.

From the earliest stages, the researcher begins to decide what is significant to the question under study and what is not, noting the regularities and patterns, and starting to formulate explanations and possibilities. These formulations need to be very lightly held to begin with—it is important to be sceptical. As the study progresses, you may refer back to your earlier notes, seek corroboration from alternative sources and refer back to documentary evidence. You may even attempt to replicate your initial findings with further data collection. These strategies are employed to test your findings for plausibility, to confirm your assumptions and to demonstrate their validity. This is a process referred to as 'saturation' (Glaser and Strauss, 1967), where our ongoing interpretations of events (hypotheses or intuitions) are repeatedly tested against the data in an attempt to falsify them. Through this continuous testing they may be rejected, modified or elaborated.

In the case of this evaluation, the analytic categories were prescribed by the national evaluation team, which had responded to a government tender specification, but more often we seek to obtain these from the data. A common strategy, if you are engaged in a small study and are not using a computer software package such as SPSS or NU*DIST, is to do the following:

- Make a copy of the data set (the interview transcripts or notes).
- Code each response to distinguish the source.
- Cut the paper so that each response is separated.
- Classify the responses into 'types'.
- Sort all of the responses into these categories.

This takes up a good deal of space (often on the floor), and a better way to do it if you have a larger sample is to use computer software. The best way to learn how to use such packages is to attend a course with some of your pilot material.

The data collected by a survey may be qualitative, but they also lend themselves to quantitative analysis. Where responses can be coded and represented as numbers, we can apply statistical tests to describe the data more effectively, to assess the significance of our findings and to test for correlations. A full account of the statistical possibilities lies beyond the scope of this chapter but readers may usefully refer to Clegg (1998). Kinnear and Gray's (1997) guide to the use of the SPSS for Windows software is also to be strongly recommended.

A common approach to validation through triangulation is to use more than one data-collection technique—for example, the validation of observational data through interview. Yet another strategy is to involve a colleague in the process of analysis. Where a group of researchers is able to share the analysis in this way we have a 'critical community', in which researchers are able to provide each other with practical support in their 'progressive re-focusing'. In the EEC case study, triangulation was employed as a validation process where the responses of parents, staff and managers were compared and contrasted with each other and with documentary and observational information. Trained volunteers recruited from the governing body carried out the parent interviews. It was the task of a researcher to carry out the analysis and to bring together multiple sources of data.

The following abstracted extracts from the case study findings touch on a small range of issues identified in the analysis. Supplementary data were collected from previous research and from other documentation, such as Social Services Inspection Reports, and in the final presentation a literature review located the study within the most relevant theoretical and research traditions that preceded it.

> All the families have a home assessment to establish the type of service required. They are expected to participate in ongoing progress meetings and to work with staff to agree on an action plan for their children's development ...
>
> The centre had introduced a programme incorporating a range of strategies to develop parents' capacities as educators, encouraging them to take a more active part in their child's learning and progress. In addition to this the centre is offering extensive education activities to the parents, to help with self-awareness, child-rearing, basic skills and more advanced courses. The vast majority of parents who were interviewed experienced success and satisfaction with what the centre offered. For a minority this meant further study and new employment opportunities but the vast majority admitted to better parenting as a result. The work with fathers still had some way to go. This was largely acknowledged in the staff questionnaires rather than the parent responses. (Sirah-Blatchford, 2000b)

QUANTITATIVE SURVEY ANALYSIS AND MIXED METHODOLOGIES

As Hughes (Chapter 3) has argued, traditionally scientists claimed that positivist knowledge was the only form of knowledge that could provide a true account of reality. But in recent years a wide range of alternative positions have been taken in opposition to positivism in the social sciences. Notable examples include critical realism (Scott, 2007), contemporary pragmatism (Thayer-Bacon, 2003) and feminist standpoint theory (Harding, 1993; Best, 2007). Another approach, adopted in the large-scale mixed-method Effective Provision of Pre-school Education (EPPE) study (Siraj-Blatchford et al. 2006), has been identified as one of scientific realism. Scientific realists consider that their approach provides a means of rejecting the excessive claims of positivism without rejecting what they consider to be the underlying discipline of the social sciences. From a scientific realist position, it is possible to reject naïve empiricism and argue that knowledge may be both fallible, partial and approximate, and yet still remain 'objective' (Bunge, 1993):

> … scientific realism is a middle-ground position between direct realism and relativism. Scientific realism is also a critical realism, contending that the job of science is to use its method to improve our perceptual (measurement) processes, separate illusion from reality, and thereby generate the most accurate possible description and understanding of the world. (Hunt, 1990)

The realism in scientific realism may therefore be considered a 'contingent' realism (Lashchyk, 1992), which holds that science makes progress—that is, that scientific theories usually get successively better. The main weakness of this position is that its findings may be considered to some degree culturally specific and that it may be unable to account for any rapid changes of understanding that occur during periods of paradigmatic revolution (for example, the adoption of a heliocentric model in astronomy, or a move from communist to capitalist social organisation). While considering the EPPE methodology, which successfully combined both qualitative and quantitative analysis without making any positivist claims or assumptions, it may also be worth considering a point made by Tashakkori and Teddlie (2003), who argue that the success of mixed-method research has contributed in part to the discrediting of the 'paradigm wars' between qualitative and quantitative methods in the United States.

SUMMARY

This chapter has provided a range of ideas that may be applied in the development of small-scale surveys. The chapter includes the broad outline account of the first part of a three-year nursery evaluation that has recently been conducted in the United Kingdom. A particular focus was placed on the use of interviews and questionnaires in collecting data on the quality of the parental partnership offered by the centre. Among the technical issues considered was the unavoidable tradeoff between reliability and validity. Alternative sampling strategies were identified and practical advice was given regarding the effective conduct of interviews. The chapter also identified a range of epistemological positions that have been developed in recent years that may be applied in support of quantitative and mixed-method analysis.

QUESTIONS FOR REFLECTION

1 What might be the key differences between a survey or questionnaire developed from your own research interests, and one based

upon a commission from some external body—for example, a local authority or a government department?

2 What are the main advantages of using one-to-one interviews instead of postal questionnaires?

3 List between three and six ideas that might increase the response rate for a postal questionnaire.

REFERENCES

Anderson, G. 1990 *Fundamentals of Educational Research*, Falmer Press, London.

Best, S. 2007 Review of Harding, S. 1998 *Is Science Multicultural?, Postcolonialism, Feminism, and Epistemologies*, Indiana University Press, Bloomington, IN, <http://web.archive.org/web/20010707065736/ http://utminers.utep.edu/best/books8.htm>, accessed 10 November 2009.

Bunge, M. 1993 'Realism and Antirealism in Social Science', *Theory and Decision*, vol. 35, no. 3, pp. 207–35.

Clegg, F. 1998 *Simple Statistics: A Course Book for the Social Sciences*, Cambridge University Press, Cambridge.

Cohen, L. and Manion, L. 1994 *Research Methods in Education*, 4th ed., Routledge, London.

Cronbach, L. 1982 *Designing Evaluations of Educational and Social Programs*, Jossey-Bass, San Francisco.

Department of Education and Employment (DfEE) 1997 *Excellence in Schools, White Paper*, DfEE, London.

Gearing, B. and Dant, T. 1990 'Doing Biographical Research', in S. Peace (ed.), *Researching Social Gerontology: Concepts, Methods and Issues*, Sage, London.

Glaser, B. and Strauss, A. 1967 *The Discovery of Grounded Theory*, Aldine, Chicago.

Harding, S. 1993 'Rethinking Standpoint Epistemology: What is "Strong Objectivity"?' in L. Alcoff and E. Potter (eds), *Feminist Epistemologies*, Routledge, New York.

Hunt, S. 1990 'Truth in Marketing Theory and Research,' *Journal of Marketing*, vol. 54, pp. 1–15.

Kinnear, P. and Gray, C. 1997 *SPSS for Windows Made Simple*, 2nd ed. Psychology Press, Hove, UK.

Lashchyk, E. 1992 'Contingent Scientific Realism and Instrumentalism: Beyond Rorty's "The End of Philosophy" and Fine's "Natural Ontological Attitude" ', *Filosofs'ka y Sotsyolohychna Dumka (Philosophical and Sociological Thought)*, nos. 11 and 12, pp. 57–69, 41–61, <www.ditext.com/lashchyk/noa.html>, accessed 10 November 2009.

May, T. 1993 *Social Research: Issues, Methods and Process*, Open University Press, Buckingham.

Miles, M. and Huberman, A. 1994 *Qualitative Data Analysis*, 2nd ed., Sage, London.

Parlett, M. and Hamilton, D. 1987 'Evaluation as Illumination', in R. Murphy and H. Torrance (eds), *Evaluating Education: Issues and Methods*, Harper & Row, London.

Pascal, C., Bertram, T., Gasper, M., Mould, C., Ramsden, F. and Saunders, M. 1999 *Research to Inform the Evaluation of the Early Excellence Centres Pilot Programme*, Centre for Research in Early Childhood, University College, Worcester.

Robson, C. 1998 *Real World Research*, Blackwell, Oxford.

Scott, D. 2007 'Resolving the Quantitative–Qualitative Dilemma: A Critical Realist Approach', *International Journal of Research & Method in Education* vol. 30, no. 1, pp. 3–17.

Siraj-Blatchford, I. 2000a *Parent and Staff Questionnaires to Evaluate Early Excellence*, Institute of Education, London.

——2000b *Annual Centre Evaluation (8301002)*, unpublished technical report, Institute of Education, London.

Siraj-Blatchford, I. and Clarke, P. 2000 *Supporting Identity, Diversity and Language in the Early Years*, Open University Press, Buckingham.

Siraj-Blatchford, I., Sammons, P., Taggart, B., Sylva, K. and Melhuish, E. 2006 'Educational Research and Evidence Based Policy: The Mixed Method Approach of the EPPE Project', *Evaluation and Research in Education*, vol. 19, No. 2, pp. 63–82.

Tashakkori, A. and Teddlie, C. (eds) 2003 *Handbook of Mixed Methods in Social and Behavioural Research*, Sage, Thousand Oaks, CA.

Thayer-Bacon, B. 2003 'Pragmatism and Feminism as Qualified Relativism', *Studies in Philosophy and Education*, vol. 22, pp. 417–38.

FURTHER READING

Blaxter, L., Hughes, C. and Tight, M. 2001 *How to Research*, 2nd ed., Open University Press, Buckingham. A very practical and accessible text that avoids unnecessary jargon to provide a valuable guide to small-scale research.

Fitz-Gibbon, C. and Morris, L. 1987 *How to Design a Program Evaluation*, 2nd ed., Sage, Newbury Park, CA. Fitz-Gibbon and Morris provide a clear step-by-step guide to the development of the most rigorous form of educational program evaluation.

Moser, C. and Kalton, G. 1985 *Survey Methods in Social Investigation,* Gower, Aldershot. A classic text on survey design, administration and analysis.

14

Interviewing young children

Maria Assunção Folque

Interviewing children presents special challenges and special rewards. The challenges include designing innovative ways of researching, where children engage purposefully with the researcher, feel free to express their own views or ideas, and are not put in situations where they are preoccupied with trying to find out the purpose of a question or activity and with responding to the adult's sometimes hidden agenda. On the other side, the rewards can include children's ability to provide thoughtful contributions to our understanding of their views and the unique way in which they read and understand their life contexts.

Focusing on interviewing children for research and practice development, in this chapter I will use data from a research project using different interview techniques with children in two Portuguese preschool classrooms. In both, a particular pedagogical model—the Portuguese Modern School Movement (MEM)—was used by the teachers. The study examined this pedagogical model for preschool education in practice and analysed how this 'cultural tool' mediated (afforded or constrained) processes associated with children's learning to learn (Folque, 2008). Children's ages in Portuguese preschools range from three to six; they remain with the same staff in these mixed-age cohorts. The contribution of children's views about some of the model's components was crucial to fully understanding the cultures of learning that were being generated in each classroom and the way the MEM pedagogy was mediating the learning cultures. Listening to children is always useful, but in this study of a pedagogy focused on communities of learning, the children's views were as important as those of the teachers and other adults.

PURPOSES FOR INTERVIEWING CHILDREN

Interviewing children has long been a part of social activity, such as in legal contexts (for example, as witnesses, parental custody), counselling (for example, child abuse) and child development research (for example, Piaget's clinical interview). Recently, though, children's interviews have been used more widely in various studies concerning children's lives. This trend has been generally grounded on the United Nations (UN) Convention on the Rights of the Child, reflecting a substantial change in the way children are viewed in our society, due to new ontological and epistemological conceptions about social research and also in terms of changing theories of learning and pedagogical approaches.

The UN Convention on the Rights of the Child Article 12 establishes the right of the child to be heard and to have a voice in their everyday life contexts: 'States Parties shall assure to the child who is capable of forming his or her own views the right to express those views freely in all matters affecting the child, the views of the child being given due weight in accordance with the age and maturity of the child.' The ethical and political imperatives of listening to the children have been discussed by several researchers (Clark, Kjorholt and Moss, 2005; Westcott and Littleton, 2005), as this is not simply a matter of allowing the child to express their views but also considering the ways in which such views will be interpreted and used, affecting children's identities and their life contexts. Many studies on quality development use interviews with children to understand how their views can be incorporated in developing the quality of educational settings (Clark, 2005; Katz, 1992; Pascal et al., 1996; Sheridan and Pramling, 2001), recognising that children have a perspective that can be different from those of adults such as parents or professionals.

This view of children as citizens relates also to a new image of the child as a competent participant in research. This change has been based on a move away from seeing children as vulnerable (powerless) and immature (lacking psychological and language competence), or constructing the child as 'human becoming' (Kjorholt, Moss and Clark, 2005), into a view of children as competent social actors. There has been a concern with children's ability to express themselves in valid ways for research purposes, implying that children are somehow limited to report, express and provide 'objective' accounts of a 'given reality'. Early years researchers have been more concerned with the researcher's competence and appropriate tools to interview children or to listen to their hundred languages (Rinaldi, 2005). Despite research projects which utilised children's views of the learning/teaching processes beginning with junior and secondary pupils (McCallum, Hargreaves and Gipps, 2000) and primary schooling (Kershner and Pointon, 2000; Rudduck and McIntyre 2007), this technique has been recently used as a method in preschools. Several studies have shown that children are competent at analysing pedagogy, expressing in a very direct way the principles of teaching and learning and the rules and power of the learning environment (Brooker, 2002; Einarsdóttir, 2007; Folque, 2008; Oliveira-Formosinho and Araújo, 2004, 2008; Pramling, 2004). Children interviewed about their educational contexts 'recognize their extensive knowledge and conscientiousness on these topics and can be a stimulating input for transformative pedagogy' (Oliveira-Formosinho and Araújo, 2006, p. 30).

Another field in which interviewing children has gained much interest in the last decade is educational research on teaching and learning, where the researcher seeks to understand and theorise about the best learning conditions and how to provide appropriate learning environments. The learning process is no longer perceived as an input/output (teaching/learning) process, but rather as a dialogical process occurring as children and adults act together and jointly create meanings. This view underlies many pedagogical discourses associated with effective learning: dialogical inquiry (Wells, 1999); sustained shared thinking (Siraj-Blatchford et al., 2003); didactics as procedures and processes that can be communicated and shared (Rinaldi, 2005); pedagogy of listening; or pedagogy of relationships (Moss et al., 2005).

Several researchers highlight the importance of interaction and dialogue with children not only to coconstruct knowledge (Pramling, 1996; Rinaldi, 2005; Siraj-Blatchford et al., 2003), but also to reflect about and to monitor how one learns and the conducive conditions to learning (Folque, 2008; Wall and Higgins, 2006). In this line, dialogues with children and pupils became central to empowering children as learners, as they become aware of their own learning strategies, and engage in meta-learning dialogues and explore their own metacognitive abilities and those of others. In this respect, interviewing children is also an educational activity that has an impact on children's learning trajectories.

INTERVIEWING CHILDREN AS AN ACTIVITY

Children's interviews (including conversations) in a sociocultural context are seen as part of educational activities going beyond the purpose of gathering data to a view of educational activity (Rinaldi, 2005; Robins, 2002). Most of the studies state that listening to children is not about having access to their untouched views, but rather is about engaging in dialogues in particular contexts. In these terms, it is a mutual constituent of data generation, where children act and express themselves in a particular activity and interactive context (Hedegaard and Fleer, 2008; Westcott and Littleton, 2005).

If we understand interviews as particular contextualised activities with rules, roles, objects, goals and tools, where children and adults create meaning together by sharing their own motives, we have to ask: 'How did all these components in the interview activity interact into the construction of discourse?' In this respect, many methodological issues have to be dealt with: issues of power relationships, roles (adult role, childlike role), the object of the activity (play, work, art, writing, explaining, learning), rules for acting, and so on. Problems with power relationships within an interview between adults and children are sometimes due to the ways in which the dialogue is framed, promoting more uneven interactions. For instance, when the interviewer knows the answer to what she is asking, the interview turns into an assessment activity—'we want to know whether you know'—leaving the child in a powerless position (Westcott and Littleton, 2005). Instead, interviewing should be aimed at knowing what is not known—Tell me how it is. Why? Can you explain to me what you think?—so that the child is the expert and is focused on sharing his or her own views rather than guessing what is on the researcher's mind.

Interviewing children as a way of accessing their views and experiences is a research strategy that has challenged researchers in methodological terms, but it is also providing researchers and practitioners with invaluable insight into the educational process, contributing to 'finding new ways of living together' (Kjorholt et al. 2005, p. 185). The study presented here demonstrates some of these methodological challenges and possibilities.

WHAT WERE YOUR RESEARCH QUESTIONS?

Two broad research questions, each with several sub-questions, framed the study:

1 What are the key features of the MEM model observed in two different contexts? To what extent do the observed practices

reflect the MEM ideals? How is learning organised in the two classrooms? What are the activities, interactions and tools that mediate the teaching/learning process? What are the roles of the participants (teachers, children, other adults)? How do teachers conceptualise the learning process, the roles of the participants and the organisation of the learning context? How do children perceive/understand their learning environment, the purposes and the processes of the learning the rules, and the roles of the different participants?

2 How does the MEM pedagogy, as practised in the two classrooms, enhance or constrain children's learning to learn? In what respects does the MEM pedagogy (as investigated in the two classrooms) promote processes associated with children's learning to learn? How do the children perceive themselves as learners and participants in the learning process? How do children move towards full participation in the MEM classroom? Which factors constrain or support greater participation?

These research questions arose from my interest in studying MEM, a pedagogical model developed by a teachers' association to which I belong. My interest in pedagogical models and how they construct sociocultural environments where learning takes place has its roots in the theoretical and practical conflicts encountered in my professional life as a teacher.

For MEM teachers, learning is thought of as an empowering process, which provides tools for autonomous and responsible citizens to actively engage in and act in the world, as well as for personal and social fulfilment. To enact this empowering process, the MEM model has certain ritual activities—'Council Meetings', 'Activities and Projects', 'Communication Time'—where children devise their own plans for the curriculum in cooperation with the group, get involved in meaningful, individual or small-group activities and evaluate them communicating to others in their group. The MEM model provides a set of piloting or orienting tools to support children's self-regulating process—the 'Diary', the 'Activities Chart', the 'Responsibilities Chart' (see below for a description).

The MEM model might look promising in terms of promoting the learning processes that empower children as lifelong learners and committed citizens; it is applied throughout the stages of education—preschool to university. However, there has been insufficient detailed research on how these practices are collaboratively reconstructed by MEM teachers with their groups of children in real early years contexts. My study took seriously the MEM pedagogy's principles that consider young children as citizens with a voice, social responsibility and active participation in their own classroom life; therefore, studying the children's views about this cultural tool and the way in which it mediates learning contexts was an imperative.

HOW DID YOU ANSWER THEM?

The inquiry employed an in-depth mixed-method case study approach with ethnographic elements. It used a multiple case study design with two MEM classrooms (which I have called Amoreira and Magnólia), purposefully selected and intensively studied over a period of nine months. Data included field notes of observations (participant observations), transcripts of videorecording, interviews with adults and children, and documents (children's work, piloting tools, curriculum documents) collected over a period of nine months.

Particular attention was paid to the way in which children in the two classrooms perceived and understood their learning environment and how they viewed themselves as learners within this context, with the researcher listening to them in many different ways. Through my participant observation of children's behaviour (action and interaction), I attempted to understand the particular ways in which children interpret and give meaning to situations, by engaging with them through interviews (including informal conversations) and listening to their explanations, opinions and experiences. The children's interviews were devised in line with the research questions, aiming to get at the children's perspectives about the learning environment of the classroom, particularly how they understood some of the features of the MEM model such as classroom organisation, routines, some key activities and the MEM piloting tools. The interviews revealed how the children perceived themselves as learners and participants in their classrooms.

STRUCTURING CHILDREN'S INTERVIEWS

The major challenge was designing interviews with activities and contexts where children were most able to display their competence in thinking and expression while minimising the constraints of adult–child power relations—that is, situations where children can make sense of the questions and the activity (interview) in which they are engaged (Donaldson, 1978). My long-term presence in the classroom helped to increase familiarity and increase the possibility for intersubjectivity between myself and the children (Hviid, 2008), who by now had developed confident relationships with me. Slowly I had become part of their classroom communities.

My role in the classroom was different from that of the teacher or the assistant in that it involved little intervention and facilitated a more balanced power relationship with the children. Still, I never opted to adopt a 'childlike' or 'least adult' role (Mandell, 1991; Warming, 2005) as a way to gain access to children's worlds. Understanding that 'the generational differences between adults and children cannot be eradicated in the context of the research' (Christensen and James, 2000, p. 6), I understood that the children should not be brought into confusion or misled; I opted to explain to them openly what I was doing in the classroom (as I did with the teachers)—saying I was getting to know what they did and how they learnt in the classroom using the MEM activities and tools. Throughout fieldwork, my role was established as a non-official adult at school (Mayall, 2000), an adult truly interested in understanding how things were done in these communities.

Interviews with children consisted of 'formal' interviews, informal conversations and guided tours of the classroom. Informal conversations occurred throughout the year in relevant situations and elicited children's meanings of those situations ('What are you doing? Can you explain how you use this?'). Data on children's views of learning and learning processes were collected through these informal conversations during classroom activities, talking with children about the purpose of school—'Why do you come to school?' or 'Why do children come to school?' These conversations had the advantage of arising organically from the context, and were therefore more conducive to getting children's natural and sensible responses to my questions.

The 'formal' interviews with the children took place outside the classroom (in places with which they were familiar and comfortable) in order to get children to focus on the interview. Children were able to choose their pair (within their same-age friends) and to decide and plan when to go for the interview, gaining some power over this activity. An extra column named 'interviews' was added to their 'Activities Chart'. This provided a more comfortable situation for the children (Woodhead and Faulkner, 2000), diluting the adult–child power relationships.

The purposes of the interviews were explained directly and sensibly to the children, helping them to be clear about my intentions (Brooker, 2001). Most of the time, the children were happy in engaging in 'formal' interviews with me, either because they felt important or because they were keen to spend time with me, although occasionally there were some children who did not feel motivated throughout the whole interview. In these cases, I ended the interview and tried to approach them later through informal conversations.

I planned two sets of interviews (November and May), aimed at understanding the extent to which the children saw themselves as learners, the school as a place to learn (or to play, or to be cared for) and their understanding of learning processes. Questions were centred on 'What have you been learning here?' and 'How did you learn these things?' I planned to repeat the same interview at the end of the year to track changes in children's perceptions of the nature and processes of learning.

A tour of the classroom (March) and another planned interview (May) were designed to gather children's views of their learning environment, how they understood the purposes of learning activities and some of the tools they used in the classrooms. These also aimed to understand the extent to which the transparency of the socio-political organisation of practice, of its content and of the artefacts engaged in practice were perceived by the children to give them opportunities for full participation (Lave and Wenger, 1991). Children were invited to share their knowledge of the classroom with me so that I would understand its organisation and the possibilities for action the children and adults had. In the tour of the classroom, children were invited to guide me through the different areas of the classroom (choosing the order), and to explain the purpose, the materials they had and activities in which they could engage. This activity enabled the children (even younger ones) to actively engage in sharing their views about the classroom.

The last interview started by focusing on time routines: 'Now that I have been here for such a long time and I am about to finish my work, can you help me to see if I understood clearly some of the things in the classroom? First, what do you do from when you first come to school in the morning until the end of the day?' I wrote down what the children said (despite tape-recording it as well) to demonstrate to the children that they were being taken seriously; this also helped the children to organise their thinking (Brooker, 2001) by sharing and cooperating in the organisation of writing (saying, for example, 'Wait, I am writing'; 'Then we go to the meeting …'; 'I have that already …'; 'So after lunch what do you do?'). In the second part of the interview, children were presented with photographs of classroom situations ('Council Meetings' and 'Communication Time') and their classroom 'Piloting Tools' ('Diary', 'Responsibility Chart' and 'Activities Chart'), and asked to choose one to explain the purpose as well as the roles of children, and teacher, and also the rules (for example, 'Who writes in the "Diary" and when?').

The point to be made here is that the researcher who wants to interview children effectively will structure those interviews to provide multiple opportunities for children to say what they know and what they think. It is important to take advantage of informal opportunities to elicit responses from children in unplanned conversations as well as formal interviews. While formal interviews can set up an activity where more vocal children engage in thoughtful dialogues with the researcher, informal conversations and participant observation might be more suitable for less confident or very young children.

WHAT SAMPLING OR OTHER RESEARCH DESIGN ISSUES WERE THERE?

The first decision concerned sampling the number of MEM preschool classrooms. Opting for two cases rather than three or more was a decision grounded on the prioritisation of depth rather than breadth. The methodological approach adopted in the study required a long period of time in each classroom to get to 'see' what was not immediately evident.

Contacts with the MEM movement were undertaken in order to find teachers who were recognised by this community as 'old-timers' and full participants within MEM, therefore ensuring some degree of confidence in their understanding and application of the MEM model. The selection process resulted in the identification of two 'typical' (Schofield, 2002) MEM teachers. The main focus of the study was on practice, using cases to illustrate, rather than to compare (see Chapter 9).

WITHIN-CASE SAMPLING

An explicit sampling frame of dimensions was developed (Miles and Huberman, 1994), grounded on the research questions and the theoretical and analytical framework. Observations of the teacher and children throughout the different activities that are part of the MEM routine were sampled and planned in order to have a representative body of data from each classroom through the year. Additionally, as the fieldwork evolved in each classroom, different foci on observation, documents and artefacts were sampled in an 'iterative' way (Miles and Huberman, 1994). Accordingly, interviews were conducted with different adults in each school, different documents were analysed, and observations of children's activities also differed according to their relevance to each individual case.

All the children in both classrooms were possible interviewees. As I had no particular interest in individual children but rather in each group of children's ideas and understandings, there was no attempt to interview every child; if a child was not attending school for interview, this was not seen as a problem for sampling. Although the study used a well-planned design and data-collection schedule, the research process required that flexibility and changes in the design had to be made in order to adjust to the classroom contexts and their priorities, even if this meant changing the research schedule.

WHAT DID YOU FIND?

By listening to the children in many different ways, including but not only through formal interviews, I came to understand that the meanings created by the children in these two MEM classrooms were sometimes in line with those of the teachers and also with the 'ideal' MEM model, but at times they differed in many ways. I will report here only those findings which highlight issues related to the child interviews.

- The children were able to articulate their own move from 'child' to 'learner' and their leading activity from playing with others to learning with others.
- Children in both classrooms expressed a clear perception of the MEM activities (for example, 'Council Meetings') and the piloting tools (for example, 'Diary', 'Activities Chart').
- Children in the two classrooms assigned different meanings to the same activities and piloting tools.
- Children were able to express the power relationships that were built in the classroom.
- Children expressed their understandings of the activities and the piloting tools, both verbally and through their actions.

CASE STUDY EXAMPLE: CHILDREN CAN ARTICULATE THE PURPOSE OF SCHOOL

The study looked at classrooms as communities of learning in accord with both the MEM model for early childhood education (ECE) and the Portuguese Curriculum Guidelines for Preschool Education. This entailed understanding a community of practice with learning as a 'shared endeavour' (Wenger, 1998), which in fact constitutes a challenge for some ECE classrooms. While an understanding of learning as the purpose of the community activity was clear for both teachers, the study revealed that this was not always clear to all the children. Towards the end of the school year (April/May), about 39 per cent of the children (mainly the youngest) included external causes in their reasons for coming to school, 30 per cent mentioned coming to school to 'do things' and about 34 per cent said they were coming to school to learn.

A.F.	Teresa, why do you come to school?
Teresa (4:1)	'Cause my mother wants me to come here.
A.F.	Filipa, why do you come to school?
Filipa (3:6)	Because I have to come to school because it is a school day.
A.F.	What for?
Filipa (3:6)	To do some drawings.
João (5:0)	Because I like to learn.
A.F.	And why do you think children come to school?
João (5:0)	To know things.
Daniel (5:6)	It's to learn how to write.

These interview extracts show that the children were picking up the individual culture of the classroom. In their interviews, the Amoreira children saw the purpose of coming to school as work (39 per cent of the younger ones) and only 17 per cent associated it with play. At Magnólia, 35 per cent of the children (of all ages) associated play with the purpose of coming to school and only two (9 per cent) referred to coming to school to work. In fact, the learning discourse in Amoreira was linked with working, practising and searching for challenges to improve. On the other hand, the Magnólia community had its focus on projects of intellectual and aesthetic quality. In addition to this central focus, to which the teacher was mostly devoted, children had many opportunities to play in a rich classroom environment.

Children's views about the 'Council Meetings' and the 'Diary'

The Council Meeting (CM) is a whole-group language-based activity central to creating a community of learning in the classroom. In the CM, children participate in the decisions about the curriculum through planning and evaluating together; it is also a time for debate and critical coconstruction of the group norms and social behaviours, helping children to live in a community focusing on their own personal and social development.

At CMs, the groups use the Diary, a piloting tool that both registers and directs the CM actions. The Diary is a weekly register of incidents, desires, conflicts or accounts of events that any group member wants to mark. It is organised in four columns: 'We didn't like', 'We liked', 'We did' and 'We want'. Any child or adult can fill in the diary at any time during the week. Children can draw or ask an adult or older child to write for them. At the end of the week, during the Friday Council Meeting, the contents are analysed and discussed within the group.

The perceived goals of the CM, according to Magnólia children, were *to plan and evaluate* and see *who behaved and who didn't*. Writing things down was seen as the main action during CMs. At Amoreira, children's perceptions of the CMs' goals included *to show, tell and write* and *to read the Diary, talk and solve problems*; planning and evaluating was also mentioned as activities done at CMs, but not as strongly as the other two. In fact, the two classrooms differed in the type of things they did in the CM as well as in the time devoted to each action. At Magnólia planning and evaluating took 50 per cent of most of the CMs' time and was done in a very structured way, while at Amoreira planning and evaluating accounted for 20 per cent of the CM. The morning CM at Amoreira included a set time to *show, tell and write*, where children would share with each other things from their lives outside school. This did not take place in Magnólia.

One striking finding in the children's interviews was the meanings the children created in relation to the part of the CMs devoted to discussing the critical incidents recorded under the columns 'We didn't like' and 'We liked'.

As stated above, the Magnólia children saw the purpose of the CM as to *see who behaved and who didn't*, while at Amoreira the children saw this purpose as being to *talk and solve problems*.

Pedro (6:4) Patrícia (teacher) is here and all the children are here at the meeting to know what is important. As Patrícia has the Diary … and the thing to mark, it is to know why people did behave very, very well and did behave very, very badly.

(Magnólia boy commenting on the CM photo)

Filipa (3:8) The meeting!

A.F. Yes, the meetings … what are they for?

Filipa (3:8) It is to see … to see … . It is to write in Diary when others hit.

A.F. Uhum, … what for?

Filipa (3:8) It's to forgive the other.

(Amoreira girl commenting on the CM photo)

Maria (5:10) And then, when it is meeting day, we … the presidents go and get the Diary … and then, … We're going to … to solve everything!

A.F. How do you solve things, Maria?

Maria (5:10) It is like that: we have to find a way so that we will never hit children anymore.

A.F. … And this meeting, what is it called? Is it the Council Meeting?

Daniel (5:8) The solving meeting!

A.F.	… what is the purpose of the Diary?
Marta (5:0)	It is to help … help children … once Teresa cried because of Filipa … 'Filipa hit me Carolina!' and Carolina said 'Teresa go and write in the Diary.' And she wrote.
A.F.	… and do you think it helped Teresa?
Marta (5:0)	Yes, it helped and we solved it.
A.F.	She was not upset anymore?
Luís (4:9)	No, now she is not, when we write in the Diary we are not sad …

(Amoreira children commenting on the Diary photo)

'Learning to solve problems' versus 'seeing who behaves and who misbehaves', were the two very different perceptions that children held about the Friday CM discussions of the 'We liked' and 'We didn't like' columns in each classroom. The latter is contradictory to the MEM philosophy of finding ways to solve problems and developing socially and personally with the support of the group, without punishing the children.

The results of the children's interviews provided a new focus of analysis and the ability to uncover issues that were not immediately understood by the researcher. Throughout the interviews, the children in the Magnólia classroom referred to the teacher many times as a 'reason for doing things' (because the teacher says, wants, tells), while in the Amoreira classroom, the teacher was rarely mentioned during the interviews. The analysis of field notes and video transcripts allowed me to identify elements of the teachers' pedagogy that were critical for the progress children had made in their personal and social development, and the construction of more equal power relationships in the classroom, as in the aims of the MEM model.

1 Throughout these examples, children's ages will be indicated x:y, where x = years of age and y = months. All names are pseudonyms.

CASE STUDY EXAMPLE: CHILDREN CAN EXPLAIN THEIR USE OF THE ACTIVITIES CHART AS A TOOL FOR REGULATING LEARNING

The Activities Chart (AC) is a graphic representation of the classroom organisation displaying the separate areas and activities (pictures and writing) in which children can engage on the top row with the children's names in the left column. Each child wrote his or her own name, using the colour of their nametag. The use of children's writing in the *names* column reveals an emphasis on individual children's ownership of the group tool, as well as an opportunity for children to use functional writing. Younger children were on the top rows so they could easily find the right place to plan and evaluate. The right-hand column had a record (code) of the colours used each day, following a fixed pattern. The AC invited not only self-evaluations but also peer evaluations of individual children and the evaluation of the group.

When prompted by the photograph of the AC, and asked what it was and what it was for, many concepts of the function of this tool emerged. Many children referred to the AC by showing how it was used, performing the actions and operations to be done and the procedures to be followed.

Andreia (6:1) It is when children do a small circle they mark here and go and occupy that activity.

Some children understood its function as supporting the choice of the activities:

Carina (4:3) It is for us to choose what we want to do.

Another function assigned to the AC was to plan and support carrying out the plan:

Daniel (5:3) It's for us to remember what we have to do.

Also, a few children expressed the use of this piloting tool to evaluate the activities that they had been choosing more frequently:

Marta (5:0) It helps us to see where we have already any circles …

Finally, the older children mentioned using such evaluation in order to plan more consciously:

Maria (5:10) [We choose different activities] so that we can learn to do all these things.

The data from the interviews seemed to indicate that only older children (five-years-olds) understood the AC as a tool for self-regulating learning, engaging in purposeful planning through the appropriation of explicit learning-oriented criteria based on assessment (see Maria (5:10) above). However, when triangulating interview data with observation data, a different picture emerged. The analysis of the language (and sometimes the gestures) children used while independently using the AC showed that children often engaged both in self-appraisal and self-management of thoughts/attitudes as well as in regulating others' informed planning. What might have been understood as an ability that only older children could display was actually emerging in younger children, as the following two transcripts show.

Daniel (5:6), Andreia (5:11) and Filipa (3:6) plan at the AC:

Daniel (5:6) — I want to go to the library.

Andreia (5:11) — You've never been to the library! (points to Daniel's column)

(Daniel marks at 'library' and goes off. Andreia also marks at the library.)

Filipa (3:6) — You've never been here, here, here (points haphazardly to different activities while she reproduces the activities regulative discourse).

Andreia (5:11) — (Taking seriously what Filipa says)—I didn't go to drawing? Have a look! (points to the drawing cell along her row) and I've also been painting.

(Amoreira, March)

Hugo (3:4) wants to go to the make-believe area and knows already where to mark his circle. Luís (4:6) tells him that he had been many times to the home corner and counts all the registered circles.

Luís (4:6) — You have to go here, or here! (Pointing to the ones that have few or no circles.

Hugo (3:4) says he wants to go to the make-believe area and marks his circle.

(Amoreira, February)

The above transcripts show how very young children started to use the regulative function of the AC. Filipa (3:6) reproduced the activities' regulative discourse promoted by the use of the AC although she did not yet seem to fully understand or use it for herself. Luís (4:6) was already displaying an understanding of the potential of the AC to regulate choices as he assumed the position of the older child peer-tutoring the younger one, Hugo (3:4), on how he was supposed to plan. None of these children (or other young ones) was seen displaying self-regulation in his or her independent planning, but still the children were starting to use it with others. At the interviews, only the older children revealed their understanding of the AC as a tool to regulate their planning. The importance of triangulating data in order to achieve validity in research results became evident. This finding calls for attention on how the way in which we listen to young children might influence our results.

HOW DID YOU INTERPRET WHAT YOU FOUND?

The interpretations of the findings from the children's interviews were not done in isolation of the other findings gathered through different data (observation, analysis of interactions, documents) collection. A systematic analysis using NVivo coding system allowed management of different data and revelation of themes and patterns across data sources.

The children's perspectives made a major contribution, as they gave an incredible account of what was happening in each classroom with great detail and sensitivity. Despite the teachers' intentions and the actual practice of the MEM organisational components, the children's views about their learning environment were, to an extent, related to the way they experienced the learning activities and the use of the piloting tools. The study revealed that the way in which the activities were structured, how the piloting tools were used (rules) and the resulting interactions were of major importance for the meanings created about the functions of each tool within its own context. The same tool was seen to provide different affordances to the children.

HOW DID YOUR PARADIGM INFLUENCE THE RESULTS?

Methodological approaches to the study of pedagogy and pedagogical models differ in considerable ways, due to the researcher's ontological and epistemological stances as well as to the kinds of question a study aims to answer.

Most studies of pedagogical models in ECE have been concerned with the link between children's experiences of a particular model (the process) and their immediate or long-term learning and development (the products or the impact) (Schweinhart and Weikart, 1997; Sylva and Nabuco, 1996). Such studies, being largely quantitative, tend to establish causal relationships between some variables of the models and some measurable outcome in terms of children's knowledge or development, aiming mainly to compare the effectiveness of different pedagogies. These evaluation studies are important in linking pedagogical models with outcomes, but they tend to be less powerful in shedding light on and explaining the processes (practices) that might account for these results.

Interpretive research sees the interchange between pedagogy and learning as a negotiation of meanings, constructs and ideas by participants, and views the reality they produce as a combination of such negotiation of meanings in a sociocultural and institutional context. In social action, individuals constantly 'negotiate with others the meanings of our own actions and circumstances, of their actions and circumstances, and of social and cultural institutions and products' (see Chapter 3).

The theoretical framework in this research combined a sociocultural theory of learning with the literature on learning to learn, and the contribution of interactions in the teaching/learning process. This theoretical background provided a means of analysis which focused on the social processes of teaching/learning mediated by cultural tools (applications of the MEM model) within two classrooms. Pedagogical models such as the MEM model are cultural tools which are reconstructed in classroom practices by teachers and children in their everyday joint activity within institutional and social contexts (Wertsch, 1998).

It is clear that the type of results presented in this study are, to some extent, generated within a research paradigm that looks at reality as complex and multivoiced. Drawing on literature on communities of practice, individual and shared goals in the two classrooms were investigated, as well as the communities' social structures: roles, rules, division of labour, and access to resources (Lave and Wenger, 1991). Some key factors were examined in particular: transparency of the socio-political organisation of practice, of its content and of the artefacts engaged in practice; access; and transferring responsibility (Lave and Wenger, 1991; Rogoff, 1998).

HOW DID YOUR RESEARCH CONTEXT INFLUENCE THE RESULTS?

Empirical research always happens in a particular context. In this respect, results have to be understood in relation to the particularities of the space in which the study is conducted. One particular condition of this research was the fact that I am a member of the MEM movement, and therefore an insider to its culture, with specific knowledge of the MEM model. This extensive familiarity with the MEM model not only permitted deeper exploration and analysis of the issues, but also facilitated my access to the teachers and classrooms and establishment of a good rapport with them. At the same time, the insider perspective of the model could impede my ability to see and question some of the features of the model that might have been visible to an outsider. Although the research process involved frequent work together with academic colleagues who were not part of the MEM movement, and in some cases not even Portuguese, I understand that the line of inquiry presented here and the 'story' told in this study cannot be separated from my professional biography. That biography includes the fact that I was a preschool teacher for twelve years. Thus it was relatively easy for me to communicate productively with the children in each classroom. Adding to this, my long-term permanence in each classroom added to the meanings created.

Within a sociocultural approach, interviews are seen as activities implying dialogues between persons in particular contexts. Using different types of interviews and different procedures, as stated before, permitted triangulation of data; furthermore, a continuous reflexive account of the interpretation of data in relation to the context where it was generated was a fundamental tool. Listening to the children entailed listening to their different languages and also included listening to the context and to myself as a researcher, avoiding what Moss, Clark and Kjorholt (2005) call the risk of the 'listener claiming to have heard and grasped the authentic voice of the person listened to, thus giving authority to the listener' (2005, p. 11).

SUMMARY

This chapter has suggested that children *are* able to provide significant data for studies about their own experience and education. Thus, it is critical that the researcher finds creative ways to enable children to express their perceptions and judgments. This study claims that interviews are more than asking a set of questions. Listening to children implies engaging with them in sustained dialogues, as well as observing and participating with them in different activities. Interviews with children can be seen as a research tool as well as a pedagogical tool, part of the learning process. I have pointed out some of the challenges in interviewing children:

- designing activities which children understand and which engage with their purpose without feeling constrained by the adult type of interaction
- finding different ways of listening to the children using different languages, and thinking about the possibilities they give to the children (of different ages) to express themselves
- engaging in sustained dialogues where meanings are created through intersubjectivity, not just being 'questioned'
- building up a relationship with the children before interviewing them—difficult in a constrained research schedule
- ensuring interviewing is an ethical activity (as in any other form of research), dealing with issues of power, consent, and their impact on the participants. (See Chapters 5, 6 and 10.)

The MEM model was where I learned many of these challenges in relation to pedagogy. In this respect, I understand listening to children as part of a pedagogy which enables children to participate in many activities in which communities engage, including research: 'listening is understood as a pedagogy and a way of researching life, a culture and an ethic, a continuous process and relationship' (Moss, Clark and Kjorholt, 2005, p. 13).

During fieldwork, I did not report back to the children the results of the research, even though listening to children's ideas and points of views contributed to the results of this study. As the results are disseminated within and beyond the MEM movement, teachers have been using these findings to change their practices and develop their pedagogy. Hopefully, other children will profit from the participation in this study of Amoreira and Magnólia's children and their views of the MEM pedagogy.

QUESTIONS FOR REFLECTION

Before starting to think about how to design your interviews with children, consider the context in which the interviews are going to occur:

1 Participants—who are the participants in the context? What kind of relationships do they have? What are the roles each play in the context? How much intimacy and/or familiarity can you reach with the children? How do these conditions affect the way in which you might be able to listen to the children?
2 How do you think you can design your questions so that the children see it as a meaningful activity in which they will engage freely? What kind of activity is it going to be? Where is it going to occur? What are the conditions that will make children feel comfortable and free to express themselves? Which languages will you use in the communicative process?

REFERENCES

Brooker, L. 2001 'Interviewing Children' in G.M. Naughton, S.A. Rolfe and I. Siraj-Blatchford (eds), *Doing Early Childhood Research: International Perspectives on Theory and Practice*, Open University Press, Buckingham, pp. 162–77.

——2002 *Starting School: Young Children Learning Cultures*, Open University Press, Buckingham.

Clark, A. 2005 'Ways of Seeing: Using the Mosaic Approach to Listen to Young Children's Perspectives', in A. Clark, A.T. Kjorholt and P. Moss (eds), *Beyond Listening: Children's Perspectives on Early Childhood Services*, Policy Press, Bristol, pp. 29–49.

Clark, A., Kjorholt, A.T. and Moss, P. (eds) 2005 *Beyond Listening: Children's Perspectives on Early Childhood Services*, Policy Press, Bristol.

Christensen, P. and James, A. 2000 *Research with Children: Perspectives and Practices*, Falmer Press, London.

Donaldson, M. 1978 *Children's Minds*, Fontana, London.

Einarsdóttir, J. 2007 'Research with Children: Methodological and Ethical Challenges', *European Early Childhood Education Research Journal*, vol. 15, no. 2, pp. 197–211.

Folque, M.A. 2008 An Investigation of the Movimento da Escola Moderna (MEM) Pedagogy and Its Contribution to Learning to Learn in Portuguese Pre-schools, unpublished PhD thesis, Institute of Education, University of London, London.

Hedegaard, M. and Fleer, M. (eds) 2008 *Studying Children: A Cultural-Historical Approach*, Open University Press, Maidenhead.

Hviid, P. 2008 'Interviewing Using a Cultural-Historical Approach' in M. Hedegaard and M. Fleer (eds), *Studying Children: A Cultural-Historical Approach*, Open University Press, Berkshire, pp. 139–56.

Katz, L. 1992 'Early Childhood Programs: Multiple Perspectives on Quality', *Childhood Education*, vol. 69, no. 2, pp. 66–71.

Kershner, R. and Pointon, P. 2000 'Children's Views of the Primary Classroom as an Environment for Working and Learning', *Research in Education*, no. 2, 64, pp. 64–77.

Kjorholt, A.T., Moss, P. and Clark, A. 2005 'Beyond Listening: Future Prospects', in A. Clark, A.T. Kjorholt and P. Moss (eds), *Beyond Listening: Children's Perspectives on Early Childhood Services*, Policy Press, Bristol, pp. 175–87.

Lave, J. and Wenger, E. 1991 *Situated Learning: Legitimate Peripheral Participation*, Cambridge University Press, Cambridge.

Mandell, N. 1991 'The Least Adult Role in Studying Children' in F.C. Waksler (ed.), *Studying the Social Worlds of Children: Sociological Readings*, RoutledgeFalmer, London, pp. 38–59.

Mayall, B. 2000 'Conversations with Children: Working with Generational Issues', in P. Christensen and A. James (eds), *Research with Children: Perspectives and Practices*, Falmer Press, London, pp. 120–35.

McCallum, B., Hargreaves, E. and Gipps, C. 2000 'Learning: The Pupil's Voice', *Cambridge Journal of Education*, vol. 30, no. 2, pp. 275–89.

Miles, M.B. and Huberman, A.M. 1994 *Qualitative Data Analysis*, 2nd ed., Sage, Thousand Oaks.

Moss, P., Clark, A. and Kjorholt, A.T. 2005 'Introduction', in A. Clark, A.T. Kjorholt and P. Moss (eds), *Beyond Listening: Children's Perspectives on Early Childhood Services*, Policy Press, Bristol, pp. 1–16.

Oliveira-Formosinho, J. (ed.) 2008 *A Escola Vista pelas Crianças* (Vol. 12), Porto Editora, Porto.

Oliveira-Formosinho, J. and Araújo, S.B. 2004 'Children's Perspectives About Pedagogical Interactions', *European Early Childhood Education Research Journal*, vol. 12, no. 1, pp. 103–14.

——2006 'Listening to Children as a Way to Reconstruct Knowledge About Children: Some Methodological Implications', *European Early Childhood Education Research Journal*, vol. 14, no. 1, pp. 21–31.

Pascal, C., Bertram, A., Ramsden, F., Georgson, J., Saunders, M. and Mould, C. 1996 *Evaluating and Developing Quality in Early Childhood Settings*, Amber Publications, Worcester.

Pramling, I. 1996 'Understanding and Empowering the Child as a Learner', in D. Olson and N. Torrance (eds), *Handbook of Education and Human Development: New Models of Learning, Teaching and Schooling*, Blackwell, Oxford, pp. 565–92.

——2004 'How Do Children Tell Us About Their Childhoods?' *Early Childhood Research & Practice*, vol. 6, no. 1, <http://ecrp.uiuc.edu/v6n1/pramling.html> accessed 1 September 2009.

Rinaldi, C. 2005 'Documentation and Assessment: What is the Relationship?' in A. Clark, A.T. Kjorholt and P. Moss (eds), *Beyond Listening: Children's Perspectives on Early Childhood Services*, Policy Press, Bristol, pp. 17–28.

Robbins, J. 2002 'Shoes and Ships and Sealing Wax—Taking a Sociocultural Approach to Interviewing Young Children', *New Zealand Research in Early Childhood Education Journal*, no. 5, pp. 13–30.

Rogoff, B. 1998 'Cognition as a Collaborative Process', in D. Kuhn and R.S. Siegler (eds), *Handbook of Child Psychology: Cognition, Perception, and Language* (Vol. 2), John Wiley & Sons, New York, pp. 679–744.

Rudduck, J. and McIntyre, D. 2007 *Improving Learning Through Consulting Pupils*, Routledge, London.

Schofield, J.W. 2002 'Increasing the Generalizability of Qualitative Research', in A.M. Huberman and M.B. Miles (eds), *The Qualitative Researcher's Companion*, Sage, Thousand Oaks, pp. 171–203.

Schweinhart, L.J. and Weikart, D.P. 1997 'The High-scope Preschool Curriculum Comparison Through Age 23', *Early Childhood Research Quarterly*, no. 12, pp. 117–43.

Sheridan, S. and Pramling, I. 2001 'Children's Conceptions of Participation and Influence in Pre-school: A Perspective on Pedagogical Quality', *Contemporary Issues in Early Childhood*, vol. 2, no. 2, pp. 169–94.

Siraj-Blatchford, I., Sylva, K., Taggart, B., Sammons, P., Melhuish, E. and Elliot, K. 2003 *Intensive Case Studies of Practice across the Foundation Stage* (Technical Paper No. 10), Institute of Education, University of London and DfES, London.

Sylva, K. and Nabuco, M.E. 1996 'Research on Quality in the Curriculum', *International Journal of Early Childhood*, vol. 28, no. 2, pp. 1–6.

Wall, K. and Higgins, S. 2006 'Facilitating Metacognitive Talk: A Research and Learning Tool', *International Journal of Research & Method in Education*, vol. 29, no. 1, pp. 39–53.

Warming, H. 2005 'Participant Observation: A Way to Learn About Children's Perspectives', in A. Clark, A.T. Kjorholt and P. Moss (eds), *Beyond Listening: Children's Perspectives on Early Childhood Services*, Policy Press, Bristol, pp. 51–70.

Wells, G. 1999 *Dialogic Inquiry: Toward a Sociocultural Practice and Theory of Education*, Cambridge University Press, Cambridge.

Wenger, E. 1998 *Communities of Practice: Learning, Meaning and Identity*, Cambridge University Press, Cambridge.

Wertsch, J.V. 1998 *Mind as Action*, Oxford University Press, New York.

Westcott, H.L. and Littleton, K.S. 2005 'Exploring Meaning in Interviews with Children', in S. Greene and D. Hogan (eds), *Researching Children's Experience: Approaches and Methods*, Sage, London, pp. 141–57.

Woodhead, M. and Faulkner, D. 2000 'Subjects, Objects or Participants? Dilemmas of Psychological Research with Children', in P. Christensen and A. James (eds), *Research with Children: Perspectives and Practices*, Falmer Press, London, pp. 9–35.

FURTHER READING

Christensen, P. and James, A. 2000 *Research with Children: Perspectives and Practices*, Falmer Press, London. This book helps us to understand the move from more traditional ways of researching children's lives to new paradigms where children are viewed as participants in their lives and in the research process, and perceiving childhood as a social construct.

Clark, A., Kjorholt, A.T. and Moss, P. 2005 *Beyond Listening: Children's Perspectives on Early Childhood Services*, Policy Press, Bristol. While it advocates listening to young children and offers important methodological information about how to go about it using different 'languages', this book offers a critical perspective of the subject identifying some dilemmas and challenges, particularly in terms of how one uses 'children's voices'.

Hedegaard, M. and Fleer, M. (eds) 2008 *Studying Children: A Cultural-Historical Approach*, Open University Press, Maidenhead. This book considers the links between methods and design and the theoretical framework of research. The authors adopt a cultural-historical theoretical approach, viewing child development as a social process deeply related to the child's social, cultural and historical context. The authors highlight the interactive nature of the research process and how the research methods and techniques might construct the reports we produce about children's lives, learning and development. A chapter on interviewing within this perspective might be of particular interest to those interested in designing ways to interview children.

15

Interviewing adults in an Indigenous community

Sue Atkinson-Lopez

Between 2003 and 2007, as an Indigenous Victorian—a Yorta Yorta woman working in the early childhood field—I interviewed 30 members of the Indigenous early childhood community to gather data for my PhD thesis, 'Indigenous Self-determination and Early Childhood Education and Care in Victoria'.

AIMS OF THE RESEARCH

The aim of this research was to explore Indigenous Victorian perspectives of early childhood education and care within Indigenous specific and non-Indigenous specific centres.

The research was guided by the following question:

> What are the theoretical, practical and political issues in constructing an Early Childhood curriculum that contributes to the self-determination of Indigenous people in Victoria?

LINKS TO THEORY AND EMPIRICAL RESEARCH

To arrive at this question, I examined current literature on approaches to Indigenous inclusion in education, and more specifically in early childhood education. I found that major silences exist in the literature on current approaches to Indigenous inclusion in early childhood education: the voices and identities of urban (Victorian) Aboriginal families and examinations of what self-determination looks like within an early childhood curriculum.

WHAT GUIDED YOUR DECISIONS REGARDING THE CHOICE OF METHODS EMPLOYED?

As an Indigenous researcher, it was particularly important for me to work within the ethics of Indigenous protocols, as the primary focus of my research was the self-determination of the Victorian Indigenous community to which I belong. Although the meaning of self-determination is debated, there is agreement amongst Indigenous activists that self-determination, with its affiliation to power and knowledge, is central to the empowerment of Indigenous people (Roberts, 1994).

The following principles, drawing on these ethics of Indigenous protocols, informed my research:

- undertaking research that benefits the Indigenous community
- consultation and collaboration with the Indigenous community throughout the research process
- respecting Indigenous community protocols
- actively acknowledging Indigenous ownership of knowledge and process
- dissemination of results in a way that is accessible to and benefits the Indigenous community (adapted from Smith, 1995).

The implications of working within this ethical framework were multiple, as I constructed a methodology informed culturally, politically, ideologically and historically by my standpoint as an Indigenous researcher.

POSITIONALITY AND PERSPECTIVES INFORMING THE RESEARCH

My position as an insider, as a member of the Indigenous community working in the early childhood profession, meant that I was participating in what I was investigating. This differentiated my work from the bulk of the investigations into Indigenous communities that have been conducted by Western academics. Until recently, before partnership models of Indigenous research emerged, the process of investigating Indigenous communities by non-Indigenous academics had taken place within a framework informed by, and subsumed in, the dominant white research culture which has seen Indigenous 'subjects' exploited and oppressed (Atkinson, et al., 1994).

This can be seen in the compensatory education movement of the late 1960s and 1970s, where the perceived 'failures' of the Aboriginal family to provide adequately for their preschool children in terms of the skills and attitudes necessary for success in a Eurocentric middle-class school system would be addressed within early childhood programs. These programs, with their roots in Western research and practice, were implemented with little consultation with or involvement of Indigenous families and communities (McConnochie and Russel, 1982). The decision-making or self-determination capacity of Indigenous communities was overlooked within this construction of Aboriginality as incompetence.

In my research project, the Indigenous voices of my local Indigenous community were positioned as knowledgable and capable in the movement towards greater self-determination. In exploring how Indigenous community members made sense of the links between early childhood education and Indigenous self-determination, I sought to inform the construction of Indigenous-inclusive early childhood programs in an enriched way, with all their complexities, multiplicities and contradictions. In this quest, a qualitative research approach was taken using several techniques I believe to be consistent with the principles of ethical conduct of Indigenous research. These included the use of an Indigenous community forum, consultation with Indigenous Victorian Elders, communicating narratives in the oral tradition through dialogues, and informing Indigenous community members of the research outcomes. Qualitative research is responsive to these principles in that it encourages the production of rich texts via dialogues that provide spaces for the complexity of voices once silenced. The broad interview questions that semi-structured these dialogues were drawn from my literature review and my own experiences as an Indigenous early childhood professional:

1 What is the early childhood centre's role in building on the identity and culture of Indigenous preschoolers?
2 How do early childhood centres plan and implement Indigenous-inclusive programs for Indigenous and non Indigenous preschoolers?
3 What understandings of Victoria's Indigenous culture do non-Indigenous early childhood practitioners hold?
4 What understandings of Victoria's Indigenous culture do Indigenous and non-Indigenous preschoolers hold?
5 How is Indigenous community consultation being implemented in the construction of an Indigenous early childhood curriculum?

Each group of participants—Elders, parents, early childhood professionals and children—had interview schedules tailored to their own positions within the early childhood community. This is in keeping with Atkinson's (2006) approach to Indigenous research, which acknowledges the diversity of the Indigenous community.

The principles around what Edwards (2001) describes as a 'self-critical awareness of the processes of research' (2001, p. 134) within qualitative research also demand that I, as the researcher, consider issues of power. Postmodern critiques of power which include an 'ethical concern for those whose experiences are being represented' (Edwards, 2001, p. 134) and a transparency about the researcher's own position were brought to this qualitative framing of the research. The issue of an unequal power relationship that often exists between researcher and subject was greatly modified in the context of interviewing many of the participants who were known to me as friends, relatives and colleagues. I was mindful that Elders were treated with respect and looked on as mentors with knowledge and experiences that younger people such as myself may not possess. I was also mindful that, although the participants would be prepared to share personal thoughts and reflections, there may have been limits to what they were willing to share as part of a public discourse.

THE PARTICIPANTS

The Indigenous community in Victoria has a well-established network of early childhood services. It was the representatives of these organisations, and the children and families who access them, who were invited to participate in this research. Therefore, the participants were chosen using purposeful sampling (Denzin and Lincoln, 2000) and convenience sampling (Mac Naughton, 2001). It was also of central importance in respecting the local Elders to invite them to participate.

In contemporary Victoria, there is no definitive definition of an Elder. However, the term is often applied to Indigenous people over 50 years of age who have particular experiences and/or knowledge upon which the community can draw when seeking guidance or advice. Including the Elders not only gave breadth to my sample, but was recognition of the place these men and women hold as teachers and mentors, and the foundations they lay in building early childhood services for Indigenous children in Victoria.

The diversity of people invited to participate also reflected the breadth and complexity of Victoria's Indigenous early childhood community. Factors such as age, family commitments, education, location in the workforce, state of origin, family background and physical appearance have an impact on the experience of Aboriginality, and understandings and experiences of self-determination. I anticipated that these diverse perspectives would also build the validity of my research by allowing analysis from multiple viewpoints.

COMMUNITY CONSULTATION

The specific research techniques used in this research were constructed to reflect the communal and collective organisation of the Indigenous community. Before beginning the collection of data, I invited local Indigenous Elders and representatives from Victorian Indigenous early childhood organisations to a community forum in March 2003. The objective of this forum was to inform the Indigenous community about the research and to receive advice. I began by advising the small but enthusiastic group about the work I had done to date. I presented my research topic and briefly described how I had arrived at this topic through a literature review and the process involved in developing a research proposal. I then advised the group about how I would gather my data; I described who I sought to interview and why; and I provided examples of the interview schedules which were constructed around five broad questions (see above).

I outlined the themes I would expect to emerge from the data, and the group was made aware of the Indigenous research ethics that were at the centre of my methodology. Strong interest was expressed in the research and participants suggested other documents I should read to strengthen my understanding of current developments in the area. These participants were pleased to form a reference group, which I consulted twice more during the course of my research.

In January 2007, I invited all the research participants and my academic supervisor to a second meeting. I outlined the eight chapters nearing completion by including the reading of anonymous quotes from data gathered from interviews. As part of checking the validity of my interpretation, participants had the opportunity to give me feedback in confidence around the use of their voices. I also described to the participants how I was broadly using the concepts of Indigenous self-determination, colonisation and decolonisation within these chapters. By attempting to define these concepts, I was aiming to clarify the goals of my research and to actively inform and respect the early childhood community, particularly the Indigenous early childhood community, as coauthors of the narrative which is my research project (Atkinson, 2006; Mac Naughton and Hughes, 2008).

The final forum was held on 22 May 2008 at a Multifunctional Aboriginal Children's Service (MACS), where members of the steering committee and the manager of the MACS were given an abstract summarising the project. Those in attendance were also given samples of how their voices had been used within extracts of two chapters and were asked for feedback regarding the accuracy of the quotes in representing their position.

This collaborative approach is in line with the ethical and methodological approaches to researching with Indigenous communities in the broader research literature, which emphasise ongoing consultation with Indigenous communities during the research process, including during analysis (Atkinson, 2006; Gower, 2003).

ANALYSIS OF DATA

That many of the interviewees were known to me as friends, colleagues and relations is reflective of the nature of Victoria's Indigenous community as a tight-knit collective. It was the informal and frequent conversations I had with many of the interviewees prior to 2000 that shaped this project. In listening to their voices, as I transcribed the interviews and as I read and reread their words, I tried to produce an authentic representation of their words that would strengthen the validity of my project. In this, I spent much time reflecting on what I had heard in what Atkinson (2006) describes as a 'deep listening' and 'hearing with more than the ears'. By engaging with complexities such as inconsistencies within and across the interviews, rather than glossing over these, I believe I have come closer to acting with fidelity around the participants' voices in more accurately representing their attitudes and ideas. In locating their voices within an academic framework, I hoped to give my local Indigenous early childhood community a stronger voice within early childhood theory and practice. I believe that embracing complexities will help to ensure that their voices will be heard. My project is more likely to withstand critical scrutiny by embracing complexities, thereby giving this project weight and authority within academia and beyond. Such validity of voice is central in attempting to move early childhood professionals, academics and policy-makers towards change around Indigenous inclusion in Victoria (Mac Naughton and Hughes, 2008).

PRESENTING MY FINDINGS

I presented my findings as a text or narrative. This, I believe, is in keeping with the Indigenous intellectual and cultural framework for the transmission of knowledge in the oral tradition. Traditionally in Australia's Indigenous community, 'secular' knowledge, religious and philosophical beliefs were transmitted across the generations using oral texts such as stories and song, supported by symbols used in art (Atkinson, Lovett and Elkner, 1991). That this oral tradition remains important in passing on a once-hidden Indigenous history is reflected in the gathering of Indigenous Victorian voices and presenting them in a written text in the oral tradition (for example, Critchett, 1998). Although five broad questions structured the interviews, they were open-ended and gave the participants plenty of scope for conversations which enabled the participants' experiences and personal and social histories to come forward. In this sense, my findings are part of a continuing historical narrative (Mac Naughton and Hughes, 2008). To make the academic interpretation of these narratives accessible to the community which produced them, I distributed a plain language version to the centres and organisations involved as coauthors.

VALIDITY

I believe my text, which is neither definitive nor final, recognised those complexities around the construction of knowledges that encompass history, race, power, hopes, dreams and the struggle for survival as Indigenous people. The authority of my text, I believe, lies in its engagement with such complexities, the ethics employed in the study, my position within the community I am studying and the potential to redefine theory and practice within early childhood education and care.

In the act of combining experience and theory, I hoped to make this work meaningful to my own community by providing an in-depth analysis of the Indigenous community's positions on self-determination and early childhood education. The validity of this work will also lie in its value for informing and reconceptualising early childhood theory and practice, and for effecting change. Until quite recently, theory and practice in the early childhood field have served and reflected non-Indigenous conceptions of Aboriginality and childhood. In placing Indigenous Victorian voices within an academic framework, we as an Indigenous community can speak more rigorously against theories or practices that rest on stereotypes rather than on critique and reflection.

Although I was aware that I was writing largely for the white academic audience who are in a position to judge the worthiness of the piece, the success of my research will also be judged by the Victorian Indigenous early childhood community in terms of how well the project followed the principles of self-determination within the researched community and how useful this project will be in the realisation of self-determination in early childhood.

SUMMARY

I began this study to explore the theoretical, political and practical issues in constructing an early childhood curriculum that contributes to the self-determination of Indigenous people in Victoria. The participants' comments around this broad question demonstrated that such issues are strongly informed by colonial constructions of Aboriginality. Such constructions are tied to the concept of the Indigenous as the distant, traditional 'other', leaving Indigenous Victorians largely marginalised in their quest to find a voice around Indigenous inclusion in early childhood education and care.

Although the Indigenous participants' statements underline the concept of a postcolonial Aboriginality which is complex, multiple and ambiguous, this is a concept with which non-Indigenous early childhood practitioners commonly struggle. Until a postcolonial understanding of Aboriginality is embedded in the early childhood curriculum, the self-determination of Indigenous communities in negotiating an inclusive place in that curriculum will be undermined.

QUESTIONS FOR REFLECTION

1. If you wish to conduct research with an Indigenous early childhood community, what initial steps must you take to ensure the research topic and proposed methodology is ethical, appropriate and respectful of that community?
2. How would you build a respectful and ethical research partnership with the Indigenous community that ensures the community has ownership of the project?

REFERENCES

Atkinson, J. 2006 '*Evidence-based Practice or Practice-based Evidence?*' paper presented to Child Safety Research Conference, Brisbane, 14–15 November.

Atkinson, M., Brabham, W., Henry, J. and James, D. 1994 *Koorie Research Program: Ethics, Protocols and Methodologies*, Deakin University, Melbourne.

Atkinson, S., Lovett, I., and Elkner, B. 1991 *Story, Music and Movement: Aboriginal Child Care Support Materials*, Victorian Aboriginal Child Care Agency, Melbourne.

Critchett, J. 1998 *Untold Stories: Memories and Lives of Victorian Koories*, Melbourne University Press, Melbourne.

Denzin, N.K. and Lincoln, Y.S. 2000 'The Fifth Moment' in N.K. Denzin and Y.S. Lincoln (eds), *Handbook of Qualitative Research*, Sage, Thousand Oaks, CA, pp. 575–86.

Edwards, A. 2001 'Qualitative Designs', in G. Mac Naughton, S. Rolfe and I. Siraj-Blatchford (eds), *Doing Early Childhood Research: International Perspectives on Theory and Practice*, Open University Press, Buckingham, pp. 117–35.

Gower, D. 2003 *Ethical Research in Indigenous Contexts and the Practical Implementation of It: Guidelines for Ethical Research Versus the Practice of Research*, paper presented at the Australian Association for Research in Education, Auckland, New Zealand, 30 November–3 December.

Mac Naughton, G. 2001 'Action Research', in G. Mac Naughton, S.A. Rolfe and I. Siraj-Blatchford (eds), *Doing Early Childhood Research: International Perspectives on Theory and Practice*, Open University Press, Buckingham, pp. 208–23.

Mac Naughton, G. and Hughes, P. 2008 *Doing Action Research in Early Childhood*, Open University Press, Maidenhead.

McConnochie, K. and Russel, A. 1982 *Early Childhood Services for Aboriginal Children*, Australian Government Publishing Service, Canberra.

Roberts, D. 1994 'Self-determination and the Struggle for Aboriginal Equality', in E. Bourke, C. Bourke and B. Edwards (eds), *Aboriginal Australia*, University of Queensland Press, Brisbane, pp. 212–36.

Smith, A. 1995 '*Indigenous Research Ethics: Policy, Protocols in Aboriginal Research*', paper presented at the Indigenous Research Ethics Conference, Townsville, Queensland, 27–29 September.

FURTHER READING

Gower, D. 2003 'Ethical Research in Indigenous Contexts and the Practical Implementation of It: Guidelines for Ethical Research Versus the Practice of Research', paper presented at The Australian Association for Research in Education, Auckland, New Zealand, 30 November–3 December. In this paper, Gower examines the National Health and Medical Council's national guidelines for the conduct of research involving Indigenous communities and looks at ethical principles identified by the Aboriginal Institute of Aboriginal and Torres Strait Islander Studies (AITSIS). Gower's discussion around such guidelines and some of the questions it raises are useful for early childhood professionals considering the complexities of researching within Indigenous communities.

Henderson, R., Simmons, D., Bourke, L. and Muir, J. 2002 'Development of Guidelines for Non-Indigenous People Undertaking Research Among the Indigenous Population of North-east Victoria', *Medical Journal of Australia*, vol. 176, pp. 482–5. Although this article is written within the framework of researching Indigenous health, the guidelines discussed can inform educational researchers' understandings and practice in building strong relationships with Indigenous communities based on culturally appropriate protocols.

16

An ethnographic approach to researching young children's learning

Iram Siraj-Blatchford

Ethnographic research has its roots in anthropological and cross-cultural study. In its broadest sense, it encompasses any study that aims to describe some aspect of the sociocultural understandings and practices of a group of people. Rather than offering a particular method for data collection, ethnography may be conducted using a wide range of methodologies. It should therefore be properly understood as providing us with a particular perspective on what counts as legitimate knowledge or, to put it in more academic and philosophical terms, as providing us with an **epistemology** for our research.

Ethnographies typically aim to provide holistic accounts that include the views and perspectives, beliefs and values of all of those involved in the particular sociocultural practice or institutional context being studied. But these broad aims are difficult to achieve in early childhood studies that are, of necessity, limited in terms of time and resources. We should therefore be cautious regarding the overall aims of, and in the claims that we make for, our studies. As Edwards suggests in Chapter 9, researchers may avoid the naïve positivism of many of the early ethnographers by limiting their efforts (and empirical claims) to that of producing what Geertz (1993) has refered to as 'local knowledge'—that is, rich information about locally embedded ways of understanding and acting in the world. In such circumstances, it is more appropriate to refer to the work as providing 'a partial ethnographic account'.

Early childhood researchers have conducted ethnographic research for a wide range of purposes. It has been applied to the study of educational outcomes for children attending early years services (Sylva et al., 1999a and b). It has also been applied to identify the different experiences of girls and of young minority ethnic children in institutional settings (Wright, 1986; Davies, 1989; Connolly, 1998); to the study of play (Feitelsen, 1977; Paley, 1984; Dau, 1999); and the study of particular early childhood programs (Kantor and Whalley, 1998; Folque, 2008).

In the context of preschool improvement and effectiveness studies, ethnographic researchers have often succeeded in getting below the surface of general evaluative characteristics identified in checklists and rating scales that look at quality (Harms, Clifford and Cryer, 1998; Sylva et al., 1999a and b). The best of these studies go a long way towards revealing the processes by which individuals and groups sustain, modify, shape, change and create their working, learning and play environments. Ethnographic forms of analysis can be especially valuable to those engaged in practice and in institutional development. But, while an increasing number of quantitative and qualitative studies, and studies employing mixed methodologies such as the UK Effective Provision of Pre-School Education (EPPE) project, do pay closer attention to the overall contexts and ethos of early childhood education settings than was previously the case, there is clearly a need for more ethnographic research that can paint in the fine-grained reality of educational processes within early childhood settings.

As Dahlberg, Moss and Pence (1999) and James and Prout (1997) have suggested, the qualitative studies currently being applied in early childhood education are also important in allowing new voices to be heard—these are the voices of teachers, other carers, families and the children themselves.

It has been suggested that the presentational task of ethnography is to 'paint pictures in words', 'capture a likeness', recreate the 'feel' of an event, 'evoke an image', 'awaken a spirit' or 'reconstruct a mood or atmosphere' (Woods, 1996). Hammersley (1999) provides a useful summary, in which he refers to ethnography as having the following features:

- People's behaviour is studied in everyday contexts.
- Data are gathered from a range of sources, but observation and/or relatively informal conversations are usually the main sources.
- The approach to data collection is 'unstructured'.
- The focus is usually a single setting or group.
- The analysis of data involves interpretation.

In fact, ethnographic study is by its very nature interpretative—that is, concerned with understanding the subjective world of human experience. The central aim of the ethnographer is therefore to provide a holistic account that includes the views, perspectives, beliefs, intentions and values of the subjects of the study. To achieve this, we focus upon human actions that are always understood as 'behaviours-with-meaning' (Cohen and Manion, 1994). 'Actions' are only meaningful to us if we can identify the intentions of the actors involved. This is often far from straightforward—a classic example of the difficulty involves considering the difference between a wink and a blink. While there may be no mechanical difference between the two acts, the cultural contexts, and the relationship between individuals that each act suggests, demonstrate that they actually constitute two significantly different actions. As Fetterman (1989) suggests: 'Anyone who has ever mistaken a blink for a wink is fully aware of the significance of cultural interpretation.' (1989, p. 28) An account that is capable of discrimination between the two actions involves what Geertz (1993), citing Gilbert Ryle, refers to as 'thick description' (1993, p. 6). A **thick description** is one that includes everything needed for the reader to understand what is happening. While a **thin description** would simply describe the rapid closing of an eyelid, a thick description will provide the context, telling the reader whether the movement was a blink caused by a piece of dust, a conspiratorial gesture or a romantic signal transmitted across a crowded room. Again, this is a tall order, and it constitutes what has been referred to as the 'paradox of familiarity' for 'insider' researchers such as practitioners conducting ethnographic studies of their own workplace.

The problem is that, while we may easily be able to apply our shared cultural framework of understanding when we *interpret* the behaviour of colleagues, parents and young children in our own 'insider' social group, for precisely the same reasons we find it very much more difficult to isolate and make these cultural principles *explicit*. As Garfinkle's (1963) classic (if problematic) experiments with student volunteers showed, individuals share a whole range of 'background expectancies' upon which social interaction and meaningful communication depend. In one study, Garfinkle instructed his students to record the responses of friends or relatives when commonplace remarks and conversation were actively (and unreasonably) pursued to obtain total clarification of their precise meanings. A short passage from one of Garfinkle's transcriptions illustrates the general idea, and a typical response:

> (S waved his hand cheerily)
> S: How are you?

> *E:* How am I in regard to what? My health, my finances, my school work, my peace of mind, my ...
> *S:* (red in the face and suddenly out of control): Look! I was just trying to be polite. Frankly, I don't give a damn how you are. (Garfinkel, 1963, p. 222)

Paley (1984) notes similar, if less dramatic discomfort on the part of a group of four-year-olds in the following interaction:

> *Teacher:* How do you play house with a Barbie doll?
> *Charlotte:* We pretend they are the sister and the mommy.
> *Teacher:* Then who are you?
> *Janie:* We're the one that acts them out.
> *Teacher:* Oh. You *are* the Barbie doll.
> *Janie:* Right. We *are* the sister or mommy.
> *Teacher:* But you're the sister and mommy even without Barbie.
> *Jill:* This is much more funner. Because you can look at her and see how she looks.
> *Teacher:* By the way, how old is she supposed to be?
> The girls blush and giggle as if I have asked an indelicate question.
> I have never seen them so ill at ease in a discussion.
> *Charlotte:* Maybe a teenager.
> But sometimes she's a mother?
> *Charlotte:* No.
> *Janie:* Yes. Uh ... I don't know. Yes, she is.
> *Teacher:* Do you ever pretend she's a mother with a baby?
> *Charlotte:* No! No! She never has a baby. Never!
> *Jill:* Of course not. No babies.
> *Janie:* But we pretend to have babies. Right, Mary Ann? Remember?
> There are more side-glances and embarrassed laughter; Barbie is not open to full analysis. By contrast, nothing is covert about superhero dolls. Why is Barbie in this sensitive category of family secrets? (Paley, 1984, pp. 11–12)

As Garfinkle (1963) argues, the stability and meaningfulness of our day-to-day communications depends upon unstated cultural assumptions about what is said and why we say it. This is as true of young children as it is of adults. If we are to provide an adequate account, it is important that all the significant, unstated assumptions are identified and stated as clearly as possible. Cross-context or cross-cultural comparison can often be useful in this respect. Schieffelin and Ochs (1998), for example, studied the use of simplified registers ('baby talk') by caregivers in different societies and came to the conclusion that these practices may be part of a more general orientation in which situations are adapted to young children's perceived needs. In societies where a simplified register is not applied, children are expected to adapt to the adult world at an early age. In such societies, caregivers direct the children to notice and respond to others, and they frequently model appropriate utterances for the child to repeat to third parties. These features of caregiver speech are therefore neither universal nor necessary for language to be acquired, although this may often be assumed.

This effort to provide an adequate account of the insider perspective provides a central challenge for ethnography. If researchers want to discover how respondents understand and rationalise their practices, they must suspend their own personal values and judgments, and identify the hidden assumptions that determine the insider perspectives and approaches. But, as we have seen, this is often a special problem for those who study institutional contexts with which they are especially familiar. The task must then be to make the familiar 'strange', to imagine yourself as an 'outsider' and to recognise that even the most common and accepted practices might be questioned or appear questionable from that outsider perspective.

Burgess (1985) cites Howard Becker (1971), who stresses the difficulties that are involved:

> It is not just the survey method of educational testing or any of those things that keeps people from seeing what is going on. I think, instead, that it is first and foremost a matter of it all being so familiar that it becomes impossible to single out events that occur in the classroom as things that have occurred, even when they happen right in front of you. I have not had the experience of observing in elementary and high school classrooms myself, but I have in college classrooms and it takes a tremendous effort of will and imagination to stop seeing the things that are conventionally there to be seen. I have talked to a couple of teams of research people who have sat around in classrooms trying to observe and it is like pulling teeth to get them to see or write anything beyond what 'everyone' knows. (1985, p. 10)

The importance of all this really cannot be overstated—a concrete example may therefore be of value. Consider Connolly's (1998) narrative account of a four-year-old boy's sexual harassment of Michaela, a five-year-old, in Mr Wallace's classroom at 'East Avenue Primary School'.

Hannah and Michaela had just been talking about Michaela's new boyfriend, which appeared to frustrate Sean as he had previously expressed an interest in Michaela as a girlfriend. Hannah was now turning her attention directly to Sean and trying unsuccessfully to engage him in conversation:

> *Hannah:* That's a nice name—'Sean'!
> *Sean:* I hate my name! [*his head remains focused on his work and he slightly turns away from her*]
> *Hannah:* [*carries on with her own work for a short while before looking up again and turning her attention to Michaela*]: You're only five and he's six [referring back to Michaela's boyfriend].
> *Sean:* [*looks up and stares at Michaela. Frustratedly*]: He sits on your knee and pulls your clothes off! [*stands up and leans over the table to Michaela, staring her directly in the face*] He sits on your knee and licks your [*whispers the rest—inaudible*].
> *Michaela:* [*appears upset and jumps up, pushes her chair under the table and walks towards Mr Wallace*].
> *Hannah:* [*anxiously sits up straight, folds her arms and momentarily puts one of her fingers over her lips in anticipation of Mr Wallace's attention*].
> *Michaela:* [*as she makes her way towards Mr Wallace, he looks up and asks her to go over and have her turn making a bumble bee with the classroom assistant. She does this, deciding not to tell Mr Wallace*] (Connolly, 1998, p. 142)

Connolly's account goes on to cite a number of other interactions that showed how the public experiences of the girls at East Avenue were significantly shaped by notions of heterosexuality and the discourse of boyfriends. It isn't difficult in this case to imagine an alternative 'thin' descriptive account that would provide no more than the surface dialogue; such an account would tell us nothing about Sean's possible sense of 'rejection' and do little to show how Michaela considers reporting, but then decides not to complain about, Sean's behaviour to Mr Wallace.

Another example of good practice in terms of thick description is taken from Paley's (1984) study of the children playing in her own classroom:

> Social action in kindergarten is contained in dramatic plots. Since the characters create the plot, actors must identify themselves. In the doll corner, if a plumber arrives, then a pipe has just broken; the appearance of a school teacher signals that the children are about to receive a lesson. The four girls in the doll corner have announced who they are: Mother, Sister, Baby, Maid. To begin with, then, there will be cooking and eating, crying and cleaning. Charlotte is the mother because, she tells the others, she is wearing the silver shoes. Leadership often goes to the child who is most confident about the meaning of symbols.

Karen: I'm hungry. Wa-a-ah!
Charlotte: Lie down, baby.
Karen: I'm a baby that sits up.
Charlotte: First you lie down and sister covers you and *then* I make your cereal and then you sit up.
Karen: Okay.
(Paley, 1984, p. 1)

Typically, small-scale studies involve an initial observation phase where various inferences may be made about what has been seen, followed by either formal interviews or less structured conversations and documentary analysis. This, in turn, will be followed with more focused observations to confirm or clarify what is happening. The process is cyclical. Ethnography is concerned with lived experiences, and to study this the researcher usually engages in participant observation. That is, they participate in the activities of the group to be studied and simultaneously record what is taking place. Field notes are often written on the spot and subsequently amplified and elaborated while the events remain fresh in the researcher's memory. Increasingly, photographic, audio and videorecordings are being used to supplement these accounts and to provide more permanent records. All of these materials may then be drawn upon in writing up the final ethnographic study.

While some readers who plan to research their own working environment may consider that the formality of gaining consent is unnecessary, we would argue that, in any form of research, permission should be sought from both the parents and the children. In fact, given the importance of participant observation in ethnography, it should be recognised that the issue of access, and the role of gatekeepers in providing/permitting access, takes on much more *ongoing* significance. Rather than the usual business of gaining formal permission in preparation for a study, in ethnography access becomes a process of continuously establishing and developing relationships with the research participants. Even where the ethnographer is an outsider, the significant gatekeepers may not be the head or manager of the centre in which you are working, but rather the more vociferous individuals (adults and children) who participate on a day-to-day basis within the setting. For an interesting account of the essentially negotiative and ongoing character, as well as the continuing tensions and problems, of participant observation, see Schatzman and Strauss (1973).

We have found that, where prior consent is required, initial access is best gained through a mutual contact that can recommend the researcher to the institutional manager. The manager will need to be reassured about confidentiality and will expect to be given assurances that the research will not be disruptive to the normal day-to-day functioning of the establishment. We have found that gatekeepers often have a vested interest in the results of the study—they may be anxious that, however anonymous the study might be, their colleagues, employees and practices are presented in a good light. If they have experience of other non-ethnographic research they may ask you to explain the hypothesis that you intend testing, and to show the interview schedules or questionnaires that you will be using. All of this may take some explaining, and it is wise to arrive at any initial meeting prepared to provide an account of the basic assumptions and philosophy of ethnography to put their minds at rest. Where concerns or suspicions are particularly great, it is a good idea to suggest the formation of an advisory committee to which you can report at significant stages of the study. Advisory committees, which may be drawn from user groups (for example, parents as well as administrators/governors, etc.), are often invaluable in providing access to documentary evidence that would otherwise be unavailable. They also provide an additional means of gaining validation through additional triangulation (see below).

Those embarking on their first ethnographic study are often nervous about the prospect of conducting participant observation, but we have found most early childhood settings to be extremely friendly and easy-going places. While the participant observation of many of those groups of interest to other social researchers (such as adult and adolescent drug-takers and other social deviants) can be problematic, many researchers find working with young children relatively easy and, as Sluckin (1981) observed in his research on playground behaviour, you can quickly become 'part of the furniture':

> Within a few weeks the children became more and more familiar with my presence and I became part of the furniture of the playground. On one occasion they used me in a game of 'all after that man there' and for fifty seconds I was mobbed, pulled and kicked by a bevy of five-year-olds. Happily, the noise was more alarming than the blows and so I concluded that this was an example of pretend fighting. On another occasion I became incorporated into a piece of rhyming word play, as two five-year-old girls revealed to each other my true identity.
>
> *Jane:* He's about that big.
> *Sophie (to me):* You're about that big.
> *Jane:* He's a dum dum.
> *Sophie:* He's daft, he's a paddy dum dum.
> *Jane:* I know what he is, I know what he is.
> *Sophie:* What?
> *Jane:* He's a lazy bugger; he never gets up in the morning.
> (1981, p. 7)

THE PLACE OF THEORY IN ETHNOGRAPHY

Connolly's (1998) study of 'East Avenue Primary School' is perhaps especially useful in identifying the place of theory in ethnographic research. Connolly applied theoretical constructs drawn from Grugeon (1993), Epstein (1997) and Walkerdine (1981), among others, in his analysis of the girls' peer relations. It hardly needs to be said that the children themselves would understand the events quite differently from the academic analysts. Given the need to obtain the world-views of those we study, it is important that we should hold back our own interpretations of what is happening to hear the explanations given by those most closely involved in the action. But, just as we have seen in the case of Schieffelin and Ochs' (1998) study, in order to understand the events some theoretical explanations may be required that go beyond the knowledge and experience of our respondents (even when they are adults). While quantitative researchers often begin with a theoretical hypothesis that is to be tested, in ethnography the aim of the researcher is to begin as far as possible with an open mind and to allow the theoretical explanations of the behaviours and statements that are being recorded to emerge from the data. This process, which Glaser and Strauss (1967) refer to as 'grounded theory', is well established and accepted by most practitioners. Ethnographic researchers do need to ground their theory in the data that they collect, but as Fetterman (1989) argues, as a study progresses we should not be too nervous about applying theory from other sources as long as it can be seen to be appropriate and offer useful explanatory power: 'Theories need not be juxtapositions of constructs, assumptions, propositions, and generalisations; they can be midlevel or personal theories about how the world or some small part of it works.' (1989, p. 17).

It is important in this context to recognise that it is neither possible nor desirable to deny our personal theories and suppositions, but what we have to do is to declare them and, where appropriate, compare and contrast them to the theories and suppositions of other theorists and our respondents. Throughout the ethnographic inquiry, there should be a continuous interplay between the observations being made and the theories being developed and introduced to explain them. A good deal of flexibility is demanded of the researcher and, as the theories become more elaborate, some degree of focused questioning or observation is to be expected. As Burns (2000) has observed, this can be particularly worrying for the novice because they are unable to predict in advance the directions the study may take.

Having selected a suitable subject for study, the researcher therefore begins by making broad descriptive observations that provide an overview of the situation being studied. The data-collection field is then narrowed down to provide more and more focused observations. The process has often been described as one of 'progressive focusing'; in the process, theories may increasingly be drawn from the researcher's previous knowledge and experience, and they may also be taken off the academic 'shelf'. As previously argued, theory has an important part to play in ethnography, but it should always be recognised that theories are invariably subject specific—they may be applied with great value to some topics but found to be entirely misleading or inappropriate to others.

It is important to capture the meanings and language of the practitioners, and a useful analytical (and recording and reporting) technique is to identify 'critical episodes' and to prepare 'vignettes' that illustrate significant behaviours. These episodes may be especially significant in explaining a common behaviour recorded, or to show something characteristic of the setting—or, for example, an educational style employed by a particular practitioner. In producing a holistic account, the researcher must be aware that the dramas being recorded are set within wider institutional and sociocultural contexts that also have to be accounted for. That said, early childhood professionals themselves recognise that norms are contextual and specific to particular settings, as Waterhouse (1991) shows in this extract from his records of 'staffroom talk': 'I've just found out that the lot I had last time were far below par for this school you know. Not half as good as they're "used to"! Quite! But I didn't realize 'cause I'd always taught in rough schools. They were all pretty good, you know. You forget what the norm is after a while!' (1991, p. 56).

Waterhouse (1991) sought to provide accounts of the day-to-day institutional practices that operated as 'self-fulfilling prophesies'—or, perhaps less controversially, as 'self-sustaining prophesies', to the disadvantage of young working-class children. Following the perspective of Sharp and Green (1973), Waterhouse focused particularly upon the construction of pupil identities, and provides a symbolic interactionalist study of the processes by which pupils as 'others' are constructed by their teachers in the early years of schooling.

REFLEXIVITY AND REFLEXIVE ABSTRACTION

In terms of learning, we all practise what Piaget referred to as 'reflexivity', suggesting that this process constituted the very basis of all conceptual learning. Piaget argued that, while empirical knowledge might be acquired simply through observation, the learning of explanatory rules and concepts relies upon a process of reflexive abstraction—the self-conscious coordination of the observed with existing cognitive structures of meaning. From this perspective, as an observation is recognised as in some way inconsistent with the individual's cognitive structure of meaning, that structure is reorganised to accommodate it. This elaborated structure of meaning may then, in turn, be applied to explain the observation, which is itself transformed in the process. In a word, the process is one of equilibration. Piaget's 'reflexive abstraction' is a mechanism of equilibration and, from this perspective, it is disequilibrium or cognitive dissonance that provides the motor for the process of learning.

But when we learn about people and about social events, the process is even more complex. Our understanding of any kind of event is conditioned by our prior knowledge, but in this case the 'object' of our interest behaves according to their own understanding of what it is they are doing. We cannot really understand why they act in a particular way unless we first discover what their intentions are. This process of determining the intentions of the authors of texts, actions or other cultural products is termed hermeneutics. While the lesson was most clearly learnt in anthropology, it is now widely recognised that a hermeneutic process must be applied in all of the social sciences. We now recognise that if we wish to describe what someone is doing, we must first understand what they think that they are doing. If this wasn't complicated enough, as social scientists we must also recognise the process that Giddens (1975) refers to as the 'double hermenuetic' (1975, p. 12), where our respondent's understanding of events changes as a direct response of our intervention. As James and Prout (1997) have observed, this is nowhere less apparent than in the study of childhood itself (1997, p. 5).

RELIABILITY, REPLICABILITY, VALIDITY AND TRIANGULATION

Reliability, replicability and validity are important in all forms of research, but they mean different things, and have different implications, in the case of qualitative research. To a quantitative researcher, reliability is to do with the degree of 'fit' between the data and their theoretical representation of it. In ethnography, we attempt to collect multiple representations, and present our research in a manner that explicitly recognises that research participants and readers may have different interpretations of the phenomenon being studied. Insofar as we are successful in engaging with this multiplicity of interpretations, reliability becomes more of a concern to the reader than the researcher. The associated problem of replicability—whether another researcher would produce the same results—is solved by providing a clear account of the research process. The reader should then be able to follow the researcher's footsteps and assess the rationale at every stage. Ideally, an ethnographer should explain their methods of data collection and analysis so clearly that another researcher could use the research report as an instruction manual to replicate the study. Four particular issues need to be addressed explicitly in the report: the application of theory, researcher status, sampling and the social context.

The application of theory

Different theoretical constructs and assumptions can lead to findings that differ widely in their emphasis and interpretation. Analytical categories and constructs must therefore be defined carefully, and their theoretical antecedents and implications outlined.

Researcher status

The ethnographic data that are collected will always depend to some degree on the social relationship that the researcher has with the research subjects. Research reports must therefore provide a clear account of the role and status that they have adopted within the group investigated.

Sampling choices

In this context, it is important to recognise that, while most ethnographies are, by their very nature, case studies, that doesn't mean that sampling isn't an issue. While you are unlikely to be making any strong claims regarding the representative nature of your sample choice, the reasons that you had for choosing the specific case still need to be justified. As Miles and Huberman (1994) argue, your sample in this case is *purposive*, and it is your research *purposes* that need to be explained (1994, p. 27). In the study of any one particular group, researchers may neglect information about the life experiences of people in other groups. In making a case for reliability, it is therefore important to identify the role and status of the people who have served as informants and to explain the decision processes involved in making your choice.

Social contexts

What people say and do always varies to some extent according to who else is present at the time. Ethnographic researchers must therefore be especially alert to the fact that they may themselves influence their respondents' behaviour, and that the data they collect may be quite different, depending upon the social contexts within which their respondents are reporting or acting. Again, a case should be made for the decisions that were taken to ensure the greatest research reliability.

To most quantitative researchers 'validity' is all about 'truth conditions', the relationship between what it is that a test measures and what it will predict (Guildford, 1954). Ethnographic researchers are more interested in what 'seems' to be true than in any objectively defined truth. But ethnographers are attempting to portray the social world as it appears to the people that inhabit it, and something therefore has to be done to ensure that it is the perceptions of the 'inhabitants', and not of the visiting researcher, that take precedence. (In discussing validity in these terms, it is significant to note that the words 'valid' and 'value' have the same etymological roots.) For an idea to have value, or to be valid, it needs to be strong and effective. Our assessments of validity are based upon our perceptions of 'worth', and hence upon our value systems. In clarifying our rationale, we are delegating this responsibility to the reader, who may accept or reject our explicit values. Quantitative researchers often present their findings as objective truth, and hence *smuggle* their values in (Siraj-Blatchford, 1994).

This is where triangulation comes in. The term is borrowed from the contexts of navigation or surveying, where two or more directional markers are used to accurately locate a single geographical feature or position. In qualitative research, to triangulate your data means to confirm their validity by obtaining data from a second or third methodological source. An observation may therefore be backed up by evidence gained in an interview and/or from documentary analysis. Brannen (1992) argues that adequate triangulation (providing multiple sources of information) involves not only methods and data, but also investigators and theories. For all of these reasons, mixed-method studies are becoming more popular. Pinnell et al. (1994), for example, compared instructional models for the literacy education of 'high-risk' six-year-olds, using qualitative analyses through videotaped data to support the largely quantitative analyses. This allowed more description and interpretation of teaching and learning processes. They concluded that: 'Solving the problems related to reading failure in the US may ultimately depend on our willingness to examine programmatic outcomes in ways that take into account the multiple, interacting factors that may mean success for our high-risk students.' (Pinnell et al., 1994, p. 36).

As Fetterman (1989) argues, in recent years there has been increasing evidence in the research literature that mixing methods is a valuable strategy for theory development and theory testing.

CONCLUSIONS

The growing popularity of ethnographic methods, as well as 'teacher research', action and collaborative research, may be seen in part as a reaction to a growing dissatisfaction with educational research that was once founded within a naïve empiricist tradition. Research at that time was conducted almost exclusively from within the various academic disciplines such as psychology, sociology and philosophy. Much of this research undoubtedly was problematic, or failed to relate its findings to educational practices and concerns. However, the controversy surrounding the academic status of ethnography and other qualitative approaches has never really been resolved. The traditional approaches to research provided at least the illusion of objectivity. Today, many ethnographers and quantitative researchers reject the suggestion that any research can be truly value free. While other writers have embraced poststructuralist and postmodern approaches that reject the very notion of objectivity, many others are still anxious to be persuasive and rigorous in their work. Researchers have responded in a variety of ways, and even the psychoanalysis of the researcher has been suggested to provide some legitimising basis for ethnography. An elaboration of my own perspective lies beyond the constraints of this chapter, but some of the founding principles may be found in Siraj-Blatchford (1994, 1997, et al. 2006).

The funding bodies that have commissioned preschool quality or effectiveness research have tended to favour quantitative measures of children's academic and social development and progress, as these measures have been seen to provide 'reliable' statistical data. The large samples and/or the longitudinal nature of many of these studies have determined the use of quantitative methods to ensure greater confidence in terms of the representativeness and the generalisability of findings. However, in selecting a particular set of instruments for quantitative study, we inevitably limit the possibilities for explanation that are open to us. Even more fundamentally, the research questions being asked and the hypotheses being tested are drawn from established paradigms and are thus value-loaded in favour of particular explanations. For an increasing number of researchers, this recognition has led to an outright rejection of any form of quantification at all. But it is important to recognise that this outright rejection of quantification may be an over-reaction. While the assumed objectivity of quantitative methods in the past has constituted (and still does constitute) some kind of metaphysical status for its hardened advocates, this aspect may be rejected without rejecting the underlying discipline. A softer, post-metaphysical, new empiricism offers the possibility of greater rigour, and the continued development of better theoretical models and paradigms (Siraj-Blatchford et al. 2006).

In this, it must be recognised that while quantitative studies provide a means of testing theory, qualitative research has a major role to play in generating and developing theory. The two should be seen as complementary rather than contradictory activities.

Many of the possibilities and limitations of ethnography were actually identified in the debate between Woods and Hammersley in the pages of the *British Educational Research Journal* in 1987. In an earlier paper, Woods (1985) had identified three phases in the development of ethnographic research: '1. description; 2. theory formulation; 3. theory testing'.

While to Hammersley (1987a) the notion of 'theory testing' could only mean the use of hypothetical deduction, Woods (1987) clearly accepted a broader definition that would include a wider range of validation strategies which might often fall short of providing any kind of definitive 'proof'. A major difficulty lay in the authors' (Woods, 1985, 1987; Hammersley, 1987a, 1987b) failure to clearly define the difference between individual studies that might include the use of various validation procedures, and the progressive development of an educational paradigm by 'a collaborative research community'. In the circumstances (and perhaps inevitably), the authors were at times 'talking past each other'.

As Sylva (1995) has suggested, we must recognise that over the past twenty or more years we have seen a major theoretical shift away from the study of the child-as-solitary-learner (Piaget) to the child-as-learner-in-social-context (Vygotsky), and narrative and ethnographic research now offer 'an exciting new vein of early years research'. Sylva (1995) therefore suggests that, in discriminating between early childhood education studies, we might usefully consider their 'fitness for purpose'. But we must also recognise that our evaluation of fitness will ultimately and inevitably depend on our choice of paradigm, and our power to impose our evaluations will depend upon the degree to which our paradigm is established. Early childhood education has traditionally occupied a marginal position in educational debate. The challenge is therefore, as always, to construct paradigms from within the everyday professional and institutional contexts that we study and to develop them, where possible, in collaboration with other researchers, parents, carers and children.

SUMMARY

In this chapter we have argued that ethnography has an important role to play in early childhood and educational research. We have considered the place of theory and argued that the ethnographer should be especially careful to consider explanations and theories other than their own. The challenges and benefits of participant observation were discussed, as well as the nature of the truth claims that may be offered. The central task must always be to provide a reasoned and critical analysis of the data.

QUESTIONS FOR REFLECTION

1. What epistemological model do you favour? How will you justify it to your readers?
2. Take a close look at a study that is presented as ethnographic or a partial ethnography. Consider the extent to which the study makes a case for reliability and validity. How might the report be strengthened in these terms?
3. If ethnographers reject any claim to (weak or strong) objectivity, what are the implications for the disadvantaged and oppressed groups about which they often write?

REFERENCES

Becker, H. 1971 'Footnote', in M. Wax et al. (eds), *Anthropological Perspectives in Education*, Basic Books, New York.

Brannen, J. (ed.) 1992 *Mixing Methods: Qualitative and Quantitative Research*, Avebury, Aldershot.

Burgess, R. 1985 *Field Methods in the Study of Education*, Falmer Press, London.

Burns, R. 2000 *Introduction to Research Methods*, Sage, London.

Cohen, L. and Manion, L. 1994 *Research Methods in Education*, Routledge, London.

Connolly, P. 1998 *Racism, Gender Identities and Young Children*, Routledge, London.

Dahlberg, G., Moss, P. and Pence, A. 1999 *Beyond Quality in Early Childhood Education and Care: Postmodern Perspectives*, Falmer Press, London.

Dau, E. 1999 *Child's Play: Revisiting Play in Early Childhood Settings*, MacLennan & Petty, Sydney.

Davies, B. 1989 *Frogs and Snails and Feminist Tails: Preschool Children and Gender*, Allen & Unwin, Sydney.

Epstein, D. 1997 'Cultures of Schooling/Cultures of Sexuality', *International Journal of Inclusive Education*, vol. 1, no. 1, pp. 37–53.

Feitelson, D. 1977 'Cross-cultural Studies of Representational Play', in B. Tizard and D. Harvey (eds), *Biology of Play*, Heinemann Medical, New York.

Fetterman, D. 1989 *Ethnography: Step by Step*, Applied Social Research Methods Series Vol. 17, Sage, London.

Folque, M. 2008 An Investigation of the *Moviemento da Escola Moderna* (MEM) Pedagogy and its Contribution to Learning to Learn in Portuguese Pre-schools, unpublished PhD thesis, Institute of Education, University of London, London.

Garfinkle, H. 1963 'A Conception of, and Experiments with, "Trust" as a Condition of Stable Social Actions', in O. Harvey (ed.), *Motivation and Social Interaction*, Ronald Press, New York.

Geertz, C. 1993 *The Interpretation of Cultures*, Fontana, London.

Giddens, A. 1975 *The Class Structure of Advanced Societies*, Harper & Row, New York.

Glaser, B. and Strauss, A. 1967 *The Discovery of Grounded Theory*, Aldine, Chicago.

Grugeon, E. 1993 'Gender Implications of Children's Playground Culture', in P. Woods and M. Hammersley (eds), *Gender and Ethnicity in Schools: Ethnographic Accounts*, Routledge, London, pp. 11–33.

Guildford, J. 1954 *Psychometric Methods*, McGraw-Hill, New York.

Hammersley, M. 1987a 'Ethnography and the Cumulative Development of Theory: A Discussion of Woods' Proposal for "Phase Two" Research', *British Education Research Journal*, vol. 13, no. 3, pp. 283–6.

——1987b 'Ethnography for Survival? A Reply to Woods', *British Education Research Journal*, vol. 13, no. 3, pp. 309–17.

——1992 *What's Wrong with Ethnography? Methodological Explorations*, Routledge in association with The Open University, London.

——(ed.) 1999 *Researching School Experience: Ethnographic Studies of Teaching and Learning*, Falmer Press, London.

Harms, T., Clifford, R. and Cryer, D. 1998 *Early Childhood Environment Rating Scale: Revised Edition*, Teachers College Press, New York.

James, A. and Prout, A. (eds) 1997 *Constructing and Reconstructing Childhood*, Falmer, London.

Kantor, R. and Whalley, K. 1998 'New Ideas and Existing Frameworks: Learning from Reggio Emilia', in C. Edwards, G. Forman and L. Gandini (eds), *The Hundred Languages of Children: The Reggio Emilia Approach to Early Childhood Education*, 2nd ed., Ablex Press, Norwood, NJ, pp. 313–33.

Malaguzzi, L. 1993 'History, Ideas and Basic Philosophy', in C. Edwards, L. Gandini and G. Forman (eds), *The Hundred Languages of Children: The Reggio Emilia Approach to Early Childhood*, Ablex, Norwood, NJ.

Miles, M. and Huberman, A. 1994 *Qualitative Data Analysis*, Sage, London.

Paley, V.G. 1984 *Boys and Girls: Superheroes in the Doll Corner* (with a foreword by Philip W. Jackson), University of Chicago Press, Chicago.

Penn, H. 1997 *Comparing Nurseries: Staff and Children in Italy, Spain and the UK*, Paul Chapman, London.

Pinnell, G.S. 1990 *Studying the Effectiveness of Early Intervention Approaches for First Grade Children having Difficulty in Reading*, Martha L. King Language and Literacy Center, Ohio State University, Columbus, OH.

Pinnell, G.S., Lyons, C., Deford, D., Bryk, A. and Selzter, M. 1994 'Comparing Instructional Models for the Literacy Education of High-risk First Graders', *Reading Research Quarterly*, vol. 29, no.1, pp. 8–39.

Schatzman, L. and Strauss, A.L. 1973 *Field Research*, Prentice-Hall, Englewood Cliffs, NJ.

Schieffelin, B. and Ochs, E. 1998 'A Cultural Perspective on the Transition from Prelinguistic to Linguistic Communication,' in M. Wood, D. Faulkner and K. Littleton (eds), *Cultural Worlds of Early Childhood*, Routledge, London.

Sharp, R. and Green, A. 1973 *Education and Social Control*, Routledge & Kegan Paul, London.

Siraj-Blatchford, I. 1994 *Praxis Makes Perfect: Critical Educational Research for Social Justice*, Education Now Books, Nottingham.

——1997 'Postmodernism', in R. Meighan and I. Siraj-Blatchford (eds), *A Sociology of Educating*, Cassell, London.

Siraj-Blatchford, J., Ashcroft, K. and Jones, M. 1997 *Researching into Student Learning and Support in Colleges and Universities*, David Fulton, London.

Siraj-Blatchford, I., Sammons, O., Taggart, B., Sylva, K. and Melhuish, E. 2006 'Educational Research and Evidence Based Policy: The Mixed Method Approach of the EPPE Project', *Evaluation and Research in Education*, vol. 19, no. 2, pp. 63–82.

Sluckin, A. 1981 *Growing Up in the Playground: The Social Development of Children*, Routledge & Kegan Paul, London.

Smith, P. and Connolly, K. 1980 *The Ecology of Preschool Behaviour*, Cambridge University Press, Cambridge.

Stenhouse, L. 1975 *An Introduction to Curriculum Research and Development*, Heinemann, London.

Sylva, K. 1995 'Research as a Medieval Banquet—Barons, Troubadours and Minstrels', Paper presented at the RSA 'Start Right' Conference, September, London.

Sylva, K., Sammons, P., Melhuish, E., Siraj-Blatchford, I. and Taggart, B. 1999a *An Introduction to the EPPE Project, Technical Paper 1*, Institute of Education and DfEE, London.

——1999b, *Characteristics of the Centres in the EPPE Sample: Observational Profiles, Technical Paper 6*, Institute of Education and DfEE, London.

Walkerdine, V. 1981 'Sex, Power and Pedagogy', *Screen Education*, vol. 38, pp. 14–24.

Waterhouse, S. 1991 *First Episodes: Pupil Careers in the Early Years of School*, Falmer Press, London.

Woods, P. 1985 'Ethnography and Theory Construction in Educational Research, in R. Burgess (ed.), *Field Methods in the Study of Education*, Falmer Press, London.

——1987 'Ethnography at the Crossroads: A Reply to Hammersley', *British Education Research Journal*, vol. 13, no. 3, pp. 291–307.

——1996 *Researching the Art of Teaching: Ethnography for Educational Use*, Routledge, London.

Wright, C. 1986 'School Processes: An Ethnographic Study', in J. Eggleston, D. Dunn and M. Anjali (eds), Education for Some, Trentham Books, Stoke-on-Trent.

FURTHER READING

Fetterman, D. 1998 *Ethnography: Step by Step, Applied Social Research Methods Series Vol. 17, 2nd Edition*, Sage, London. An excellent and authoritative introduction written from the perspective of a practising anthropologist. The book provides a very user-friendly introduction to the main issues as well as some valuable references to further reading.

Folque, M. 2008 An Investigation of the *Movimento da Escola Moderna* (MEM) Pedagogy and Its Contribution to Learning to Learn in Portuguese Pre-schools, Unpublished PhD thesis, Institute of Education, University of London, London.

Kantor, R. and Whalley, K. 1998 'Existing Frameworks and New Ideas from Reggio Emilia Experience: Learning at a Lab School with 2- to 4-year-old Children', in C. Edwards, L. Gandini and G. Forman (eds), *The Hundred Languages of Children: The Reggio Emilia Approach—Advanced Reflections*, Greenwood Press, San Francisco, pp. 313–35.

Paley, V.G. 1984 *The Boy Who Would be a Helicopter*, Harvard University Press, New York. While any contemporary academic text would be expected to engage more fully in the extant relevant research literature, this text is recommended as an exemplar of good practice.

Siraj-Blatchford, I., Sammons, P., Taggart, B., Sylva, K. and Melhuish, E. 2006 'Educational Research and Evidence Based Policy: The Mixed Method Approach of the EPPE Project', *Evaluation and Research in Education*, vol. 19, no. 2, pp. 63–82.

Woods, P., Boyle, M. and Hubbard, N. 1999, *Multicultural Children in the Early Years: Creative Teaching, Meaningful Learning*, Multilingual Matters, Clevedon. A two-year study of children's experiences on their transition to school. Teachers' values and beliefs are explored and a number of practical opportunities and constraints identified.

17

Action research

Louise Taylor

WHAT WAS THE OVERALL AIM OF THIS RESEARCH?

The aim of this research was to *reimagine* professional learning for early education teachers. The research was carried out for my PhD, and was conducted with a small group of early education teachers in New Zealand using action research. The term 'early education teachers' refers to those teaching in both the early childhood and primary school sectors, working with children from birth to eight years of age. My interest in professional learning grew over many years as a result of my experiences working as an early education teacher, tutor, professional learning facilitator and education consultant.

When I began the research in 2000, I had been working in education for almost 30 years, and up until this time I had encountered very little professional learning that had truly inspired me. Rarely had I engaged in the kind of critical inquiry that had caused me to think differently about teaching, or had led to life-changing experiences. Most of my professional learning had been directed at the technical aspects of teaching, and over the years I had developed a growing sense of dissatisfaction with this. I began to explore alternatives and was drawn to the writings of Freire and bell hooks. Their work helped me to believe that a different kind of learning was possible.

Freire and hooks challenged me to consider emancipatory learning, which hooks (1994) describes as the kind of learning where 'paradise can be created' (1994, p. 207); a space of possibility, where an open inquiring mind and a desire for progressive social change are at the heart of the learning process. The more I read of their work, the more I wanted to experience this kind of learning and to share it with other teachers. Freire and hooks encouraged me to believe that I could reimagine professional learning, and that it was possible to realise an emancipatory vision in my own practice. My doctoral thesis recounts the changes that occurred as I sought to work differently with teachers, and this chapter discusses some aspects of this work.

WHAT WERE YOUR MAJOR RESEARCH QUESTIONS?

My research was guided by the following broad question:

> How can we expand our ways of understanding and practising professional learning for individual and social change in early education?

To break this question down, I focused more specifically on knowledge, the learner and change using the following sub-questions:

- What constitutes professional early education knowledge, who owns it and how can it be generated?
- What are the needs and challenges facing early education teachers as learners, how are these being addressed, and how can professional learning be supported in the future?
- What influences teacher change and how can it be supported in early education professional learning programs?
- How can professional learning in early education become a force for progressive social change?

Investigating these questions helped me to deconstruct professional learning and to reimagine this within emancipatory ideals. I framed the research using poststructuralist feminist theory and the work of Foucault, and conducted the project using action research.

LINKS TO THEORY AND EMPIRICAL RESEARCH

A survey of the literature revealed a plethora of work on professional learning in general, but no significant research using poststructuralist feminist theory for a conceptual framework, which my study did. Most of the research and initiatives in professional learning were, and still are, about curriculum delivery, programs or initiatives that can be reproduced, and ways to improve teacher practice (Taylor, 2007). Furthermore, I found a noticeable lack of interest in gender issues and/or social justice, so my research fitted nicely within this gap.

I framed my project around three theoretical perspectives: critical pedagogy, poststructuralist feminist theory and the work of Foucault (e.g. 1980a, 1980b, 1980c, 1990a, 1990b, 1995). While each of these bodies of work had something different to offer, they complemented each other and were all used to add focus and depth to my work in both the design and analysis phases. It was the work of Freire and bell hooks in particular that motivated me to think about teacher professional learning differently, and as already noted this gave purpose and direction to the research. The ideas of Freire continued to give momentum to what we did in our action research group sessions throughout the entire project.

Poststructuralist feminist theory and the work of Foucault were used to frame the way action research was enacted, and provided specific tools with which to view and analyse the data. These theories also added an alternative perspective to the majority of work on critical pedagogy, which is still largely dominated by male writers and modernist thinking (e.g. Lather, 1998; Parker, 1997). I believe that the blend of theoretical perspectives brought a fresh approach to the existing work on teacher professional learning.

DECISIONS REGARDING THE CHOICE OF METHODS

I wanted a research methodology that would allow me to work with teachers on their professional learning over time. I wanted the process to involve collaborative active engagement, especially as I was seeking to understand more about emancipatory education in my own practice. I was guided by Lather (1991), who contends that any research with an emancipatory vision needs to be open-ended, dialogically reciprocal, grounded in respect for humanity, sceptical of common sense and intent on transforming structures of inequality. Taking note of these ideals, I chose to use an action research methodology, believing that this was most closely aligned with the overall aims of this project and the emancipatory vision embedded within it.

Action research is a qualitative research approach with critical theoretical origins dating back to postwar America and the work of Lewin (e.g. Burns, 1997; Carr and Kemmis, 2002; Kemmis and McTaggart, 1988). In general terms, those employing action research are intent on achieving a more socially just world (Carr and Kemmis, 2002; Fay, 1987; Mac Naughton, 1996; Taylor 2007). Action research is a collaborative process which involves groups of people working together in social/

educational settings to bring about social change. Because it is action oriented, it is particularly suited to disrupting oppressive structures as they are encountered (Mac Naughton, 2005). In its most rudimentary form, action research involves working through a repetitive process of *planning, acting and observing, then reflecting* on outcomes and making changes in the *here and now.* Action research is more about researching *with* others rather than researching *for* or *about* them.

The collaborative, action-oriented and evolving nature of action research meant that I could work with teachers on the design of the project and the directions it took throughout. In this way, teachers were active participants for almost the entire project, and their input was far greater than it would have been had I just interviewed or observed them. I began by conducting semi-structured interviews with ten participants (who were easy to recruit), with the simple objective of hearing about their professional learning experiences. From this group of ten, eight teachers decided that they would like to meet with others to explore their professional learning in more depth. The plan was to meet monthly for one year, but this extended into three years with seven of the eight remaining with the project for its entirety. At these meetings we made collective decisions about our meetings and we discussed the data and my ongoing reflections on this. Teachers layered their reflections on to my own reflections, sometimes disputing understandings and interpretations with me.

This very open-ended approach to researching meant that the project did not lose momentum but continued to evolve. In the second and third years, we spaced out our meetings more; however, we never tired of things to discuss. As I progressed with my analysis and writing, our discussions often were about the content of my writing. Sometimes our different perspectives created tension, but it was by negotiating through these tense moments that we experienced the most change. At its core, action research is about activism and working towards emancipation and social justice (Mac Naughton, 2005), and as a methodology it requires much of both the participants and the researcher. It is change-oriented, and anyone involved must be prepared to confront themselves and each other and be changed—and we *were* changed by each other (Butler, 2004).

As a researcher, participant, teacher and facilitator of professional learning, I changed. I was fully immersed in the project. I could not retreat to an ivory tower to ponder the data and then report on my findings from a distant position, and this immersion 'meant being willing to critique myself and change what I thought and did' (Taylor, 2007, p. 90). As a result, I sometimes felt exposed and vulnerable, but this only helped others to share and learn in a similar way to me. My perspective became one of the whole, and this challenged me to listen, learn and act differently. Employing action research changed me, and it gave value to the opinions and experiences of others. Choosing to use action research made it possible for me to begin to realise my emancipatory vision for education.

HOW DID PARADIGM ISSUES INFLUENCE YOUR RESEARCH?

At the beginning of my doctoral research, my supervisor (Glenda Mac Naughton) asked me to think about whether or not I would be working within a modernist or postmodern paradigm. At the time, I didn't understand the importance of this question but as I progressed through my work I realised that my response became fundamental to how I thought, acted and wrote about my project. Modernism and postmodernism have different perspectives on knowledge production, validity and data representation, all of which were core elements of my thesis and the findings that I chose to write about. As action research has its roots in modernist thinking, and I had chosen this as my methodology, I had to consider whether I would work within its traditions or whether I would use a reconceptualised approach.

Modernist research essentially seeks to uncover or find *truth* or the *right* answer/s to questions of life and practice. Knowledge is believed to be *something* that can be uncovered, or discovered, and contained. It can also be proven through rational objective analysis. Modernist researchers believe that knowledge gained through research can be applied across many contexts, often universally, and those who create this knowledge are typically known as experts. Postmodernist researchers, by contrast, reject the notion of truth itself, believing instead that knowledge can only ever be partial and context dependent, and as a result claims to universal applicability are not made. Postmodernists argue that knowledge, perceived as truth, is most often determined by *who* is speaking rather than what is being said, and because of this they question the assumption that research can be validated as true or proven to be so.

I chose to work within a postmodern paradigm, and this shaped all aspects of the project including how the project was designed, what data was selected, how the data was analysed, and how the findings were represented. Reconceptualising action research within postmodernism also meant re-defining some key methodological stances, two of which were knowledge and validity.

Reconceptualising knowledge

A reconceptualised perspective on knowledge meant that I did not expect my research findings to produce universally applicable theory. The purpose wasn't to provide new knowledge on professional learning that could be applied over many contexts, or to present a model that could be reproduced. Instead, the findings and interpretations were presented as local and partial to the project, and used to generate discussion points about how professional learning might be reimagined in other contexts. I did not work to show consistency of findings or to present a rational objective argument. Instead of coherence and certainty, I highlighted inconsistencies and incongruence. I didn't eliminate or conceal the anomalies, contradictions or contentions, but brought these into the open because it was these that opened up the possibility of a different way of thinking. In short, I sought to portray the complexities within the world (Lather, 1991), rather than provide answers to these.

Often it was the small pieces of data, the moments in our discussions when a fracture or disruption occurred, that caused us to halt our usual patterns of thought. It was these moments that I thought about the most and it was these that I then played around with and wrote about. These disruptions were not a hindrance to the production of knowledge; they disrupted knowledge itself by throwing open the possibility that things could be different. Actively seeking out the obscure and the disruptive helped me to avoid the use of grand narratives and totalising statements, and guarded me from presenting only privileged and majority viewpoints. We did see things differently, and it was the richness in this diversity of thought that became the focus of my work.

Writing this way was not always easy. Along with other postmodern researchers, I sometimes doubted that I could ever talk about anything with the kind of strength and confidence that is necessary to complete a doctorate. I troubled over how I would represent the storylines of others without taking these out of context and fixing them in time and space. And this created a sense of burden on my authorship (Geertz, 1988, cited in St Pierre, 2000) with which I had to learn to work. It helped when I wrote myself and my doubts and struggles into my work—in postmodern action research, this is not only allowed but is expected. It was not necessary for me to be the objective and dispassionate researcher, and this gave freedom to my thinking and writing and enabled me to be more playful and experimental in my work.

Reconceptualising validity

In modernist research discourses, the emphasis on validity gives priority to reaching consensus about what data and knowledge are valid, presupposing the notion that it is possible to prove the truth value of data. This is problematic when researching within a postmodern paradigm, as I was. Early on, I realised that if I was to challenge knowledge and truth itself, then I would not be able to claim that my findings had verifiable proof. So validity for me became more about being trustworthy (e.g. Kincheloe and McLaren, 1994; McTaggart, 2005) with what participants had said rather than proving the truth of my work. This meant working with them on the meanings I gave to their words and being respectful about their changing positions. This also meant including alternative perspectives so that I illuminated, rather than hid, counter-patterns (Lather, 1991).

One way in which I worked towards trustworthiness was to create opportunities for multiple readings of the data (Ryan and Campbell, 2001) and the interpretation that I was bringing to this. Discussions on the data and any emerging themes became a regular part of our dialogue together, and while this sometimes created contention over meanings, it also brought inclusiveness. Participants did not always have the last say, but they did have a voice, and their opinions were valid and included as much as possible. Often teachers had changed their perspective or position over time and did not want to be held to something that was a passing comment. One way I negotiated with them over this was to present their changing perspectives and shifting positions as thoughts in progress (Taylor, 2007). The final words were mine, but in every possible way I included others in order to build trustworthiness, and this kept me grounded in my emancipatory ideals.

WHAT SAMPLING OR OTHER RESEARCH DESIGN ISSUES WERE THERE?

Two main issues arose for me in regard to research design. One was a dilemma I faced when participants chose a directional path that created problems for me, and the other was with respect to anonymity.

Dilemmas over direction

I chose action research largely because it is a collaborative research method, but at one point in the cyclic process when we were deciding the next phase, I faced an internal dilemma. When we began working as a group, we were meeting together monthly. We were from different backgrounds, so to encourage dialogue we began by choosing individual projects from our workplaces to work on. The intention was that we would all explore an area of our practice that we wanted to deconstruct and reimagine. However, in session four when we were reflecting on the process and making decisions about the next step, participants made it quite clear that they no longer wanted to work on projects but instead just wanted to meet and talk—about *anything!*

In my thesis, I write about how at this point I was challenged to consider how collaborative I was prepared to be. Taking this direction meant more uncertainty than I had planned for, and opened up the possibility that I would be faced with disconnected and incoherent data. Even though I expected this to a degree as a postmodernist researcher, when faced with the prospect of this on the scale that these teachers wanted, I was unnerved. I went with the group decision, however, and as a result of this decision the neat cycles that I had anticipated 'dispersed into many cycles, with all operating simultaneously and with each converging on the other' (Taylor, 2007, p. 96). At one point, the group described this as rather like tossing a ball of string around the room and watching it unravel and tangle as the fibres intersected (Taylor, 2007). We made our way through this dilemma and my troubling became part of the findings.

Anonymity

Formal institutional ethics committees have specific requirements of researchers, and one is that you will assure participants of their anonymity. This was one ethical rule that I broke outright! During the first year of meeting together, the group members made a decision to speak at a research conference together. I had planned to go to this conference and share about my doctoral work, but because I was working with adults I felt uncomfortable sharing their storylines for them—I wanted them to *speak for themselves.* So I invited them to join me, which they did (each one), even though this was at personal expense for each of them (for example, plane fares, motel accommodation and conference fees). At this conference, my *data spoke for itself*, and this broke the anonymity of all of the participants. Working with consenting adults made this possible and the decision to speak at the conference became a highlight not only for me, but also for participants. One of the teachers in the project had been teaching for over 50 years, and after the conference she said 'the conference that we did was one of the highlights of my professional development' (Taylor, 2007, p. 92). I would do the same again, without hesitation.

WHAT WERE THE MAIN OUTCOMES OF YOUR RESEARCH?

My research provides openings for discussion around the professional learning of early education teachers. It challenges some of the current trends in professional learning and highlights how some common practices work against innovation and progressive social change. While the findings are local to the project, they nevertheless showcase some of the processes that were used to open up dialogue and create contexts for disrupting the normal to make space for otherness.

Challenges to the status of the New Zealand curriculum Te Whārikia

One of the main challenges made by my research was to the status that the New Zealand early childhood curriculum, Te Whāriki (Ministry of Education, 1996), now has in New Zealand. Te Whāriki has been hailed as the first bicultural curriculum in New Zealand (Ritchie, 2002; Haggerty, 2003), and it permeates all legislation, training, governance, professional learning and research in the New Zealand early childhood sector. This has resulted in Te Whāriki gaining what poststructuralist feminists and Foucault scholars term the *status of truth* (Foucault, 1980c), making it very difficult for teachers (and professional learning facilitators) to move outside of this. The truth status of Te Whāriki affected the group's ability to think and act differently because Te Whāriki was used as the ultimate guide to what is right, normal and best practice.

In this project, there were teachers from both the early childhood and primary school sectors, so perspectives on curriculum varied and tensions arose over understandings. One such moment was in a discussion over what it means to be bicultural. On this occasion, the early childhood teachers assumed a position of knowing based on their understanding and practice of Te Whāriki. The early childhood teachers proceeded to teach others how to put biculturalism into practice, and the discussion became a closed subject as the *knowers* taught those who *did not know* what they *needed to know*. There was no debate and no suspicion cast over Te Whāriki, even though this was an opportunity for something *other* to be considered. Suspicion of all written documents is necessary according to Rhedding-Jones (2002), as this generates the kind of critical inquiry necessary for progressive social change. But in the instance described in my thesis, the opportunity for creating *other* understandings of biculturalism became lost in the truth of Te Whāriki.

Challenges to the standardisation of teaching practice

My research also challenged the worldwide trend towards standardisation in teacher professional learning. I did not refute the positive aspects of this, noting that in some contexts, such as the United States, the advent of standardisation has brought more qualified teachers into needy communities (Fromberg, 2006; Lubeck and Jessup, 2001). But I did raise an awareness of the impact that this trend is having on the profession's ability to innovate and encapsulate diversity. Standardisation has a tendency to position teachers as technicians, and minimises engagement in critical inquiry. Technicians follow set models and patterns and methods, and focus on putting into practice what others have mandated. Critical inquirers do not accept the world at face value but continue to question and deconstruct and investigate the origins and effects of decisions.

The teachers in this research shared how they had become resigned to many of the government requirements that they felt had been put upon them. They told of instances when they had disagreed but were just too tired to make a stand. They said that they just didn't have the energy needed to think about teaching differently, so they just *got on with it*. They also talked of how much energy goes into continually improving their practice against predetermined standards, and of how little time there is for professional discussions beyond the everyday practical routines of teaching. In this project, we created the time and space for a different kind of learning, where professional dialogue became the objective. Time was given to lengthy discussions and there was space to experiment and just experience. This provided a context for innovative thought and resulted in some intimate connections with otherness.

Learning to work differently in professional learning

My thesis told a story of how I changed the way I worked with teachers and the effects of these changes on others. I did not state how professional learning should be done, but gave an honest account of the issues with which I grappled and the disruptions that occurred in my own practice. Writing myself into my work enabled me to take my reader with me as I reconstituted myself as a woman, teacher, researcher and professional learning facilitator. Readers could take whatever they chose to from this, and from there create their own journey. I changed what I counted as worthwhile to know and what I valued in the professional learning opportunities that I created for others. I challenged my use of time and space, and critiqued how I had used these as a function of power to sanction some discourses and silence others. I learnt to work with tension so that I might trouble truth and I grew to appreciate the invisibility of change in the process of reconstitution. I developed great faith in the learning process, and therefore provided breathing spaces for movement and 'pleasurable curiosity' (Taylor, 2007, p. 191), all of which allowed for a shifting of positions. I learnt how to move forward in my work for social justice and began to realise my vision for emancipatory education in my practice; this was the greatest outcome for me.

HOW DID YOU INTERPRET YOUR FINDINGS?

Data analysis started immediately the data collection phase began, so that this could inform the next cycle of the project. The first form of data collection was a semi-structured interview and the reflections from these interviews influenced the makeup of the learning discussion group that followed. The first three meetings were planned around the themes and concerns that came out of the initial interviews and then during the next phase of the action research this happened collaboratively. Once underway, analysis went on all the time at different levels. First, the process and direction were constantly monitored and critiqued by the whole group. Group discussions always began with questions such as 'How are we going?', and changes in direction came from these discussions. Second, there were reflections on the discussions that went on in the sessions, and all were invited to contribute to these—which they did. Sessions were transcribed and these, along with my reflections, were circulated. Participant reflections were then added to my reflections and so on, creating a layering of data and reflections on data.

To start with, I looked for emerging themes and then I sought anomalies, contradictions and inconsistencies. To interpret the data, I was guided by three main bodies of theory:

- critical pedagogy—as a reminder of purpose
- the work of Foucault—as a way to locate and question
- poststructuralist feminist theory—as a means towards understanding.

Critical pedagogy: A reminder of purpose

Critical pedagogy reminded me of my emancipatory ideals and my desire to contribute to progressive social change. This meant deliberately challenging the historical, social and political factors influencing education and professional learning, both in the group sessions and in my interpretation of data. It also meant being prepared to critique my own intentions and actions. The goal was always to seek out oppressive practices in order to challenge these, even though at first some of my actions unintentionally worked against this goal. Keeping critical pedagogy at the forefront of my thinking reminded me of my purpose.

The work of Foucault: A way to locate and question

I used the work of Foucault to locate the function of power on many levels and to examine the interrelatedness of power, knowledge, the learner and change. Using Foucault's notion that power is not purely negative, but also productive (e.g. Foucault, 1980a), I questioned the effects of this function of power within the research group meetings and examined the impact of this on our professional learning and my desire for emancipatory education. I asked questions of the group processes as well, and of my own actions. One way in which I did this was to locate points of resistance in discussions because, according to Foucault (1980b), these highlight moments when what is *known to be true* comes into contest. I located tensions and disruptions and actively looked for a privileging of discourses. Foucault's work taught me how privileged discourses can reach the status of truth (Foucault, 1980a) and this helped me to understand how Te Whāriki had functioned as such, and the normalising affects this had.

Foucault devoted much of his work to how subjects are constituted, and more specifically how they become normalised through discourse. I found his work on sexuality particularly helpful for highlighting the complex disciplinary systems that permeate society to regulate behaviour. I used his work on the problematisation of sexuality (e.g. Foucault, 1990), for example, to locate ways in which teachers had learnt to conduct themselves in appropriate ways and used these locations to question how this could be disrupted. Doing this developed my understanding of how knowledge is produced and how the regulation of discourse works in the process of normalisation. This all helped me to begin to imagine professional learning differently.

Poststructuralist feminist theory: A means towards understanding

Poststructuralist feminist theory was the lens through which I viewed the data. In addition to the general tenets of postmodernism, poststructuralist feminist theory focuses on the subject, who is believed to be *always in the process of becoming* (Davies, 2000), continually taking up and resisting the discourses that give shape to their being. So this is what I focused on—the discourses that shaped our expectations of what it meant to be a woman teacher and how these were negotiated. This negotiation, and the takeup, resistance and subversion of discourses, became crucial to my analysis and overall findings. An example of this is the teacher who had taken up for herself discourses (from childhood) about what it meant to be the ideal teacher; her storyline highlights how she struggled to live these discourses even when she was challenged with the impossibility of such a dream (Walkerdine, 1990).

Locating such instances in the storylines and then examining them through a poststructuralist feminist lens gave me insight into some of the ideals that I held myself as a woman teacher and professional learning facilitator. This in turn helped me to reconstitute myself and the way in which I practised professional learning. Layer upon layer, the data and the ongoing interpretations of this gave way to changing perspectives, during the project and beyond.

QUESTIONS THAT COULD BE USED TO GUIDE ANALYSIS IN POSTMODERN ACTION RESEARCH

- What conflicts are arising?
- What discourses are privileged?
- How is power working on multiple levels?
- Where are the tensions?
- Where are the points of resistance?
- What practices have become normalised?
- How have beliefs been shaped?
- What contests exist over interpretations?
- Who can speak?
- Who is silenced?
- How might things be disrupted?

HOW DID POLICY AND/OR PRACTICE CONTEXTS INFLUENCE YOUR RESULTS?

As previously noted, research that is conducted within a postmodern paradigm is always context dependent and localised. While the processes that I described in my findings may be relevant in a wider context, the project was nonetheless context specific to the New Zealand teaching community. This was particularly so as I devoted a considerable portion of the thesis findings to a discussion that occurred around biculturalism and the status given to the New Zealand early childhood curriculum Te Whāriki during this discussion. This, however, does not detract from the potential of this work to generate discussion about teacher professional learning in other contexts.

RESEARCH LIMITATIONS

Some researchers may find postmodern research limiting because it is so context dependent and local. Those working within this paradigm, however, would argue that this is not a limitation but rather a safeguard against accepting generalised knowledge that may be used to create normalising standards. Remaining focused on the local added rigour to my work and helped me to be trustworthy (Taylor, 2007) in my representation of the storylines of others. Because I avoided grand theories about what was said, I kept storylines in context, and this showed respect for the time and space when these were shared. This allowed participants to move on from their storylines into new contexts as life shifted for them. I found this a very positive aspect of postmodern research.

One of the limitations that challenged me, but also kept me rigorous, was presenting the data as partial, even though I fully assented to this. In some ways it would have been easier to pinpoint change and then make assumptions about what, specifically, had contributed to this. But as the project really was only part of the whole that made up the experiences of these teachers, this was not an option. This made it difficult for me to provide verifiable proof that change had occurred, and as a result I could not provide evidence of what precipitates change. Unfortunately, policymakers want evidence (e.g. Alton-Lee, 2003, 2004; Mac Naughton 2003; Ministry of Education, 2006) and I could not provide this. I was always conscious that what occurred in the research project was partly obscured and to present my findings as otherwise would have been misleading.

FUTURE DIRECTIONS

My research was about creating openings for discussion around professional learning, and it is my hope that this will happen. The biggest change to come out of this project was in the way I understood and now practise professional learning, and because of this my thesis continues to influence my work with teachers. I no longer work in early childhood but rather with youth and adults in *second-chance education*, and the experiences that changed my practice throughout this project have helped me to work in more socially just ways in a different setting. During my research, I developed a greater respect for humanity, I learnt at first hand the importance of extended dialogue and debate, and I discovered ways to actively disrupt knowledge. These are just a few of the lessons I am taking with me into my future.

SUMMARY

This chapter summarises some of the key aspects of my doctoral research which was undertaken in order to reimagine professional learning for early education teachers in New Zealand. This was an action research project that was reconceptualised within a postmodern paradigm. Critical theory, poststructuralist feminist theory and the work of Foucault were used to shape the project, including its design, the selection of data, analysis and representation. The findings of this project should open up discussion about how an emancipatory vision might be realised in the practice of professional learning.

REFLECTIVE QUESTIONS

1 In what situations would action research be a preferable methodology?
2 What are some of the dilemmas that a researcher can face in action research?
3 What are some of the ways that participants can have input into interpretations?
4 How can researchers address validity in postmodern research?
5 What are some of the challenges of postmodern research?
6 How might curriculum be scrutinised in your own setting?
7 What kind of professional learning opportunities do you value most?
8 What could you do differently in your own setting?

REFERENCES

Alton-Lee, A. 2003 'Quality Teaching for Diverse Students in Schooling: Best Evidence Synthesis', prepared for the New Zealand Ministry of Education, <www.minedu.govt.nz>, accessed 9 March 2007.

——2004 *Improving Educational Policy and Practice Through an Iterative Best Evidence Synthesis Programme*, Paper presented at the OECD-US Seminar, Evidence-based Policy Research, April, Washington, DC.

Burns, R.B. 1997 *Introduction to Research Methods,* Addison Wesley Longman, Melbourne.

Butler, J. 2004 *Undoing Gender,* Routledge, New York.

Carr, W. and Kemmis, S. 2002 *Becoming Critical: Education, Knowledge and Action Research,* Deakin University Press, Melbourne.

Davies, B. 2000 *A Body of Writing 1990–1999*, Alta Mira Press, Walnut Creek, CA.

Fay, B. 1987 *Critical Social Science*, Cornell University Press, Ithaca, NY.

Freire, P. 1973 *Education for Critical Consciousness*, Seabury, New York.

——1994 *Pedagogy of Hope*, Continuum, New York.

——1996 *Pedagogy of the Oppressed* (1970), Continuum, New York.

Foucault, M. 1980a 'Truth and Power', in C. Gordon (ed.), *Power/Knowledge: Selected Interviews and Other Writings 1972–1977 by Michel Foucault*, Pantheon, New York, pp. 109–33.

——1980b 'Power and Strategies', in C. Gordon (ed.), *Power/Knowledge: Selected Interviews and Other Writings 1972–1977 by Michel Foucault*, Pantheon, New York, pp. 134–45.

——1980c 'Truth and Power' in C. Gordon (ed.) *Power/Knowledge: Selected Interviews and Other Writings 1972–1977 by Michel Foucault*, Pantheon, New York, pp. 109–33.

——1990a *The History of Sexuality: An Introduction*, Volume 1, Vintage, New York.

——1990b *The Use of Pleasure: The History of Sexuality*, Volume 2, Vintage, New York.

——1995 *Discipline and Punish: The Birth of the Prison*, Vintage, New York.

Fromberg, D.P. 2006 'Kindergarten Education and Early Childhood Teacher Education in the United States: Status at the Start of the 21st Century', *Journal of Early Childhood Teacher Education*, vol. 27, no. 1, pp. 65–85.

Haggerty, M. 2003 'Reconceptualising Notions of Curriculum: The Case of Te Whāriki', *New Zealand Research in Early Childhood Education*, no. 6, pp. 35–49.

hooks, b. 1994 *Teaching to Transgress: Education as the Practice of Freedom*, Routledge, New York.

Kemmis, S. and McTaggart, R. 1988 'Introduction: The Nature of Action Research', in S. Kemmis and R. McTaggart (eds), *The Action Research Planner*, Deakin University Press, Melbourne, pp. 5–28.

Kincheloe, J.L. and McLaren, P.L. 1994 'Rethinking Critical Theory and Qualitative Research', in N.K. Denzin and Y.S. Lincoln (eds), *Handbook of Qualitative Research*, Sage, Thousand Oaks, CA, pp. 138–57.

Lather, P. 1991 *Getting Smart: Feminist Research and Pedagogy with/in the Postmodern*, Routledge, New York.

——1998 'Critical Pedagogy and Its Complicities: A Praxis of Stuck Places', *Educational Theory*, vol. 48, no. 4, pp. 487–97.

Lewin, K. 1948 *Resolving Social Conflicts: Selected Papers on Group Dynamics*, Gertrude W. Lewin (ed.), Harper & Row, New York.

Lubeck, S. and Jessup, P. 2001 'Globalisation and its Impact on Early Years Funding and Curriculum: Reform Initiative in England and the United States', in T. David (ed.), *Promoting Evidence-based Practice in Early Childhood Education: Research and Its Implications*, Elsevier Science, London, pp. 227–49.

Mac Naughton, G. 1996 'Researching for Quality: A Case for Action Research in Early Childhood Services', *Australian Journal of Early Childhood*, vol. 21, no. 2, pp. 29–33.

——2003, 'Researching Together to Make a Difference: Possibilities and Provocations', keynote paper presented with Smith, K. and Taylor, L. at the 3rd Centre for Equity and Innovation in Early Childhood International Conference, Melbourne, November.

——2005 *Doing Foucault in Early Childhood Studies: Applying Poststructuralist Ideas*, Routledge, New York.

McTaggart, R. 2005 'Is Validity Really an Issue for Participatory Action Research?' in B. Cooke and J.W. Cox (eds), *Fundamentals of Action Research, Volume III: Social Change Applications, the Practitioner and Action Research Knowledge*, Sage, Thousand Oaks, CA, pp. 395–421.

Ministry of Education 1996 *Te Whāriki: He Whāriki Mātauranga mō ngā Mokopuna o Aotearoa/Early Childhood Curriculum*, Learning Media, Wellington.

——2006 'Educate: Ministry of Education Statement of Intent 2006–2011', <www.minedu.govt.nz>, accessed 9 March 2009.

Parker, S. 1997 *Reflective Teaching in a Postmodern World: A Manifesto for Education in Postmodernity*, Open University Press, Philadelphia, PA.

Rhedding-Jones, J. 2002 'An Undoing of Documents and Other Texts: Towards a Critical Multiculturalism in Early Childhood Education', *Contemporary Issues in Early Childhood*, vol. 3, no. 3, pp. 90–116.

Ritchie, J. 2002 'Bicultural Development: Innovation in Implementation of Te Whāriki', *Australian Journal of Early Childhood*, vol. 27, no. 2, pp. 32–7.

Ryan, S. and Campbell, S. 2001 'Doing Research for the First Time', in G. Mac Naughton, S.A. Rolfe and I. Siraj-Blatchford (eds), *Doing Early Childhood Research: International Perspectives on Theory and Practice,* Open University Press, Buckingham, pp. 56–63.

St Pierre, E.A. 2000 'Nomadic Inquiry in the Smooth Spaces of the Field: A Preface', in E.A. St Pierre and W.A. Pillow (eds), *Working the Ruins: Feminist Poststructuralist Theory and Methods in Education*, Routledge, New York, pp. 258–83.

Taylor, L. 2007 Re-imagining Professional Learning in Early Education, Unpublished PhD thesis, University of Melbourne, Melbourne.

Walkerdine, V. 1990 *School Girl Fictions*, Verso, New York.

FURTHER READING

hooks, b. 1994 *Teaching to Transgress: Education as the Practice of Freedom*, Routledge, New York. If you want to read a book that inspires you to think differently about education, then this book is a must! It challenges readers to think about how education can be emancipatory, and encourages those in education to make the work of social justice a priority.

Cherry, N. 1999 *Action Research: A Pathway to Action, Knowledge and Learning*, RMIT University Press, Melbourne; Hinchey, P.H. 2008 *Action Research*, Peter Lang, New York. These two books give an overview of action research and are particularly useful for anyone who is new to this field. Both explain the principles of action research clearly and both are easy to read.

Mac Naughton, G. 2005 *Doing Foucault in Early Childhood Studies: Applying Poststructural Ideas*, Routledge, New York. This book by Mac Naughton is an excellent introduction to the work of Foucault and postructuralism. As well as defining some key concepts this book provides practical ways these can be applied in early childhood. The book includes many examples from practitioners working in the field.

18

Direct observation

Sharne A. Rolfe and Susan Emmett

Direct observation—appraisal of the social and physical environment based on our own direct perceptions—is something we do all our waking lives. Our survival depends on it. Even infants are careful, systematic observers, and children are explicitly taught observational skills from an early age—for example, how to discriminate household objects that are permissible and safe to touch from those that are not; how to use signs and other signals as a guide to safety and direction; and how to identify among strangers those people who may be trusted. Careful observation also underpins skilled communication and promotes learning.

Perhaps for these reasons, some people think it ought to be easy and straightforward to do observational research, and that specialised skills and knowledge are unnecessary. However, every novice researcher quickly becomes aware of how daunting a task it can be to collect accurate and systematic observational data. Discussing this in their guide to observing behaviour, Martin and Bateson (2007) reassure us that: 'The truth is that measuring behaviour *is* a skill, but not one that is especially difficult to master, given some basic knowledge and an awareness of the possible pitfalls.' (2007, p. 1)

Early childhood professionals (ECPs) first encounter the challenges and pitfalls of **systematic observation** during pre-service training. Good observation is fundamental to the task of good teaching. The observational techniques ECPs use to gain information about children—

including running and anecdotal records, checklists, rating scales and time and event sampling—can be equally well applied in observational research. There are numerous books that describe these techniques (e.g. Bentzen, 2009; Pellegrini, Symons and Hoch, 2004; Sharman, Cross and Vennis, 2007). We will overview some in this chapter, but our main focus is on the issues that arise when direct observation is used to gather data in early childhood research. Among other things, we will consider why a researcher might choose direct observation, what is needed to achieve reliable data, and what considerations guide the choice of one observational technique over another.

Two observational studies of young children in child-care services (Emmett and Rolfe, 2009; Rolfe, 2007) will be used to illustrate these issues and the strengths and challenges of direct observation as a data-gathering tool in early childhood research.

OVERALL AIM OF THE RESEARCH

Despite the significance of child care as a developmental context, and the pivotal importance of secure attachments during early childhood for psychological well-being (Rolfe, 2004; Sroufe et al., 2005), there is much we do not know about the attachment experiences of infants and young children in child-care services. There is also limited research on how the principles of attachment theory (AT) are best taught in pre-service early childhood education courses.

Using direct observation, Rolfe (2007) and Emmett and Rolfe (2009) explored the nature of the interactions and relationships between young children and ECPs in child-care services. Using concepts drawn from AT and the emotional availability (EA) framework (Biringen, Robinson and Emde, 2000; Bornstein et al., 2008), Rolfe (2007) compared the interactions of infants and their mothers and fathers at home with interactions between the same infants and ECPs in child care. In their study, Emmett and Rolfe (2009) evaluated the impacts of a new AT-focused pre-service education initiative on attachment practices and behaviours enacted by students during practicum placements and later when participants were employed.

MAJOR RESEARCH QUESTIONS

Rolfe (2007) was primarily concerned with how the interactional experiences of infants differed between home and child-care settings, and whether the caregiving prescursors of secure attachment were evident in the way ECPs interacted with infants in child care. The major research question addressed was:

> Are there differences in the way mothers, fathers and ECPs interact with infants—in terms of sensitivity, structuring, nonintrusiveness, enjoyment and restrictiveness—and does infant positive affect and responsiveness differ according to adult partner?

Over a 30-month period, Emmett and Rolfe (2009) followed the professional journeys of fifteen participants who took part in a new attachment-focused pre-service education initiative in the final year of their early childhood pre-service diploma. The study comprised Stage 1, when the participants were final-year students, and Stage 2, when they were qualified ECPs employed in child care. One of the major research questions addressed was:

> To what extent do participants sustain an attachment focus in their professional practice two years after the education initiative is completed?

LINKS TO THEORY AND EMPIRICAL RESEARCH

Rolfe (2007)

The importance of secure attachments with primary caregivers—including mothers, fathers and ECPs—for infants and young children is now beyond question. Founded on the seminal work of John Bowlby (1973, 1980, 1982, 1988), AT has generated an impressive empirical literature linking social-emotional well-being and resilience to the experience of secure attachments in early childhood (e.g. see Cassidy and Shaver, 2008).

Building on the careful observational work of Mary Ainsworth and her colleagues (Ainsworth, 1967; Ainsworth et al., 1978), attachment researchers have described the key features of caregiving that promote attachment security, these being caregiver sensitivity and responsiveness. Parallel work on the concept of EA provides detailed descriptions of the core features of quality caregiving, and an observational measuring instrument—the Emotional Availability Scales—to assess them. The 3rd edition of these Scales (Biringen, Robinson and Emde, 2000) describes six dimensions of EA, four to do with parental/caregiver behaviour—sensitivity, structuring, non-intrusiveness and non-hostility—and two to do with child behaviour—responsiveness and involvement.

Whilst the links between EA and secure attachment outcomes have been emphasised (e.g. see Easterbrooks and Biringen, 2000), relatively little is known about the dynamics of EA in child-care services. In one of the few studies to investigate this topic, Zimmerman and Fassler (2003) found differences in the quality of mother–infant and ECP–infant interactions, although the small sample size and the young age of mothers limited the generalisability of the outcomes. Rolfe (2007) extends this work using an assessment instrument developed by the author that combines interactional characteristics drawn from both AT and EA frameworks.

Emmett and Rolfe (2009)

The research literature is also meagre in regard to the ways in which AT might best be taught during pre-service early childhood education courses. It is important, for example, that students fully understand AT and its implications for the practices they enact with young children. Furthermore, it is important that these attachment-focused practices continue not only to be enacted by new graduates, but to be sustained over the long term of employment. AT incorporates many complex concepts, and ECPs-in-training may grapple to understand this body of theory and the subtleties of translating it into practice. Furthermore, once employed, ECPS may encounter challenges and tensions in the workplace if, for example, other ECPs under-value attachment-based practice.

Emmett and Rolfe (2009) set out to develop and then evaluate a semester-length program focusing on AT for final-year students completing a pre-service diploma in early childhood education. The program—which students voluntarily elected to undertake—included seminar-based content on AT as well as some one-to-one sessions between the first researcher and each student, exploring their attachment history and the practice implications of different attachment states of mind. The seminar content was carefully integrated with issues of attachment history to emerge from the individual sessions and both were explicitly linked to practicum-based experiences. Teaching staff worked individually and collectively with participants to identify, discuss and enact examples of AT-based practices of increasing complexity and subtlety.

Direct observation

All research data are based on observation. That is, if we define observation broadly as one person's perception or measurement of something about someone or something else, then data from interviews, surveys, questionnaires and even physiological recordings are all in some way observational. This chapter focuses specifically on direct observation. As the term implies, this involves researchers recording the data of interest directly, based on their own perceptions and impressions, rather than indirectly—for example, from a questionnaire that the participant or someone else completes. Most direct observation is of behaviour: children's behaviour, parents' behaviour or the behaviour of ECPs. The kinds of behaviour observed depend on the researcher's aims and interests. In both our studies, our interest lay primarily in the nature of dyadic interactions between young children and the adults who care for them, and in the case of Emmett and Rolfe (2009), whether we could influence the nature of these interactions through training.

Behavioural observations are not solely directed at understanding the development of children, although they are very useful in this regard. Observation may also be used to assess early childhood service quality, curricula or the effectiveness of diverse kinds of interventions. Direct observation can be time consuming, but the richness of data achieved and the insights that come from this form of data more than compensate.

CHOICE OF METHODS

When researchers are interested in understanding or explaining everyday behaviours as they occur, or these data are helpful in evaluating the quality of a service or the effectiveness of an intervention, then direct observation is worth considering. Because our primary research interest lay in the nature of child–adult interactions as they occur in everyday settings (home and/or child-care service), direct observation seemed ideal. It also fitted with the skills, knowledge and research paradigms we brought from our respective academic disciplines: psychology (Rolfe) and early childhood education (Emmett).

A brief overview of different techniques of direct observation

Although we were clear that direct observation was the method of choice to answer our research questions, there were a number of well-tested techniques to consider and then choose between before data collection could begin. Different authors may refer to the same technique by a different name. To avoid confusion, it is best to focus on what the technique involves (that is, how it is done) rather than the specific name given to it.

The technique with which ECPs are most familiar—and which potentially provides one of the richest accounts of ongoing behaviour—is the

running record, otherwise called a specimen record or narrative description. The observer, who usually knows ahead of time when, how and why the observation is being made, writes down in longhand everything seen as it occurs—for example, what a child does and says over a specified period of time. If this technique is chosen, the aim is usually to get as detailed a picture as possible of the participant's behaviour. Objectivity is emphasised by avoiding interpretations, inferences or evaluations. **Anecdotal records** are similar, but are considered by some to be better suited to recording atypical rather then typical behaviours.

It is tempting to assume that, given enough time and minimal distractions, an observer could record everything using one or other of these techniques. This is not so. Perceptual overload can occur. Martin and Bateson (2007) note that: 'It simply is not possible to record everything that happens, because any stream of behaviour could, in principle, be described in an enormous number of different ways.' (2007, p. 26). Further, Bentzen (2009) warns:

> Our brains enable us to see in ways that far exceed the camera's ability to 'see'. But observation becomes complicated precisely because we do more with sensory information than the camera is able to do ... what and how much information we perceive varies from person to person, and even within the same person from one time to another. So it is that two individuals can be visually aware of the same object or event but visually aware in different ways. (2009, pp. 5–6)

Another technique is the **checklist**. These are prepared prior to observing. The form a checklist takes is only limited by the interest and ingenuity of the observer. Checklists may be simple, with behaviours listed down in a column on the left-hand side of the page with spaces or boxes to the right that can be ticked when they are observed. Some checklists leave room for more detailed comments about behaviour—such as the context or setting, when it occurred and what happened before and after it. Checklists can also be used to document characteristics of a curriculum or an early childhood service. It is important to remember that lengthy observations prior to checklist completion may at times be needed to ensure accuracy and to avoid premature conclusions.

Rating scales share some essential features with checklists, but the phenomenon of interest is recorded in terms of where it fits along a continuum, rather than whether it is present or not. A judgment is required. For example, we may prescribe a numerical value—such as 1, 2, 3, 4 or 5 on a five-point Likert scale—according to the frequency or intensity of a behaviour. Usually scale points are given names, such as 'very high' through 'medium' to 'very low'. There are many rating scales available for use by the early childhood researcher, covering a diverse range of topic areas, so it is not always necessary to develop your own, although of course you can.

Two further observational techniques are commonly used. These are **event sampling** and **time sampling**. These are useful when we wish to take a sample of ongoing behaviour rather than observe everything that occurs over a period of time. In event sampling, we wait for a particular event to occur (for example, aggressive behaviours in preschool setting) and then we record something about it—for example, what happens first, who does what, how long the event lasts, what brings it to a conclusion. What we try to achieve is a sufficient sample of the event to make generalisations. As Nicolson and Shipstead (2002) write:

> Event sampling permits the observer to collect data about the targeted behaviour in an efficient manner because it concentrates his or her attention on only that behaviour. Although an observer is not able to see every targeted event of interest over an indefinite period of time, a sample of observations over a limited period should serve to represent the behaviour. (2002, p. 203)

In time sampling, occurrences of the behaviour(s) of interest are recorded for set time periods. These can be very short (every five seconds) or relatively long (each half-hour). Time sampling allows us to measure the relative frequency of the behaviours by counting up the number of time samples in which they occurred.

> **QUALITATIVE OR QUANTITATIVE?**
> Techniques of direct observation include both qualitative and quantitative measures. Anecdotal and running records are qualitative because they involve narrative (word-based) descriptions. Checklists, rating scales and time sampling yield quantitative data—that is, numbers relating to extent, frequency, and so on.

Choosing between different observational techniques for research data collection

Once the decision is made to use direct observation, the choice of observational technique should be guided by the research questions to be addressed. If your research calls for detailed descriptions of all the behaviours that occur over a time period in a particular setting, then running records will achieve this richness, or something close to it. Running records or anecdotal records may be particularly useful if you are interested in the minutiae of what occurs at a specific time point—for example, when the child first enters the early childhood service, at sleep time or on departure. Keeping a detailed account of all the behaviours that occur from when the parent and child first enter the room to when the parent leaves can prove a wealth of information missing from a score on a rating scale of separation distress. A rating scale score might be quite sufficient, however, and be potentially less intrusive and time consuming for certain research questions. If a single numerical score is all you require to answer your question, there may be little justification for more detailed recording.

ACHIEVING HIGH-QUALITY OBSERVATIONAL DATA

In any research using direct observation, a central consideration is how to achieve high-quality data that meets the criteria of **observational reliability**. Data must be recorded in such a way that other observers would produce the same recordings if they did the observations. Also, observers need to be consistent in their recordings over time.

Characteristics of the observer

Nicolson and Shipstead (2002, pp. 25–6) provide an example showing how two observers using the same technique (running records) and recording at the same time produce two very different three-minute observations of a preschool child playing outside in the sandpit. The reason for this is the **subjectivity** inherent in direct observation.

As human observers, it is inevitable that our feelings and interpretations influence what we see or don't see. The behavioural record reflects, to a greater or lesser extent, our 'experiences, biases, emotions, and even cultural and social norms' (Nicolson and Shipstead, 2002, p. 25). In other words, we see the world around us through a lens. What I see and how I interpret it may not be the same as what you see or how you interpret it. We may notice different behaviours, focus on certain events or interactions more than others, or simply 'miss' certain behaviours because we are distracted or interrupted—even for a brief period of time. Two people may generate different records if behaviours are defined in very general terms, such as 'aggression' or 'sociability'. How do we decide what behaviour is 'aggressive' and would you and

I necessarily agree? The less well defined the target behaviours are, the more likely it is that observer bias will influence the data. If we approach our study with specific hypotheses, there is also the danger that we may see what we want to see in order to support our expectations. Observer training and careful definition of target behaviours may increase **objectivity** and reliability.

Reliability

Reliability refers to the consistency of observations, across time and between observers, and in research studies it is very important to establish the reliability of your observations. Inter-observer reliability (IOR) is a measure of the extent to which two (or more) observers obtain the same results when observing the same behaviours at the same time. It is calculated by dividing the total number of observer agreements by the number of agreements and disagreements, and is usually represented as a percentage. The more reliable the observational data, the closer the IOR is to 100 per cent. Intra-observer reliability measures how consistent an observer is over time.

In Rolfe (2007), two observers scored all videotapes independently, achieving an IOR of 96 per cent. Since 70 per cent agreement or higher is usually taken as the metric for acceptable reliability (Martin and Bateson, 2007), we were able to have confidence in the data collected. Intra-observer reliability was measured in Emmett and Rolfe (2009). Based on observational recordings by Emmett of three practice videotapes at two time intervals, two months apart, an acceptable intra-observer reliability of 84 per cent was achieved. A more technical description of different ways of assessing the reliability of observational data can be found in Martin and Bateson (2007, pp. 72–85).

WHAT SAMPLING OR OTHER RESEARCH DESIGN ISSUES WERE THERE?

The main sampling issue in our studies arose in relation to the behaviours of our participants: how to determine which behaviours were most relevant to the study aims and how to then code them. The main point to remember in observational research is that behaviour is 'a continuous stream of movements and events' (Martin and Bateson, 2007, p. 33). To measure behaviour, these movements and events must be broken down into categories that should preferably be defined in such a way that different observers viewing the same sequence would produce the same behavioural record.

Having considered the various options, in Rolfe (2007) the decision was taken to use a rating scale that measured different qualities of adult–infant interactions. The scale was developed by the researcher and incorporated elements of both AT and EA frameworks. Developing the rating scale was preceded by many hours observing infant–adult dyads in the course of other research studies and in pilot work for this study. In its final form, the rating scale focused on six characteristics of adult interactional behaviour:

- sensitivity
- structuring
- intrusiveness
- enjoyment
- restrictiveness
- interaction tempo.

These were listed down the left-hand side of the observer's sheet. Next to each characteristic, there was a five-point Likert scale (1 = Very Low to 5 = Very High) to be completed by the observer. Three characteristics of infant behaviour were also listed, each one also to be scored on a five-point scale (1 = Very Low to 5 = Very High):

- responsiveness to adult
- positive affect
- interest level.

The ratings were scored after viewing two three-minute interactional play samples videotaped for each infant–adult dyad in the study: mother and infant at home; father and infant at home; and ECP and infant at the child-care centre. Eighteen infants were observed in each of the settings. The decision to sample interactions in this way was based on previous research indicating that this period is long enough to capture the nature of everyday interactions. Adults were given a small number of age-appropriate toys and invited to play with the infant as they normally did. In centres, arrangements were made to relieve the ECP of responsibilities for other children for the duration of the observation and the infant–ECP dyad was observed in a relatively quiet area away from distractions. This enabled ECPs to focus on the infant, approximating as closely as possible the conditions under which parent–infant dyads were observed at home. Only the ECP most familiar with the infant was observed.

In Emmett and Rolfe (2009), a similar approach was initially used to develop a rating scale of professional practice, based on many hours observing ECPs in a range of early childhood services and drawing on key EA literature, including Biringen et al. (2000) and AT (e.g. Marvin et al., 2002). In addition, three 90-minute videorecordings of children's interactions with professional caregivers within three child-care centres were made and reviewed several times to finalise caregiver and child attachment-focused practices and behaviours. The following categories were rated on a five-point Likert scale (1 = Very Low to 5 = Very High):

- responsiveness of ECP to child
- ECP's ability to interpret child's signals
- ECP builds and sustains warm, affectionate relationship with child
- ECP balances the child's freedom to explore with safe supports
- ECP displays a relaxed, calm and flexible demeanour that is in tune with the child's pace and rhythms
- ECP communicates with coworkers about the importance of sensitive, responsive and consistent caregiving practices and appropriate strategies to implement this
- responsiveness of child to ECP
- child uses adult as secure base and explores environment
- child displays contented and relaxed demeanour.

In that part of the study to do with evaluating the education program after the participants had been employed in the field for two years, running records of ongoing ECP and child behaviours were collected over two six-hour observation sessions for each participant. Great care was taken to avoid inferences and interpretations at this stage of data collection, and the observer tried to record as thoroughly as possible all she saw of relevance to the aims of the study. Each running record was then reviewed and analysed by the researcher to develop evaluations. These evaluations were then used to complete the rating scale for each participant. The method of running records rather than videotaping was used at this point in the study due to the long observation periods. It was also considered crucially important that the observer remain as unobtrusive as possible.

MAIN RESEARCH OUTCOMES

Statistical analyses using two-way ANOVAs comparing adult (mother, father and ECP) and episode (1 vs 2) were completed for each of the nine measures in Rolfe (2007). These analyses revealed that there were no significant differences between mothers, fathers and ECPs in terms of sensitivity, intrusiveness, restrictiveness and tempo of play, and all the observed interactions were on average moderately to highly sensitive, very low to low on intrusiveness, highly non-restrictive and of moderate tempo. However, highly significant differences emerged on two adult measures—enjoyment and structuring. Parents showed significantly more enjoyment in their interactions with their infants, $F(2,50) = 10.08$, $p < .001$. Mothers and fathers also structured the play interactions more than ECPs, with mothers the most highly structuring of all, $F(2,50) = 11.27$, $p < .001$.

All three measures of infant behaviour differed significantly according to adult partner. Infant responsiveness was significantly higher during play with parents than ECPs, $F(2,50) = 8.16$, $p < .001$. Infants showed more positive affect during play with parents, $F(2,50) = 5.33$, $p < .01$; and the interest levels of the infants were higher with parents, particularly when the play partner was their mother, $F(2,50) = 6.06$, $p < .01$.

In order to explore the nature of interactions in more detail, the frequency of each rating category in each dyad was calculated for each of the statistically significant measures. This showed that only one mother and one father showed low levels of enjoyment in either play episode, whereas six (of eighteen) ECPs showed low levels of enjoyment in both episodes. Six ECPs showed low levels of structuring, a key teaching-oriented strategy, whereas the majority of parents showed moderate to high levels of structuring. In terms of infant behaviours, infants were only scored as highly unresponsive in episodes with ECPs and the majority of infant interactions with ECPs were coded as unresponsive to moderately responsive. The majority of infants showed dampened/flat affect (neither positive nor negative) during interactions with ECPs, whereas the majority of interactions with parents were scored as highly positive in infant affect. Interest levels showed a similar pattern.

In Emmett and Rolfe (2009), non-parametric statistical analyses across the three time periods—before the education program, immediately after the education program and two years after beginning professional employment—revealed that, although participants' depth of knowledge in relation to AT and their ability to operationalise this knowledge increased significantly pre- to immediately post-program, these benefits were not sustained two years after participants entered early childhood services as qualified practitioners. Whilst this longitudinal study used a variety of data-gathering techniques including questionnaires, interviews and personal narratives (participant and researcher), direct observation in the child-care setting was essential to the insights gained about the longer-term impacts of the training program.

INTERPRETATION OF FINDINGS

The results of Rolfe (2007) add to those of other studies that have uncovered differences in the way parents and ECPs interact with infants (e.g. Stith and Davis, 1984; Caruso, 1989) and reveal that infants, for their part, differ in how they interact with parents and ECPs. We are unable to be sure about the direction of effects—that is, whether the infants are responding to differences in adult ways of interacting, or whether adults respond differently because of how infants are interacting with them. What we now need to determine is whether it is possible to bring the interactions of infants and ECPs closer to what occurs in parent–infant interactions, since these latter interactions evidenced greater quality and would be expected, on the basis of theory and empirical work, to offer optimal pathways to emotional security and positive learning outcomes. One possibility is that ECPs become desensitised by exposure to high infant:adult ratios in early childhood services, and this leads to a style of interacting that is more routinised and less spontaneous and joyful.

Clearly, understanding the role of professional training and experience in this process is crucial. Importantly in this regard, Emmett and Rolfe's (2009) data reveal that knowledge, insights and behaviours developed through a semester-length program during the final year of tertiary study impact significantly and positively on practice at the time, but are not retained two years into professional employment. We have some evidence that the nature of the workplace and the practices enacted there impact strongly on participants' emerging practices once employed. Over time, participants appeared to develop a style of interacting with and caring for young children that mirrored established practices within their employment setting, rather than sustaining what they had learnt during their period of training.

In both studies, there are limitations of both research process and design. In the main, these relate to small sample sizes. Also, in Emmett and Rolfe (2009), resource limitations meant that one researcher collected all the direct observation data. Whilst intra-observer reliability was established, the findings would have been further strengthened if two observers had collected the data so that inter-observer reliability could be established.

IN WHAT WAYS DID ISSUES OF PARADIGM INFLUENCE THE RESULTS?

In Rolfe (2007), the aim was to determine whether and in what ways the interactions between parents and infants differed from those between ECPs and infants. This question and the use of quantitative methods of data collection arose from the positivistic paradigm brought by the author to the research endeavour. In contrast, an interpretist paradigm, sometimes termed a constructivist philosophical approach, underpinned the study of Emmett and Rolfe (2009). An inductive research methodology was used. Themes emerged from the data and a story was gradually constructed. Data were analysed after each time interval and results of Stage One influenced the development of Stage Two data collection tools.

For example, the results that revealed the transformation in student participants' ability to understand and operationalise attachment-focused practice in Stage One led to the formulation of Stage Two research questions. Research tools were then constructed to answer these questions. The study therefore engaged an iterative design that involved repeated data collection and analysis. This recursive process embodies the interpretist paradigm, whereby analysis is employed all the way through a study to facilitate the generation of new theory.

HOW DID POLICY AND/OR PRACTICE CONTEXTS INFLUENCE THE RESULTS?

In many ways, the naturalistic nature of the research context elicited data that encapsulated the natural flow of behaviour. However, this is never completely the case. The participants, other people in the observational environments (home and early childhood service) and the children all influence one another and all are, to some extent, influenced by the presence of the observer, even if the observer remains as inconspicuous as possible. The presence of an observer and techniques such as videotaping may change the dynamics of behaviour to an extent that may be difficult to quantify and in ways that are challenging to predict.

It is as well for those conducting observational research to consider carefully how the presence of the observer may influence the results. It is possible to discuss this aspect directly with adult participants, and even with children. Participants can be encouraged to comment on how being observed affected them and how it may have changed their usual behaviours. These insights can be added to the data set and discussed at the point where results are interpreted.

LIMITATIONS AND FUTURE DIRECTIONS

For us, a major insight from the two research studies was the value of using different observational techniques in order to understand better the phenomenon of interest. It also led us to reflect on two practical issues that need to be considered in planning observational research.

To videotape or not?

Videotaping can be a useful way to record observations. Videotapes can then be coded later. The main advantage is that you can replay behaviour sequences again and again. There are computer packages available to assist in recording video-based observations of this kind. However, there are time and resourcing implications in using video. It takes a lot more time to record from videotapes than recording *in situ*. Your project will need to purchase the videotapes and may need to acquire a video camera, playback monitor and a computer package. Finally, the camera is highly intrusive and a focus of ongoing interest to the children, well past the time when interest in a human observer likely fades.

How much observational data is 'enough'?

For us, this was determined by practical considerations, such as how long we had to complete the studies and how much time each week we had to collect our data. If you are doing the study by yourself with limited funding, you also need to consider the time required to analyse the data. Observational data, especially of a qualitative type, can take a long time to analyse, and the written records need to be transcribed and often then recoded into some quantitative form.

SUMMARY

This chapter has considered direct, systematic observation as applied in early childhood research. Decision-making around choice of observational method (from anecdotal and running records to category coding using time and event samples) was considered. Issues to do with operationalising behaviour categories, sources of observer bias and error, and ways of establishing observer reliability have been discussed. Using a combination of methods of direct observation may be a useful way forward in many early childhood studies.

QUESTIONS FOR REFLECTION

1 Do you think you are a good observer? Why or why not?
2 What are the main differences between systematic observation

and the sort of observation we do as a normal part of everyday living?

3 Why is subjectivity in observational data a problem and what can we do about it?
4 In what ways can we establish the reliability of our observations?
5 What topic areas or potential questions of interest to you could be researched using direct observation?

REFERENCES

Ainsworth, M.D.S. 1967 *Infancy in Uganda: Infant Care and the Growth of Attachment*, Johns Hopkins Press, Baltimore, MD.

Ainsworth, M.D.S., Blehar, M.C., Waters, E. and Wall, S. 1978 *Patterns of Attachment: Assessed in the Strange Situation and at Home*, Lawrence Erlbaum, Hillsdale, NJ.

Bentzen, W.R. 2009 *Seeing Young Children: A Guide to Observing and Recording Behaviour*, 6th ed., Thomson Delmar Learning, Clifton Park, NY.

Biringen, Z., Robinson, J.L., and Emde, R.N. 2000 'Appendix B: The Emotional Availability Scales (3rd ed., an Abridged Infancy/Early Childhood Version)', *Attachment and Human Development*, vol. 2, pp. 256–70.

Bornstein, M.H., Putnick, D.L., Heslington, M., Gini, M., Suwalsky, J.T.D., Venuti, P., de Falco, S., Giusti, Z. and de Galperin, C.Z. 2008 'Mother–Child Emotional Availability in Ecological Perspective: Three Countries, Two Regions, Two Genders', *Developmental Psychology*, vol. 44, pp. 666–80.

Bowlby, J. 1973 *Attachment and Loss: Vol. 2. Separation, Anxiety and Anger*, Basic Books, New York.

——1980 *Attachment and Loss: Vol. 3. Loss, Sadness and Depression*, Hogarth Press, London.

——1982 [1969] *Attachment and Loss: Vol. 1. Attachment*, 2nd ed., Basic Books, New York.

——1988, *A Secure Base: Clinical Implications of Attachment Theory*, Routledge, London.

Caruso, D.A. 1989 'Quality of Day Care and Home-reared Infants' Interactions Patterns with Mothers and Day Care Providers', *Child and Youth Care Quarterly*, vol. 18, pp. 177–91.

Cassidy, J. and Shaver, P.R. 2008 *Handbook of Attachment: Theory, Research and Clinical Applications*, 2nd ed., Guilford Press, New York.

Easterbrooks, M.A. and Biringen, Z. 2000 'Guest Editors' Introduction to the Special Issue: Mapping the Terrain of Emotional Availability and Attachment', *Attachment and Human Development*, vol. 2, pp. 123–9.

Emmett, S. and Rolfe, S.A. 2009 'A New Attachment-focused Pre-service Training Initiative for Professional Caregivers of Infants: A Longitudinal Study of its Effectiveness', Paper presented at the 12th World Congress of the World Association for Infant Mental Health, Leipzig, Germany, 29 June–3 July.

Martin P. and Bateson, P. 2007 *Measuring Behaviour: An Introductory Guide*, 3rd ed., Cambridge University Press, Cambridge.

Marvin, R., Cooper, G., Hoffman, K. and Powell, B. 2002 'The Circle of Security Project: Attachment-based Intervention with Caregiver-Pre-school Dyads', *Attachment and Human Development*, vol. 4, pp. 107–24.

Nicolson, S. and Shipstead, S.G. 2002 *Through the Looking Glass: Observations in the Early Childhood Classroom*, 3rd ed., Merrill Prentice Hall, Upper Saddle River, NJ.

Pellegrini, A.D., Symons, F.J. and Hoch, J. 2004 *Observing Children in Their Natural Worlds: A Methodological Primer*, 2nd ed., Lawrence Erlbaum, Mahwah, NJ.

Rolfe, S.A. 2004 *Rethinking Attachment for Early Childhood Practice: Promoting Security, Autonomy and Resilience in Young Children*, Allen & Unwin, Sydney.

——2007 'Professional Carers as Attachment Figures? Two Studies of the Relationships Between Early Childhood Professionals and Infants in Australian Child Care Centres', paper presented at the 3rd International Attachment Conference, University of Minho, Braga, Portugal, 11–13 July.

Sharman, C., Cross, W. and Vennis, D. 2007 *Observing Children and Young People*, 4th ed., Continuum, London.

Sroufe, L.A., Egeland, B., Carlson, E.A. and Collins, W.A. 2005 *The Development of the Person: The Minnesota Study of Risk and Adaptation from Birth to Adulthood*, Guilford Press, New York.

Stith, S. and Davis, A. 1984 'Employed Mothers and Family Day Care Substitute Caregivers: A Comparative Analysis of Infant Care', *Child Development*, vol. 55, pp. 1340–8.

Zimmerman, L. and Fassler, I. 2003 'The Dynamics of Emotional Availability in Childcare: How Infants Involve and Respond to their Teen Mothers and Childcare Teachers', *Infants and Young Children*, vol. 16, pp. 258–69.

FURTHER READING

Nicolson, S. and Shipstead, S.G. 2002 *Through the Looking Glass: Observations in the Early Childhood Classroom*, 3rd ed. Merrill, Upper Saddle River, NJ. This book is written for early childhood students and staff who wish to apply observation in their professional setting. It is useful for students of research because of the detail it provides about each observational technique. It includes discussions of the strengths and weaknesses of each technique, ethical considerations and issues of authentic assessment.

Pellegrini, A.D. 2004 *Observing Children in Their Natural Worlds: A Methodological Primer*, 2nd ed., Erlbaum, Hillsdale, NJ. This book considers observation as a research tool, describing in detail issues such as the setting of the observations, reliability and validity, designing observational research, how to categorise behaviours, indirect observational methods, computer-assisted recording and observational software programs and writing research reports.

19

Case study

Teresa Vasconcelos

> Scientific and methodological options must be guided by criteria of coherence and opportunity regarding the object of the study and not by any aprioristic decision about validity of theories or practices of research. (Nóvoa, 1991, p. 18)

WHAT WAS THE OVERALL AIM OF THIS RESEARCH?

According to the nature of the problem we need to investigate, it is important to choose adequate methods and procedures (see the chapters in Part II of this volume for additional discussion on this issue). This is key to understanding the epistemology of research generally, and the nature of case studies specifically. In my own case study research (Vasconcelos, 1995, 1997, 2005a and b, 2006; Vasconcelos and Walsh, 2001; Vasconcelos et al., 2003), presented in this chapter, each study had different aims. The aim of the first case study I present, 'The Story of Ana' (Vasconcelos, 1995, 1997), was to give an ethnographic, in-depth description of the practice of an excellent early childhood practitioner as a 'community builder' and promoter of rich group life. The second example is a multiple case study (Vasconcelos et al., 2003), which examined a successful borough (surroundings of Lisbon) in terms of the process of expansion of early childhood coverage (90 per cent coverage) and explored issues of equity through in-depth observations in four early childhood settings (public, semi-public, charity and private for-profit).

WHAT WERE YOUR MAJOR RESEARCH QUESTIONS?

> Perhaps the most difficult task of the researcher is to design good questions, research questions that will direct the looking and the thinking enough and not too much. (Stake, 1995, p. 15)

To choose issues as primary research questions, 'in order to force attention to complexity and contextuality' (Stake, 1995, p. 16), is key to case studies. According to Stake, 'issues are not simple and clean, but intrinsically wired to political, social, historical, and especially personal contexts' (1995, p. 17). In the multiple case study mentioned above (Vasconcelos et al., 2003), an example of an issue was 'equity'. This issue provided a good conceptual structure for organising the case studies. Then we looked at the issue in terms of different layers and dimensions, and in even more detail within each setting examined.

In the most recent case (Vasconcelos et al., 2003) the major research questions involved:

- how to provide coherence between political decision-making and its corresponding implementation;
- how to define equity provided by services from the viewpoint of parents, professionals, children and supervisors;
- how to provide better attention to 'children in most need' (Vasconcelos et al., 2003) and families considered to be more vulnerable.

In the first case study, of Ana (Vasconcelos, 1995, 1997), the issues and layers of the study were:

- What degree of commitment and competence distinguishes 'Ana' as an excellent teacher?
- What 'epiphanies' (Denzin, 1989) or turning points have shaped Ana's life as an early childhood teacher?
- How does she organise the daily activities involving children, parents, the teacher aides and other teachers?
- How does 'Ana' understand and describe the significance of her work with young children?
- How does she create 'community' and 'democracy' in her classroom? (Vasconcelos, 1995; Vasconcelos and Walsh, 2001)

WHAT GUIDED YOUR DECISIONS REGARDING THE CHOICE OF METHODS YOU EMPLOYED?

Stake (1995) considers that:

> ... a case study is expected to catch the complexity of a single case ... We study a case when it itself is of very special interest ... A case study is the study of the particularity and complexity of a single case, coming to understand its activity within important circumstances. (1995, p. xi)

Therefore, a case study is considered to be 'the study of the particular' (Stake, 1994). A case study is not a methodological choice; rather, it is a choice of the object to be studied. In the case that looked at issues of equity in four early childhood settings, we were concerned about how the 'good intentions' of the recently approved Framework Law for Preschool Education (Organisation for Economic Co-operation and Development, February 1997) were expressed in the concrete field. Therefore we conducted a larger case study which 'zoomed' into four settings using ethnographic instruments to describe and 'see' the issues of equity. We found deep inequities (Vasconcelos et al., 2003; Vasconcelos, 2005a). Yet at the same time we found an 'exemplary setting' in terms of *equity* (Vasconcelos, 2006). Only through case study research could we have gained such detailed information.

The best metaphor to explain what case studies are is a very simple one: a funnel. Bogdan and Biklen (1992) explain why they use this metaphor:

> Good questions that organize qualitative studies are not too specific. The start of the study is the wide end: the researchers scout for possible places and people that might be the subject or the source of data, find the location they think they want to study, and then cast a wide net trying to judge the feasibility of the site or data source for their purposes. They look for clues on how they might proceed and what might be feasible to do ... They continue to modify the design and choose procedures as they learn more about the topic of the study ... They work to develop a focus. The data collection and research activities narrow to sites, subjects, materials, topics and themes. From broad exploratory beginnings they move to more directed data collection and analysis. (1992, p. 62)

Walker (1981) sees a case study as 'the examination of an example in action'—*examination* because it observes something in detail in order to look for understanding; *example* because it refers to a unity, a particular study; and *action* due to its dynamic and interactive characteristics. In educational science, case studies have been shown to be a vital tool for people who aim to describe and deeply understand the context of teaching and learning.

Yin (1994) defines a case study as 'an empirical inquiry' that researches a present event within its context, especially when the boundaries between the event and its context are not clearly defined. A case study illustrates a concrete educational situation in the present and in its context, therefore contributing to the identification of its specific characteristics. Case studies are mainly descriptive; the researcher aims at describing and delivering a situation as it is. Therefore, a case study uses what cultural anthropologist Clifford Geertz (1973, referring to the works by Gilbert Ryle) calls 'thick description'. Denzin (1989) describes 'thick description' as follows:

> A thick description does more than record what a person is doing. It goes beyond mere fact and surface appearances. It presents details, context, emotion, and the webs of social relationships that join persons to one another. Thick description evokes emotionality and self-feelings. It inserts history into experience. It establishes the significance of an experience, or the sequence of events, for the person or persons in question. In thick description, the voices, feelings, actions and meanings of interacting individuals are heard. (1989, p. 83)

Case studies are therefore systematic, based on facts and literal. They are not just descriptive, because they also produce deep analytical meaning. They can question a situation or confront it with pre-existing theories. They can help to generate new theories and new questions for future research.

The researcher, besides understanding and interpreting facts, aims at discovering the uncovered sense of actions and the meanings given to them by the actors involved. Therefore, some authors use the metaphor of the onion: there are many layers of meaning to be uncovered, from the various viewpoints of the actors involved. Each layer of context presents the research question in a new light, just as the research question highlights new aspects of each layer of context. This interplay between the research question and the context reflects a variety of opportunities for defining the actual case. The case, therefore, never stands apart from its context; the identification of the actual case points to a unique context that forms part of the case. This is why it is considered a 'bounded system'.

Time is an important factor in this kind of research. Woods (1996) considers that there is a need for a lengthy period in the field and extensive work to create knowledge, competencies and trust that will allow the researcher to enter 'the most deep sanctuaries' and augment the level of trust needed to understand the situation at first hand. Knowledge is both local and total because 'it rebuilds local cognitive projects highlighting its exemplarity and, by that way, it transforms them into total illustrated thinking' (Canário, 1997, p. 109).

FITTING YOUR CASE STUDY TO YOUR RESEARCH STUDY

There are many many ways of doing case studies. (Stake, 1995, p. xii)

According to Stake (1995), there are three kinds of case studies: intrinsic, instrumental, and multiple or multi-site case studies.

Intrinsic case studies aim to understand a concrete situation in depth by recognising what is specific and unique in that situation. A singular situation is analysed in order to document its singularity. When we studied Ana the early childhood teacher (Vasconcelos, 1995, 1997; Vasconcelos and Walsh, 2001), we did so because of the intrinsic value of her teaching. The aim of our research was simply to describe and document her teaching in all its various dimensions.

In *instrumental* case studies, the aim is the in-depth comprehension of a question or problem, having in mind the development or refinement of a theory or generic explanation. According to Stake (1994), the case plays a 'supportive role, facilitating our understanding of something else' (1994, p. 237). When Wigfall and Moss (2001) wanted to study a multi-agency child-care network, they had a clear issue they wanted to study: 'networking'. The case described plays a 'supportive role' in order to provide a better understanding of the issue.

Finally, in *multi-site* or *multiple* case studies, the instrumental perspective is always important. By multiplying the contexts being studied, the researcher aims at a broader understanding and verisimilitude in constructing theories or generalisations. When Vasconcelos et al., (2003) developed a set of case studies in the same borough (Vasconcelos, 2005a, 2006), they were looking at the same issue: equity. However, we wanted to illustrate different settings according to the general national typology: private non-profit, private for profit, public and semi-public. Each setting provided an example of that typology, so we chose to develop a multi-site case study. In the same way, when we studied different cases where ISSA (International Step by Step Association) network was operating, despite being guided by the same issues, the cases were intrinsically different (Stake, 2006).

WHAT RESEARCH DESIGN ISSUES ARE THERE IN CASE STUDY RESEARCH?

Generalisation

Case study seems a poor basis for generalization. (Stake, 1995, p. 7)

Case studies look at particularisation; generalisation is not the aim—rather, the emphasis is on uniqueness and understanding. Therefore, interpretation is the aim of a case study: 'We emphasize placing an interpreter in the field to observe the workings of a case, one who records objectively what is happening but simultaneously examines its meaning and redirects observation to refine or substantiate those meanings. Initial research questions may be modified or even replaced in mid-study by the case researcher.' (Stake, 1995, pp. 8–9) In the case study that looked at issues of equity, only by doing a multiple case study could we have access to the information in the field. In the case of Ana, we were not at all interested in issues of generalisation but in the specificity of Ana's practice.

Information-gathering

> Data are not there, waiting, like tomatoes on a vine, to be picked. Data must be generated before they are collected. (Graue and Walsh, 1998, p. 91)

From broad exploratory beginnings, case study researchers move to more directed data collection and analysis, looking for a variety of information collected in a set of different situations and with a diversity of informants. In the beginning, data are impressionistic; later, they are refined, focused and reorganised. This is how the 'funnel' operates. According to Stake (1995) 'absolutely essential parts of a data-gathering plan are the following: definition of a case, list of research questions, identification of helpers, data sources, allocation of time, expenses, intended reporting' (1995, p. 51). In our own case studies, we experienced the data-gathering process as a multi-layered and very dynamic process. As we were organising and reconstructing our fieldnotes and putting them into a log, we realised the importance of 'thick description' (Denzin 1989, p. 83): it provides context, emotion and multiple layers of significance.

Documentation

Documentation is an important means of information-gathering in order to select documents that may be useful to the research. It is also important to be open to any emerging documents that might be relevant. Document analysis can become a means to find frequencies or contingencies of a certain question. Two kinds of documents may be useful: official documents and personal documents (Bogdan and Biklen 1992). Official documents may indicate the official perspectives, of the administrative and organisational structure of the study. Personal documents refer to productions in which the subject, in the first person, narrates actions, experiences or beliefs. This material may provide elements about the vision their authors have of the world and how they establish relationships. In the case of Ana, we analysed her 'lesson plans' and her own personal reflections that she kept almost daily in a journal. A case should include a list of contextual items that could be included as 'exhibits' in the case. A selection of these can be 'boxed' within the text or appended to the case. Such contextual items could include: other research documents and statistical data; maps of the area; names and addresses of associated organisations; photographs; archival and historical documents; copies of associated policies, procedures, laws and statutes; newspaper/journal articles; personal records, and so on. Journal articles were important in the mid-1990s when we studied Ana. At that time, central government was not paying much attention to the early childhood field, despite the reform of the educational system. Teacher unions were on the streets (I 'shadowed' Ana in teacher demonstrations) in order to create political pressure. In fact, after elections in 1995, the government reconsidered its investment in the early years, and made it a priority. Collecting newspaper articles about these street demonstrations was part of the process of documenting our own research.

Interviews

Interviews are a direct process of gathering information concerning the phenomenon under study, based on the formulation of questions to the people involved on it. Their answers, as they reflect different perceptions and interests, will provide a framework that is representative of the absence or occurrence of the phenomenon, and will therefore provide a basis for its interpretation. Stake (1995) considers that the interview is a fundamental strategy for accessing multiple realities. He advises the researcher to have a detailed plan of what he or she needs to know. Yet he considers that, in case studies, interviews should be done when the researcher cannot retrieve the required information directly from field observation. Therefore, interviews are always complementary to the direct observation data. Interviewing is one of the most powerful means for trying to understand other human beings. The most common form of interviewing is individual, face-to-face interaction, though group interviews are also used frequently. The interview requires mastery and is considered to be something of an art. The interviewer must have an attitude that calls forth an intention to be 'on the skin' of the interviewee, therefore allowing the dialogue to become an understanding and capturing of the other. Stake advises the researcher to be clear about what they need to know in order to avoid irrelevant data collection. Interviewing Ana (Vasconcelos, 1995, 1997) after many hours of observation of her work with young children was key for Ana to have her own voice brought into the study. Ana could check my own fieldnotes, clarifying and even correcting some of my assumptions, thus giving her own interpretation of the facts. Interviewing Ana led us to other interviews: Ana's daughter was interviewed, but so were the inspector in the area and the leader of her teachers' movement, the MEM (Vasconcelos 1997, 1995). Therefore, we could gain different perspectives on the same issues as well as different layers of meaning.

Observation

Atkinson and Hammersley (1994) consider that:

> … all social research is a form of participant observation because we cannot study the social world without being part of it … participant observation not being a specific technique of research, but a way of being in the world that is key to qualitative researchers. (1994, p. 250)

Stake (1995) explains the need for helping the reader to be present in the study:

> To develop vicarious experience for the reader, to give them a sense of 'being there', the physical situation should be well described … There should be some balance between the uniqueness and the ordinariness of the place. (1995, p. 63)

Erickson (1996) explains: 'we paid particular attention to both the immediate and the larger cultural context' (1996, p. 119), attempting to examine multiple layers of contexts and the different points of view of the actors involved. Some key observations need to be triangulated. According to Stake et al., (1991), 'dialogue and contextual detail are chosen not only to portray the event but to develop issue-based assertions' (1991, p. 11). In our multiple case study research (Vasconcelos et al., 2003), because we were several observers in different settings, we were able to triangulate observations with each other. We also gave the product of our observations back to the directors and teachers of the settings for them to help us to have a better 'vicarious experience'.

Data-storage system

> Constructing a data record is drudgery—tedious, demanding work often done into the night. The temptation to focus on fieldwork at the

> expense of constructing a data record can be strong. (Graue and Walsh, 1998, p. 129)

In our study using multiple case study methods (Vasconcelos et al., 2003), looking for issues of equity in four early childhood settings, classroom field notes were logged by activity (for example, daily routines, rituals, large-group meetings, small-group work, interactions with individual children), according to Graue and Walsh (1998). The four case study reports were developed according to the equity indicators identified by Sall and Deketelle (1996). These indicators were simplified and synthesised in four comparative tables that provided a parallel reading of the information of the four settings, completed with detailed indicators to analyse the pedagogy of the classrooms (1996, p. 131).

It is important to keep a personal diary, including calendar, telephone numbers, observation notes and expenses. It is also important to gain the permission of participants on the basis of a brief written description of the intentions of the case study. Written permission should be obtained from parents (if the study involves young children), but also from school authorities and local inspectors.

Access and entry

Steve Ball (1990) establishes an interesting difference between 'entry' and 'access'. 'Entry' implies that conditions were established to develop the study in the chosen setting: written permissions, information on the study, and so on. But 'access' only emerges when true trust is gained and participants are willing to open themselves completely to the study, prepared to cooperate and be open to the presence of the researcher. 'Access' implies that a level of intimacy was gained. In our study of Ana (Vasconcelos, 1995, 1997) we describe the slight difference between access and entry. Despite having gained entry, we only gained access when the three teachers at the kindergarten (including Ana) understood what they could gain from our research.

QUESTIONS OF ETHICS

> Fabricating data or distorting data is the ultimate sin of the scientist. (Bogdan and Biklen, 1992, p. 164)

As in any research, issues of harm, betrayal of trust, consent, deception, dissimulation, invasion of privacy and confidentiality of data need to be at the core of any case study. In an interpretive study, the subjects become extremely vulnerable and need to be respected, so they must be protected from harm.

Therefore, in addition to usual ethical protocols for research (see Chapter 5), ethical norms for a case study involve paying close attention to the issues of respect, reciprocity, responsibility, justice, codes and consent and informed consent. A case researcher should also follow very simple general guidelines in order to protect subjects' identities, treat subjects with respect and seek their cooperation in research, never lie, inform them of the terms of agreement of study, and tell the truth when writing.

Usually we are the:

> ... guest of the people we are studying, in some ways intruding into a space that is by custom a private place. We are coming *intending* to make it public. We believe this risk is worth taking: problems, shortcomings, and personal dismay are essential to understanding but we are pained to think that we sometimes may leave a site having made it more difficult for the educators to carry out their responsibilities. (Stake et al., 1991, p. 12)

We must deal with many ethical issues in our case studies, particularly, what information to use in the writing of the case and what should remain private. Subjects have trusted us, and it is up to us, as the researchers, to make discerning decisions about what can become public. Subjects (or better, actors) have trusted us, and they should be protected. From our own experience, the ultimate line is that respect for the subjects is more important than the quality of our research: if those two issues ever conflict, we must choose respect. This happened with Ana in the process of turning my research from the original English language into Portuguese (Vasconcelos, 1995, 1997), and with the teachers who collaborated in our multiple case study (Vasconcelos et al., 2003).

HOW DID YOU INTERPRET WHAT YOU FOUND?

Analysis and interpretation

> Interpretation is a productive process that sets forth the multiple meanings of an event, object, experience, or text. Interpretation is transformative. It illuminates, throws light on experience. (Denzin, 1994, p. 500)

Doing analysis is a matter of giving meaning to first impressions as well as to final compilations. According to Stake (1995), analysis essentially means 'taking something apart' (1995, p. 71) in order to make sense of it.

Stake (1995) considers that case study findings are not so much discoveries but experiences, which, in part, we ourselves have constructed. According to him, the search for meaning is often a 'search for patterns, for consistency within certain conditions, which we call "correspondence"' (1995, p. 78).

In our own study (Vasconcelos et al., 2003) the interpretive description was a result of repeated reading of the four institutional reports and of looking at the comparative tables developed further on. This description gave a picture of four very different settings (2003, p. 132). Then, on 'a leap of interpretation', the metaphor of a *ghetto* came to our mind, especially as we looked at the school for the 'Roma' children and the exclusive school for the rich families. Those children were deprived of the privileges of the mainstream and, despite goodwill, generous intentions and right philosophies, those schools were not demonstrating equity practices. After this leap of interpretation, 'emergent themes' were discussed. Knowing that case studies are not meant for generalisations, lessons can be learned and issues can be developed out of the cases. This is what we call 'emergent themes'. In this particular study, the 'emergent themes' were as follows:

- leadership and organisational structures
- pedagogies and pedagogical actions
- local policies of emancipation and self-realisation (Vasconcelos et al., 2003).

Interpretation is a major part of a case study. Erickson (1996) speaks of 'assertions', a form of generalisation. According to Stake (1995), 'for doing assertions we draw from understandings whose derivation may be some hidden mix of personal experience, scholarship, assertions of other researchers' (1995, p. 12). And he insists that: 'A case study is noninterventive and empathetic ... We try hard to understand how the actors, the people being studied, see things ... We try to preserve the multiple realities, the different and even contradictory views of what is happening.' (1995, p. 12) According to Stake, 'naturalistic generalizations are conclusions arrived at through personal engagement in life's affairs or by vicarious experience so well constructed that the person feels as if it happened to themselves' (1995, p. 85).

Triangulation

The concept of triangulation, as in the action of making a triangle, may be traced to the Greeks and the origins of modern mathematics. The metaphor of radio triangulation, 'determining the point of origin of a

> radio broadcast by using directional antennas set up at the two ends of a known baseline', aptly illustrates this concept. (Denzin, 1970, p. 234)

By triangulating information, the researcher is trying to clarify the meaning of the information gathered, by reinforcing or questioning it. On the other side, the researcher tries to identify complementary or alternative meanings that will provide a better understanding of the complexities of the study.

By doing triangulation, the researcher multiplies methods of collecting information—observation and interviews around the same issue, for example. He also multiplies modes of producing data: diversified times, different people, different circumstances. Another form of triangulation is to diversify models of analysis, using different theoretical backgrounds to investigate the same phenomenon. Additional observations give us grounds for revising our interpretation. Having other researchers look at the same scene or event may help with triangulation. Denzin (1970) speaks of 'theoretical triangulation', and suggests choosing reviewers from alternative theoretical viewpoints. (See Chapter 9 for a more detailed discussion of triangulation.)

Writing

> The practice of writing is undertaken at every step of the research process—the researcher is authoring both her own experience and her understanding of others as she generates data, formulates interpretations, and develops a case for others to read. (Graue and Walsh, 1998, p. 208)

Writing is part of the interpretive act in research. Case study researchers are constantly writing, with the final writing of the case report being just one parcel of that writing. Writing is also part of the analytical process, a reflection on what the observer has been seeing and feeling. According to Graue and Walsh (1998), 'writing is not a neutral activity, reporting the facts. It is strategically undertaken to tell a particular story to a particular audience.' (1998, p. 211) They continue: 'writing is not just telling what it is—it is shaping and contouring perspectives in ways that have implications for all involved' (1998, p. 212).

Stake (1995, p. 123) gives us an example of how to organise a case study report (see Table 19.1).

When writing a case study report, it is important to provide the reader with examples of short dialogues, vignettes and fragments of

Table 19.1: Case Study Reporting

Entry vignette	I want my readers immediately to start developing a vicarious experience, to get the feel of the place, time.
Issue identification, purpose and method of study	Although most of my readers care little about my methods, I want to tell them something about how the study came to be, who I am, and what issues I think will help us to understand the case.
Extensive narrative description to further define case and contexts	I want to present a body of relatively uncontestable data, not completely without interpretation, but a description not unlike they would make themselves had they been there. I have controversial data to present, I am likely to present them, if I can, as views of a contender or witness.
Development of issues	Somewhere, perhaps in the middle, I want to carefully develop a few key issues, not for the purpose of generalising beyond the case but for understanding the complexity of the case. It is often here that I will draw on other research or on my understanding of other cases.
Descriptive detail, documents, quotations, triangulating data	Some of the issues need further probing. This should be the place for the most confirming experiential data. I will indicate not only what I have done to confirm the observations (my triangulations) but what I have done to try to disconfirm them
Assertions	It is my intent to provide information that allows the readers to reconsider their knowledge of the case or even to modify existing generalisations about such cases. Nevertheless, having presented a body of relatively uninterpreted observations, I will summarise what I feel I understand about the case and how my generalisations about the case have changed conceptually or in level of confidence.
Closing vignette	I like to close on an experiential note, reminding the reader that the report is just one person's encounter with a complex case.

Source: Stake (1995, p. 123).

interviews. Those are part of the 'evidence' which needs to be provided. The following example provides the 'feeling' of a place:

> The gate is accessible and invites us to enter. The wooden building has windows with curtains and, on the corner of the entrance, a round table decorated with flowers creates a home-like atmosphere. Wall panels,

> displaying carefully children's art work and texts, also present information for the parents. Some staff do the cleaning, others prepare the meal (smells of home-made food), everyone busy knowing what they are doing. (field notes, Vasconcelos, 2006, p. 172)

Vignette writing is an important process in providing evidence. Vignettes, according to Graue and Walsh (1998), are a 'way to sharpen analysis and to crystallize issues deemed important by the researcher for the reader' (1998, p. 208). They are 'snapshots or mini-voices of a setting, a person, or an event. They tell a story that illustrates an interpretive theme within a research paper. Vignettes sketch images that through their detail illuminate ideas that seem inherently related to "being there".' (1998, p. 220). Vignettes are:

> … crystallizations that are developed for telling—they are communication tools that help leverage understanding for both the reader and the writer. For the reader they do what stories have always done for teaching—vignettes put ideas in concrete context, allowing us to see how abstract notions play out in lived experience … The vignette is illuminative for the writer as well. Writing vignettes help to prompt certain kinds of understanding. (1998, p. 221)

We present here the transcription of an interesting dialogue among children and teachers about birds that demonstrates processes of making sense, and illustrates what a vignette may be:

> Birds fly? (child)
> How do they fly? (teacher)
> They have feathers, beaks and wings.
> Some have nails like the eagles and a certain type of dinosaur.
> Birds are born from eggs like dinosaurs.
> They have feathers not to be cold.
> And to be able to fly!
> I also think that it is because they become beautiful with feathers and the females like them!
> We want to see a feather with a microscope!
> When we arrived into our classroom we separated the feathers that we picked up, but it was difficult. We liked seeing X … (another child) paying attention.

> We listened to the music of the 'Swan Lake' by Tchaikovsky. (Vasconcelos, 2006, field notes)

According to Stake (1995):

> ... finishing a case study is the consummation of a work of art. A few of us will find a study, excepting our family business, the first work of our lifetime. Because it is an exercise in such depth, the case study is an opportunity to see what others have not yet seen, to reflect the uniqueness of our own lives, to engage the best of our interpretive powers, and to make, even by its integrity alone, an advocacy for those things we cherish. (1995, p. 136)

WHAT WERE THE MAIN OUTCOMES OF YOUR RESEARCH?

In studying Ana (Vasconcelos, 1995a, 1997; Vasconcelos and Walsh, 2001), the outcome of our research was the publication of the report in the Portuguese language (Vasconcelos, 1997). Ten years after its publication, this book is still being sold, and Ana has become a reference for the early childhood field in Portugal, and especially for younger practitioners. Ana's practice 'around the Large Table', despite Ana herself having retired, is still an inspiration and a lesson for those who want to learn how to become 'good' teachers.

In the multiple case study (Vasconcelos et al., 2003; Vasconcelos, 2005a, 2006), recommendations were made to central and local governments. What most interested the educational authorities were not so much the 'happy statistics' of the borough coverage in services for young children, but the specific cases. The ethnographic zoom, with its detail, emotion and descriptions of classroom life, the vignettes and the discourse ('voices') of teachers and parents were key to understanding the issues of equity so important in the recent law.

In summary, the use of case studies shed light on and brought detail to general problems. Recommendations could be made on how to promote equity at a local level (Vasconcelos, 2005a) and descriptions were provided of good equity practices (Vasconcelos, 2006)—even if equity is represented by small utopias (2006, p. 180).

QUESTIONS FOR REFLECTION

1 What type of case study seems most relevant to your particular research question and context?

2 What challenges do you foresee in gaining access for your planned case study research?
3 What are your planned strategies for documenting your case study?

REFERENCES

Atkinson, P. and Hammersley, M. 1994 'Ethnography and Participant Observation' in N.K. Denzin and Y.S. Lincoln, (eds), *Handbook of Qualitative Research*, Sage, Thousand Oaks, CA, pp. 248–61.

Ball, S. 1990 'Self-doubt and Soft Data: Social and Technical Trajectories in Ethnographic Fieldwork', *International Journal of Qualitative Studies in Education*, vol. 3, no. 2, pp. 157–71.

Bogdan, R.C. and Biklen, S.K. 1992 [1982] *Qualitative Research for Education: An Introduction to Theory and Methods*, 2nd ed., Allyn & Bacon, London.

Canário, R. (ed.) 1997 Formação e Situações de Trabalho (Formation and Work Situations), Porto Editora, Porto.

Denzin, N. 1970 *The Research Act*, Prentice-Hall, London.

——1989 *Interpretive Interactionism*, Sage, Newbury Park, CA.

——1994 'The Art and Politics of Interpretation', in N.K. Denzin and Y.S. Lincoln (eds), *Handbook of Qualitative Research*, Sage, Thousand Oaks, CA, pp. 500–15.

Denzin, N.K. and Lincoln, Y.S. (eds) 1994 *Handbook of Qualitative Research*, Sage, Thousand Oaks, CA.

Erickson, F. 1996 'Qualitative Methods in Research on Teaching', in M.C. Wittrock (ed.), *Handbook of Research on Teaching*, Macmillan, New York, pp. 119–61.

Geertz, C. 1973 *The Interpretation of Cultures*, Basic Books, New York.

Graue, M.E. and Walsh, D. 1998 *Studying Children in Context: Theories, Methods and Ethics*, Sage, Thousand Oaks, CA.

Merriam, S.B. 1988 *The Case Study: Research in Education*, Jossey-Bass, San Francisco.

Nóvoa, A. 1991 'As Ciências da Educação e os processos de mudança (Educational Sciences and the Changing Processes)', in *Ciências da Educação em Portugal*, Sociedade Portuguesa de Ciências da Educação, Porto, pp. 17–33.

Organisation for Economic Co-operation and Development 1997 Ministry of Education, Department of Basic Education, *Education and Care Policy in Portugal*, Background report, <www.oecd.org/dataoecd/48/51/2476551.pdf>.

Sall, H.N. and Deketelle, J.M. 1996 'Évaluation du rendement des systèmes éducatifs: Approches Conceptuelle et Problematique' (Evaluation of Educational Systems: A Conceptual and Problematizing Approach), draft paper.

Spodek, B. and Saracho, O.N. (eds) 2005 *International Perspectives on Research in Early Childhood Education*, Information Age, Greenwich, CT.

Stake, R.E. 1994 'Case Studies', in N.K. Denzin and Y.S. Lincoln (eds), *Handbook of Qualitative Research*, Sage, London, pp. 236–47.

——1995 *The Art of Case Study Research*, Sage, London.

——2006 *Multiple Case Study Analysis*, Guilford Press, London.

Stake, R., Bresler, L. and Marby, L. 1991 *Custom and Cherishing: The Arts in Elementary Schools*, National Arts Education Research Center, University of Illinois, Urbana, IL.

Vasconcelos, T. 1995 'Houses and Fields and Vineyards Shall Yet Be Bought in this Land': The Story of Ana, a Public Kindergarten Teacher in Portugal, PhD dissertation, University of Illinois at Urbana-Champaign, IL.

——1997 *Ao Redor da Mesa Grande: Prática Educativa de Ana* (Around the Large Table; Ana's Educational Practice), Porto Editora, Porto.

——2005a 'Early Childhood Education and Equity Issues in Portugal', *Journal of Early Childhood Research*, vol. 2, no. 2, pp. 127–48.

——2005b 'Research in Early Childhood Education in Portugal', in B. Spodek and O.N. Saracho (eds), *International Perspectives on Research in Early Childhood Education*, Information Age, Greenwich, CT, pp. 259–91.

——2006 'Children's Spaces as Sites for Ethical Practices: A "School-as-a-Tree" in an Economically Impoverished Neighbourhood', *International Journal of Early Years Education*, vol. 14, no. 2, pp. 169–82.

Vasconcelos, T., D'Orey, I., Homem, L. and Cabral, M. 2003 *Educação de Infância em Portugal: Situação e contextos numa perspectiva de promoção de equidade e combate à exclusão* (Early Childhood Education in Portugal: Situation and Contexts Under the Perspective of Promoting Equity and Overcoming Exclusion), Conselho Nacional de Education (National Board of Education), Studies and Reports, Lisbon.

Vasconcelos, T. and Walsh, D. 2001 'Conversations Around the Large Table: Building Community in a Portuguese Kindergarten', *Early Education and Development*, vol. 12, no. 4, pp. 499–522.

Walker, R. 1981 'Three Good Reasons for Not Doing Case Study Research', paper presented at the annual meeting of the British Educational Research Association at Crewe and Alsager College of Education, Cheshire.

Woods, P. 1996 *Researching the Art of Teaching*, Routledge, London.

Yin, R. 1994 *Case Study Research: Design and Methods*, 2nd ed., Sage, Thousand Oaks, CA.

Examples of case studies (in English)

Ayers, W. 1989 *The Good Preschool Teacher: Six Teachers Reflect on Their Lives*, Teachers College Press, New York.

Leavitt, R.L. 1994 *Power and Emotion in Infant–Toddler Day Care*, State University of New York Press, New York.

Pianta, R.C. and Walsh, D.J. 1996 *High-Risk Children in Schools: Constructing Sustaining Relationships*, Routledge, London.

Stake, R., Bresler, L. and Marby, L. 1991 *Custom and Cherishing: The Arts in Elementary Schools*, National Arts Education Research Center, University of Illinois, Urbana, IL.

Tobin, J., Wu, D.Y.H. and Davidson, D. 1989 *Preschool in Three Cultures: Japan, China, and the United States*, Yale University Press, London.

Wigfall, V. and Moss, P. 2001 *More Than the Sum of Its Parts? A Study of a Multi-agency Child Care Network*, National Children's Bureau, London.

FURTHER READING

Stake, R.E. 1995 *The Art of Case Study Research*, Sage, London. This is a classic for case study researchers. Using his own work as he was developing a workshop on case study at a Swedish university, Bob Stake develops a step-by-step course (with notes for instructors and researchers) on how to develop case studies, and uses one of his case studies as an illustration.

——2006 *Multiple Case Study Analysis*, Guilford Press, London. In his more recent work, Bob Stake describes the complexities and possibilities of drawing conclusions from multiple case analysis, respecting the specificities of each context. This is also a rather 'pedagogical' step-by-step textbook.

20

Quasi-experimental research

Liane Brown

Studies that use a quasi-experimental design, as the name implies, have many features in common with those utilising an experimental design. **Quasi-experiments** are in many respects like **experiments**. They seek to evaluate the impact of some factor (such as a particular intervention) or set of factors on participants, and they aim to test hypotheses based on prior research. Experiments and quasi-experiments are both founded on a positivistic paradigm which espouses the belief that it is possible to assess cause and effect, to predict outcomes and to control the effect of random, confounding or intervening variables (see Chapter 3).

Quasi-experiments differ from experiments in one key feature: they lack random assignment of participants to experimental and comparison (control) groups (Campbell and Stanley, 1963). Therefore, the researcher cannot infer the equivalence of groups prior to the intervention treatment, and in important ways this limits what conclusions can be drawn when the study is completed. Because of the complex nature and ethical concerns inherent in doing research in education and the social sciences, truly random assignment of participants is usually impossible, and quasi-experiments are probably the most one can aspire to in these disciplines (see Chapter 7). The quasi-experiment is therefore an important design for consideration by early childhood researchers.

There are many forms that quasi-experiments can take, including the regression-discontinuity, equivalent time samples and counterbalanced designs (see Campbell and Stanley, 1963; Robson, 2002). Quasi-experimental designs exist for both multiple- and single-group studies. In this chapter, I focus on a quasi-experimental design called the interrupted time series and illustrate it with an example of research undertaken as part of my Doctorate in Education (Brown, 2009). This study utilised the **interrupted time series design** to evaluate an attachment-based parenting program developed for parents with children in the early and middle years of school (Brown, 2007).

WHAT WAS THE OVERALL AIM OF THIS RESEARCH?

My particular area of interest is parenting education. As part of my Doctorate in Education, I developed a parenting program grounded in attachment theory (AT) (Brown, 2007). The program targeted parents with children in early and middle childhood, covering the preschool (age four) and primary school (ages five to twelve) years. The overall aim of the research was to investigate the impacts of this parenting program on parental sensitivity, parental assertiveness, child behaviours and the parent–child relationship.

WHAT WERE YOUR MAJOR RESEARCH QUESTIONS?

My research questions were:

> Does this program increase parental sensitivity? Parental sensitivity is defined as responsiveness that consistently and accurately recognises, accepts, validates and reciprocates the expression of a child's emotions in a timely manner (Brown, 2007). This is in contrast to dismissing minimising and discouraging the child's emotional signals.
>
> Does the program increase parental assertiveness? Assertiveness is defined as communication that consistently and non-aggressively expresses the parent's own needs in a clear, calm, confident way, sets appropriate limits, and follows through with consequences (Brown, 2007). It is linked to age-appropriate parenting that is firm, yet non-threatening.
>
> Does the program increase child prosocial behaviours and decrease child behavioural difficulties as perceived by the parent? Child behavioural difficulties are behaviours perceived by the parent to be difficult to manage; prosocial behaviours benefit others, including being kind, being considerate, helping and sharing.

> Does the program improve the parental perception of the parent–child relationship? The parent–child relationship is defined as the 'degree of happiness, all things considered' of parents' relationships with their children.

HOW DID THESE QUESTIONS LINK TO THEORY AND EMPIRICAL RESEARCH?

For a number of years, I had been working as a parenting educator, running various well-known group programs such as the Positive Parenting Program (Group Triple P), Parent Effectiveness Training, Steps Towards Effective Parenting and How to Drug Proof Your Kids. These **community-based programs** do not target particular at-risk groups and are designed for the population at large. Only one of these community programs, Triple P, had sound **empirical evidence** to support its claims of effectiveness (e.g. Sanders, 1999); the others reported international, anecdotal success (*About Gordon Training International* n.d.; Dinkmeyer et al., 1997; *How to Drug Proof Your Kids*, n.d.).

The main focus of Group Triple P for children aged two to twelve years is the promotion of parental assertiveness. Having been introduced to AT and research on emotional intelligence, I felt that an effective parenting program needed to promote not just parental assertiveness to manage children's behaviours, but most importantly parental emotional sensitivity. From a theoretical perspective, parental sensitivity is expected to enhance the relationship between the parent and the child generally (e.g. see Ainsworth et al., 1978), and the resulting secure relationship would be maintained even as children's challenging behaviours were being dealt with by the parent (van Zeijl et al., 2006).

The new program I developed, called The Essence of Parenting, had its theoretical foundations in AT (Bowlby, 1969, 1973, 1980). One possible way to explore the impacts of the program systematically was to use a quasi-experimental research design.

WHAT GUIDED YOUR DECISIONS REGARDING THE CHOICE OF METHODS YOU EMPLOYED?

With many parenting programs available, how do government bodies, non-government organisations in the mental health sector or preschool directors select which interventions they will support, partner or fund? One fundamental criterion is that programs be empirically validated (e.g. see *Triple P Procedure Manual*, 2002). Evidence needs to be provided that the interventions are effective.

In consultation with design specialists, it was decided that the best-suited methodology for evaluating the impacts of The Essence of Parenting was the quasi-experimental interrupted time series design. This design involves a single experimental group. Measurements, observations or tests are taken before and after the experimental treatment. The number of data collection points required to establish patterns of change in the time series can be as high as 50 or even more (Robson, 2002), especially in the physical sciences and biology (Campbell and Stanley, 1963). My research involved parent self-report questionnaires. Clearly it would be unreasonable, and perhaps unethical, to expect parents to complete questionnaires 25 times before and after the parenting program. Robson (2002) suggests that adding even one pre- or post-test to a small-scale, one-group pre-test/post-test design is advantageous. This is because the trends that we can begin to see in the data help to counter several of the threats to **internal validity**. Internal validity is the rigour of the study, and the extent to which alternative explanations for causal relationships have been accounted for.

For example, let's say that parental assertiveness was high at the end of the intervention. We could not deduce that it was due to the program because the parents may have begun the program with already high assertiveness scores. Adding a pre-test would help because we would then be able to compare pre- and post-intervention scores. However, even if assertiveness started low and ended high we could still not assume that changes were due to the program. Differences could be due to history, testing, statistical regression or maturation, to name a few (Robson, 2002). History refers to changes occurring in participants' environments, other than those changes directly related to the parenting program. For instance, if the government sent out parenting pamphlets to all households around the time that the parenting program was being conducted, or if there was a television campaign about parenting behaviours, then it could be the pamphlets or television drive rather than the program that was effecting changes in parents' assertiveness. Testing describes changes that could be due to practice and experience resulting from having completed the test/measuring instrument before. The questions on a pre-test measure could, for example, alert parents to thinking about their behaviours and this, rather than the program itself, could be the cause of differences on the post-test measures. Regression refers to the tendency for participants with extreme marks to score closer to the mean when retested. Maturation is the growth, development or change occurring in participants that is unrelated to the program. For instance, some parents might find that their parent–child relationship improves as the child grows older, perhaps because the child is less dependent on them.

These various rival **hypotheses** are all possible threats to the internal validity of the pre-test/post-test research design, and the researcher must adopt strategies to strengthen the design.

One way of improving the pre-test/post-test single-group design is to add an additional pre-test and post-test. By having two pre-tests, we can see whether scores are the same pre-program, as we would expect them to be. By adding an extra post-test, we can see whether post-program changes are maintained, or whether they regress with time once the program is completed. In this study, the interrupted time series employed four time points: twelve weeks pre-program (T1), two weeks pre-program (T2), immediate post-program (T3) and six months post-program (T4). The first three time points were evenly spaced, ten weeks apart.

WHAT SAMPLING OR OTHER RESEARCH DESIGN ISSUES WERE THERE?

Participants were recruited through local preschools and primary schools in the Melbourne metropolitan region to participate in The Essence of Parenting program. After signing up for the intervention, parents were then invited to participate in the research project, requiring them to participate in the full program and, in addition, complete questionnaires before and after it. One of the inherent problems with volunteers as research participants is selection bias—that is, their characteristics may differ from those who choose not to volunteer. For example, motivation for change, engagement and adherence to what is taught may vary between these groups. Of the parents who signed up for the parenting program, 78 per cent (n = 115) agreed to participate in the research component.

Where mailout questionnaires are being used, an important issue to consider is that of non-response. In Chapter 13, John Siraj-Blatchford reports on expected response rates from the original dispatch and subsequent follow-ups of postal questionnaires. In my research, questionnaires were mailed out to participants at T1, T2 and T4, and they were returned via mail. At T3, there was personal delivery and return of the questionnaires during the final session of the program. If a participant was absent during this final session, then the mode of delivery was mailout/mail-return. Although multi-mode delivery has been criticised for having different effects on responses, it can aid with increasing response rates. Follow-ups for non-response of the postal questionnaires was via a courtesy email reminder the morning after a due return date, a second email reminder two days later where necessary, and finally a phone call reminder.

Another aspect to consider for data collection is increasing the rate of your usable data. In this research, returned questionnaires were skimmed to check that all questions had been completed. For incomplete questionnaires, an email was sent asking the respondent to complete the relevant questions. Where no email address was available, a phone call was made. Wording during the phone call followed the exact instructions provided as the written text on the questionnaire. Using this method, the need to average scores for missing data was minimised. Furthermore, response rates were not diminished by unusable questionnaires in which there were many missing items.

In this interrupted time series, the pre-program measures were at T1 and T2. However, some parents signed up too late to complete the questionnaires at T1, twelve weeks before the intervention commenced. They were only able to complete measures T2–T4. **Chi-square analyses** showed no statistically significant proportional differences in gender, ethnicity, educational attainment, socioeconomic status (SES) or employment status between those who signed up with enough time to complete data for T1 (T1–T4: n = 74) and the fifteen participants who signed up too late (T2–T4: n = 89). Furthermore, when analyses were conducted separately for these two groups, the results were consistent.

WHAT WERE THE MAIN OUTCOMES OF YOUR RESEARCH?

Statistical analyses using a single-factor within-subjects repeated measures ANOVA (Analysis of Variance) showed that The Essence of Parenting improved parental sensitivity, parental assertiveness, child behaviours and the parent–child relationship as perceived by the parent (Brown and Rolfe, 2009). Some sub-scales were more amenable to change than others. For example, the encouragement of emotional expression improved but there were no significant changes in problem-focused responses.

AN EXAMPLE OF SUB-SCALES

The Coping with Children's Negative Emotions Scale (CCNES; Fabes et al., 2002) was used to measure parental sensitivity. Nine scenarios are presented in which a child is experiencing anger, sadness or anxiety. Each scenario provides six possible parental responses that represent six sub-scales: emotion-focused responses, problem-focused responses, encouragement of emotional expression, minimisation reactions, punitive reactions and personal distress reactions.

HOW DID YOU INTERPRET WHAT YOU FOUND?

I used both EXCEL and SPSS to analyse data from this research project. EXCEL is beneficial as a spreadsheet with many worksheets, and for manipulating data. For example, computations are simple for recoding scores or summing columns of individual items to calculate an overall score for a sub-scale. I later transferred the data to SPSS for the statistical analyses such as running repeated measures, comparing ANOVAs, generating pairwise comparisons, and comparing means from complete and incomplete data sets.

Unequivocal findings were inferred for the following sub-scales in which (a) there were no pre-program changes, (b) there were significant pre- to post-program improvements, and (c) results at six months post-program were either maintained or showed further significant improvements:

1 *Sensitivity—encouragement of emotional expression:* high effect at immediate post-program and modest effect six months later.
2 *Assertiveness—inconsistent discipline:* large decreases six months after The Essence of Parenting had finished.
3 *Assertiveness—corporal punishment:* modest effect decreases six months post-intervention.
4 *Child behaviours—prosocial behaviours:* modest increases six months post-program.
5 *Child behaviours—conduct problems:* modest decreases six months after The Essence of Parenting had finished.
6 *Parent–child relationship:* generally modest effect increases at six months post-program with very large effects for parents who began with low satisfaction scores just prior to the commencement of the intervention.

As discussed earlier, completing questionnaires on more than one occasion can sometimes result in score changes even before an intervention has taken place. In this study, some of the sub-scales showed statistically significant changes between T1 and T2 (for example, minimisation and punitive reactions). This meant that, even when there were statistically significant improvements pre- to post-program (at the $p < .001$ level with large effect sizes), no conclusions about the effectiveness of the intervention on these sub-scales could be drawn. It was simply impossible to tease out the extent of the impact from testing versus the program itself.

Results such as these, while unexpected and on face value disappointing, are by no means unhelpful. To the contrary, they are valuable for the program developer. They suggest the possibility that some parenting behaviours (as defined by those sub-scales that changed pre-program) might be altered by participating in mailout questionnaires alone, without parents needing to attend a program. That would enable precious time in the program to focus on those parenting behaviours that are more difficult to alter, and for which reading material would be insufficient for change. Of course, further research would need to be conducted to see whether changes due to testing or other written material were maintained long term if there were no intervention.

INTERPRETING SOME UNEXPECTED FINDINGS

An unexpected outcome related to one aspect of parental sensitivity as measured by the CCNES (Fabes et al., 2002). In this instrument, some of the sub-scales are negatively related (for example, minimisation of children's emotions) and some of them are positively related (for example, the encouragement of children's emotional expression). One sub-scale, emotion-focused responses (EFR), is considered positive in the CCNES—that is, higher scores indicate greater sensitivity. However, results from my study showed statistically significant *decreases* on this subscale pre- to post-program. In The Essence of Parenting, EFR are considered important responses in which parents should be skilled. Why, then, did this measure decrease rather than, not increase as a result of the program?

One possibility is that EFR are part of what might be called a sensitivity process. If viewed this way, then it could be argued that EFR should only occur *after* the encouragement of emotional expression and validation of a child's feelings, in an appropriately timely manner. Were a parent to immediately respond to a child's signals with EFR, having omitted to encourage emotional expression and validate the child's feelings, it could be considered *not* emotionally sensitive within the model. For example, if a child had sadly revealed to her parent that she had been left out of a game at preschool, and the parent's immediate response was to get the child to think of other happier things, this would be considered not sensitive. The CCNES does not take into account precisely where in such a sensitivity sequence a particular response is employed. It is quite possible that in responding to the CCNES, parents in the study reported on how they would initially respond to a child's signals. Considered in this way, it could be argued that EFR should decrease post-program, as it did.

Another unanticipated result was that child prosocial behaviours showed not just maintenance, but continuing improvements that were statistically significant (p = .007; d = .3) from immediate post-program to six months post-program. In interpreting this result, one possibility is that it takes time for the effects of a program focusing on parental changes to flow through to child outcomes. Parents' behaviours may transform, but only some time after the program has finished and the children are accustomed to the new parenting behaviours do the effects become fully evident.

In interpreting the results, I had to be mindful that the findings in this research applied to this sample and could not be generalised to the population. This sample was high achieving in both educational level and SES. It was predominantly Caucasian (70 per cent). Seventy-five per cent of the participants were female and more than 90 per cent were aged 30–49 years. Further research will need to incorporate low education and SES groups, diverse ethnicity, an equitable number of males and representation from a variety of parenting age groups, including teenagers.

IN WHAT WAYS DID ISSUES OF PARADIGM INFLUENCE YOUR RESEARCH?

Approaching the research from a **positivist paradigm** predisposed it to a **quantitative** methodological design. This influenced the kinds of research questions I investigated, the methods of data collection, the type of analyses used and ultimately the results.

HOW DID YOUR RESEARCH CONTEXT INFLUENCE YOUR RESULTS?

The research context influenced the type of results that were found. Within the quantitative framework, the research questions were very much of a *yes–no* nature. For example, *Does the parenting program increase parental sensitivity?* The complexity and diversity of an individual's experiences before, during or after the program were not scrutinised by this approach. Rather, the study evaluated how the program impacted parents generally. Had the research been **qualitative**, a vastly different set of research questions could have been asked. Some attempt was made to access this sort of complexity in the study (see box).

A QUALITATIVE APPROACH

Following is a sample of three qualitative questions that parents were asked once they had completed the program, along with some of their responses.

1. *Think about your child's behaviour. In what way(s) has this program changed how you view your child's behaviour generally?*
   N: I can see that my daughter's behaviour is in response to other issues, to her feelings that she cannot yet express maturely and what she is looking for from me ...
   H: Some behaviour is through my parenting and not being prompt to follow up.
2. *Think of a behaviour that you found particularly challenging in your child before you did this program.*
   (a) Briefly describe the behaviour as it was before the program began.
   S: My child wouldn't turn off the computer game when I say it is time to turn it off.
   E: Tantrums, yelling at me when she didn't get her way, argumentative, uncooperative, becoming completely irrational and unable to calm down.
   M: The morning routine to get out the door on time and my child being asked numerous times to do various things to be ready.
   (b) As a result of participating in the program, have you changed your understanding/interpretation of the child's behaviour? If so, how?
   S: Yes. I actually changed my way of telling him. I go to him, talk to him in an arm's distance, give him five minutes finishing off time. Then, come back in five minutes to tell him it is time to turn it off. And he does turn it off!
   E: I feel she was unable to communicate her feeling and wants, therefore lashing out, resulting in the tantrums and irrational behaviour. Through sensitive listening and discussion, building a space of trust and acceptance, she was able to explain to me she was experiencing some bullying at school. I feel that this also led to some of her behavioural issues.
   M: Yes, yes, yes, yes, yes!!! So many things I could do to help things run smoothly. For example, not yell from the kitchen, follow up, give five minute warning, encourage her to do herself instead of taking over and doing it for her, etc., etc., etc.
3. *Think of your own parenting behaviour. In what way(s) has this program changed how you view your parenting behaviour?*
   S: I was too super sensitive [emotionally intrusive].

Now, after the program I learned that I also need to be assertive.

B: I feel I was far too heavy on assertiveness and light on sensitivity. I listen much more to my children and they often come up with their own solutions to various problems instead of me jumping in and doing it for them.

L: The parenting program has made me more sensitive in my parenting—emotionally I feel I am kinder to my children and giving them more time. I am also validating their emotions.

V: Making sure the consequences are related to the behaviour.

These responses provide insight into how the program impacted some parents and ultimately their children. Clearly there are differences, with some parents becoming more emotionally sensitive and others becoming more assertive. However, we cannot be sure whether these responses reflect the experiences of only a few or whether they represent the majority of parents who participated in the program. Quantitative approaches, by comparison, can reveal the impacts for the whole sample.

WHAT LIMITATIONS DID YOU IDENTIFY AND WHERE MIGHT THIS RESEARCH NOW LEAD?

Data in the study were based solely on self-report measures. Future research needs **triangulation** of data that includes observations of parental behaviour and measures of the child's perspective of parental behaviours. On a broader scale, methodological triangulation could also be helpful, in which quantitative and qualitative approaches are combined.

Investigating six-month effects of the program was appropriate for the time restrictions in this initial study. Incorporating longer follow-up periods would provide additional evidence for the long-term impacts of the program.

Some scientific journals have a preference for publishing research with random assignment of participants to groups. A follow-up study of this parenting program could use a Solomon four-group design. Apart from incorporating **randomisation** and **control groups**, the Solomon four-way design could alleviate some of the uncertainty arising from the pre-program changes observed in the present study.

THE SOLOMON FOUR-GROUP DESIGN

This experimental design considers **external validity** factors. The combined effects of testing, maturation, and history can be noted. Participants are randomly assigned to one of four groups (see Table 20.1). Two of the groups are intervention groups, one with pre-testing and one without pre-testing; they both have post-testing. Two of the groups are control groups, one with two tests and one with only one test. For **ethical** reasons, the control groups should be waitlisted to receive the intervention at a later date.

The Solomon four-group design would need to have a much larger sample size than what was available in this study, so that adequate statistical analyses can be conducted with each of the four sub-groups.

Table 20.1: Diagrammatic representation of groups in a Solomon four-group design

Group	Test	Intervention	Test	Intervention for wait-listed control group
1	✓	✓	✓	
2		✓	✓	
3	✓		✓	✓
4			✓	✓

SUMMARY

This chapter has described the place for quasi-experimental designs in early childhood research. I focused on the interrupted time series design, using recent research on the impacts of a parenting program on parent behaviours, child outcomes and the parent–child relationship to illustrate this type of design. Some points to remember are:

- quasi-experimental designs are frequently used in the social sciences and education where true experimental designs may not be feasible
- there are several types of quasi-experimental designs
- countering threats to validity is particularly crucial for quasi-experimental designs
- the interrupted time series design is useful for experimentation with a single group; it is an extension of the one-group pre-test/post-test design

- one benefit of the interrupted time series design is that it shows trends in the data both pre- and post-intervention
- when researching the impacts of a program, ideally there should be no pre-intervention change; where significant change is found, the effects of repeated testing, maturation, history, or regression must be considered
- some possible post-program (for example, immediate post- to six months post-intervention) effects are that scores (a) stay the same, suggesting that the new behaviour is relatively permanent; (b) alter a little in the direction of pre-program scores so that although there is some regression, the new behaviour is more or less learned; (c) alter considerably in the direction of pre-program scores indicating that new behaviours are actually not maintained with the passing of time; or (d) keep improving, suggesting a delayed positive effect on behaviours.

QUESTIONS FOR REFLECTION

1. List as many types of quasi-experimental design as you can.
2. What is the purpose of the interrupted time series design?
3. What advantages and limitations can you anticipate for an interrupted time series design?
4. What might be some threats to validity for this design?
5. How could you overcome these threats?
6. What sorts of experimental conditions will be well suited to the interrupted time series design?
7. What sorts of research topics will be well suited to the interrupted time series design?
8. What are some advantages and disadvantages of self-report questionnaires?

REFERENCES

About Gordon Training International, n.d. <www.gordontraining.com/about-gordon-training-international.html>, accessed 21 June 2009.

Ainsworth, M.D.S., Blehar, M.C., Waters, E. and Wall, S. 1978 *Patterns of Attachment: A Psychological Study of the Strange Situation*, Lawrence Erlbaum, Mahwah, NJ.

Bowlby, J. 1969 *Attachment and Loss: Attachment*, Pimlico, London.

——1973 *Attachment and Loss: Separation, Anxiety and Anger*, Pimlico, London.

——1980 *Attachment and Loss: Loss, Sadness and Depression*, Pimlico, London.

Brown, L. 2007 'Introducing "The Essence of Parenting": A Parenting Program Drawing on Attachment Theory', *Post-Script: Postgraduate Journal of Education Research*, no. 8, pp. 61–73.

——2009 The Essence of Parenting: Impacts of an Attachment-based Group Intervention for Middle Childhood on Sensitive-assertive Parenting, Child Behaviours, and the Parent–Child Relationship, unpublished PhD thesis, the University of Melbourne.

Brown, L. and Rolfe, S. 2009 'The Essence of Parenting: Promoting "Sensitive-assertive" Parenting in Early–Middle Childhood', paper presented at the Biennial Meeting of the Society for Research in Child Development, Denver, Colorado, 2–4 April.

Bryman, A. and Cramer, D. 2009 *Quantitative data analysis with SPSS 14, 15 and 16: A Guide for Social Scientists*, Routledge, Abirydon.

Campbell, D.T. and Stanley, J.C. 1963 *Experimental and Quasi-experimental Designs for Research*, Rand McNally, Chicago.

Dinkmeyer, D.S., McKay, G.D. and Dinkmeyer, D.J. 1997 STEP: *Leader's Resource Guide*, American Guidance Service, Circle Pines, MN.

Fabes, R.A., Poulin, R.E., Eisenberg, N. and Madden-Derdich, D.A. 2002 'The Coping with Children's Negative Emotions Scale (CCNES): Psychometric properties and Relations with Children's Emotional Competence', *Marriage and Family Review*, no. 34, pp. 285–310.

How to Drug Proof Your Kids: About: International partners, n.d. <www.drugproofyourkids.com/about/A000000005.cfm>, accessed 21 June 2009.

Robson, C. 2002 *Real World Research: A Resource for Social Scientists and Practitioner-Researchers*, Blackwell, Oxford.

Sanders, M.R. 1999 Triple P—Positive Parenting Program: Towards an Empirically Validated Multilevel Parenting and Family Support Strategy for the Prevention of Behavior and Emotional Problems in Children', *Clinical Child and Family Psychology Review*, vol. 2, no. 2, pp. 71–90.

Triple P Procedure Manual 2002 New South Wales Department of Health, <www.health.nsw.gov.au/pubs/2001/pdf/ParentingProgram.pdf>, accessed 22 June 2009.

van Zeijl, J., Mesman, J., van IJzendoorn, M.H., Bakermans-Kranenburg, M.J., Juffer, F., Stolk, M.N., Koot, H.M. and Alink, L.R.A. 2006 'Attachment-based Intervention for Enhancing Sensitive Discipline in Mothers of 1- to 3-year-old Children at Risk for Externalizing Behavior Problems: A Randomized Controlled Trial', *Journal of Consulting and Clinical Psychology*, vol. 74, no. 6, pp. 994–1005.

FURTHER READING

Bryman, A. and Cramer, D. 2009 *Quantitative Data Analysis with SPSS 14, 15 and 16: A Guide for Social Scientists*, Routledge, Abirydon. This step-by-step guide for the novice researcher is non-technical and user friendly. It covers basic statistical techniques that can be computed by SPSS for Windows. Rather than reading it cover to cover, you could go directly to the chapter that is relevant for your inquiry.

Campbell, D.T. and Stanley, J.C. 1963 *Experimental and Quasi-experimental Designs for Research*, Rand McNally College, Chicago. Although very old, this book is considered a classic. It is a useful guide to both experimental and quasi-experimental research designs. It provides a description of each design along with its advantages and limitations.

Robson, C. 2002 *Real World Research: A Resource for Social Scientists and Practitioner-researchers*, Blackwell, Oxford. This easy-to-read book is a must for anyone considering doing research in the social sciences. It is very practical.

Appendix 1: Getting our terms right

The language used in the research literature can sometimes be confusing for the novice researcher. Discussions can feature uncommon specialist terms, such as 'methodology' and 'paradigm', which are used commonly by academics but might be new to practitioners. Sometimes, researchers use terms such as 'method', 'technique' and 'significance' that are common in everyday language but give them specialist meanings. To add to the confusion, different researchers sometimes use the same term to mean different things. For example, one researcher may use 'paradigm' to refer to what another researcher may call a 'theory' and another may call a 'frame'.

Table A.1 sets out how some key terms in the research literature have been used in this book. It lists these key terms roughly in the order in which a researcher would use them when discussing the research process or planning a research project. Thus, the researcher's first task is to choose the paradigm within which to work; and their choice effectively shapes the sort of theory they set out to investigate and methodology through which to do so. From that base, the researcher then designs the project, specifying its approach, the methods to be used and the techniques of using them. Finally, a researcher will describe how the data will be analysed, reflecting the project's paradigm, methodology and approach.

Table A.1 Getting our terms right

Term	Definition in this book	Examples	Chapters that feature this term
Paradigm (also known as frame or—erroneously—as theoretical framework)	A way to 'see' the world and organise it into a coherent whole. Each paradigm has three elements: • a belief about the nature of knowledge—what it means to say that we know something • a methodology—what to investigate, how to investigate it, what to measure or assess and how to do so • criteria of validity—how to judge someone's claim to know something. Any research project always happens within a particular paradigm that will be more or less overtly acknowledged by the researcher.	Positivism Interpretivism Structuralism Poststructuralism	Chapter 1 Chapter 2 Chapter 3 Chapter 7 Chapter 10
Theory (also known as theoretical perspective or theoretical framework)	An abstract explanation of something (e.g. an event, a behaviour, a relationship) that can either be proved or disproved.	Feminist theories seek to explain relations within and between genders. Developmental psychology theories seek to explain how children's skills, understandings and cognitions change over time.	Chapter 2 Chapter 6
Methodology (also known as methodological approach)	The rules governing how to produce knowledge within a specific paradigm. The rules concern what to investigate, how to investigate it, what to measure or assess and how to do so. More complex than 'method', and therefore not synonymous with 'method'.	Induction Deduction	Chapter 2 Chapter 3

Design (also known as plan)	A statement of how a research project will be conducted. It specifies what will be researched, how, when and where the research will occur, the participants, what data will be collected and how they will be analysed.	Experimental, quasi-experimental or non-experimental Retrospective or prospective Longitudinal or cross-sectional	Chapter 7 Chapter 8 Chapter 9 Chapter 10 Chapter 11 Chapter 12
Approach	The type or form of knowledge produced and how it is collected, presented, analysed and interpreted.	Qualitative Quantitative	Chapter 2 Chapter 3 Chapter 7
Method	A way to investigate, examine or otherwise collect information about something (e.g. an event or behaviour).	Interviews Observations Surveys Experiments Database searches	Each case study chapter uses a particular method.
Technique (also known as tool or procedure)	The practicalities of a method.	*Interviews:* Open questions, Closed questions, Internal cross-checking, Funnelling. *Observations:* Running records, Anecdotal records, checklists, Time sampling, Event sampling, Rating scales.	Each case study chapter discusses the techniques of its featured method.

Glossary

Aboriginal sovereignty is the power inherent in the rights of Aboriginal people as the First Peoples of a particular country and inherent in the relatedness of Aboriginal people to all things in this country of past, present and future.

Agency is seen in the extent to which people are able to make choices for themselves in any given circumstance.

Analytic memos are written records of interpretations of the evidence collected, usually one or two pages in length. They should be written regularly, and used as signposts to indicate the developing analysis of the evidence. They contain notes on how to interpret evidence using the theoretical frameworks of the study, new questions that arise, cross-references to evidence already gathered and reminders about the focus to be taken in future data collection.

Assumptions are the taken-for-granted, often unconscious ways in which a person views the world.

Autonomy is self-rule. As used in discussions of ethics, it means that individuals should have the right and responsibility to determine the kind of life they wish to live.

Bias occurs when researchers make prejudiced judgments about any aspect of the research process.

Biological racism is the unsubstantiated belief that certain biological traits and racial characteristics make white people superior to black people. This ideology was prominent from the eighteenth century but persists today in underpinning social, political and economic relationships of governments, groups and individuals.

Causation is the principle behind cause-and-effect relationships. Causation is established when there is a sufficient degree of association between the cause (the independent variable) and the effect (the dependent variable), when the cause is shown to precede the effect, and when there can be no other reasonable cause to explain the outcome.

Chi-square analysis is a type of statistical analysis for non-parametric measures. The fit between a theoretical frequency distribution and a frequency distribution of observed data for which each observation may fall into one of several classes, is tested.

Closed-ended questions are questions that ask the respondent to choose between responses determined by the interviewer. For instance, 'Did you feel happy or sad when that happened?'

Cluster random sampling is a random selection of groups rather than individuals.

Collaborative Aboriginal research is research 'with' Aboriginal people that seeks their involvement as anything other than objects of research and aims to achieve Aboriginal agency. The extent to which this occurs is limited by methodology and data-collection methods. The researcher's assumptions and positioning are often not made conscious, examined or addressed.

Colonialism constitutes the social, cultural, intellectual, political and ideological mechanisms by which non-Aboriginal governments and nation states have invaded Aboriginal lands and managed Aboriginal people. It is enforced in hierarchical structures such as legislation, politics, health services and welfare, and agencies and structures of knowledge reproduction such as schools, universities and research.

Community-based programs are interventions available to all parents as opposed to specific clusters such as at-risk groups.

Content analysis is a method of data analysis used by qualitative researchers who want to explore and label patterns of behaviour or text. Researchers decide on a unit of analysis such as a behaviour, a grouping of words or a broad stream of conversation and the descriptors that might be applied to each unit of analysis. The descriptors (or labels) may be derived from previous research, or a specific theoretical framework.

Contingency table is a table, comprising rows and columns, that shows the relationship between two nominal or ordinal variables. Each cell in the table shows the frequency of the occurrence of that intersection of categories for each of the two variables.

Control group is a group that does not receive the independent variable (or treatment) in an experiment, but is treated 'as usual'.

Critical race theory emanates from critical theory to interrogate and address power in any given relationship that involves the race, ethnicity, culture and identity of the researcher and the research participants.

Cross-sectional designs compare different age groups at a single time.

Cultural inventions are artefacts, technologies, knowledge and concepts that are created by a particular group of people.

Daily research plans are made before a study begins and focus on what the researcher aims to do each day during fieldwork.

DCSF Department for Children, Schools and Families

Decolonisation is the sets of understandings, processes and practices involved in the deconstructing and restructuring of relationships of power, entrenched as normal, between non-Aboriginal and Aboriginal people.

Deductive research methodology is used when the researcher develops clear statements about the expected outcomes of the study (hypotheses) based on theory and prior research, and designs the research study to test these hypotheses in a controlled and systematic way. Data are generally not analysed until data collection is complete.

Degrees of freedom (*df*) is a value that represents the extent to which data are 'restrained' by the analysis and/or the total number of subjects. Calculated in different ways, depending on the method of analysis being used, the principle is to calculate *df* as *N*–1, where *N* represents the number of subjects or the number of groups.

Dependent relationship is a relationship between researcher and subject where the researcher has some power over, or can supply some benefit to, the subject—for example, teacher/student, parent/child, professional/client, manager of child-care centre/parent.

Dependent variable is a characteristic of subjects that is measured to determine the effect on them of the variable manipulated by the experimenter (the independent variable).

Direct observation involves the researcher recording the data of interest directly from their own observations rather than indirectly (for example, via questionnaire or other objective test). Most direct observation is of behaviour: children's, parents' or that of early childhood staff.

Discourses are the emotional, social and institutional frameworks through which we make sense of our desires, practices and understandings.

Effect size is an objective assessment of the magnitude of an observed effect. Measures of effect size include Pearson's *r* for correlations, Cohen's *d* for the difference between two means, eta^2 for ANOVA.

Empirical evidence is results that are verifiable or proven by observation or experiment; it is practical as opposed to theoretical evidence.

Epistemology is any philosophical theory of knowledge that provides an account of what counts as legitimate knowledge.

EPPE Effective Provision of Pre-School Education project

Equity is about justice and fairness, and therefore often requires moving beyond making things equal.

ESRC Economic and Social Research Council

Essentialism is the belief in possession of intrinsic or characteristic properties that constitute the true nature of something.

Ethical research considers the effects of the research on the rights and well-being of all those who may be affected by the research.

Ethics refers to a consideration of the effects of the research on the rights and well-being of all those who may be affected by the research.

Ethograms are inventories of observed behaviours (defined in terms of the anatomical movements involved) for particular groups in particular contexts. They were originally developed by ethologists to study the behaviour of non-human species in natural environments.

Eurocentric research is based on the 'use of the White middle class (male) as the standard and its adherence to the comparative approach in conducting research' (Padilla and Lindholm, 1995, p. 110). *See also* Deficit model.

Experiments are data collections under conditions that control as many relevant variables as possible, while manipulating a treatment variable (the independent variable) and measuring its effect or outcome (the dependent variable). Experiments involve random assignment to groups.

External validity refers to the extent to which the results of a study can be generalised to the wider population. It requires attention to sample representativeness, replication of test conditions, replication of results, sample sensitisation to the research procedures, and bias in the sample or the research process.

Feminism(s) is a range of theories critiquing patriarchal structures and highlighting the inability of existing social texts to represent lived experience.

Feminist criminological theory theorises how the lives of women are regulated by men on behalf of the state and seeks to makes visible their experience.

Feminist poststructuralist theory theorises the mechanisms of power and how meaning and power are organised, enacted and opposed in society, and places the social construction of gender at the centre of its inquiry.

Generalisability is the extent to which results from a research study apply to and/or can explain the phenomenon in general, for the population as a whole, and under real-world conditions.

Grand narratives are 'big pictures' about humanity's 'progress' on its 'journey'.

Heterogeneity is characterised by diversity, containing variety and difference.

Homogeneity is when aspects or characteristics of people/groups are the same, or seen to be the same.

Hypotheses are predictive statements containing a possible explanation of some phenomenon and its likely causation.

Illumination research allows researchers and practitioners to interpret and respond aspects of the field with gazes informed by the insights of previous research.

Independent variable is something that is manipulated by the experimenter to determine its effect on the subjects. Subjects are grouped according to the level of the independent variable that they receive/experience.

Indigenist research is a research paradigm based on Aboriginal world-view, knowledge and values that has relatedness as a core assumption. As such, it seeks Aboriginal sovereignty in all decisions and all relationships.

Internal reliability is the degree to which the indicators or items that make up a scale—for example, from a questionnaire—are consistent and intercorrelated.

Internal validity refers to the extent to which an assessment tool correctly represents a phenomenon of interest—that is, how well the construct is defined by the measure. Internal validity requires attention to the content of a measure.

Interpretivists believe that we continually create and recreate our social world as a dynamic system of meanings by continually negotiating with others the meanings of our actions and circumstances and theirs, and the meanings of social and cultural institutions and products.

Interrupted time series design is a quasi-experimental design involving a single experimental group on which a series of tests, observations or measurements are made, both before and after an experimental intervention.

Knowledge-power regimes are institutionally articulated systems of meaning (knowledge) that regulate what we think is the normal, right and desirable ways to think, feel and act in a particular situation and that enable particular groups of people to exercise power in ways that benefit them.

Lifestory data are usually collected through a series of several in-depth interviews which encourage detailed recall of previous and current events and current interpretations of these events, and how these identities shape the beliefs and behaviours of the person whose lifestory is being described.

Longitudinal research is a design that allows investigation of naturally occurring changes, on repeated occasions over a substantial period of time.

Mandated means required by law to fulfil particular requirements.

Measurement error refers to the discrepancy between the measurements that represent a concept/construct and the actual value of that concept. Measurement error is inversely related to the reliability and validity of the measurement tool.

Measurement validity refers to the extent to which an assessment tool correctly or truly represents a concept/construct. Measurement validity requires attention to the content of the measure.

Mirroring or reflective probe is a follow-up question that reflects the participant's testimony back to them; it is used by an interviewer to clarify or verify participant testimony.

Native title began in 1993 when the *Native Title Act* was legislated by the Commonwealth Government of Australia. This legislation acknowledged the prior occupation of Aboriginal people before 1770, denouncing the *terra nullius* edict upon which the land was claimed by the British.

Non-judgmental questions and responses are interviewer questions and responses that do not, either in tone or content, seek to estimate or decide the merits of things.

Non-parametric statistics are used when the assumption of normal distribution cannot be met. In most cases, this occurs when variables are not quantified but are based on nominal or ordinal groupings.

Objectivity in observational research refers to the extent to which observer bias is minimised, mainly through observer training and careful definition of behaviour categories.

OMEP Organisation Mondiale pour l'Education Prescolaire (World Organisation for Early Childhood Education)

Open-ended questions are interviewer questions that have no pre-determined responses and seek to avoid directing the participant to answer in a particular way—for instance, 'How did you feel when that happened?'

Operational definition is a specification of a construct or variable in measurable terms that gives meaning to a variable by identifying how it is to be measured.

Paradigm is a way to 'see' the world and organise it into a coherent framework. Each paradigm is a specific collection of beliefs about what constitutes knowledge and about our relationships with it, together with practices based upon those beliefs.

Parametric statistics are used when variables are measured as a quantity—that is, as a parameter. Measures must be based on interval scales. Parametric tests assume that the sample scores are normally distributed—that is, are symmetrical about the mean.

Participant observer is a data-collection strategy in which the researcher takes part in the activities of the individuals being studied. As a participant observer, the researcher has the opportunity to actively gain access to information from the 'inside' rather than passively from the 'outside'.

Policy is multidimensional, value-laden, social and political phenomena comprising policy texts and processes.

Policy contexts are the situation of policy players in complex and often contested social, cultural and historical sites.

Policy research is the process of understanding policy-making contexts, policy players, policy texts, policy processes and policy outcomes.

Positivists are researchers who try to explain and predict their surroundings in terms of cause-and-effect relationships between apparently random events and appearances, and an underlying order of universal laws.

Postmodernism includes theories used by researchers who 'see' human societies as fundamentally incoherent and discontinuous, rather than regarding each society as at a particular stage of 'development' or 'progress'.

Postpositivist paradigms assume that only partially objective accounts of the world can be produced.

Poststructuralism refers to a set of theories that assume language, meaning, and subjectivity are never fixed and therefore, can never be fully revealed or understood by the research process.

Poststructuralists are researchers who 'see' the individual and their circumstances as fundamentally incoherent and discontinuous, and try to explain this constant instability without attempting to 'capture' or stabilise it.

Praxis is practice informed by theory and vice versa.

Qualitative approaches involve collection of data that are non-numerical in form—usually text-based data. These methods are favoured (but not necessarily used exclusively) by researchers following an inductive research process that seeks understanding rather than explanation and encourages diversity and complexity in the data rather than experimental control.

Quantitative approaches involve collection of data that are numerical in form. These methods are favoured (but not necessarily used exclusively) by researchers following a deductive research process based on careful experimental design and control to determine and/or explain relationships between independent and dependent (outcome) variables.

Quasi-experiment is a research design with an experimental approach but in which random assignment to treatment and comparison groups is not used.

Random sample is a sample selected in a manner that ensures that every member of a population has an equal chance of selection.

Randomisation is random assignment to treatment or comparison groups. *See also* **Random sample**.

Rapport is a positive interpersonal climate between interviewer and participant necessary for the fruitful conduct of the interview.

Reciprocity refers to a data-gathering technique where meaning and power are negotiated between the researcher and researched and between data and theory.

Reflexive abstraction is the self-conscious coordination of the observed with existing cognitive structures of meaning

Reflexivity refers to responsiveness to the evidence gathered in the field.

Relevant variables are variables that the researcher takes into account as possible influences on pre-existing differences in the sample population.

Reliability usually refers to the consistency, accuracy and stability of the measurements used or observations collected in the study, a positivistic paradigm.

The more reliable the measurement or observation, the more 'error-free' it is considered to be. There are various ways in which reliability can be assessed by calculation of so-called 'reliability coefficients'.

Replication is the process of repeating an experiment, ideally with different researchers, in different laboratories.

Research briefs are detailed outlines about the research completed before a study begins.

Research designs can be thought of as a set of procedures developed to guide an entire study, from formulating research questions to disseminating results.

Research diaries are useful tools for both action researchers and those working with qualitative data more generally. Diaries allow researchers to keep track of the development of ideas as a study progresses, through their written reflections on the research process.

Research relationships are the conscious and unconscious relationships that exist between researcher and research participants. These are often predetermined by the research paradigm, researcher positioning and especially the methodology.

Researcher assumptions are the often unconscious ways in which a researcher sees the world and then brings and applies these assumptions and taken-for-granted views within research.

Researcher positioning consists of the cultural, social, political and historical ways in which a researcher comes to know, give meaning to and construct a particular topic in research. It emanates from the researcher's assumptions and is evident in the type of research paradigm and its methodology used in the research.

Researcher reflexivity is a process of thinking about the research process, including data generation, power relationships and initial analysis.

Sampling is a process of selecting a portion of a defined category—usually people, though it can be applied to other aspects of the research design such as settings or events—that is in some ways representative of the defined category as a whole (the 'population').

Single case study design is a research strategy aimed at explaining, describing, illustrating, and/or exploring contemporary phenomenon within a real-life context of a single individual, group, event, institution or culture.

Small-scale studies include projects where data collection occurs over a short period of time, when a small number of participants are involved in a study, or when few data-collection methods are used to answer a research question.

Stratified random sampling is a sampling technique that selects individuals from sub-groups in proportion to their represention in the population.

Structuralism is the theoretical approach used by researchers who believe that meaning doesn't lie *within* something, waiting to be discovered through careful observation. Instead, meaning lies in the non-observable system of relationships *between* that 'something' and something else.

Subjectivity is used in positivist research to refer to the extent that the observer's own feelings, biases and interpretations influence what they observe and record, or don't observe and record. It is used in poststructuralist theory to describe an individual's conscious and unconscious thoughts, sense of self and understanding of their relation to the world. One's subjectivity is socially constructed through discourses and language.

Systematic observation is a process of collecting observational data, usually about the behaviour of children and/or adults, using predefined behaviour categories and standard observational techniques by observers trained to an acceptable criterion of observational reliability. Systematic observations in natural settings (such as homes, preschools or parks) are referred to as naturalistic observations; those in observer-controlled settings (for example, laboratories) are called structured observations.

Telos refers to a 'journey' by humanity towards some ill-defined 'goal' or 'end-point'.

Terra nullius is a Latin term meaning 'land belonging to no one' or 'empty land'.

***Terra nullius* Aboriginal research** is research 'on' or 'to' Aboriginal people. It is based on the assumption that Aboriginal people do not need to be consulted in research and they are erased within this form of Aboriginal research.

Theory-building refers to qualitative research that relates closely to the modernist 'moment' outlined in Chapter 9. In this sense, it is the process of constructing coherent patterns from analyses of evidence from the field using these patterns to form the basis of a grounded theory which can be generalised across other similar settings and events.

Thick description is a description that includes everything needed for the reader to understand what is happening.

Timelines sketch out the entire research project, paying close attention to the role of the researcher and the timeframe.

Traditionalising in Aboriginal research is research 'about' or 'of' Aboriginal people. The researcher's assumptions are not made conscious and the positioning is objective towards both the research knowledge and Aboriginal people.

Treatment group is a group that receive the independent variable (or treatment) in an experiment.

Triangulation is a research practice of comparing and combining different forms, or different sources, of information in order to reach a better understanding of processes or perspectives. An example would be using the views of both teachers and pupils to gain an informed view of school processes, or using classroom observations as well as teacher interviews to learn about teachers' practices.

True experiment *See* Experiments.

Trustworthiness involves judgments about the quality and credibility of the research design, enactment, analysis, findings and conclusions.

UNESCO United Nations Educational, Scientific and Cultural Organization.

Validity is the process of establishing the 'truth' of the research outcomes. Each paradigm has its own validity processes as summarised in Chapter 3.

Index

Page numbers in *italics* refer to figures.